All Necessary Measures

PENNSYLVANIA STUDIES IN HUMAN RIGHTS

Bert B. Lockwood, Jr., Series Editor

A complete list of books in the series is available from the publisher.

ALL NECESSARY MEASURES

THE UNITED NATIONS AND HUMANITARIAN INTERVENTION

Carrie Booth Walling

PENN

UNIVERSITY OF PENNSYLVANIA PRESS

PHILADELPHIA

Published by
University of Pennsylvania Press
Philadelphia, Pennsylvania 19104-4112
www.upenn.edu/pennpress

Printed in the United States of America on acid-free paper
10 9 8 7 6 5 4 3 2 1

Library of Congress Cataloging-in-Publication Data
ISBN 978-0-8122-4534-9

To Dayne, Bennett, and Emery

Contents

Chapter 1

Constructing Humanitarian Intervention

It is important that when civilians in grave danger cry out, the
international community, undaunted, is ready to respond.
—UN Security Council, 17 March 2011

On the evening of 17 March 2011, members of the United Nations Security
Council (UNSC) met to discuss the deteriorating security situation in
Libya. It was the fourth Security Council meeting on Libya in a month
following the outbreak of violence between Colonel Muammar Qadhafi's
regime and the opponents to his rule. What started out in mid-February
as peaceful protests against arbitrary arrest and extrajudicial killing by the
government quickly deteriorated into an armed rebellion to overthrow
Qadhafi and remove his regime from power. In the face of early rebel advances in the western region of the country, Qadhafi's son Saif al-Islam
Qadhafi had threatened that "rivers of blood will run through Libya" and
casualties would increase from the dozens into the thousands if protesters
refused to accept regime-initiated reforms.[1] Hours before the 17 March
Security Council meeting, Colonel Qadhafi's forces were poised to retake
the rebel-held city of Benghazi. Qadhafi warned Benghazi's residents that
his forces would come that night and "they would show no mercy or com-
passion" to the opponents of his rule.[2] The Security Council, in United
Nations (UN) headquarters in New York, was contemplating the text of a
draft resolution submitted by France, Lebanon, the United Kingdom (UK),
and the United States (U.S.). The resolution proposed the creation of a no-
fly zone in the airspace of Libya and authorized member states to take "all
necessary measures" to protect civilians and civilian populated areas under

threat of attack, including Benghazi. Proponents of the resolution, including the ambassador of the UK, argued that the Charter of the United Nations protected the rights and values that civilians in Libya were advocating for, and that the Security Council had a responsibility to protect civilians from the violence perpetrated against them by their own government: "The central purpose of the resolution is clear: to end the violence, to protect civilians and to allow the people of Libya to determine their own future, free from the tyranny of the Al-Qadhafi regime. The Libyan population wants the same rights and freedoms that people across the Middle East and North Africa are demanding and that are enshrined in the values of the United Nations Charter. Today's resolution puts the weight of the Security Council squarely behind the Libyan people in defence of those values."[3] Ten Security Council members voted in favor of Resolution 1973, paving the way for a humanitarian intervention in Libya that was remarkable both for the expansive mandate provided by the resolution and for the swift adoption by the Security Council.

Humanitarian intervention in Libya marked an important evolution in an already remarkable shift in Security Council practice and state justifications for the use of military force that began in the 1990s. Faced with a mounting humanitarian crisis along the border of Iraq with Turkey and Iran in 1991, the Security Council permitted the creation of a no-fly zone to protect Iraqi Kurds and Shi'as from government attack because Saddam Hussein's repression was causing a refugee crisis that was destabilizing the region and threatening the sovereignty of Iraq's neighbors. By mid-decade, however, the UNSC began to justify its use of enforcement action under Chapter VII of the Charter by referring directly to human rights norms, rather than their effects on neighboring sovereign states.[4]

Humanitarian intervention had been impermissible during the Cold War as human rights were considered to be within the domestic jurisdiction of each state and beyond the purview of the UNSC. In the 1970s, the Security Council did not address internal situations of mass killing but instead criticized UN members that intervened militarily to halt the bloodshed in neighboring states, despite positive humanitarian motives or effects.[5] For example, in 1979 when Vietnam intervened militarily in Cambodia, effectively ending the murderous regime of Pol Pot and the Khmer Rouge, Vietnam was condemned by the council for its intolerable breach of UN rules, despite its potential positive humanitarian effects. France's ambassador to the Security Council argued that using military force, even against a detestable regime, was dangerous to international order: "The notion that because a regime is detestable foreign intervention is justified and forcible overthrow is legitimate is extremely dangerous. That could ultimately jeopardize the very maintenance of international law and order and make the continued existence of various regimes dependent on the judgment of their neighbors."[6] At that time, references to human rights were inappropriate and illegitimate for Security Council deliberation. International order took precedence over justice. In direct contrast, in the month leading up to the passage of Resolution 1973 on Libya, UNSC members, including states as diverse as Brazil, Bosnia-Herzegovina, and the Russian Federation, condemned Libyan authorities for their violations of international human rights. At least thirty references to human rights were made in the Security Council chamber and within the council's public documents on Libya during that period.[7] Indeed, the formal meeting records indicate that those members supporting the resolution did so primarily on the basis of the "Libyan authorities' disrespect for their obligations under international humanitarian and international human rights law" and the threat this posed to international peace and security.[8]

More than three decades after the French statement criticizing the Vietnamese intervention in Cambodia, the French minister for foreign affairs urged council members to quickly pass Resolution 1973, which would authorize all necessary measures to protect civilians from egregious violations of their human rights, in effect authorizing humanitarian intervention. "We do not have much time left. It is a matter of days, perhaps even hours. Every hour and day that goes by means a further clampdown and repression for the freedom-loving civilian population, in particular the people of Benghazi. Every hour and day that goes by increases the burden of responsibility on our shoulders. If we are careful not to act too late, the Security Council will have the distinction of having ensured that in Libya law prevails over force, democracy over dictatorship and freedom over oppression."[9] In 1979, the Security Council criticized illegal intervention against a rights-abusing regime. Humanitarian justifications were deemed inappropriate and illegitimate in the venue of the Security Council. In 1999, the Security Council declined to criticize or censure members of the North Atlantic Treaty Organization (NATO) for another illegal intervention against a rights-abusing regime (to stop Serbian government led ethnic cleansing in

Kosovo) *precisely* because it was humanitarian justification that, the council deemed, made the action legitimate. In 2011 in the case of Libya, the Security Council legally authorized its members to use military force against a sovereign state member of the UN because it was violating the human rights of its own population.

The UNSC is known as a realm of great-power politics and historically it did not consider human rights protection as a legitimate purpose of military force. How did the UNSC become concerned with human rights and willing to occasionally use military force to end or punish gross human rights violations in sovereign states without their consent? Humanitarian intervention by the UNSC signals that state observance of minimal human rights standards is an increasingly significant component of state responsibility within international society. As these examples illustrate, however, this has not always been the case. The legitimacy of humanitarian intervention and the authority of the Security Council to undertake it had to be actively socially constructed. This book's purpose is to illustrate how the increasing legitimacy of human rights norms is changing the meaning of state sovereignty and the purpose of military force at the United Nations by examining Security Council behavior and justifications for that behavior. The central claim is that the arguments that international actors make about the cause and character of conflict and the source of sovereign authority matter: they shape the likelihood that military force will or will not be used in defense of international human rights.

Skeptics may protest that language has more potential to conceal than to reveal motive and that the primary determinant of humanitarian intervention is the selfish interests of powerful states. In this book, I challenge the claim that discourse is epiphenomenal in international relations. By using both a single historical narrative designed to compare evolution of norms over time and by examining a series of qualitative, comparative case studies, I demonstrate precisely how norms and discourse have real-world explanatory power. By tracking changes in discourse alongside changes in behavior, I demonstrate that Security Council members have mixed motives; that norms and strategic interests interact; and that shifting stories about human rights, sovereignty, and war alter humanitarian intervention policy at the UN. This survey of cases also shows that UNSC humanitarian intervention behavior does not map neatly onto a set of a priori interests of intervening states. Rather, humanitarian intervention is costly and imposes foreseen material costs on intervening states. It is through their interaction that norms and interests are mutually constituted and thus have the potential to evolve over time. As this study demonstrates, both human rights and sovereignty norms have coevolved such that a minimal conception of the former is now encapsulated in the latter. Power in the UNSC at the start of the twenty-first century is no longer simply about whose military can win but also about whose story can win.[10]

The United Nations and Military Force

The UNSC is charged with maintaining international peace and security and regulating state sovereignty. The UN Charter empowers it with the political and legal authority to identify aggression and to regulate the use of military force in international affairs in response to threats to, or breaches of, international peace. The Security Council has the sole legal responsibility to authorize enforcement measures against state members of the UN, including the use of military force under Chapter VII. The Charter preserves a state's right of individual or collective self-defense in the event of an armed attack in Article 51 but even a state victim of attack must report its defensive actions to the council and defer to its authority and responsibility for the maintenance of international peace and security. The Security Council also has the power to recommend new members for admission to the UN. In effect, the Security Council regulates both international legal sovereignty (the mutual recognition between states) and Westphalian sovereignty (the state's effective control over its people and territory without external interference).[11]

The Security Council comprises fifteen members: the five permanent members of China, France, Russia, the UK, and the U.S.; and ten nonpermanent or rotating members that are elected on a regional basis for two-year terms. Currently five nonpermanent members are drawn from the regions of Africa and Asia, two from Latin America, two from western Europe, and one from eastern Europe.[12] Permanent members have veto power over any substantive resolution or decision that comes before the UNSC. This means that the UN cannot undertake any collective measures on international security without the consent or acquiescence of its permanent members. Although this prevents the UN from taking any action that might bring its most powerful members to the brink of war, it also allows permanent members to act as spoilers, preventing UN action in some cases of mass atrocity like Kosovo in 1999 and Syria in 2011–12. Despite the unequal power dynamic in the council, the five permanent members cannot act without the support of nonpermanent members. Decisions of the Security Council require nine affirmative votes and no permanent member veto—only then are they binding on all UN members (Article 25 of the Charter). The working methods of the UNSC allow nonmembers to participate in council meetings. Rule 37 of the Security Council's *Provisional Rules of Procedure* permits any UN member that is not a member of the Security Council to participate in its formal meetings without a vote. Like the members of the council, nonmembers publicly justify their policy positions in formal meetings—they communicate directly with one another but also to domestic publics and third-party states. They do so to publicly register their views with external audiences but also to attempt to shape the debate and the policy options available for consideration. Rule 39 of the *Provisional Rules of Procedure* allows the Security Council to invite members of the Secretariat or other persons it deems competent to provide information and assistance when the council is examining issues within their competence.[13] It has become common for special representatives to the secretary-general, the under-secretary-general for political affairs, and representatives from the offices of the Department of Peacekeeping Operations and the Department of Humanitarian Affairs, among others, to brief the UNSC.

Since the end of the Cold War, the east-west rivalries that once divided the Security Council have diminished and relations among permanent members have improved considerably. There has been a significant reduction in the use of the veto and a culture of accommodation has developed among the five permanent members, whereby they seldom bring draft resolutions with permanent member opposition forward for public vote.[14] The number of resolutions passed by the UNSC dramatically spiked at the end of the Cold War and has remained significantly high since. The same is true for Chapter VII resolutions, and most sanctions regimes and peacekeeping operations also were established in the post–Cold War period.[15] Increasing UNSC action reflects both the altered political environment within the council among its members and dramatic change in international society. Not only has the number of armed conflicts increased—peaking in the early 1990s with only a minor decline in the subsequent decade—the character of these conflicts has changed from primarily interstate to intrastate.[16] Changes in Security Council behavior and the council's justifications for that behavior suggest that the meaning of sovereignty and the purpose of military force have shifted since the end of the Cold War and continue to evolve. These changes have not occurred without contestation, however. Severe disagreement on the source of sovereign authority and the character of violence in target states as well as the appropriate military response have seriously strained relations among permanent members and can temporarily block Security Council action, as the chapters on Kosovo and Libya will demonstrate.

In contemporary international politics, the Charter of the United Nations provides the normative framework through which contestation over the legitimate use of force occurs, and the Security Council is the forum in which that debate takes place. According to the Charter, there are only two legal justifications for the use of military force: self-defense (protected by Article 51) and with the authorization of the UNSC under Chapter VII. Historically, other resort to military force was considered aggression because protecting state sovereignty was considered the heart of the legal regime of the UN. Article 2 affirms the sovereign equality of states, proscribes the threat or use of military force against the territorial integrity or political independence of states, and prohibits the UN from interfering in matters that fall within the domestic jurisdiction of states. Nonetheless, the core principles and purposes of the UN outlined in the preamble and Chapter 1 of the Charter include the achievement of international cooperation in solving international humanitarian problems and the reaffirmation of fundamental human rights, in addition to the prevention of war and maintenance of international peace and security. Changes in the international political and normative context since 1989 have prompted debate within the Security Council about other purposes for which military force should be used. Originally, different organs were created to achieve the UN's diverse purposes. The Charter tasks the UNSC with maintaining international peace and security and regulating sovereignty, whereas the encouragement and monitoring of human rights was assigned to the Economic and Social Council and its Commission on Human Rights, which was replaced by the Human Rights Council in 2006. A strict separation of responsibility was largely maintained between the two bodies until 1991, when the subject of human rights entered the UNSC for the first time during the Gulf War. This sparked rancorous debate among council members: China and India argued that addressing human rights concerns was not within the competency of the council and therefore inappropriate, citing the division of labor created by the Charter.[17] Despite these concerns, the UNSC passed Resolution 688 with ten affirmative votes, defining the transborder effects of human rights violations in Iraq as a threat to international peace and security and bringing human rights concerns within the purview of the Security Council for the first time. Human rights concerns that pertain to international peace and security have continued to be a legitimate subject of Security Council deliberation ever since.

The United Nations, Human Rights, and Sovereignty

The Universal Declaration of Human Rights was adopted by the United Nations General Assembly in 1948 and has been essential to "establishing the contours of the contemporary consensus on internationally recognized human rights."[18] Indeed the Universal Declaration was created to define more clearly and completely what the drafters of the Charter meant when they referenced human rights in the preamble and identified promoting human rights as a purpose of the UN. Contemporary human rights norms are generally accepted to be the rights of individuals that are codified in the Universal Declaration and the United Nations' other human rights instruments, including the International Covenant on Civil and Political Rights and the International Covenant on Economic, Social, and Cultural Rights, which together with the Universal Declaration make up what is commonly termed the International Bill of Human Rights. The Convention on the Prevention and Punishment of the Crime of Genocide (or the Genocide Convention) is also cited by members of the UNSC as providing both the humanitarian and human rights justification for the use of force. Martha Finnemore argues that contemporary beliefs about human rights at the domestic and international level have transformed understandings of the legitimate use of military force to include responding to humanitarian crises and stopping mass atrocities.[19] Only since the early 1990s has humanitarian intervention become a legitimate response to human rights violations reaching the gravity of crimes against humanity or genocide in sovereign states.

Sovereignty, in addition to being well defined in the Charter, is considered to be the *grundnorm* of international society.[20] According to Robert Jackson, sovereignty is "a legal institution that authenticates a political order based on independent states whose governments are the principal authorities both domestically and internationally."[21] The core notion of sovereignty has been enduring but its practices are "periodically renovated" to respond to historical changes in circumstances.[22] Daniel Philpott conceptualizes sovereignty in terms of "revolutions" or periods of conceptual change where notions of authority are revised in significant ways, despite the permanence of the institution.[23] Because sovereignty is a social construct rather than a material condition, Bruce Cronin argues, it is the "subject of interpretation and re-interpretation by the participants in the nation-state system."[24]

While sovereignty became an institutionalized political norm in the twentieth century, in practice there remained a significant tension over whether sovereignty should be determined on a territorial basis—where historical borders are sacrosanct even when they do not match the demographic facts of the state within those borders—or based on the political desire for self-rule of a distinctive group of people.[25] Indeed this unresolved tension about what constitutes legitimate statehood is often a cause of the massive human rights violations that elicit humanitarian interventions. Internationally sanctioned military intervention as a response of the international community to state-led ethnic cleansing represents a revision in sovereignty—one that demands more stringent guarantees of individual rights within a state.[26] This revolution in sovereignty reemphasizes the nation-state as the primary actor in international politics rather than displaces it because it problematizes *legitimate* state authority over people and borders rather than that state authority itself.

The meaning of sovereignty derives from the international community of sovereign states because state sovereignty requires mutual recognition. Members of the broader global system of states have consistently placed constraints on sovereign independence. Despite enduring commitment to state sovereignty as a principle, in practice, the revocation, temporary suspension, or violation of sovereignty rights has regularly occurred in the international society of states.[27] Since the end of the Cold War, however, the revocation or temporary suspension of sovereignty has been justified on the basis of violations of fundamental human rights and international humanitarian law. Indeed the current and past three secretaries-general of the United Nations—Ban Ki-Moon (2007–present), Kofi Annan (1997–2006), Boutros Boutros-Ghali (1992–1996), and Javier Pérez de Cuéllar (1982–1991)—have all recognized that "the evolution of international human rights standards and support for their implementation has now reached the stage where norms of non-intervention, and the related deference to sovereignty rights, no longer apply to the same extent in the face of severe human rights or humanitarian abuses."[28] This contradicts the practice throughout much of the UN's history, during which it regarded the state's treatment of its own population to be within the domestic jurisdiction of states. The balance between these two normative values has shifted in response to several factors at the end of the twentieth century, including the end of the Cold War, an increase in intrastate conflict and a dramatic rise in mass atrocity crimes, the growth of the human rights movement and the growing legitimacy of human rights norms, and revolutions in information technology including the emergence of the twenty-four-hour news media and internet communications.[29] The chapters that follow illustrate how sovereignty norms and human rights norms are mutually constituted and coevolving at the United Nations and trace that process across two decades of decisions.

As international human rights norms become increasingly legitimate and widespread, gross violations of human rights have been defined as threats to international peace and security; and militarily stopping ethnic cleansing has become legitimate. In cases of armed conflict characterized by mass atrocity, these two core norms have the potential to come into conflict with one another: the protection of state sovereignty and the protection of international human rights. When human rights violations are defined as a threat to international peace and security, Security Council members may face competing normative claims. Protecting state sovereignty has traditionally demanded a policy of nonintervention in domestic affairs; whereas, protecting human rights norms introduces the possibility of the use of military force to stop violence occurring within the borders of sovereign states. Unless these two sets of norms can be conceptually reconciled, council members must act in a complex normative environment characterized by multiple and often competing normative claims about the appropriate response to mass violence.[30]

The perceived inability of the UNSC to appropriately respond to this ethical dilemma prompted Secretary-General Kofi Annan to demand that the UN reconsider how it responds to the political, human rights, and humanitarian crises affecting much of the world. Annan's 1999 annual report to the General Assembly was largely motivated by the twin failures of Rwanda and Kosovo. In 1994, the UNSC failed to protect the Tutsi population during the Rwandan genocide and in 1999 NATO intervened militarily to protect Kosovo's Albanian population from ethnic cleansing without the required Security Council authorization. Annan challenged the UN "to forge unity behind the principle that massive and systematic violations of human rights—wherever they may take place—should not be allowed to stand."[31] He argued that two concepts of sovereignty were developing at the UN: state sovereignty and individual sovereignty: "State sovereignty, in its most basic sense, is being redefined by the forces of globalization and international cooperation. The State is now widely understood to be the servant of its people, and not vice versa. At the same time, individual sovereignty—and by this I mean the human rights and fundamental freedoms of each and every individual as enshrined in our Charter—has been enhanced by a renewed consciousness of the right of every individual to control his or her own destiny."[32] Annan recognized that these parallel developments did not provide easy interpretation but that the answers could be found in the Charter. The failures to reconcile sovereignty and human rights were not caused by deficiencies in the Charter, he reasoned, but by the difficulties its members had in applying its core principles to a new era in which traditional notions of sovereignty "did not do justice to the aspirations of people to attain their fundamental freedoms."[33] Sovereignty and human rights were often in tension throughout the 1990s, as they had been traditionally, but Annan suggested that conceptually they did not need to be.

In 2001 the International Commission on Intervention and State Sovereignty (ICISS) released a groundbreaking report, *The Responsibility to Protect*, in direct response to the secretary-general's challenge. At its core, the responsibility to protect embodies the idea that states have a responsibility to protect their own populations from catastrophic harm and violations of fundamental human rights but that when they are unable or unwilling to do so, the international community must share in the fulfillment of that responsibility.[34] Sovereignty, when conceived as responsibility, incorporates a minimal conception of human rights, easing the tension between the two norms in the worst circumstances—large-scale loss of life or ethnic cleansing caused by state commission or omission.[35] Responsibility to protect seeks to create normative coherence between sovereignty norms and human rights norms by conceptualizing the former to incorporate the latter. The cases in this book, however, illustrate that throughout the 1990s, the UNSC largely conceived of sovereignty and human rights in opposition. Humanitarian intervention by the Security Council generally occurred where the perceived tension between sovereignty norms and human rights norms could be eliminated—in cases where the perpetrators of mass atrocity were nonstate actors or state actors without recognized sovereignty. In cases where the perpetrators were sovereign state members of the UN—as in Rwanda and Kosovo—humanitarian intervention by the Security Council was not forthcoming.

In 2005, a limited version of the responsibility-to-protect principle was officially endorsed by the membership of the UN in paragraphs 138 and 139 of the World Summit Outcome document. These paragraphs affirm that states have a responsibility to protect their own populations from genocide, war crimes, ethnic cleansing, and crimes against humanity.[36] They also affirm that the international community, acting through the UN, has a responsibility "to use appropriate diplomatic, humanitarian and other peaceful means, in accordance with Chapters VI and VIII of the Charter" in responding to these same crimes. Only when these measures fail and state authorities "manifestly fail to protect their populations" will the UNSC consider collective action under Chapter VII on a "case by case basis."[37] Later the responsibility to protect was reaffirmed by the Security Council in a series of thematic and case-specific resolutions. Despite these and subsequent affirmations of responsibility to protect both in formal documents and the public discourse of the council, in practice, perceived conflict between sovereignty norms and human rights norms continued to bar humanitarian intervention until March 2011. It was groundbreaking when the UNSC authorized the use of "all necessary measures" under Chapter VII to protect civilians and civilian protected areas in Libya, marking the first time that it authorized humanitarian intervention against a state perpetrator, and justifying it using responsibility-to-protect language.

Evolving Norms and Changing Practices in International Relations

While norms of sovereignty and human rights have been a central concern of the UN since its founding, their conceptual meaning has changed over time. Social constructivists argue that norms—standards of appropriate behavior for an actor with a given identity—are derived from shared moral, causal, or factual belief.[38] Norms are both regulative and constitutive because they restrain and enable actors while also shaping their identities and interests. Norms, then, are not simply given. They must be actively created, diffused, and internalized, and they evolve over time, sometimes strengthening and sometimes weakening. Persuasion or norm advocacy by norm entrepreneurs is central to the effective emergence of new norms or alterations in an existing norm's meaning. Successful new norms are typically legitimized by proponents' peers, receive the support of prominent states, and are adjacent or linked to existing norms; this link to existing norms has to be actively constructed by proponents.[39] Social constructivists argue that humanitarian intervention has become possible as human rights norms have become increasingly legitimate and widely held beliefs in international society.[40] In short, the legitimacy of human rights creates a permissive normative environment for the practice of humanitarian intervention. The emergence of new ideas about humanitarian intervention, however, did not displace sovereignty norms. Instead, ideas about human rights exist alongside sovereignty and nonintervention norms within the culture of the UN. Thus, decisions by the UNSC shape how both human rights norms and sovereignty norms are interpreted and applied over time.[41]

In contrast, rationalist approaches to international relations understand norms to be primarily regulative.[42] These approaches posit that norms constrain or order behavior but do not shape actors and their identities. Norms, then, reflect rather than create national interests and are often conceived as reflecting the values and interests of powerful states that are then imposed on weaker states. In the realm of the United Nations, this suggests that UNSC decisions about humanitarian intervention reflect the combined total of individual members' national interests and level of power more than any particular commitment to new norms of human rights. Rationalist scholars argue that humanitarian intervention is explained by the material interests of the five permanent members, the most powerful ones, who only engage in humanitarian intervention when their national interests are at stake. According to this approach, humanitarian intervention is a guise that provides ideological cover for otherwise nonhumanitarian motives.[43]

Though this approach is appealing for its simplicity and intuitiveness, when a strictly rationalist approach is applied on a case-by-case basis to conflicts characterized by mass atrocity, claims of purely material motivations for humanitarian intervention are not convincing. Material self-interests, national security concerns, and geopolitical calculations seem to figure prominently in situations where Security Council humanitarian intervention has been absent but are largely lacking in situations where humanitarian intervention has occurred. Rationalist approaches partially explain cases where humanitarian intervention is absent, as in Rwanda and Darfur. For, example, lack of national and material interests in Rwanda by most powerful members of the Security Council resulted in a marginal and contingent commitment to the UN peacekeeping mission there. In contrast, France as a political and military ally of the perpetrator government had significant interests in the political outcome of UN involvement in Rwanda and intervened both in decision making and in the field in ways that benefited French national interests (see Chapter 5). In another example, China often shielded Sudanese president Omar al-Bashir and his regime (and simultaneously Chinese oil interests) during council meetings on the situation in Darfur (see Chapter 7). Nonetheless, the influence of human rights norms was also present in both of these cases, as evidenced by the creation of the International Criminal Tribunal to prosecute perpetrators of genocide in Rwanda and the referral of the situation in Darfur to the International Criminal Court (ICC).

Rationalist approaches with their emphasis on material power and interests cannot explain why powerful states would undertake elective military intervention at all. Humanitarian intervention is costly to intervening states, which typically pay a high cost in blood and treasure and become bound to some form of international administration for security protection indefinitely. This is why Chaim Kaufmann and Robert Pape consider humanitarian intervention "a costly international moral action—one that advances moral principle rather than selfish interest."[44] There is little tangible material benefit for humanitarian interventions in places like Somalia and Sierra Leone. So while Western powers lacked security interests in Rwanda and Darfur (where they did not intervene), they also lacked security interests in Somalia and Sierra Leone (where they did intervene). Even when humanitarian intervention occurs in places within the regional security interests of powerful permanent Security Council members as in Bosnia-Herzegovina, national security interest is not a compelling explanation. For example, while Bosnia was largely considered to be in the Western sphere of influence and the war there was considered a regional security threat, western European states were initially reluctant to intervene. Instead, non-Western states were the strongest and most consistent advocates for humanitarian intervention in Bosnia during Security Council meetings, and support for intervention was widespread throughout the international community (see Chapter 4).

These brief examples challenge the idea that humanitarian intervention is a tool used by the strong against the weak for selfish purposes. They preview what the chapters of this study show: material explanations of humanitarian intervention behavior, while important, are incomplete. Interests and material power matter to Security Council decision making, but interests are shaped by normative values, and power takes many forms—the power of ideas, the power to define norms, and the ability to tell a convincing story are just as important for shaping outcomes in Security Council decision making as material power. The emergence of human rights ideas in the UNSC demonstrates the power of ideas to reshape understandings of national interests and international security interests.[45] The cases in this study bear this out—principled ideas and normative values shape UNSC decision making and are just as influential as power or interests. Yet little scholarly literature in international relations takes seriously the influence of norms in places of hard power like the United Nations Security Council or illustrates how discourse in international relations has real explanatory power. This book does so by surveying the major UN humanitarian interventions—both successes and failures—in order to show how discourse creates the conditions for military action in defense of human rights.

This book takes a decidedly social constructivist approach to the question of humanitarian intervention, one that focuses on the mutual constitution and coevolution of human rights norms and sovereignty norms. While attentive to the material interests of Security Council members and how they influence decisions, this study draws attention to the interaction of norms, interests, and power–and not competition between them, as is common in much international relations scholarship. The cases that follow illustrate how Security Council discourse creates and forecloses opportunities for humanitarian intervention in cases of armed conflict characterized by mass atrocity crimes. They also show how Security Council members struggle to reconcile sovereignty norms and human rights norms in the context of specific conflicts. My analysis demonstrates that human rights are increasingly linked to international peace and security and that normative ideas about human rights, sovereign authority, and state responsibilities to their populations shape council decision making about humanitarian intervention as much as material and geostrategic considerations. Thus, I also illustrate the ways that norms and interests interact and are mutually constituted throughout the debates that accompany each case.

Researching Humanitarian Intervention

A project of this character—one that seeks to generalize and explain how Security Council discourse creates the possibility of humanitarian intervention—is fraught with challenge. Political by design, the UNSC examines the question of humanitarian intervention on a case-by-case basis. The council maintains a strong resistance to standard-setting requirements and intends to avoid creating precedent or developing discernible patterns in behavior.[46] In fact, political contingency is central to how the UNSC was designed to function. Thus, faced with tensions between legal and moral principles, as in situations of conflict characterized by mass atrocity crimes, political considerations *ought* to and often do weigh heavily on members of the Security Council when they are making decisions about humanitarian intervention.[47] This project is attentive to the political contingency in each case of examination, yet specifically draws attention to important but overlooked patterns in discourse that map onto Security Council humanitarian intervention behavior. The project builds theory to explain how UNSC humanitarian intervention becomes possible in some cases of mass atrocity but not others, given a permissive normative environment.

I define humanitarian intervention as *the use of military force by a group of states inside a sovereign state without the formal consent of its authorities for the purpose of preventing, halting, or punishing widespread and gross violations of the fundamental human rights of individuals.*[48] For the purposes of theory building, I selected my cases with variation in humanitarian intervention outcomes. Examining armed conflicts where UNSC humanitarian intervention has happened alongside similar situations where it might have been expected but did not occur illustrates otherwise obscured patterns of intervention behavior. The comparison of "cases" and "noncases" of humanitarian intervention also helps to identify or challenge interpretations of Security Council behavior.

To create a data set of cases of expected humanitarian intervention, I used the Political Terror Scale—a yearly report that measures physical integrity rights violations (murder, disappearance, and torture) by states against their domestic populations.[49] The scale measures levels of political terror and violence in a particular year using a five-point ranking. The most severe score is a level 5, which denotes one of two situations: (1) a situation of political terror where murders, disappearances, and torture are a common part of life for the whole population and where leaders place no limits on the means or thoroughness with which they pursue their personal or ideological goals; or (2) a level of widespread terror so great that although it is only aimed at certain segments of the population it still constitutes a level 5 ranking.[50] The scale's coders draw data from the annual country reports of Amnesty International and the U.S. Department of State Country Reports on Human Rights Practices. I draw my data only from the scale's codes for Amnesty International reports to protect the integrity of the data from conflict of interest, because the United States is a permanent member of the Security Council.

Compiling the data on all the states between 1989 and 2010 that received a level 5 ranking of political terror for two or more consecutive years on these reports resulted in 26 states.[51] Because humanitarian intervention is an elective use of force and must have a reasonable prospect for success, interveners will not mount an elective military intervention against a nuclear state, reducing the complete set of possible cases of expected humanitarian intervention between 1989 and 2010 to 22 states including: Afghanistan, Algeria, Angola, Bosnia-Herzegovina, Brazil, Burundi, Chad, Colombia, Congo, Democratic Republic of Congo, Ethiopia, Iraq, Liberia, Myanmar, Peru, Rwanda, Sierra Leone, Somalia, South Africa, Sri Lanka, Sudan, and Yugoslavia (Serbia and Montenegro). As this sample alone makes clear, despite the increasing legitimacy of humanitarian intervention, its occurrence is rare. Cases of Security Council humanitarian intervention from this set include only Bosnia, Sierra Leone, and Somalia. Several other cases, including Burundi, Democratic Republic of Congo, and Sudan have hosted large peacekeeping operations but the involvement of the UNSC falls short of humanitarian intervention.

I chose to examine the three cases of Security Council humanitarian intervention from the set above—Bosnia, Sierra Leone, and Somalia—and an equal number of cases from this set where the Security Council might have been expected to use humanitarian intervention but did not—Rwanda, Kosovo (Yugoslavia), and Darfur (Sudan).[52] The conflicts in Somalia, Bosnia-Herzegovina, and Rwanda occurred simultaneously, and the practice of UNSC-authorized humanitarian intervention first emerged during this period (1991–95). The conflicts in Kosovo (Yugoslavia), Sierra Leone, and Darfur (Sudan) occurred in a later period (1996–2010)—a period marked by significant debate over whether the Security Council had a responsibility to stop ethnic cleansing.

These cases had useful attributes for both initial theory building and subsequent theory testing.[53] The cases were characterized by human rights abuses of relatively equal severity across similar time frames but had different humanitarian intervention outcomes. Process tracing and discourse analysis revealed that these cases had significant variation in terms of characterization of the conflict by the UNSC and the source of sovereign authority in a target state. The cases of Bosnia and Darfur provided significant within-case variation over time. Most of the cases have intrinsic importance to the study of humanitarian intervention, including Somalia, Bosnia, Rwanda, and Kosovo. All of the cases are data-rich and there is an abundance of primary documentation and secondary source literature for each. The cases also resemble current situations of policy concern, allowing for ease of testing these findings across an even broader set of cases. Finally, because of the severity of the human rights violations involved in Rwanda and Darfur and their geographic location in Africa, explaining the absence of Security Council humanitarian intervention in these particular cases creates a hard test for a theory of norm change and potential support for an alternative explanation of state interest.

In addition to the six cases drawn from the data set above, my study begins with an examination of the situation in Iraq (1991–92) and ends by testing my findings in the most recent case of humanitarian intervention as of this writing—in Libya (2011). First, the case of Iraq is groundbreaking for a study of Security Council humanitarian intervention. Resolution 688 defined the effects of the Iraqi regime's human rights violations as a threat to international peace and security and was the first Security Council resolution that referenced human rights concerns in relation to Chapter VII, paving the way for eventual use of military force in defense of an internal humanitarian crisis with cross-border effects. Second, in 2011, the UNSC engaged in an unprecedented humanitarian intervention in Libya—the first in over a decade—discrediting the argument that humanitarian intervention during the 1990s was a temporary deviation in Council practice. Libya provides a useful test case for the theory advanced in this book: that Security Council discourse about the character of conflict and sovereign authority in target states creates and forecloses opportunities for humanitarian intervention. Importantly, the level of violence that preceded the humanitarian intervention in Libya was far lower than in the other cases of this study, which suggests a potential widening of the prospective cases of future humanitarian intervention.

The Role of Argument and Storytelling in the Security Council

Arguing, scholars have shown, has an impact on the practice of world politics, and the UNSC is a realm of political argumentation.[54] Indeed the UNSC is the primary venue in international politics where authoritative decisions are made about what events constitute threats to international peace and security, the legitimate source of sovereign authority, and the purpose of military force. Because the Security Council is a political institution, the application of Charter principles is mediated by politics. The UNSC is a forum of "heated and unsystematic, but often principled debate about appropriate standards of international behavior and the extent and limits of the council's authority to regulate that behavior."[55] The Security Council is also a quasi-legal institution with dense patterns of interactions—its decisions are binding on member states and it is vested with the authority to judge the legality of the use of military force in international affairs. Because it gains its authority through the legitimacy conferred on it by other UN members, the arguments and justifications that council members make about the topics on their agendas, particularly the use of force, not only are significant but also relate to particular international norms.[56] Consequently, some arguments are more acceptable and credible than others during council debates. To be legitimate and persuasive, Security Council members and others appearing before the council frame their arguments according to the legal norms enshrined in the Charter of the UN or according to widely shared international moral norms. Arguments that appear prejudiced—generated purely by self-interest—are viewed skeptically and are often disqualified by other actors. These limitations on appropriate discourse impose some constraint on UNSC action: members will incur reputational costs if they act without a defensible position or advance arguments that do not reasonably justify their conduct in relationship to legal or moral norms.[57]

Members of the Security Council struggle over the power to define norms. Control over the interpretation of the norms and principles of the Charter, in particular, is markedly important. Thus, the effective framing of issues is essential.[58] Framing involves creating a template that identifies a problem and offers a solution to it. An attractively framed argument viewed as legitimate by other members of the Security Council is more likely to be persuasive and gain necessary widespread support. Emotional appeals and narratives are just as important and sometimes more compelling than appeals to logic. Narratives identify some facts as more important than others. The influence of the agent advancing the narrative matters but so do the perceptions of those states that the narrative is directed toward.[59] The discursive representation of conflicts and related human rights violations by Security Council members has the potential to create and foreclose opportunities for humanitarian intervention: ". . . . Discourses are understood to work to define and to enable, and also to silence and exclude, for example by limiting and restricting authorities to some groups, but not others, endorsing a certain common sense, but making other modes of categorizing and judging meaningless, impractical, inadequate or otherwise disqualified."[60] Classifying mass killing into categories like *ethnic cleansing* or *genocide* may make certain courses of action (such as humanitarian intervention) more possible than others like *human rights abuses, civil war*, or *ethnic conflict*.[61] Early decisions in the naming and framing of conflicts may determine the range of possible policy outcomes.[62] Yet actors cannot simply choose frames or stories—they are limited by existing legal and political norms; and their stories must resonate with their target audience in order to be persuasive.

When Security Council members face competing normative demands, like the tension between sovereignty and human rights, they argue about the cause of conflicts, the character of violence, sovereign authority in the target state, and how to interpret relevant norms. For this reason, I pay attention to the ways that council members justify their positions on the potential use of military force. In research for this study, I examined the public documents produced by the UNSC for each of my case studies. This includes transcripts of formal meetings, resolutions, presidential statements, and formal mission reports. The UNSC makes its decisions in formal meetings that are on the public record, but much of the actual decision making takes place in "informal consultations" that are off the record and held behind closed doors.[63] In many cases, individual Security Council members have already decided how they will vote, and they often prepare the text of their formal statements in advance. In many cases, proposed resolutions that do not have the support or acquiescence of permanent members never make it to the council chamber. Nonetheless, formal meeting records remain the most useful documents for identifying how individual states characterize conflicts and the violence that accompanies them as well as their justifications for the decisions about the use of military force.

Despite the pro forma character of official proceedings, the public statements made by Security Council members offer revealing justifications for decisions precisely because they are scripted in advance and for public consumption. Security Council members take considerable care to select the words that they deem appropriate and they argue about the language used in resolutions and presidential statements because they are in the public record.

Security Council Resolutions are meticulously negotiated documents because they are binding on all member states of the United Nations. The way that council members vote and their justifications for that vote illustrate the degree to which the resolution is supported by each state, making the resolution a useful measure of areas of Security Council agreement, or lack thereof. Presidential statements are advisory rather than binding but they are consensus documents, as are the formal mission reports of the UNSC. This means that the content and wording of each of these texts has received the unanimous approval of council members before being publicly issued. I examine two types of evidence found in these documents: Security Council decisions about the use of military force in cases of mass atrocity; and debates about, and justifications for, humanitarian intervention or its absence across the entire set of cases. By analyzing these texts and comparing them to actual Security Council behavior, I demonstrate how the discourse of Security Council members produces opportunities for humanitarian intervention. Finnemore asserts that "when states justify their interventions, they draw on and articulate shared values and expectations that other decision makers and other publics in other states hold. Justification is literally an attempt to connect one's actions with standards of justice, or perhaps more generically, with standards of appropriate and acceptable behavior."[64] The arguments of council members and their justifications for humanitarian intervention provide clues about the normative context in which decisions about humanitarian intervention are made in addition to illustrating how the practice is discursively constructed as legitimate.

A Theory of Causal Stories

Security Council texts rely on formulaic presentations, therefore it is easy to identify systematic patterns of problem definition and the policy solutions that flow from them. Through a method of content analysis that carefully examines Security Council discourse, I generated a typology of causal stories that explains how council members struggle to control interpretations of conflicts and how the narratives they advance open and foreclose the possibility of using military force in defense of human rights. These frames, which I call causal stories—a concept that I borrow from public policy scholar Deborah Stone[65]—are created, changed, and contested in the UNSC. They compete against alternatives until one becomes predominant. The predominant causal story has direct implications for Security Council decision making about the use of military force.

In order to trace the emergence and diffusion of Security Council stories, I analyze the signification processes of its members using predication analysis, which focuses specifically on the "language practices of predication—the verbs, adverbs and adjectives that attach to particular nouns."[66] I study how predications construct nouns like *conflict, war*, and *human rights violations* as a particular type of *conflict, war*, and *human rights violation*. For example, Security Council deliberations alternately describe the situation in Darfur as an "ethnic conflict," "tribal war," or "genocide." The fighting is characterized by "civilian casualties," "ethnic cleansing," or "chaos." I create a list of the predications that are attached to threats to international peace and security that the Security Council constructs—wars, conflicts, and human rights violations—and clarify the relationships between them; both what distinguishes how these subjects are constructed and how these constructions are related to each other.[67]

Policy debate, including the deliberations among Security Council members, presumes that to solve a political problem, it is necessary to find its root cause or causes.[68] Causal arguments, then, are at the heart of problem definition in international politics. "Causal theories," Stone argues, "like other modes of problem definition, are efforts to control interpretations and images of difficulties. Political actors create causal stories to describe harms and difficulties, to attribute them to actions of other individuals and organizations, and thereby to invoke government power to stop the harm. Like other forms of symbolic representation, causal stories can be emotionally compelling; they are stories of innocence and guilt, victims and oppressors, suffering and evil."[69] Through their statements, Security Council members are telling stories to one another, domestic publics, and third-party states about the conflicts on their agenda. These stories describe the causes and character of conflicts and attribute blame for human rights violations. Research across the eight cases examined in this study reveals that Security Council members regularly articulate three types of stories that explain the cause of conflicts characterized by mass atrocity crimes: intentional, inadvertent, and complex (see Table 1.1). They are called causal stories not because they have a direct causal link to subsequent council action (though discourse makes certain courses of action more likely than others) but because they are stories about causation—about the cause of conflict and the character of violence within that conflict.

Intentional causal stories explain situations where "action was willfully taken by human beings in order to bring about the consequences that actually happened."[70] They identify a specific actor or actors as responsible for knowingly and willingly causing harm to others, making it a story of perpetrators and victims. Intentional stories are the most effective type of story for changing perceptions of harm from the realm of fate to the realm of political agency because they identify a plausible candidate to take responsibility for the problem.[71] When applied to situations of conflict, intentional stories detail systematic repression where conflict is largely one-sided and premeditated. These stories characterize human rights violations as deliberate, targeted, and widespread because perpetrators are conceived of as having direct control over their actions. There are three constituent elements of an intentional story when applied to conflict situations: identification of an intentional perpetrator, characterization of the violence as deliberate and naming it in a way that demonstrates this intentional character, and identification of a targeted victim group. *Genocide, ethnic cleansing,* and *aggression* display characteristics of an intentional story, particularly when they identify perpetrators and name victims. Because violence is characterized as both deliberate and systematic, the policy implications of an intentional story focus on interdiction of violence and protection from harm because there is a perpetrator that can be stopped or a single point of leverage to address the problem. Punishment and accountability are also likely because the harms imposed are perceived as flagrant violations of widely accepted international legal norms. The intentional causal story corresponds to a specific normative script in international relations—that of international law and specifically international humanitarian law and international human rights law.[72] The norms of justice and accountability anchor the intentional story and give rise to interpretations of state sovereignty that privilege a minimal level of state responsibility for human rights.

Table 1.1. Discourse Analysis of Security Council Records

	Character of Conflict	Character of Human Rights Violations	Constituent Elements	Sample Discourse	Principle and Values	Policy Implications
Intentional causal story	Systematic repression; conflict is one-sided with premeditated attacks.	Systematic, targeted, deliberate, and widespread; perpetrators have direct control over their actions.	Narrative of perpetrator-victim: (1) identifiable perpetrator; (2) knowingly and willingly causing harm; (3) innocent civilian victims.	Aggression Repression Genocide Ethnic cleansing War crimes Crimes against humanity	Justice International law	Punishment Interdiction Protection Accountability
Inadvertent causal story	Two or more parties involved in cycle of violence and reprisal; deaths are foreseen but not purpose of violence.	Foreseen but unintended; indiscriminate; acts of omission; control is mediated by intervening conditions.	Narrative of moral equivalency: (1) multiple responsible parties who are perceived as morally equivalent; (2) deaths are predictable but unintended; (3) responsibility is diffuse.	Civil war Ethnic conflict Religious war All parties	Neutrality Impartiality Sovereign equality Domestic noninterference	Assistance Palliation Protection Observation

| Complex causal story | Multifaceted, complicated, and tragic situation with multiple and fragmenting actors/groups; responsibility for violence is diffuse. | Result of combination of structural, historical, and political decision-making factors. | Narrative of complexity or confusion: (1) multiple, fragmented perpetrator groups; (2) deaths are combination of structural factors, collateral damage and intentional harm; (3) no single point of leverage to fix the problem. | Tragedy Chaos Complex(ity) Mayhem Intertribal warfare | State Sovereignty Stability Status quo | Appeals Condemnation Good offices Observation Documentation Reporting |

Inadvertent causal stories recount situations where purposeful action has foreseen but unintended consequences. In situations of conflict, inadvertent stories describe situations where two or more parties are involved in a cycle of violence and reprisal in which deaths can be predicted but are not the purpose of the conflict. There is a perceived moral equivalency between parties to the conflict who are mutually culpable for human rights violations that are expected, as collateral damage, but result from indiscriminate action or acts of omission on the part of the parties, rather than being deliberate.[73] The constituent elements of an inadvertent story include multiple responsible parties are perceived to be morally equivalent, deaths associated with the fighting are predictable but unintended, and responsibility for those deaths is diffuse. Inadvertent stories are typically depicted discursively as *civil war* or *ethnic conflict*, terms that carry connotations of shared responsibility but diffuse culpability. In situations of gross human rights violations, inadvertent stories foster policy recommendations for the protection of civilians. Most Security Council action in these instances incorporates efforts at palliation of the harm, assistance to the parties in ending the conflict, or observation and monitoring of human rights violations or the humanitarian crisis. The underlying normative script is the sovereign equality of states and nonintervention in their domestic affairs. This suggests that council members should be neutral and impartial in their dealings with the parties to the conflict, particularly if they are states.

As Deborah Stone observes, "Complex causal stories are not very useful for solving problems in politics precisely because they do not offer a single locus of control . . . or a point of leverage to fix the problem."[74] Rather, complex stories describe multiple sources of causation (structural or social) or situations where harms result from complex systems of interaction or complicated institutional or historical patterns. Complex stories lack an identifiable actor that exerts control over the entire system or web of interactions that produce the harm. In absence of control there can be no purpose and thus no responsibility for the harms that result.[75] When applied to situations of conflict, complex stories describe multifaceted, complicated, and tragic situations in which multiple and often fragmenting groups are responsible. The accompanying violence results from a combination of both structural factors—beyond the realm of individual human control—and political decision making. Thus there is evidence of both collateral damage and intentional harm. Indeed, complex causal stories have unclear boundaries, often incorporating characteristics associated with the competing intentional and inadvertent causal stories at the same time. Complex conflicts are described as *confusing, chaotic,* or *tragic*. The policy implications of violence that lacks a single point for interdiction take two forms: (1) appeals for an end to violence, including strong verbal condemnation of cease-fire violations and human rights violations and the use of good offices to broker the conflict's peaceful resolution; and (2) observation, documentation of, and reporting on the violence, including mass atrocities and cease-fire violations. The complex story privileges the status quo—its underlying normative script is one about respect for international order and for a traditional Westphalian conception of sovereignty in which the state has control over its people and territory and is free from external interference in its domestic decision making.

Causal stories are powerful because they can lead to actions that protect the existing social order or upend it. By identifying causal agents they also assign responsibility for problems and with it the possibility of punishment, and at the same time they legitimize and empower other agents to fix the problems.[76] Causal stories are not necessarily right or wrong, nor are they mutually exclusive. Though they impute "true cause," political conflicts over causal stories extend beyond competing empirical claims—they are literally fights to control the policy agenda and to assign responsibility.[77] In the Security Council, members are fighting for the power to define threats to international peace and security and assign responsibility for conflicts as well as to control the interpretation of relevant norms like those of sovereignty and human rights. Security Council texts show that the stories articulated by members change over time and that the members regularly argue about how to characterize conflict. Tracing the emergence and diffusion of causal stories—who articulates them, under what circumstances, and the direction of diffusion—reveals important factors that mediate this contestation process. By comparing points of disjuncture and agreement in council deliberations against conditions on the ground, I identify patterns that explain why one story eventually predominates. The most important factors are the prominence of a story's proponents, including their visibility and material and normative power; and the story's consistency with expert testimony, media imagery, and forensic evidence. A causal story can be considered successful when it resonates with the domestic populations of states and when it becomes a dominant belief or guiding assumption of Security Council members.

The predominant story shapes Security Council decision making, and each story type has a different propensity to trigger the use of military force.

The discursive representation of a conflict as intentional creates opportunities for humanitarian intervention while its discursive representation as either inadvertent or complex forecloses such opportunities. Each characterization of the conflict and its attendant human rights violations appeals to preexisting normative scripts and has specific policy implications. Intentional stories identify a perpetrator(s) who intentionally and often systematically inflicts harm on a specific group of victims. Because this perpetrator can be identified and stopped, thus preventing atrocities from continuing, an intentional story is more likely than its alternatives to foster the use of military force. According to senior UN officials, support for humanitarian operations can be garnered in the Security Council only if it can be clearly shown that "a good guy–bad guy situation" exists.[78] Likewise, Kenneth Roth, executive director of Human Rights Watch, argues that complex stories are ineffective at prompting UNSC humanitarian intervention: "Conflict situations that seem like chaos do not invite humanitarian intervention. Intervention needs a clear bad guy who is going to be stopped. . . . While you could say at a certain point that even chaos deserves intervention, it is both politically and pragmatically more difficult. Politically, because it is easier to mobilize political support if there is a clear bad guy and you can stand up and say we are going to stop this bad guy; practically, because no international body wants to be in the middle of chaos."[79] Politically, rendering a cause complex is one of the most effective ways for actors to avoid action, blame, or reform.[80] Inadvertent stories, like complex stories, are unlikely to create opportunities for humanitarian intervention because the violence is understood as a foreseen by-product of the fighting and not the purpose of it. There are multiple culpable parties and they share moral responsibility rendering responsibility diffuse. When contestation persists among members about the appropriate causal story, the result will be inaction. In sum, the Security Council decision-making patterns in the cases of this study show that the Security Council is unlikely to engage in humanitarian intervention in absence of its widespread acceptance of, or acquiescence to, an intentional story with an identified, intentional perpetrator that can be stopped from inflicting harm on its targeted population.

Security Council members not only tell stories about the cause and character of conflict and their associated human rights violations, they also tell stories about sovereignty. Sovereignty stories vary by the status of sovereign authority in the target state, the actor that is the referent for sovereignty, and the norm's theoretical underpinnings. Council members regularly tell three types of stories about sovereign authority in conflict states: (1) sovereign authority is legitimate, (2) sovereign authority is illegitimate, or (3) sovereign authority is lacking, either because it is contested, has been temporarily suspended, or is absent. In many cases, the target state itself is the referent for Security Council stories about sovereignty but in others the referent can be third-party states as in the case of Iraq, deposed governments as in that of Sierra Leone, or the people living within the territory of the target state as in those of Somalia and Libya. Finally, Security Council stories about sovereignty are grounded within different theoretical or conceptual aspects of sovereignty, including Westphalian sovereignty, international legal sovereignty, popular sovereignty, and sovereignty as responsibility. Despite these variations, what is consistent across the cases examined here is that humanitarian intervention only occurs in situations when sovereignty is discursively constructed by the Security Council as consistent with, and complementary to, the promotion of human rights.

Humanitarian intervention is likely where sovereign authority in the target state is discursively constructed as lacking or where the referent of sovereignty would benefit from human rights protection. Humanitarian intervention also becomes possible where the existing governing authorities are deemed illegitimate and sovereign authority is conceptually transferred to the people of that state. In such cases, the council can advance human rights and promote sovereignty at the same time. In contrast, when the status of sovereign authority is uncontested and the governing authorities are deemed legitimate by the Security Council, the promotion of human rights through humanitarian intervention has the potential to bring sovereignty norms and human rights norms into direct conflict. In situations of contestation between norms, the stronger, more internalized norm (state sovereignty) wins over the weaker, less developed norm (human rights). Yet the tension between human rights norms and sovereignty norms can be eliminated when Security Council members discursively construct them as complementary by appealing to different theoretical underpinnings like popular sovereignty and the idea of sovereignty as responsibility associated with the responsibility to protect. Security Council stories about sovereignty are evolving across time, particularly in the way that they address human rights violations committed by perpetrator states. In short, sovereignty norms and human rights norms are mutually constituted.

Organization of the Book

Approaching these conflicts on a case-by-case basis, I illustrate how discourse shapes the likelihood that the UNSC will engage in humanitarian intervention. I also examine the interaction between sovereignty norms and human rights norms as well as how norms and interests are mutually constitutive in each case. What results is a distinct pattern linking problem definition, articulated through the medium of causal stories, to UNSC humanitarian intervention decisions. These cases also detail a twenty-year evolution in the international norms of sovereignty and human rights. Each chapter tells an important part of this broader story yet also explores the contours, contingencies, and nuances of each individual case. Chapter 2 details important precursors to humanitarian intervention: passage of Security Council Resolution 688, which defined the consequences of Iraqi human rights violations as a threat to international peace and security, and the subsequent enforcement of a no-fly zone over Iraqi territory to protect civilians. Iraq is a necessary starting point for a study on the coevolution of human rights norms and sovereignty norms because it is the site of several important UNSC innovations: the emergence of human rights discourse in formal deliberations, the definition of a humanitarian crisis as a security threat, passage of a Security Council resolution explicitly dictating how a UN member-state should treat its domestic population, and the temporary suspension of the sovereignty of a member-state over a portion of its territory for humanitarian purposes. It is in Iraq that the goals of UN military force start to change in response to powerful human rights claims made in the UNSC.

In Somalia, the Security Council used humanitarian intervention to respond to a humanitarian crisis within the boundaries of an essentially failed state. Importantly, it did so with little attention to cross-border effects. Chapter 3 examines how an internal humanitarian catastrophe was defined as a threat to international peace and security and how the United Nations Operation in Somalia II became the first peacekeeping mission authorized to undertake enforcement action under Chapter VII of the UN Charter. Chapter 4 examines the war in Bosnia and demonstrates how human rights norms transformed understandings of international peace and security and state sovereignty in the UNSC, eventually leading to humanitarian intervention. The Security Council debates about the appropriate response to the war in Bosnia reflected widespread international concerns about how to resolve situations of contested state sovereignty, the obligations of the UNSC in cases of intrastate war, and how to reconcile the promotion of human rights with state sovereignty when the two come into conflict.

Chapter 5 examines the Security Council's decision to reduce the presence of UN peacekeeping personnel during the genocide in Rwanda, rather than authorize humanitarian intervention to stop it. In Rwanda, a state member of the United Nations perpetrated systematic human rights violations against its own people. When drawn into direct conflict with one another, sovereignty norms can become a blocking mechanism to the protection of human rights norms. The chapter on Rwanda introduces a perverse finding: when the state is deemed perpetrator, humanitarian intervention is less likely to follow. At stake in the Security Council debate over the killing in Kosovo four years later was clarifying the limits of state authority over populations and territory in an era marked by the increasing legitimacy of human rights norms. Chapter 6 shows that permanent members of the UNSC disagreed on the character of the conflict and what constituted the sovereign responsibilities of the state. Permanent members adopted irreconcilable causal stories, which stymied UNSC action. Humanitarian intervention by NATO, in the absence of Security Council authorization, provoked an intense dispute among council members about the meaning of sovereignty, the relationship between human rights and international security, and the legitimate authority and purpose for the use of force. Comparing the council's response to events in Kosovo with its response to mass atrocity in Sierra Leone underscores the importance of council stories about the cause and character of conflict and the source of sovereign authority to the council's humanitarian intervention decisions. Despite different humanitarian intervention outcomes, both illustrate the increasing importance of human rights norms within the Security Council.

The conflict in Darfur, the subject of Chapter 7, has been characterized by both significant contestation between Security Council members over the cause and character of the conflict and widespread agreement over the sovereign authority of President Omar al-Bashir's regime. Both factors precluded UNSC humanitarian intervention. Nonetheless, Security Council members, some motivated by responsibility to protect, adopted alternative policy measures to promote human rights when the use of military force was blocked, including the controversial referral of the Darfur case to the International Criminal Court—the first time the Security Council exercised its authority under Article 16 of the Rome Statute. In Chapter 8, I test my theory about Security Council stories—both causal stories and stories about sovereign authority—against the recent humanitarian intervention in Libya. The Libyan intervention marks a significant evolution in the council's response to mass atrocities—it represents the first time that the UNSC adopted an intentional story in the face of gross human rights violations committed by a perpetrator state member of the UN. The international normative context has changed such that it is now easier to justify humanitarian intervention than to justify failure to respond to mass atrocities. In Chapter 9, I argue that Security Council discourse provides important clues about how council members make decisions about humanitarian intervention. The adoption of particular causal stories by the council leads to different humanitarian intervention outcomes. Contestation between competing causal stories is mediated by the relationship between sovereignty norms and human rights norms, the material and normative power of causal story proponents, and fit between causal stories and expertise. Humanitarian intervention is a legitimate military action in the contemporary permissive normative environment. Humanitarian intervention does not become possible for the Security Council, however, unless most council members are unified in support of an intentional story in which they identify a perpetrator that is deliberately and systematically harming a specified victim group; and they can discursively construct the promotion of human rights as consistent with state sovereignty.

The Emergence of Human Rights Discourse in the Security Council: Domestic Repression in Iraq, 1990–1992

Between March and August 1988, the government of Iraq launched a series of lethal poison gas attacks against Kurdish villages in northern Iraq. Western media covered the effects of the chemical weapons attack on the town of Halabja: "Ghastly scenes of bodies strewn along Halabja's streets, families locked in an embrace of death, lifeless children, doll-like with blackened mouths, eyes, and nails, and the upended carcasses of domestic animals."[1] The international human rights organization Middle East Watch characterized the Iraqi attacks against its Kurdish population as genocide.[2] The U.S. State Department publicly condemned Iraq's use of chemical weapons, and the Senate Foreign Relations Committee issued a report concluding that there was "overwhelming evidence" that Iraq had used chemical weapons against Kurdish citizens. The United States, the Soviet Union, and at least eleven other states petitioned the UN Secretary-General, Javier Pérez de Cuéllar, to investigate Iraq's possible use of chemical weapons against Iraqi Kurds, but both Iraq and neighboring Turkey, where large numbers of Kurdish refugees had fled, rejected the UN's request for access to Kurdish survivors.[3] The UN deferred to the sovereign authority of both states and refrained from further interference in their domestic affairs—no formal condemnation of Iraq by the Security Council was forthcoming.

In contrast, during that same period, Iraq also was accused of using chemical weapons in its ongoing war with Iran. On 26 August 1988, the United Nations Security Council passed Resolution 620 (1988) condemning the use of chemical weapons in the Iran-Iraq War, which violated the

1925 Geneva Protocol and Security Council Resolution 612. Though both Resolutions 620 and 612 condemned use of chemical weapons in interstate warfare, neither resolution criticized or even mentioned Iraq's use of chemical weapons against its domestic population. Yet three years later in March 1991, army troops loyal to Iraqi president Saddam Hussein and his elite Republican Guard used helicopter gunships, tanks, and artillery to indiscriminately attack northern Iraqi Kurds and Muslim Shi'a in the south. Hundreds of thousands of Iraqis panicked, fled the country, and became stranded in the mountains between Iraq and Turkey and along the border with Iran, creating a humanitarian crisis. This time, only one month later, the UNSC passed Resolution 688 defining the effects of Iraq's human rights violations as a threat to international peace and security, and France, the UK, and the U.S. enforced a no-fly zone in northern Iraq to prevent the Iraqi regime from attacking the Kurdish people. Between 1988 and 1991, there was a dramatic shift in Security Council responses to Iraqi government attacks against its own population. In 1988 the council concerned itself solely with interstate threats and aggression, but by 1991 it began considering the domestic practices within states and their effects on international peace and security. Human rights considerations lacked legitimacy in Security Council deliberations in 1988, but a series of decisions in 1991 allowed for the limited consideration of human rights concerns in the Iraq case with the unintended consequence of both legitimizing human rights norms as a subject of council debate and laying the groundwork for future humanitarian intervention. This initial deviation in Security Council practice was made possible by a dramatically changed historical and political context and contingencies specific to the Iraq case.

In August 1990, Iraq invaded and occupied Kuwait. Within hours, the UNSC held an emergency meeting and passed Resolution 660, which condemned the Iraqi invasion and demanded an immediate and complete withdrawal of Iraq from Kuwait. This was how the Security Council was designed to work—to respond quickly and decisively to acts of aggression. Yet during the Cold War, the council had rarely exercised its enforcement powers under Chapter VII of the UN Charter.[4] In fact, only 7 percent of all Chapter VII resolutions passed by the Security Council between 1946 and 2002 occurred during the Cold War, which means an astonishing 93 percent were adopted after 1989.[5] Indeed, it was the Security Council's perceived ability to respond effectively, and in concert, to Iraq's aggression against Kuwait in August 1990 that ushered in a new era of optimism about the role of the UNSC in maintaining international peace and security. During formal meetings, council members celebrated the newfound international climate of cooperation among them.[6] The broader UN membership believed that the Security Council was finally beginning to function as originally intended, and expectations grew that the UNSC would now maintain international peace and security by quickly and decisively responding to aggression and protecting the sovereignty and territorial integrity of weak states.[7]

Studying the case of Iraq is an important starting point for a study of Security Council humanitarian intervention because prior to Iraq's invasion of Kuwait, human rights discourse was considered inappropriate for council discussion. Its inclusion in council debates in 1991 and 1992 had dramatic, if unintended, political effects. Because discourse has the power to both create and foreclose policy options, incorporating human rights norms into formal debates about state sovereignty and international security fundamentally altered the council's view of the legitimate purpose of military force.

International problem solving relies on problem construction. Policymaking in the Security Council—as in other policymaking forums—is a discursive struggle over the appropriate way to classify political events, the boundaries of problem categories, and the conceptual framing of issues with a view to creating a shared meaning that motivates decision makers to act.[8] Members of the UNSC united quickly around an intentional story to characterize the war. The intentional story described Iraq's invasion of Kuwait as an external aggression against an independent and sovereign state member of the United Nations—a clear violation of Article 2.7 of the UN Charter. Clarity about the cause and character of the conflict, combined with widespread agreement that the Iraqi regime was the perpetrator of international crimes against Kuwait and its people, made it possible for the Security Council to swiftly reverse the aggression. An unprecedented level of unity persisted for the duration of Operation Desert Storm—the war authorized by the UNSC to reverse Iraq's occupation. This unity combined with the military success of the operation created a political context in which the UNSC could reexamine the legitimate purpose of military force in international relations, including the use of Chapter VII enforcement powers to address the cross-border impact of a regional humanitarian crisis. The documentary record on Iraq also demonstrates that the arguments that international actors make about the cause and character of conflict and the source of sovereign authority matter because they shape the likelihood that military force will or will not be used in defense of human rights.

The extraordinary maltreatment of the Iraqi people by Iraqi president Saddam Hussein in the aftermath of his defeat by coalition forces caused an unprecedented humanitarian disaster as millions of Iraqi Kurds and Shi'as fled across Iraq's borders into neighboring Iran and Turkey.[9] This humanitarian crisis, occurring during a traditional interstate war, created a context in which it was possible for Security Council members to consider the relationship between human rights and international security. During formal deliberations, the UNSC incorporated Secretariat briefings on Iraq's domestic human rights situation—breaking with past practice that excluded such considerations. Because the effects of Saddam Hussein's human rights violations were threatening both regional peace and security and the sovereignty of Turkey and Iran, the UNSC passed Resolution 688, which condemned Iraqi violations of human rights and demanded international access to Iraq's population and territory. The passage of Resolution 688 was a watershed moment—it was the first Security Council resolution to define domestic human rights violations as a threat to international peace and security because of its trans-border effects. In part, Resolution 688, "*condemns* the repression of the Iraqi civilian population in many parts of Iraq, including most recently in the Kurdish-populated areas, the consequences of which threaten international peace and security in the region."[10]

By dictating the terms of the Iraqi government's treatment of its own population and curtailing its freedom of movement, Resolution 688 challenged the traditional meaning of sovereignty by interfering in the internal affairs of the Iraqi state and by linking minimal standards of human rights protection to the meaning of legitimate sovereign authority. This interference was limited to Iraq, however, and only became possible because Iraq's own sovereignty had been temporarily suspended by the UN after it had violated core Charter principles. The use of military force against Iraq was an unquestionably straightforward exercise of Chapter VII to reverse international aggression. The cease-fire imposed by the UN "was one of the most intrusive since the Second World War," demonstrating the seriousness of Iraq's transgression of international norms.[11] Absent this context, it is highly unlikely that Iraq's treatment of its marginalized and minority populations would have garnered Security Council attention at all, let alone intrusive enforcement action to stop it. Widespread agreement about Iraq's pariah status, the suspension of Iraqi sovereignty, and the impact on security of the Iraqi government's human rights violations together created an environment in which a once impermissible practice—the linking of human rights and international security by the UNSC—became possible. Changing council behavior marked a new period of international openness to debating the meaning of sovereignty and the relationship between protecting human rights and maintaining international peace and security. Successful military action in Iraq, the peaceful end of the Cold War, and the inclusion of human rights discourse into Security Council decision making in 1991 created a political opening for subsequent debates about humanitarian intervention in Somalia and Bosnia-Herzegovina.

Security Council Involvement in Iraq, 1990–1992

The Baath Party began its rule of Iraq in 1968 and Saddam Hussein became the regime's president in 1979. Hussein's regime was repressive, with "virtually every important liberty, except the freedom of worship, denied to the country's 17 million people."[12] The *mukhabarat*, Arabic for secret police, ensured that no political dissent was publicly expressed. Its power over the population extended beyond Iraq's borders—its agents were responsible for many assassinations of and assassination attempts on exiles who engaged in political activity in opposition to the governing regime.[13] The civilian and military leadership of the Baath regime were disproportionately dominated by Sunni Muslims and by members of Saddam Hussein's family and allied tribes and clans. Saddam Hussein's personal autocracy was characterized by the political exclusion of a majority of Iraq's population. The non-Arab Kurdish population in the north (who made up 25 percent of the population) and the Shi'a Muslim population in the south (50 percent of the population) were excluded from power and accused of separatism by the regime. Because of regime fears of disloyalty, both populations were politically and economically disadvantaged and subject to significant political violence committed by the regime.[14] The Kurdish population was particularly vulnerable to regime repression, particularly after the Islamic fundamentalist regime in Iran headed by Ayatollah Khomeini allowed Kurdish guerillas who opposed the Iraqi regime to operate across the border from bases in Iran.[15]

The Kurdish minority in Iraq numbered between three and four million and lived primarily in the mountainous northeast part of the country adjoining the Kurdish-populated regions of Turkey and Iran. Combined, the numbers of Kurds living within the three states numbered approximately 20 million but international borders made them minority populations in each.[16] Violent oppression of the Kurds by the Iraqi regime was persistent since the early 1980s and included mass disappearances, arbitrary arrest and extrajudicial detention, forced resettlement in an effort to change the demographics of the northern region, extrajudicial killings, chemical weapons slaughter, and many other forms of persecution.[17] The most devastating was the 1987–88 *Anfal* or "spoils" campaign, which had long-lasting demographic, economic, and psychological effects on the Kurdish population.[18] During this period, the Iraqi regime destroyed approximately five hundred Kurdish villages in northern Iraq, killing between 50,000–100,000 Iraqi Kurds in an attempt to permanently defeat an internal Kurdish insurgency movement as well as to destroy Kurdish culture and way of life.[19] International human rights organizations characterized the Iraqi regime's campaign against the Kurds as genocide.[20] In the particularly egregious incident described at the beginning of the chapter, 5,000 civilians living in Halabja near the Iranian border died following a chemical gas attack on the area by Iraqi armed forces in March 1988.[21]

On 2 August 1990 Iraq invaded Kuwait and overthrew the Kuwaiti regime—only two years after acceptance of a UN-brokered cease-fire that ended its eight-year war with Iran. Saddam Hussein initially tried to justify his invasion of Kuwait as "invited," but the underlying motive for Iraq's "forced coup" was based in large part on a long-standing border dispute between the two countries.[22] Iraq sought control of the Khaur Abd Allah Channel to expand territorial access to the gulf. This control was particularly important in August 1990 because of the closure of the Shatt al-Arab River due to war-related damage from the Iran-Iraq War. The Shatt had carried nearly two–thirds of Iraq's nonoil cargo.[23] Additionally, Iraq was facing significant economic problems as a result of the Iran-Iraq War including cash shortages and mounting foreign debt. Iraq was pushed to the brink of a financial crisis in February 1990 when the price of oil dramatically decreased, and the Iraqi regime blamed Kuwait for driving the price of oil down by refusing to stick to its oil production quotas, even accusing Kuwait of intentionally harming Iraq by stealing oil and manipulating oil prices. Saddam Hussein was further angered when Kuwait refused to cancel Iraq's debts and offered no financial assistance despite Iraq's financial crisis.[24] Saddam Hussein's treatment of Kuwaiti citizens and other residents of Kuwait in the immediate aftermath of the invasion mirrored his treatment of his domestic population. Hundreds were killed and wounded, thousands detained, and hundreds of thousands forced to flee Kuwait. The human rights violations leveled against Kuwait's civilian population included extrajudicial executions, torture, rape, and large-scale arbitrary imprisonment.[25]

The international response to the Iraqi invasion and its treatment of Kuwaiti civilians was openly hostile. During an emergency meeting on 2 August that convened at 5:10 A.M. in New York, the UNSC unanimously passed Resolution 660 condemning the Iraqi invasion of Kuwait, identifying it as a breach of international peace and security, and demanding immediate and complete Iraqi withdrawal.[26] In total, the council passed twelve resolutions between 2 August and 29 November 1990 affirming the sovereignty and territorial integrity of Kuwait and demanding that Iraq withdraw its armed forces from Kuwaiti territory. Security Council resolutions became increasingly punitive as Iraqi noncompliance continued. In addition to condemning Iraqi violations of international law and demanding compliance with its past resolutions, Resolution 660 created an economic, military, and financial embargo of Iraq. Resolution 660 has been described as "one of the most sweeping ever produced by the United Nations" because it prohibited trade with Iraq and banned financial transfers except for food, medicine, and basic necessities.[27] Subsequent resolutions froze Iraqi assets, established a naval blockade of Iraq, and enacted a restrictive sanctions regime backed by force.[28]

On 29 November 1990, the Security Council passed Resolution 678, authorizing member-states of the United Nations cooperating with the government of Kuwait "to use all necessary means to uphold and implement resolution 660 and all subsequent relevant resolutions and to restore international peace and security in the area" under Chapter VII of the Charter.[29] Iraq was given until 15 January 1991 to comply with this and all preceding resolutions or face military force. Resolution 678 passed with the approval of twelve Security Council members (see Table 2.1). Only Cuba and Yemen opposed the resolution, while China abstained. China justified its abstention based on its principled opposition to the use of force to settle international disputes but explained that since Iraq had acted forcefully against Kuwait, China would abstain rather than veto the resolution.[30]

The near unanimity of the council's condemnation of Iraqi aggression and its defense of Kuwait were notable. Both permanent and nonpermanent

Table 2.1. Security Council Support for Key Resolutions, Iraq

	Subject	*Votes in Favor*	*Votes Against*	*Abstentions*
Resolution 660 (1990)	Condemns Iraqi invasion of Kuwait and demands immediate withdrawal	Canada **China** Colombia Côte d'Ivoire Cuba Ethiopia Finland **France** Malaysia Romania **USSR** **UK** **U.S.**	None	None
Resolution 678 (1990)	Authorizes all necessary means under Chapter VII to reverse Iraqi aggression against Kuwait	Canada Colombia Côte d'Ivoire Ethiopia Finland **France** Malaysia Romania **USSR** **UK** **U.S.** Zaire	Cuba, Yemen	**China**
Resolution 688 (1991)	Condemns repression of Iraqi civilian population; demands its end; and permits humanitarian organizations access to Iraqi territory	Austria Belgium Côte d'Ivoire Ecuador **France** Romania **USSR** **UK** **U.S.** Zaire	Cuba Yemen Zimbabwe	**China**, India

Permanent members of Security Council are in bold type.

members regarded the Security Council response as "historic" for the United Nations because the council was "rediscovering its true mission"— the maintenance of international peace and security and the use of enforcement action to reverse aggression.[31] For example, the U.S. secretary of state, James Baker, made the following statement preceding the vote on Resolution 678:

> With the Cold War behind us, we now have the chance to build the world which was envisioned by the founders of this organization— the founders of the United Nations. We have the chance to make this Security Council and this United Nations true instruments for peace and justice around the globe. . . . But if we are to do so, we must meet the threat to international peace created by Saddam Hussein's aggression. And that is why the debate that we are about to begin will, I think, rank as one of the most important in the history of the United Nations; It will surely do much to determine the future of this body.[32]

Addressing Iraqi aggression was deemed so important that the UNSC convened at the ministerial level twice, which doubled the previous number of Security Council meetings at the foreign ministerial level.[33] Indeed, the resort to force against Iraq would mark "the start of a new era for the United Nations" because it would transform the collective security system and create a flexible interpretation of Chapter VII.[34] It also transformed the UNSC in unintended and unanticipated ways, namely by creating an opening for human rights concerns in Security Council deliberations.

When the 15 January 1991 deadline arrived and Saddam Hussein had not withdrawn the Iraqi military from Kuwait, a coalition of thirty-four countries headed by the United States launched the authorized military attack to reverse Iraqi aggression against Kuwait. Operation Desert Storm began on 17 January 1991 with a massive air assault. Weeks of intensive bombing were followed by a ground offensive that was launched on 24 February 1991 and lasted only one hundred hours. Security Council resolutions did not authorize Coalition forces to take military action beyond liberating Kuwait, as the objective of the war was to remove Iraq from Kuwait and simultaneously damage Saddam Hussein's offensive military capabilities.[35] This limited objective was necessary for maintaining cohesion in the coalition. The defeat of the Iraqi Army was swift and definitive. Honoring the limited objectives of the military campaign supported by the UNSC, Coalition forces did not enter Baghdad or require the removal of Saddam Hussein as a condition of surrender. Nonetheless, the terms of the cease-fire outlined in Resolution 686 were severe. They included the acceptance of all previous Security Council resolutions, mandatory reparations for war damages, the release of POWs, the return of stolen property, and mainte-nance of the sanctions regime.[36] Resolution 687, which passed on 3 April 1991, imposed further obligations, including international demarcation of the Iraq-Kuwait border and the establishment of a UN peacekeeping opera-tion to monitor it and the destruction of all Iraq's nuclear, chemical, and biological weapons, which would be overseen by international inspection teams.[37] The sanctions regime, including the trade embargo and ban on oil sales, would remain in effect until Iraq had achieved total compliance with all aspects of the resolution. Resolution 687 has been described as "the longest and most comprehensive in UN history" with its provisions placing much of Iraq's economy and military under international control.[38]

The war with Coalition forces had further devastating economic and political effects on Iraq. The war had destroyed much of Iraq's industry and infrastructure and the sanctions regime had eliminated nearly all trade. The ban on oil sales severely diminished Iraq's income and most states, includ-ing the most powerful, had severed diplomatic relations with Iraq. Region-ally, Iraq was viewed as a pariah. Domestically, the regime faced internal threats from disaffected military personnel and an increasingly frustrated civilian population. Years of repression combined with nearly a decade of war and economic hardship had taken a toll on Iraq's domestic population, particularly in the northern and southern regions of the country. By March 1991 spontaneous, unruly, and unorganized rebellions led by returning sol-diers and urban Iraqi youth threatened government control of fourteen of Iraq's eighteen provinces.[39] Yet by April, the uprising was over and what started out as a seemingly straightforward military operation to reverse Iraqi aggression and reaffirm Kuwait's sovereignty and territorial integrity took a decidedly radical turn when the Security Council shifted its focus from Iraq's behavior in Kuwait to its behavior within its own borders.

At the beginning of March 1991, just days after the humiliating defeat of the Iraqi Army by the Coalition forces, Iraqi Army deserters, disaffected soldiers, and local residents of the southern Shi'a city of Basra revolted against Hussein's rule. Taking advantage of what they thought was a tempo-rary power vacuum, opponents sought to attack the regime while it was still on the defensive and while extensive dislocation remained in Baghdad. The revolt spread quickly and spontaneously throughout southern Iraq, from Basra to Karbala, Najaf, Hilla, Nasiriyya, and al-Amar.[40] During the revolt, rebel troops aided by urban youth and civilians targeted symbols of the Iraqi regime including the Baath Party and security forces headquarters, prisons, and military barracks. According to Middle East Watch, semiorganized opposition groups received a spontaneous outpouring of support from civilians who were angry about government repression and the devastation of multiple wars fought by the regime.[41] The rebels were unable to build a broader base, however, because interference from Iranian fighters gave the rebellion an unpopular ideological cast and the chaos, destruction, and brutal retribution leveled against members of the regime frightened Sunnis and more moderate elements of the population.[42] The rebels also underestimated the strength of the Iraqi regime, which quickly stamped out the uprising when the military refused to join the rebels and international actors failed to intervene. Hussein had remained both powerful and attentive to internal threats to his power. Using his elite Republican Guard and support from the army, he regained control of southern Iraq on 13 March 1991. Saddam Hussein's retribution was swift and harsh. Middle East Watch reported,

> Those who remained in the south were at the mercy of advancing government troops, who went through neighborhoods, firing indiscriminately and summarily executing hundreds of young men. . . . Refugees alleged to Middle East Watch and others that Iraqi helicopters dropped a variety of ordnance on civilians, including napalm and phosphorus bombs, chemical agents and sulfuric acid. Representatives of human rights and humanitarian organizations who saw refugees with burn injuries or photographs of such injuries were unable to confirm the source of these burns. However, doctors who examined wounded Iraqis said that some of their burns were consistent with the use of napalm.[43]

Iraqi troops engaged in widespread atrocities against the civilian population. The violence was particularly heavy in the southern marshes, where much of the local Shi'a population had congregated rather than face extensive risks in escaping the country in the flat, exposed terrain of the south.[44]

While Hussein's Republican Guard was battling revolt in the south, northern Iraqi Kurds rose up against the regime on 5 March 1991 in Rani- yya. As in the south, this revolt spread rapidly as the local population joined. The uprising in the north was characterized by a higher degree of organization and leadership due to the participation of formal Kurdish party organizations and the Fursan—Kurdish military forces that had pre- viously been allied with the Iraqi government but switched sides during the uprising. By 21 March, Kurdish insurgents controlled every major city in its territory except for Mosul, capital of the Nineveh Province.[45] Yet the revolt was reversed nearly as suddenly as it began. Once the violence in the south was quelled, the loyalist army troops and Republican Guard mobi- lized in the north, using helicopter gunships, tanks, and artillery to indis- criminately attack the Kurds. The regime's counterattack reopened the wounds of the Anfal campaign, provoking panic among the Kurdish popu- lation, who exited the country en masse. Within days, hundreds of thou- sands of Kurds became stranded in the mountains between Iraq and Turkey as they sought to escape the repression.

The result of intensified fighting between Iraqi insurgents and the gov- ernment of Saddam Hussein was a humanitarian catastrophe. According to Middle East Watch, over 1.5 million Iraqis escaped the attacks in the cities during the months of March and April. Yet many of the displaced were injured or died during their flight from Iraq because of poor conditions. For example, at least 5,000 were killed by land mines as they attempted to cross the mined border between Iraq and Turkey.[46] By the beginning of April, at least 400,000 Kurdish refugees were pushed into the mountains between Turkey and Iraq. The death toll for these refugees was estimated to be 1,000 per day. In addition to the Kurds who sought refuge in Turkey, up to 1 million Kurdish refugees crossed the border into Iran at the begin- ning of April, along with 70,000 Shi'a refugees.[47]

The Intentional Causal Story

Security Council members told two different sets of causal stories about Iraqi violence: one about its violence against Kuwait and one about its violence against its own domestic population. Council deliberations about the cause and character of Iraq's military action against Kuwait were marked by incredible unanimity. Members of the Security Council articulated only a single causal story—an intentional story—to describe the conflict. The intentional story characterized the war as an external aggression by Iraq against the sovereign state of Kuwait in violation of the United Nations Charter and international legal norms. States as diverse as Canada, Colombia, Malaysia, and Finland as well as all five of the permanent members of the Security Council condemned "the naked Iraqi invasion of Kuwait's territory."[48] Resolution 660, which defined the conflict as international aggression and demanded its reversal, was passed unanimously by the UNSC (see Table 2.1). Even prior to the passage of Resolution 660, the Russian Federation described Iraq's actions as a "violation of international peace and security." China, which is generally resistant to the use of enforcement measures, likewise endorsed this and subsequent resolutions condemning Iraqi behavior, abstaining only from resolutions that authorized "all necessary measures" or addressed the domestic practices of the Iraqi government.[49] In fact, the only state on record that objected to the intentional story about the war against Kuwait was Iraq itself. This unprecedented level of unity around an intentional story of conflict made the Security Council's Chapter VII authorization to use military force possible. Indeed, because the intentional story appeals to principles of justice and international law, its policy implications include protection, interdiction, or punishment. The intentional story persisted in the UNSC throughout Operation Desert Storm.

Security Council endorsement of an intentional causal story softened only when a majority of its members used it to characterize the Iraqi regime's violence against its own population in April 1991. The move to discuss Iraq's internal practices was both highly controversial and unprecedented in Security Council practice. Yet a majority of council members (eleven members) articulated an intentional story to describe Iraqi violence against its own Kurdish and Shi'a populations. Seven council members (Belgium, Côte d'Ivoire, France, India, Romania, the UK, and the U.S.) articulated a strong intentional story about brutal repression and the indiscriminate use of force by the Iraqi regime against its Kurdish and Shi'a populations in contravention of international humanitarian law and the Geneva Conventions. These members argued that violations of international humanitarian law constituted a threat to international peace and security.[50] For example, France argued that Iraq's repression of its minorities garnered international interest because it was at such proportions as to be considered a crime against humanity.[51] This story was embraced by an additional seven states, primarily European, whose representatives spoke as nonvoting participants during the council meeting.[52] Germany advocated a particularly strong version of the perpetrator-victim narrative when it argued that Saddam Hussein's violence against the Kurdish minority was a harbinger of genocide.[53]

Four Security Council members (Austria, Ecuador, Russia, and Zaire) articulated a softer version of the intentional story. They agreed that Iraq was violating international humanitarian law but noted that Iraq's behavior was primarily internal. Nonetheless, because of its external effects, this internal violence warranted international attention and condemnation.[54] Presumably for these members, in absence of transborder effects, Iraq's domestic practices would not have warranted Security Council attention. In contrast, China, Cuba, Yemen, and Zimbabwe argued that the Security Council had no right to intervene in the internal matters of a sovereign state, citing Article 2.7 of the UN Charter. They strongly objected to Iraq's domestic behavior being discussed at all, yet they did not articulate an alternative story to describe the situation nor did they dispute the cause or character of the regime's violence, only its relevance to Security Council deliberations.

International Security, Human Rights, and the Purpose of Military Force

Unity in the UNSC around an intentional causal story allowed deliberations to quickly shift from the cause and character of the conflict to the relationship between human rights and international security. After Coalition forces successfully reversed the Iraqi occupation, Security Council members began to debate whether humanitarian and international human rights concerns were relevant to council business, and in turn whether international humanitarian law and international human rights law were changing the purpose of military force. On 5 April 1991, Turkey and Iran requested that the UNSC respond to the mounting humanitarian crisis on their borders. They argued that the rapid flow of refugees out of Iraq and into their sovereign territory threatened to destabilize their regimes and the entire region. The effects of Iraq's military repression of its civilians, they argued, were a threat to international peace and security. During deliberations, Turkey informed the Security Council that nearly one million Iraqi refugees were heading toward the Iraqi-Turkish border, arguing that no single country could cope with such a massive influx of destitute people. Turkey described the mounting humanitarian crisis as a "grave threat to the peace and security of the region" both because of "the scale of the human tragedy" and because Iraqi mortar shells were landing on the Turkish side of the border.[55] Iran asserted that it expected to receive half a million Iraqi refugees in subsequent days. Echoing the concerns of Turkey, Iran argued that the crisis inside Iraq had international dimensions because it threatened the security of neighbor countries with the potential of further destabilizing the entire region. Iran urged the Security Council to deal "both with the cause of the crisis and with its immediate symptoms."[56]

Convinced that the effects of Saddam Hussein's brutal repression were threatening the sovereignty and security of Iraq's neighbors, the Security Council passed Resolution 688, which defined the *consequences* of Iraq's repression of its civilian population as a threat to international peace and security. Resolution 688 demanded that the Iraqi regime cease violating human rights and international humanitarian law and open its territory to humanitarian relief organizations and military observers.[57] As Table 2.1 illustrates, Resolution 688 was the most divisive of the key resolutions passed by the UNSC on the situation in Iraq. It received only ten votes in favor in contrast to unanimous support for Resolution 660. Three members opposed the resolution and two others abstained, reflecting division within the council on the relevance of human rights to Security Council work. Nevertheless, the passage of Resolution 688 was monumental—never before had the Security Council defined the effects of a state's domestic behavior as a threat to international peace and security. Its passage signaled the growing legitimacy of international human rights norms and an emergent Security Council interest in humanitarianism. Yet the appeal to human rights norms was conditional and nuanced. Nearly all council members, even supporters of Resolution 688, reaffirmed their commitment to state sovereignty and noninterference in the domestic affairs of states. Condemnation of Iraq's domestic behavior was only possible because the Iraqi regime's sovereignty had already been suspended by the Security Council in response to Iraq's blatant disregard for international legal norms, including its violations of sovereignty norms and the ban on the use of force without Security Council authorization. With its sovereign authority suspended, there was no direct conflict between sovereignty norms and human rights norms. Indeed, the protection of human rights in this case reaffirmed and protected the sovereignty and territorial integrity of Iraq's neighbors that were the referents for Security Council action. Resolution 688 simultaneously redefined regional and international security interests to include the protection of human rights and reaffirmed Article 2.7 of the Charter of the United Nations. The Security Council's demand for immediate and unlimited access to Iraq's sovereign territory was revolutionary but possible only because Iraq's domestic repression had destabilizing effects outside its borders.

References to human rights during Security Council deliberations marked a significant change in council behavior, however tentative and nuanced those affirmations of human rights were. The 5 April meeting record shows that a majority of Security Council members and nonvoting participants articulated a direct link between human rights and their national and international interests. Eighteen of the thirty-one participating states described Iraqi human right violations and the resulting humanitarian tragedy as a threat to international peace and security. These states included nine of the fifteen Security Council members—Austria, Belgium, Côte d'Ivoire, Ecuador, France, Russia, the UK, the U.S., and Zimbabwe— and nine nonvoting participants—Canada, Denmark, Germany, Iran, Luxembourg, Netherlands, Pakistan, Sweden, and Turkey. Human rights concerns were relevant, they argued, because of the transborder impact of refugee flows. Ten of these eighteen states simultaneously registered their strong support for Charter principles that protect the domestic jurisdiction of states from external interference, which suggests that it was the extraordinary nature of the Iraq situation that justified Security Council action to address the root causes of regional instability within the borders of Iraq rather than a transformation in the normative standing of the nonintervention principle. Council members emphasized the contingencies of the Iraq situation as justification for this unusual deviation. The representative from Belgium summed it up this way: "As far as Belgium is concerned, such support is in this case justified by the very specific considerations arising from an exceptionally serious situation which threatens peace and security in the region."[58] Cognizant of the implications of such a radical departure from previous Security Council behavior, the majority of members appeared eager to distinguish the Iraq case as unique in the hopes of discouraging the creation of precedent. Ecuador, for example, drew attention to the inherent tension between two relevant principles in the Charter: the unrestricted respect for human rights and nonintervention in the internal affairs of states. Ecuador reasoned that because the human rights situation extended beyond the borders of Iraq it moved beyond the sphere of Iraq's internal affairs, eliminating the tension between these Charter principles and justifying an international response.[59]

The statements by France, Germany, Norway, and the UK were exceptional because they justified Security Council interference inside of Iraq's borders based on the nature of the atrocities alone, independent of the transborder security impact. According to the UK, the protection of civilians mandated by the Geneva Conventions was sufficient justification for Security Council action.[60] Norway argued that Iraqi actions contravened internationally accepted human rights standards and norms of behavior.[61] France asserted that the human rights violations observed in Iraq assumed "the dimension of a crime against humanity," and Germany said they "harbor[ed] danger of genocide."[62] Germany also argued that the Security Council could only be successful in returning peace and security to the region if domestic peace was assured inside of Iraq, drawing an explicit link between human rights and international peace. Thus it was "the legitimate right of the international community to call for respect for human rights," according to Germany.[63] No matter how striking these statements are from a human rights perspective, they represented a minority opinion among the participants in the Security Council meeting, the vast majority of whom argued that internal human rights issues were *only* relevant if they had international effects.

Cuba, Yemen, and Zimbabwe articulated strong disagreement with any Security Council involvement in the internal affairs of Iraq. They argued that it was not within the competence of the Security Council to address the humanitarian crisis. For example, Cuba asserted: "The Security Council simply has no right to violate the principle of non-intervention. It has no right to intervene unduly in the internal affairs of any State. It has no right to intervene unduly in matters within the competence of other organs of the United Nations."[64] Yemen argued further that the resolution politicized a humanitarian issue because it focused primarily on a small segment of the affected Iraqi population—the Iraqi Kurds—while neglecting the Shi'a. India, which abstained, advanced a more nuanced argument. While the crisis warranted international attention, India reasoned, other organs of the UN were better suited to address humanitarian needs. China remarked that the question was one of "great complexity" because both the internal affairs of a country and the stability of its neighbor states were involved. China suggested that the international aspects of the question "should be settled through the appropriate channels," by which it suggested that the UNSC was not the appropriate venue for addressing human rights or humanitarian crises.[65] Yet none of the opponents of Security Council involvement disputed that human rights violations were occurring or justified the Iraqi regime's behavior. Instead, they argued that the UNSC was not the appropriate venue to address the crisis. This suggests that the growing legitimacy of human rights norms meant that detractors did not wish to be seen as condoning human rights violations.

In sum, the Security Council made a strong break with past practice when it integrated human rights norms into Security Council decision making. The inclusion of human rights in Security Council discussions, however, diminished the unity among its members, who were divided about their relevance to council deliberations. Resolution 688 reflected a compromise position that was supported by most council members and nonvoting participants. It reaffirmed the national jurisdiction of states but argued that the human rights situation caused by Iraq was no longer an internal matter of the Iraqi state. The inclusion of human rights in Security Council decision making on Iraq was a watershed moment, yet the embrace of human rights norms was situational and contingent on Iraq's prior invasion of Kuwait and the effects of human rights violations on neighbor states that appealed to the UNSC for help.

From Resolution 688 to No-Fly Zones: Divisions on Human Rights Enforcement

On 10 April 1991, France, the UK, and the U.S., three permanent members, declared a "no-fly" zone in northern Iraq above the thirty-sixth parallel, creating a safety zone that covered almost ten thousand square kilometers of Iraqi territory.[66] Its purpose was to provide protective cover for humanitarian aid agencies and Coalition forces to safely enter refugee camps on Iraqi territory and to protect Iraqi Kurds from air attacks by Iraqi military forces. Resolution 688 had demanded an end to Iraqi repression and mandated that Iraq permit international humanitarian organizations access to its population. Resolution 688 did not reference Chapter VII, which authorizes the use of military force, but the three permanent members argued that their use of enforcement measures was a necessary response to extreme humanitarian need and tacitly permitted by the resolution.[67] They argued that because the no-fly zone was necessary to the fulfillment of Resolution 688, any enforcement action undertaken for this purpose was legitimate even if it had not been expressly authorized by the Security Council. Other council members did not publicly weigh in on these attempts to further link humanitarian and human rights concerns to international security and the purpose of military force until well over a year later.

On 11 August 1992 the Security Council met to discuss continued Iraqi noncompliance with council resolutions but the meeting quickly developed into a debate among members about the legitimacy of human rights in council work. The debate proceeded in two parts: (1) the appropriateness of the participation of Max van der Stoel, the special rapporteur of the Commission on Human Rights for Iraq, in a formal meeting of the Security Council, and (2) the human rights situation inside Iraq and what, if any, relevance it had to Security Council operations. Security Council members uniformly condemned Iraqi regime's repression of its population but were divided over the continuing intrusion of human rights concerns into their meetings. Council members divided into three groups: norm promoters who actively sought to incorporate human rights concerns; norm detractors who denied the relevance and appropriateness of human rights concerns to the Security Council; and norm instrumentalists who supported the inclusion of human rights on a conditional, instrumental basis—only when such information would help the council execute its Charter mandate.

On 11 August, Belgium, France, the UK, and the U.S. invited Van der Stoel to brief the UNSC on recent human rights developments in Iraq, citing rule 39 of the *Provisional Rules of Procedure*, which reads, "The Security Council may invite members of the Secretariat or other persons, whom it considers competent for the purpose, to supply it with information or to give other assistance in examining matters within its competence."[68] Anticipating the potential push back from norm detractors, they emphasized that the Security Council would receive Van der Stoel in his personal capacity and not as the special rapporteur for Iraq appointed by the Commission on Human Rights. States that took an instrumental approach to the norms debate, like Ecuador and Zimbabwe, argued that normally it would be inappropriate for the Security Council to examine or take a stand on the human rights report written by Van der Stoel because it would undermine the division of responsibility within the UN system. However, because the Security Council had already passed Resolution 688, information that would help it execute its mandate was within the purview of the council. Norm instrumentalists consented to the request by the norm promoters for Van der Stoel's participation based on the understanding that he would be speaking in his personal capacity.[69] Detractors like China and India noted their strong reservations, arguing that matters pertaining to human rights should appropriately be discussed in the Commission on Human Rights.[70] India argued, "It is the consistent position of the Indian delegation that the various organs and bodies of the United Nations should restrict their deliberations and actions within their respective spheres of competence as defined in the Charter. . . . The Council can focus its legitimate attention on the threat or likely threat to peace and stability in the region but it cannot discuss human rights situations per se or make recommendations on matters outside its competence."[71] In the end, Van der Stoel was permitted to testify in his personal capacity, in large part because permanent members are not permitted to veto procedural matters.

Van der Stoel's testimony reaffirmed the intentional story about Iraq's internal behavior whereby the government was engaged in a systematic attempt to repress and kill large portions of the southern Shi'a and northern Kurdish populations.[72] Van der Stoel argued that the Iraqi regime's economic blockade of the north was threatening a new humanitarian catastrophe as hunger became widespread. He also testified that humanitarian relief to the southern marshes was restricted by the Iraqi government in violation of the Covenant on Economic, Social and Cultural Rights, to which Iraq is a party, and paragraph 3 of Resolution 688, which demanded immediate access to all Iraqis in need of humanitarian assistance.[73] The Iraqi regime was engaged in a major military offensive against civilians in the southern marshes using artillery bombardment and fixed-wing aircraft. Van der Stoel reminded the council that international passivity in the late 1980s had allowed Iraq to exterminate part of the Iraqi Kurd population and urged the council to avoid repeating that tragedy.[74] In short, his testimony encouraged the UNSC to expand its engagement with the Iraqi civilian population deep inside the borders of Iraq and not just in the border areas where neighbor states might be threatened.

As in the meeting preceding the passage of Resolution 688 the year before, the debate following Van der Stoel's briefing in August 1992 was not about the cause or character of the violence in Iraq or its resultant human rights violations. Rather, it was about whether the Security Council had a responsibility or a right to respond to them, and whether human rights violations were linked to the maintenance of international peace and security. Detractors of the linkage between human rights and international security were noticeably quiet in the subsequent debate and declined to speak on the public record in response to Van der Stoel's briefing. Only nine Security Council members—all of whom articulated a direct link between the protection of human rights and the maintenance of international peace and security—made formal statements in response to the briefing. States like Hungary, Japan, and Austria argued that gross and systematic human rights violations alone warranted Security Council attention. Hungary underscored this point: "[There is a] link that exists between the way a Government treats its own citizens and the way that it acts in the international arena as well as [a] link between enforcing respect for human rights and maintaining international peace and security."[75] Similarly, Austria argued,

> The protection of human rights and, in particular, of the rights of ethnic minorities too, has had an important impact on the development of peaceful relations between states. There is a direct connection between democratic processes within countries and the evolution of a political culture which is conducive to the peaceful settlement of disputes. From our own history, we know that peace was most threatened when human rights were abolished and minorities persecuted and when democratic processes gave way to totalitarian practices. Human rights, minority rights and democracy, are, therefore, important cornerstones of our common endeavour.[76]

The political implication for the Security Council was that respect for human rights was more than a legal or humanitarian question; rather, respect for human rights was also "an integral part of international collective security." Thus, the Security Council should take an "unambiguous and clear cut stand for the protection of those rights whenever and wherever they are flagrantly violated."[77] In short, protecting human rights and international humanitarian law was central to the primary functions of the UNSC.

The majority of Security Council members took the more instrumental approach by emphasizing that human rights were a concern of the Security Council *only* in such instances when human rights violations directly threatened international peace and security. According to this view, human rights violations were duly addressed by other UN organs unless their consequences had a direct bearing on international or regional peace and security. For example, France reasoned that the Security Council had an obligation to prevent massive human rights violations in the southern marshes as a means of preventing a mass exodus of refugees, which would further threaten security in the region.[78] Belgium, Russia, the UK, and the U.S. each argued that the Iraqi government's flagrant defiance of Security Council directives and especially those of Resolution 688 made the human rights behavior of Iraq relevant to council consideration. Russia emphasized the necessity of states to follow Security Council directives:

> The Russian Federation attaches great importance to the full and consistent implementation of the resolutions of the Security Council which are intended to eliminate the consequences of the Iraqi aggression against Kuwait and to establish a lasting peace and security in that region. Accordingly, we, like other Council members, are very seriously alarmed by reports of a continuing policy of repression against the civilian population in various parts of Iraq, which constitutes a direct violation of the demand, contained in resolution 688 (1991), that Iraq, as a contribution to the removing of the threat to international peace and security in the region, should end the repression against its own civilian population.[79]

Iraqi defiance of Security Council resolutions, and in particular the directive to stop repressing its population as detailed in Resolution 688, made its human rights practices an appropriate subject of Security Council discussion. In passing Resolution 688 the Security Council had determined that the consequences of Iraqi repression threatened international security. Because Resolution 688 demanded that Iraq cease the repression of its civilian population, evidence of the Iraqi regime's compliance, or lack thereof, was integral to Security Council deliberation. At minimum, both groups agreed that when human rights violations affect the security of other sovereign states they become relevant to Security Council deliberations. Fifteen days after this discussion, on 26 August 1992, France, the UK, and the U.S.

imposed a "no-fly" zone in southern Iraq (Operation Southern Watch) below the thirty-second parallel to protect the Shi'as from further aerial attacks as those nations had done previously with the Kurds in the north in April 1991.

The Interplay of Interests and Norms During Security Council Deliberations

Human rights norms were incorporated into Security Council meetings in 1991 specifically because the Iraqi refugee crisis posed a direct threat to both the international security interests and normative values of a majority of the council members. France, the UK, and the U.S. were particularly susceptible to increasing domestic and international pressure to address the tragedy, which was directly linked to Operation Desert Storm and was vividly captured by Western media and broadcast worldwide. Because Turkey was a member of the North Atlantic Treaty Organization, any security risk to it was a threat to the entire alliance, which was obligated to defend it. Despite these interests, however, Security Council members from Europe and the Americas also viewed the crisis as a threat to their core values—the promotion of freedom, human rights, and the rule of law. Ambassador Diego Arria of Venezuela, for example, described his country's motivations this way: "The concern of my country in this debate is founded on its unswerving solidarity and concern in respect of a subject of primary importance for humankind, namely, the defence of human rights wherever they are violated or trampled underfoot, and on its aspiration to see peace and harmony restored in a region whose people are traditionally friends of Venezuela."[80] Failure to address the crisis threatened the shared vision of the new world order that was so anxiously anticipated by UN members at the end of the Cold War, and particularly by France, the UK, and the U.S.

Security Council members from democratic states also were susceptible to the humanitarian impulse of their populations. Growing domestic and international pressure to respond to the unfolding tragedy came from three sources: the international media; independent experts, including officials of human rights organizations; and compelling eyewitness testimony, which had a significant impact. First, the international media presence in the region was substantial because of previous coverage of Operation Desert Storm. Live television images and photographs of the utter devastation of the Kurdish community were broadcast internationally, causing the domestic populations of Coalition states to pressure their governments to respond to the crisis, in part because they believed the war was a cause of the rebellion.[81] The extensive media attention to the plight of the Kurds elicited public outrage in the U.S. and threatened to overshadow the military success of Desert Storm. The U.S. government was motivated to respond, in part, because the crisis directly threatened the political aims of the war.[82] In short, the humanitarian crisis threatened U.S. national interests by detracting from U.S. accomplishments in the Persian Gulf. Nonetheless, it is also true that while media coverage and popular opinion added to the pressure and urgency for the U.S. to respond, President George H. W. Bush had "declared his intention to intervene before the public could find its voice."[83]

Second, independent experts like those from international human rights organizations used this opportunity to release extensive reports detailing the Iraqi regime's past human rights violations, including the Anfal campaign. They linked ongoing Iraqi repression to its past genocidal behavior.[84] At the very time that Saddam Hussein's military was indiscriminately attacking Iraqi Kurds in northern Iraq, Middle East Watch presented compelling evidence to the international public of his past genocidal efforts to destroy the Kurdish minority. Middle East Watch chastised the allied powers and in particular the United States for failing to assist the Kurds of Halabja in 1988 or to punish the Iraqi regime until *after* it had invaded Kuwait.[85] The pressure exerted on the U.S. and European states was twofold: they were criticized for past failures to prevent or punish human rights abuses against the Kurds in Iraq, and they were pressured to stop the Iraqi regime's abuses against the Kurds in the present and punish it for those abuses. In short, these advocacy groups publicly urged Security Council members to make their foreign policy behavior consistent with their professed values.

Third, the eyewitness testimony of U.S. secretary of state James Baker, who visited the refugee encampments along the Turkish border, was crucial for gaining Bush administration support for Operation Provide Comfort and the creation of the no-fly zones. In early April 1991, Baker witnessed the precarious situation of the displaced Kurds after being urged by then assistant secretary of state Margaret Tutwiler to make a personal visit to the camps. Baker was hesitant to go but Tutwiler had argued that it was necessary to demonstrate in a dramatic way that the U.S. had not abandoned the region at the end of the war.[86] Baker's motives for the visit were shaped primarily by domestic and foreign policy interests. Yet these interests were threatened by the administration's perceived failure to live up to the normative expectations of domestic and international publics who believed the U.S. had a responsibility to protect human rights and to respond to the suffering of the Iraqi population.

Talking with a delegation of Kurdish refugees who had survived Saddam Hussein's repression and had witnessed the slaughter of family members had a visceral impact on the secretary of state. Baker later said that he had "witnessed the suffering and desperation of the Iraqi people and that their experiences of cruelty and human anguish defied description."[87] He identified his personal experience of meeting Kurdish refugees as the principal motivation for the subsequent U.S. approach to Iraq policy:

> My experience on that rugged hillside was not only the catalyst for a huge expansion of American and international relief to the Kurds that came to be known as Operation Provide Comfort: it also galvanized me into pressing for a new policy, announced by the President on April 16, of establishing safe havens for the Kurds in northern Iraq-refugee camps secured by U.S. forces and administered by the United Nations. . . . It was the largest military relief operation ever undertaken, and delivered millions of dollars in food and supplies to more than 400,000 refugees.[88]

It is clear that political and military interests merged with human rights values and humanitarian concerns to produce an unprecedented U.S. and ultimately Security Council response. Compelling expert testimony, graphic television and photographic imagery, and their impact on international public opinion had a particularly strong influence on the Security Council.

The character of the military intervention itself demonstrates that both material interests and humanitarian considerations shaped Security Council decision making. If the three permanent members had been solely concerned with Turkish sovereignty and stability, sealing the Iraqi border to protect its neighbors from the negative effects of Iraq's repression would have been sufficient. Relative to sovereignty and stability, it was unnecessary to undertake a far-reaching humanitarian relief effort deep within the borders of Iraq. Further, the initial preoccupation with the situation of the Kurds and the establishment of the no-fly zone in the north but not the south betrays the underlying national security interests of those three permanent members, yet material interests cannot explain the decision to extend that same protection to the southern Shi'as over a year later when they did not pose a cross-border security threat. Moreover, while domestic pressure and international media attention were significant factors in the establishment of the no-fly zone in the north in 1991, they were not significant factors in the decision to extend the no-fly zone to the south in 1992. Indeed, in August 1992 there was little international attention devoted to the plight of the unprotected Shi'a relative to the focus on humanitarian tragedies happening in Somalia and Bosnia-Herzegovina at that same time. Nonetheless, the Security Council expanded its protection to the southern Iraqi Shi'a. In sum, domestic security interests were necessary to produce humanitarian action by France, the UK, and the U.S.; but humanitarian values and human rights norms in turn helped to constitute those national interests.

The Competing Normative Demands of State Sovereignty and Human Rights

Defining human rights violations as a threat to international peace and security has the potential to expose Security Council members to competing normative demands. The council is charged with two principal tasks: regulating state sovereignty and maintaining international peace and security. Protecting the norm of state sovereignty often leads to a policy of nonintervention in the domestic affairs of sovereign states. Maintaining international peace and security often involves enforcement action under Chapters VI, VII, and VIII of the Charter. When human rights violations are defined as a threat to international peace and security, the protection of human rights may require enforcement action within the sovereign boundaries of a state without its permission, bringing sovereignty norms and human rights norms into conflict. Norm research shows that when two norms come into conflict, the stronger, more institutionalized norm generally wins out over the newer, less established norm.[89] As a result, it is expected that when these two sets of norms conflict in a place like the UNSC, sovereignty norms should trump human rights. This did not happen in Iraq in 1991 and 1992 because Security Council members had temporarily suspended Iraqi sovereignty and discursively constructed the protection of human rights as complementary to the preservation of Turkey and Iran's sovereignty, eliminating the tension between the two norms.

Although Resolution 688 was unprecedented for redefining international security interests to include the protection of human rights, it also reaffirmed the principle of noninterference in the internal affairs of member states, despite demanding immediate and unfettered access to Iraq's sovereign territory and the end to human rights violations against its citizens. The UNSC reconciled this inherent tension between sovereignty and human rights norms by reasoning that the internal human rights situation extended beyond the border of Iraq, moving it beyond the realm of domestic affairs, and thereby justifying an international response.[90] In effect, Resolution 688 reaffirmed the domestic jurisdiction of states over their peoples and territories while portraying the human rights situation as no longer an internal matter of the Iraqi state. Thus the resolution cited Article 2.7 of the Charter of the United Nations (which protects state sovereignty), the preamble of the Charter (which identifies the protection of human rights as a function of the United Nations), and Chapter VII (which authorizes enforcement action to protect international security) simultaneously.

The prior reversal of Iraq's occupation of Kuwait by Coalition forces acting under UNSC authority created the unusual conditions necessary for a small group of powerful members to extend enforcement action to include the protection of human rights in northern and southern Iraq. Iraq was viewed as a pariah state because it had violated the highly internalized norms of state sovereignty and territorial integrity when it invaded Kuwait. Since Iraqi sovereignty had already been temporarily suspended for its breach of international norms, it was easier to garner political support in the Security Council for an expansion of its mission for humanitarian purposes. The promotion of human rights norms in Iraq occurred within the context of a conventional war in which the sovereignty of the aggressor state had been temporarily suspended, removing the tension between the protection of state sovereignty and the promotion of human rights norms.[91] In this sense, the promotion and protection of human rights was no longer in conflict with the sovereignty and nonintervention norms so deeply revered by the council. Further, Security Council members described Kuwait, Turkey, and Iran as the proper referents of sovereignty in this case and not Iraq. Thus, it was the threat to regional security and the sovereignty of neighbor states posed by Iraq's violation of international human rights norms, and not human rights norms themselves, that enabled the passage of Resolution 688.

Despite the largely instrumental application of human rights norms in Security Council Resolution 688, their inclusion had profound, if unintended, effects on the meaning of state sovereignty and the legitimate purpose of military force. In May 1991 the United States' representative to the Security Council, Thomas Pickering, drew attention to changing normative expectations: "The response to the plight of the Kurds suggests a shift in world opinion towards a re-balancing of the claims of sovereignty and those of extreme humanitarian need. This is good news since it means we are moving closer to deterring genocide and aiding its victims. However, it also means we have much careful thinking to do about the nature of, and the limitations upon, intervention to carry out humanitarian assistance programs where States refuse, in pursuit of 'policies of repression,' to give permission to such assistance."[92] Similarly, UN secretary-general Pérez de Cuéllar wrote in his 1991 report to the General Assembly that the ability of states to hide their human rights abuses behind the shield of state sovereignty was diminishing: "It is now increasingly felt that the principle of non-interference within the essential domestic jurisdiction of States cannot be regarded as a protective barrier behind which human rights could be massively or systematically violated with impunity."[93] Security Council action in Iraq ushered in a new normative context where human rights norms were growing in their international legitimacy and changing the meaning of state sovereignty and by extension the legitimate purpose of military force.

Conclusions

The Iraq case demonstrates that Security Council unity around a common causal story (in this case an intentional story about interstate aggression) that resonates with an international audience and has the backing of powerful proponents makes the use of military force possible. Justifications for the subsequent coercive response to Iraqi violations of human rights illustrate the growing legitimacy of human rights norms and their ability to shape UNSC decision making alongside considerations of national and international security interests and other powerful international norms such as sovereignty and nonintervention. Resolution 688 marked a fundamental shift in council behavior—the linkage of human rights norms to the maintenance of international security and the use of enforcement measures to curtail human rights violations being perpetrated by a state member of the United Nations against its own people when it negatively affected the security and stability of neighboring states.

Defining the effects of human rights violations as an international security threat was a radical departure from previous Security Council behavior, yet the council sought to maintain its commitment to existing Westphalian conceptions of sovereignty and nonintervention norms. The UNSC was able to promote human rights and protect state sovereignty simultaneously because Iraqi sovereignty had been temporarily suspended and because its referents for sovereign authority were Kuwait, Iran, and Turkey. Human rights mattered to the Security Council in 1991 but largely because their violation had negative consequences for other sovereign states. Most Security Council members articulated an instrumental conception of human rights—they were a means to some other end (international peace and security) rather than an end in themselves. Yet the instrumental adoption of human rights norms by the Security Council created precedent and a political opening for members who believe that the gross and systematic human rights violations warrant Security Council attention. The Security Council response to the situation of Iraq demonstrates that human rights norms and sovereignty norms are coevolving. Ideas about human rights, combined with the Security Council response to Iraqi repression, altered the meaning of sovereignty and introduced a new possibility for the legitimate use of military force—enforcement action in defense of human rights. The passage of Resolution 688 created a precedent for future Security Council humanitarian intervention that would be exercised in Somalia, Bosnia-Herzegovina, Sierra Leone, and Libya.

State Collapse in Somalia and the Emergence of Security Council Humanitarian Intervention

When Somalia made it onto the United Nations Security Council agenda in January 1992, the council members were newly optimistic about their ability to react promptly and effectively in concert with one another to threats to international peace and security. Just the year before, the council had reversed Iraq's occupation of Kuwait and stopped the Iraqi regime from violating the human rights of its population. As a result, the meaning of state sovereignty, the relationship between human rights norms and international security, and beliefs about the legitimate purpose of military force were evolving. In 1992, however, the post–Cold War order that council members collectively desired and expected was challenged by mounting threats to international peace and security originating from conflicts raging within states rather than between them. Indeed, eleven of the sixteen situations on the 1992 Security Council agenda were characterized as intrastate conflicts. This represents nearly 70 percent of the situations on the 1992 Security Council agenda compared to only 27 percent at the start of the Iraq-Kuwait crisis in 1990.[1] The Security Council was being called on to create the political conditions necessary to end conflict and no longer to simply observe and monitor peace agreements after conflicts had ended. In another example of this changed context, the Security Council recommended the admission of more new states as members of the United Nations between 1990 and 1992 than in the previous fifteen years; and nearly three-quarters were the result of the breakup of states.[2] This represented the greatest spike in UN membership since the period of decolonization in the 1960s. In short, the UNSC faced a changing international context characterized by civil wars, gross human rights violations, and mass death, which demanded new and innovative responses at the very moment it had started to fulfill its original purpose—to maintain international peace between states.

The crisis in Somalia had to compete for Security Council attention with other internal crises on the council's agenda, including Angola, Bosnia-Herzegovina, Cambodia, El Salvador, Liberia, Rwanda, and South Africa. In the competition for attention, some Security Council members and many African states complained that Somalia received scant attention and disproportionately fewer UN resources than the crisis in Bosnia. Indeed, the council met more than one hundred times to discuss the situation in Bosnia compared to less than twenty to discuss Somalia between 1992 and 1995. Nonetheless, humanitarian intervention happened in Somalia more than two years before the serious use of military force to defend Bosnian Muslims occurred in Bosnia. For reasons explained in this chapter, Security Council members decided that a robust military response to the Somalia crisis would demonstrate the international community's resolve to respond to new post–Cold War security threats. The decision to authorize the use of military force under Chapter VII of the UN Charter was different from preceding UNSC justifications for the use of force, resulted in the enhanced legitimacy of human rights norms, and led to the emergence of a new Security Council practice—humanitarian intervention.[3] The case of Somalia marked an important advance in the emerging idea that the international community in general, and the Security Council in particular, had a responsibility to respond to humanitarian crises caused by conflict in order to end human suffering. At the same time, it raised questions about the UN's ability to do so effectively, with serious implications for subsequent cases.

Humanitarian intervention became possible because Security Council members were united around a causal story about the cause and character of the conflict and because Somalia was essentially deemed a failed state. The absence of a legitimate sovereign authority eliminated potential tensions between protecting humanitarian values including human rights, intervening militarily into a domestic humanitarian crisis, and protecting state sovereignty. Initially, members were divided between an inadvertent story about civil war and a complex story that also included armed banditry, gang violence, and interclan fighting. The Chapter VII authorization in December 1992 coincided with the complex story, in large part because of the absence of a legitimate state structure, the Security Council was forced to choose between responding to the humanitarian crisis or letting it continue unabated. The latter seemed like an impossible and unnecessary choice fresh off the victory in Iraq. Nonetheless, once military forces were on the ground and the UN became the target of hostilities, the causal story held by the council changed to an intentional story in June 1993. The use of enforcement action broadened and became more aggressive with the adoption of an intentional story in which specific clan factions were identified as perpetrators of gross human rights violations leveled against both Somali civilians and UN personnel.

During formal meetings, Security Council members debated whether or not its actions in Somalia should constitute a precedent for future council action. The council was divided between members who specifically sought to use the Somalia case to set new standards of response for the council and to serve as a warning to perpetrators in other places and those who emphasized that the conditions in Somalia were sui generis, warranting an exceptional and non-precedent-setting Security Council response. As later chapters illustrate, the Security Council response in Somalia did become a precedent, often cited by members in meetings on other conflicts. Yet it was exactly because the characteristics of the Somalia crisis were sufficiently different from other internal conflicts, namely that it lacked a legitimate government, that the UNSC was able to undertake early forcible military action there in defense of humanitarian principles when it was not prepared to elsewhere in the early 1990s.

The Somalia intervention, its successes and failures, helped to delineate the conditions under which the emerging practice of humanitarian intervention would and would not become possible in future conflicts. The most prominent of these factors include the importance of widespread agreement among council members on the causal story, and after Somalia around an intentional story and the degree to which new ideas about humanitarian intervention brought human rights norms into conflict with highly internalized norms of state sovereignty. The sequencing of Security Council decisions is also important with regard to humanitarian intervention. In the early stages of norm emergence, the factors required to trigger the application of a new norm against prevailing path-dependent behavior may be more numerous and significant than the conditions that are necessary when the norm has become more developed. As Martha Finnemore and Kathryn

Sikkink write, "new norms never enter a normative vacuum but instead emerge in a highly contested normative space where they must compete with other norms and perceptions of interest."[4] When norm entrepreneurs seek to promote a new norm, they must do so within the standards of appropriateness already created by existing norms, even when those standards are exactly the behavior that is being contested.[5] In Somalia, humanitarian intervention was possible because of Security Council unity and because the exercise of human rights norms and the emerging practice of humanitarian intervention did not significantly challenge existing sovereignty norms.

The Humanitarian Crisis in Somalia

The people of Somalia share the same ethnicity, language, religion, and culture but are distinguished by clan affiliation—that is, by their lineage and family custom. Clan and subclan loyalties are important to Somali identity and politics and have fostered a culture of decentralization.[6] Their manipulation by power-seeking leaders has been a source of political and social instability since Somali independence in 1960. Initially, Major General Mohammed Siad Barre, who seized power in a 1969 coup, sought to erode the clan system and replace it with a form of "scientific socialism," but he ultimately relied on clan loyalty to maintain his personal power.[7] Three clans of the Darod clan-family—his own, his mother's, and his son-in-law's—largely controlled the Somali state, which exacerbated interclan tensions. Barre's military support for Ogadeni revolutionary forces inside neighboring Ethiopia in 1977 and their crushing defeat caused an upsurge in interclan tensions as Ogadeni refugees crossed into Somalia and occupied Isaq pastoral lands.[8] Barre survived a coup attempt the following year and tightened his grip on power but opposition to his rule continued to grow among disaffected clans, including the organized Isaq and Hawiye.[9] Barre stayed in power by using divide-and-rule tactics internally and by externally supporting insurgent groups fighting in neighboring Ethiopia. In January 1991 the twenty-one-year dictatorship of Barre ended when he was forced from office by a Hawiye rebel group, the United Somali Congress (USC). By the time Barre was removed from power, the entire country was awash in small arms. Barre had maintained his rule by manipulating clan loyalties and fostering rivalries among them, then arming them to fight one another. He had outlawed opposition parties, suppressed civil society, and destroyed all independent institutions.[10] Thus his removal created a political vacuum in which competing rebel groups and their factions vied for political control throughout the country. After 1991, Somalia was a state without a legitimate sovereign authority. The USC, which had removed Barre and controlled the capital city Mogadishu, splintered into two rival factions, one headed by Ali Mahdi Mohamed, a wealthy Somali businessman who declared himself the interim president of Somalia, and the second headed by General Mohamed Farah Aideed, the main military commander of the USC and Mahdi's competitor for political power. By mid-November, full-scale war between the two factions of the USC erupted in Mogadishu, primarily over which group would control the presidency and the territory that included Mogadishu. The conflict between them resulted in an estimated fourteen thousand deaths and thirty thousand wounded in Mogadishu alone.[11]

The factional fighting in Mogadishu was replicated throughout the country—scorched earth tactics, looting, and violent attacks against members of rival clans, including the rape of women and the killing of the elderly and children. Civilians were at risk of death from two primary sources: the hostilities and the food scarcity that resulted from a combination of years of fighting, the destruction of farmland, and drought. In March 1992, Africa Watch and Physicians for Human Rights issued a report that described the character of the conflict and its human cost:

> Mogadishu has become a place of unpredictable death, with no one in authority and no one capable of enforcing a social commitment to order. Everyone appears armed. Whoever draws first carries the day, since there is no civil authority to punish someone who robs or kills. Many people are short-tempered, stressed by hunger and fear and many men—and boys—are consuming too much qat (a widely used mild stimulant that comes as a chewable green leaf) which is more powerful when eaten on a hungry stomach. In this climate of marginally contained chaos, the ICRC and NGO community working in Mogadishu are stretched to the limits of their own endurance and institutional integrity.[12]

The World Food Program described the situation in Somalia as "an unparalleled disaster" and estimated that half of the population of the south central region had died by mid-1992.[13] In July of that year, Secretary-General Boutros Boutros-Ghali warned, based on figures provided by the UN high commissioner for refugees, that one million Somali children were at immediate risk of starving to death.[14] The International Committee of the Red Cross (ICRC) estimated that 95 percent of Somalia's population suffered from malnutrition and almost 70 percent suffered from severe malnutrition and disease.[15] Although international humanitarian relief organizations were on the ground working to alleviate the hunger, warlords restricted their movement and armed gangs regularly looted food and relief supplies intended for Somali civilians. Violence interfered with the distribution of humanitarian aid—by December 1992 it was estimated the half of all Somali children under the age of five had already died.[16]

Security Council Involvement in Somalia, 1992–1995

The character of the Security Council response to Somalia can be described as having three distinct phases: the use of nonmilitary enforcement measures (January–November 1992), forcible military humanitarian intervention (December 1992–January 1994), and reversal of enforcement measures and UN withdrawal (February 1994–March 1995). The first phase began in January 1992 when the Security Council passed Resolution 733 establishing an arms embargo. Then in April 1992, Resolution 751 established the United Nations Operation in Somalia (UNOSOM)—a traditional peacekeeping operation with primarily humanitarian ends. The Security Council response changed from a traditional peacekeeping mandate to a forcible military intervention in December 1992 when Resolution 794 established the U.S.-led United Task Force (UNITAF). UNITAF was authorized to use "all necessary means" to establish a secure environment for humanitarian relief operations. Resolution 814 transferred authority back to the UN in March 1993, and also expanded the size of the force and the scope of mandate denoted by the revised name of the UN mission, UNOSOM II. The use of forcible measures continued under UNOSOM II with an emphasis on the coercive disarmament of Somali factions. The third phase of UN involvement was characterized by a dramatic reversal in policy when in February 1994 the Security Council revised the UNOSOM II mandate, reducing its military functions and transitioning back to a more traditional peacekeeping operation. In March 1995 UN forces completely withdrew from Somalia, despite the persistence of war.

Three causal stories emerged during Security Council deliberations, but they did not coincide neatly with the three phases of council action in Somalia. The inadvertent story described an internecine civil war in which all parties to the conflict were causing harm to civilians. The complex story identified multiple clans, characterized by fragmenting interclan rivalries, warlords, armed thugs, and criminal gangs, as responsible for inflicting terror on the civilian population. The intentional story characterized the violence as deliberate and planned—naming perpetrators including the Somali National Assembly (SNA), General Aideed, and the United Somali Congress who were deliberately inflicting violence on UN peacekeeping personnel and the civilian population of Mogadishu. Initially, Security Council members were split between those who articulated an inadvertent story about civil war in which all parties were called upon to cease hostilities and a complex story about fighting between multiple factions accompanied by vigilantism and armed banditry. Despite this division, the language of early Security Council resolutions articulated the inadvertent story. By December 1992, however, the complex story dominated the Security Council until June 1993 when the intentional story emerged to compete with it. The use of military force by UN troops qualitatively changed as the intentional story gained traction in the Security Council, evolving from the forcible but largely neutral protection of humanitarian aid to the highly punitive and aggressive use of military force against specific parties to the conflict. Regardless of the story, all the resolutions passed by the UNSC expressed concern with the unfolding humanitarian tragedy and characterized its own action (both military and nonmilitary) as a humanitarian response. Security Council members devoted significantly more time debating the appropriate humanitarian response to the crisis in Somalia than to understanding its underlying cause and character—its causal story.

Non-Military Enforcement Measures and Contestation Between Inadvertent and Complex Stories

In January 1992, the Security Council passed Resolution 733, which urged "all parties" to the conflict to cease hostilities and agree to a cease-fire and imposed an arms embargo against Somalia. The resolution was passed in absence of formal deliberation but the text reflected an inadvertent story and the moral equivalence between parties that this implied. In March, only three members articulated the inadvertent story (Morocco, Nigeria, and the United States); they described the conflict as "fratricidal" and mutually destructive to the parties that were described as unwilling to create the conditions necessary for the delivery of humanitarian relief to their own peoples.[17] In contrast, Secretary-General Boutros-Ghali and five members of the Security Council (Belgium, Japan, Hungary, India, and Zimbabwe) described the conflict as tragic and complex. The remaining council members declined to comment publicly on the cause and character of the conflict but joined the others in expressing concern about the plight of suffering civilians and linking the humanitarian crisis to international security. Security Council members pressed for an active UN presence in Somalia despite the failure of the Somali parties to abide by a cease-fire and in the absence of formal consent. The four reasons articulated in March 1992 were the magnitude of the humanitarian tragedy, the implications of continued fighting and famine for neighboring states, the unconventional nature of the conflict, and an appeal for equity in UN dealings with Africa in comparison to other regions.[18]

Unlike in Iraq, members of the Security Council were more concerned with the humanitarian tragedy unfolding within the borders of Somalia than its implications for neighboring states, and public comments emphasized the human suffering of the Somali people. For example, the United States described the situation as "a tragedy of heartbreaking magnitude" with Belgium, Zimbabwe, and Ecuador similarly noting its "tragic" character.[19] Belgium described the increasing numbers of dead, injured, and displaced persons: "All the information emanating from Somalia coincides on one point: the humanitarian situation there is a tragic one. The number of dead, injured and displaced persons continues to increase, and famine is taking firm hold."[20] Its ambassador warned that the complex political and military situation was impeding the provision of humanitarian relief and that widespread famine was impending, necessitating an international response.[21] Hungary noted its concern over "the magnitude of the human suffering brought about by the conflict" and asserted that "the continuation of this tragic and alarming situation constitutes a threat to international peace and security."[22] The Kenyan representative, speaking on behalf of the African group, called attention to "the vicious coexistence of war and famine in Somalia."[23] It is clear from statements like these that the humanitarian tragedy had captured the attention of council members. Yet members likewise were concerned with the potential regional impact of the conflict. Nigeria noted that refugees from Somalia have "consequential implications for neighboring states," while France, Australia, India, and Zimbabwe argued that both the ongoing violence and its impact on civilians threatened peace and stability in the entire region.[24] Despite this expressed concern about regional impact, however, Resolution 746 defined the continuation of the *internal* humanitarian crisis in Somalia as a threat to international peace and security, rather than its cross-border effects. "*Deeply disturbed* by the magnitude of the human suffering caused by the conflict and concerned that the continuation of the situation in Somalia constitutes a threat to international peace and security," the resolution proclaimed.[25] This same humanitarian language was repeated in Resolution 751, which established UNOSOM on 24 April 1992. The Security Council made no formal references to interstate dimensions of the conflict, transborder refugee flows, or the risk of regional spillover in either Resolution 746 or 751. Instead, nontraditional conceptions of security—that international security is affected by the violation of human rights—shaped initial UNSC reaction to the conflict. Only later did Resolutions 767 and 775, of July and August 1992 respectively, acknowledge that the provision of humanitarian assistance in Somalia was important to council efforts to restore international peace and security in the region.

Security Council engagement in Somalia was also motivated by the unconventional nature of the conflict. Council members argued that the simultaneous tragedy of fighting and famine in the absence of legitimate government authority demanded "new and innovative methods" of response.[26] Several members described the combined military and humanitarian tragedy as unconventional. Secretary-General Boutros-Ghali, in both his report to the council and in a statement to the media, argued, "Somalia presented a special challenge, as an extraordinarily complex, tragic situation that had so far eluded conventional solutions."[27] It was the unique, nonstate character of Somalia that made the use of military force possible since the need for consent was eliminated and humanitarian intervention would not challenge state sovereignty.

Forcible Military Humanitarian Intervention and Shifting Causal Stories

The second phase of UN involvement in Somalia marked another historic shift in Security Council action with regard to intrastate conflicts. When the council passed Resolution 794 in December 1992 and Resolution 814 in March 1993 (Table 3.1), it authorized the use of "all necessary means" to create the conditions necessary to ensure the delivery of humanitarian aid and to foster political reconciliation. The authorization of the use of force under Chapter VII marked an important step in the emergence of the practice of humanitarian intervention. For the first time in its history, the UNSC authorized armed intervention for a strictly humanitarian cause.[28] Unlike Resolution 688, which authorized UN protection for Iraqi Kurds and Shi'a because of the transborder impact of Iraq's human-rights-violating behavior, Resolution 794 defined the internal humanitarian crisis itself as a threat to international peace and security.[29] This Security Council innovation became possible due to a high degree of unity around a causal story and because the use of coercive force in this case posed little threat to established and highly internalized norms of state sovereignty.

During the debate preceding passage of Resolution 794, Security Council members articulated a complex story that identified multiple causes for the humanitarian crisis. Only Kenya and Nigeria, both nonvoting participants in the Security Council debate, articulated an inadvertent story. They argued that while multiple factions within Somalia were engaged in combat with one another for political control of the country, human suffering was an indirect consequence of the fighting and was compounded by drought. Morocco and Zimbabwe, both Security Council members, used the phrases "fratricidal conflict" "fratricidal tragedy" and "internecine war" to characterize the conflict but both also used words like "chaotic" and "complex," respectively.[30] The stories that they articulated described both complexity and inadvertent action simultaneously. This is consistent with a complex story that identifies multiple causal factors, frequently employing discourse from alternative causal stories at the same time (see Table 1.1). Proponents of the complex story emphasized the complicated interplay of multiple factors in causing the humanitarian crisis, including but not limited to the civil war. India described the "complex" and "chaotic" character of the situation: "The Secretary-General's report on Somalia . . . graphically depicts the complexity of the situation. The fighting in Mogadishu between two factions of the same Somali movement is compounded many-fold by hostility between political factions and movements in other parts of Somalia, fractures and struggles within these movements themselves, secessionist movements in the north and uncontrolled armed elements on the rampage everywhere."[31] The U.S. argued that what was occurring in Somalia was characteristic of the political disorder and complexity of the post–Cold War

Table 3.1. Security Council Support for Key Resolutions, Somalia

	Subject	*Votes in Favor*	*Votes Against*	*Abstentions*
Resolution 746 (1992)	Expresses concern that the continuation of human suffering in Somalia constitutes a threat to international peace and security	Austria Belgium Cape Verde **China** Ecuador **France** Hungary India Japan Morocco **Russia** **UK** **U.S.** Venezuela Zimbabwe	None	None
Resolution 794 (1992)	Authorizes all necessary means under Chapter VII to establish a safe environment for humanitarian relief and establishes UNITAF	Austria Belgium Cape Verde **China** Ecuador **France** Hungary India Japan Morocco **Russia** **UK** **U.S.** Venezuela Zimbabwe	None	None
Resolution 814 (1993)	Expands the mandate under Chapter VII to include disarmament and transfers authority from UNITAF to UNOSOM II	Brazil Cape Verde **China** Djibouti **France** Hungary Japan Morocco New Zealand Pakistan **Russia** Spain **UK** **U.S.** Venezuela	None	None

world.[32] China, Morocco, and Russia described Somalia as a situation of "total chaos" characterized by terror, blackmail, banditry, and devastation.[33] Resolution 794 explicitly articulated the complex story, asserting that in "*recognizing* the unique character of the present situation in Somalia and *mindful* of its deteriorating, complex, and extraordinary nature," the council believed it "required an exceptional response" (emphasis original).[34] Resolution 794 was passed unanimously by the Security Council (see Table 3.1).

Even after five new nonpermanent members joined the Security Council at the start of 1993 (Brazil, Djibouti, New Zealand, Pakistan, and Spain), the complex story dominated. In March 1993 the Security Council passed Resolution 814, which transferred authority from the U.S.-led UNITAF to UNOSOM II—a United Nations operation with an expanded force and mandate that emphasized disarming Somalia factions. During the debate preceding its passage, Djibouti argued that Somalia was beset by "ever-deepening anarchy" and Brazil described the complex situation as unique.[35] In the narrative of complexity and chaos, there is no single perpetrator or perpetrator group that can be held culpable for atrocities. In Somalia, the perpetrators were identified generically as warlords, armed gangs, and bandits but they were deemed only partially responsible for the ensuing humanitarian crisis. In addition to the difficulty of linking specific perpetrators to specific crimes, their harmful actions were characterized as foreseen but not the purpose of the fighting. The Security Council struggled to identify a point of leverage to disrupt the violence. The statement by Cape Verde captured the frustration of council members as they tried to stop atrocities in a context where the perpetrators could not be clearly connected to their crimes. "We are bound to admit that we have now reached a situation in which the law of the jungle is tending to prevail over the action of the international community."[36]

Despite the lack of intentional causality, the strength of human rights norms and the pull of the humanitarian impulse—the natural human desire to help those in life-threatening circumstances caused by armed conflict—rallied the Security Council toward forcible intervention.[37] Members argued that the very survival of the Somali state and the Somali people was at risk, constituting a threat to international peace and security. It was the magnitude of a human catastrophe that "defies words and imagination," according to Austria; and the absence of legitimate authority within the country propelled the Security Council to take radical new action—the use of military force to interrupt "total chaos" and create safe conditions for humanitarian relief.[38]

As Somali factions continued to obstruct humanitarian convoys and undermine efforts toward peace, UNOSOM II engaged in ever more coercive disarmament actions. Tensions heightened dramatically between UNOSOM II forces and General Aideed, the leader of the Somali National Assembly (SNA) faction of the now divided USC, who worried about being politically and militarily marginalized by the UN. Shortly after the transfer of authority from the U.S. to the UN mission, Aideed began offensive operations against UN personnel. In response, on 5 June 1993 UN peacekeepers raided a weapons storage facility of the SNA at Radio Mogadishu. Hiding behind angry crowds of civilian supporters, the SNA militia engaged the Pakistani peacekeepers in hostilities. After hours of fighting, American and Italian armored units succeeded in breaking off the confrontation.[39] By then, twenty-four Pakistani peacekeepers had been killed and fifty-six more injured, making this the heaviest single incident of UN casualties ever in a peacekeeping operation.[40] The Security Council was outraged and called an emergency meeting on 6 June.

In the aftermath of the deadly attack on the Pakistani peacekeepers, Security Council support for the complex story broke down. Consensus shifted to a newly emerged intentional story that characterized the violence as deliberate and premeditated. Members specifically identified the perpetrators, who were characterized as willingly and knowingly attacking Somali civilians and the international community through a "calculated and premeditated series of cease-fire violations."[41] The tone of the debate was openly hostile. Pakistan described the perpetrators as "petty warlords," "dictators," and "international thugs" and called for the Security Council to act swiftly to bring them to justice for their "murderous defiance of the Council's authority."[42] Similarly, the U.S. advocated for a renewed focus on "the disarming and detention of persons posing a threat to UN forces or obstructing their operations."[43] Djibouti described the perpetrators as "uncivilized" and "criminal elements."[44] France, the UK, and Venezuela were more specific and identified the Somali National Assembly, the Somali National Congress, and General Aideed by name.[45] Venezuela said that Aideed was "nationally and internationally recognized as primarily responsible for the destruction of Somalia and for thousands upon thousands of crimes against his people."[46] While the Somali people continued to be identified as victims, the overwhelming tone emphasized that the UN and its peacekeeping personnel were now the primary victims. In total, ten Security Council members specifically called for the authors of the crimes against Pakistani peacekeepers to be punished by the UN.

On 6 June 1993, Resolution 837 condemned the attacks on UN personnel; reemphasized the importance of disarming Somali parties; reaffirmed the authority of the UN to investigate, detain, and prosecute perpetrators; and encouraged both the accelerated deployment of more UN troops and enhanced military capability to confront and deter perpetrator attacks. Reflecting the shift to an intentional story, Resolution 837, which the council passed unanimously, had a decidedly more confrontational tone than previous resolutions. As an example, in December 1992, Resolution 794 had characterized the conflict as "complex" and a "tragedy." It identified perpetrators in the broadest of terms as "all parties, movements and factions in Somalia." Finally, it condemned their obstructionist behavior, which it described as the "deliberate impeding of the delivery of food and medical supplies essential for the survival of the civilian population."[47] In stark contrast, Resolution 837 described "calculated and premeditated attacks" against UN personnel and identified the perpetrators by name as "the SNA faction of the United Somali Congress led by General Aideed." Resolution 837 specifically authorized UNOSOM II forces "to confront and deter armed attacks" against UN personnel and reaffirmed its authorization to take "all necessary measures against those responsible for the attacks" on the Pakistani peacekeepers.[48] The resolution called for the neutralization of radio broadcasts inciting violence against peacekeepers and urged donations of heavy weaponry to the mission, "including armoured personnel carriers, tanks and attack helicopters, to provide UNOSOM II the capability appropriately to confront and deter armed attack directed against it in the accomplishment of its mandate."[49] The shift in story was paralleled by shifts in action on the ground. Inadvertent stories lend themselves to policies of palliation and protection while intentional stories, because they identify a perpetrator of calculated and premeditated violence, lend themselves to policies of interdiction and punishment. After the adoption of the intentional story, UN forces in Somalia became more aggressive. Whereas previous military force was used primarily in protection of humanitarian aid convoys, UN troops began regularly employing more offensive means of force. The result was an increasingly aggressive emphasis by UN personnel on the coercive disarmament of factions, the capture of Aideed, and the political isolation of the SNA. More and more, the UN came to be seen as a party to the conflict rather than its mediator. Peacekeepers were drawn into frequent gun battles with the SNA on the streets of Mogadishu and suffered more casualties. As support for the intentional story grew, coercive disarmament of Somali factions and the removal of General Aideed from influence became part of the overall UN effort to restore peace, order and security to Somalia. During a 22 September meeting, UNSC members articulated different and conflicting stories. For the first time, members fundamentally disagreed on the cause and character of the conflict—whether it was complex and multifaceted or whether it was the result of intentional acts by a particular Somali faction.

In October 1993, U.S. rangers launched a military raid intended to capture General Aideed. Full-scale fighting erupted between SNA supporters and the U.S. military forces. During the firefight, American attack helicopters were shot down and sixteen U.S. soldiers were killed. The bodies of some of the American soldiers were mutilated by angry Somalis and dragged through the streets of Mogadishu. The gruesome images were captured by television cameras and broadcast throughout the world. Within days, and acting under significant domestic pressure, the presidential administration of Bill Clinton announced that it would temporarily increase forces in Somalia but that the U.S. would withdraw completely from the operation within six months. The president had decided that the humanitarian intervention was too costly to continue but his administration wanted to withdraw gradually with honor.[50]

Reversal of Mandate and Withdrawal: Defining the Limits of Humanitarian Intervention

By November 1993, responsibility for the tragic situation in Somalia seemed to shift again but this time to the Somali people themselves. The remarks of the UK reflect the predominant sentiment of the council at that time: "The future lies in their own hands. . . . The people of Somalia bear the ultimate responsibility for national reconciliation and the reconstruction of their country. We can help but we cannot do it for them."[51] During previous meetings, blame for the crisis was placed squarely on the shoulders of the factions. Now the people of Somalia themselves bore ultimate responsibility, according to Resolution 886: "The people of Somalia bear the ultimate responsibility for national reconciliation and reconstruction of their own country."[52] The UNSC argued that it had achieved its humanitarian purpose but not its political one, and the council unanimously decided to terminate UN operations in Somalia.

The final phase of UN involvement in Somalia was characterized by an increasingly difficult military situation on the ground. In February 1994 the Security Council passed Resolution 897, which reversed its policy of coercive disarmament and revised the UNOSOM II mandate from peace enforcement to a traditional peacekeeping operation. Nine months later, the council unanimously passed Resolution 954, setting the operation's termination date for 31 March 1995. During the particularly somber meeting, delegations took turns characterizing the humanitarian operation as a success while acknowledging that the political mission had failed because of the intransigence of Somali political factions. Members as diverse as Argentina, Brazil, France, New Zealand, Nigeria, Pakistan, and the UK argued that while it was unpleasant to withdraw with unfulfilled objectives, the financial and human costs were too high when the UN faced humanitarian crises elsewhere and the Somali operation held little prospect for success.[53] In general, Security Council meetings during this period (February 1994–March 1995) took a reflective tone as its members sought to reexamine their motives and objectives for the Somali intervention as well as to discover lessons for future humanitarian interventions.

The Somalia case demonstrates that lack of unity in the Security Council precludes the use of coercive force. Once members no longer agreed on the causal story or whether the mission should continue, the use of military force became untenable even before the official change in mandate. By September 1994 the United States actively advocated for a complete UN withdrawal of the Somali mission, arguing that "UNOSOM is draining away scarce human and financial resources that would be better used by the international community elsewhere."[54] Oman also argued in favor of the dissolution of the Somali mission but suggested that the financial resources allocated to the military presence in the country could be "channeled to humanitarian purposes in that country."[55]

The Security Council also learned that complex situations were not amenable to humanitarian intervention. It is challenging to interdict chaos, especially without legitimate partners on the ground to work with. According to Brazil, "One should not conceal the fact that the Security Council has taken too long to realize that, against the backdrop of an extremely complex political situation, it could not bring peace to Somalia."[56] Spain remarked that the decision to shut done UNOSOM was "evidence that without the effective cooperation of the parties involved, any peacekeeping operation will be unable to reach all of its objectives."[57] The Security Council needs a perpetrator to stop but it also needs a domestic ally to work with like President Ahmad Kabbah in Sierra Leone (see Chapter 6) or the rebel forces in Libya (see Chapter 8). Complexity, then, became understood as not amenable to political solution because in a situation of chaos the perpetrators and potential strategic partners are not identifiable. In the absence of a government with which to negotiate, the Security Council was forced to decide between appeasing political actors that possessed military power or to oppose them with force.[58] Conflicts with multiple sources—both structural and human—and characterized by multiple factions with fissures within and between groups, as in Somalia and later in Darfur, were no longer viewed as good candidates for humanitarian intervention. Instead, complex stories would render conflicts more amenable to policies that reaffirmed stability than those that significantly challenged the status quo.

The Importance of Sovereign Authority to Security Council Decision Making

Two factors at the international level help to explain why humanitarian intervention was authorized first in Somalia and not elsewhere. First, council members initially were unified in their interpretation of the conflict or causal story—its causes, character, and victims—allowing them to act in concert. Second, the Somalia case was different than either Bosnia or Rwanda, which were occurring at the same time, precisely because Somalia lacked a legitimate government. Somalia's very viability as a state was in question, easing the inherent tension between Article 2.7 and human rights principles. Humanitarian intervention happened first in Somalia because it lacked sovereign authority. Djibouti remarked in March 1992: "Somalia is in many ways a modern anomaly, a land with no effective mechanism for governance. No operational institutions of any kind exist—financial institutions, government offices, schools, hospitals, police, military or political organs of government. It is in key respects a non-State."[59] Belgium described Somalia as an "atypical situation" and "a country without government, without administration, with no source of authority, where factions and gangs hold sway."[60] Council members representing every region of the world agreed that Somalia's lack of government was an "extraordinary situation" requiring an "exceptional response."[61] Ecuador proposed that in the absence of a legitimate government, sovereignty should be vested in the Somali people who were seeking international assistance. Speaking to the council before the vote on Resolution 794, Ecuador's representative said, "In Somalia there is no Government that can be interlocutor of the United Nations for the purpose of agreeing upon a humanitarian-assistance operation. But the Somali people—solely sovereign in the respect of its destiny—is our interlocutor, and we are heeding its call."[62] Ecuador's story appealed to theoretical conceptions of popular sovereignty wherein the state has a responsibility for the protection of the population for whom the state exists.

New norms are more likely to be acted on and strengthened when they are consistent with existing internalized norms, rather than when they are in conflict with them. Coercive humanitarian intervention in the case of Somalia did not raise the sovereignty concerns for council members that intervention elsewhere might have because the use of military force there did not transgress the sovereignty rights of a state and the principal perpetrators were illegitimate state actors. Security Council members discursively constructed the promotion of humanitarian values as consistent with or at least not opposed to sovereignty. Statelessness in a world of sovereign states was perceived as more threatening than humanitarian intervention.[63]

Norms, Interests, and Humanitarian Intervention

Security Council members were largely acting on a humanitarian impulse when they decided to use military force in Somalia. Yet they also reaffirmed the growing connection between the promotion of human rights and the protection of international security that had motivated the Security Council response in Iraq. Although the regional impact of the humanitarian crisis was profound, there is little evidence that national or international security interests were the driving motivation behind the Security Council's intervention. Rather, the justificatory discourse of members and the behavior of UN personnel on the ground demonstrated that principles of humanitarianism and ideas about human rights shaped and were shaped by collective international security interests. Norms and interests were mutually constituted.

UNSC deliberations were characterized by frequent references to the humanitarian situation and its impact on the Somali population. Council members expressed outrage at the level of starvation and violent deaths. Belgium captured the level of Security Council concern when it described the stakes of the humanitarian intervention as about "the very survival of the Somali people."[64] Ecuador argued that values were the principal motivation for its support for humanitarian intervention: "Solidarity and interdependence—principles that underly [sic] our international order—do not permit us to remain impassive in the face of human tragedy, regardless of where it may occur. Ecuador wants to live up to its moral responsibilities to this Organization and, as a member of the Security Council feels obliged to contribute to a settlement of the Somali conflict."[65] According to Ecuador, the UNSC had a moral responsibility to respond to the Somali crisis that complemented its responsibilities for the maintenance of international peace and security. New Zealand also supported the intervention despite the absence of national interests: "We have almost no historical or other connections with it. But we are particularly sensitive to and supportive of requests that the collective security mechanisms of our Organization be equally available for the benefit of the small and underprivileged as they are for the larger and more powerful."[66] According to this logic, the principle of sovereign equality required the UNSC to devote time and resources to addressing humanitarian crises whether they occurred in places of strategic interest or not. Indeed the very passage of Resolutions 746 and 794 underscored the presence of humanitarian motives. Resolution 746 was remarkable because it defined the continuation of the *internal* humanitarian crisis in Somalia as a threat to international peace and security, rather than its cross-border effects as Resolution 688 on Iraq had done. Justifying its vote in favor of Resolution 746, Hungary commented, "The Republic of Hungary is deeply concerned by the continuous deterioration of the situation in Somalia and by the magnitude of the human suffering brought about by the conflict. The continuation of this tragic and alarming situation constitutes a threat to international peace and security, and consequently, it demands effective action on behalf of the Council."[67] Then, in Resolution 794, the UNSC authorized for the first time the use of armed force under Chapter VII for a strictly humanitarian cause. The text identified the internal humanitarian crisis as sufficient to be defined as a threat to international peace and security: it made clear references to the importance of respect for international humanitarian law for achieving security, and it defined both the threat to life caused by the conflict and the obstacles posed to the distribution of humanitarian assistance as threats to international peace and security.[68] Indeed Kenya, one of Somalia's neighbors, criticized the council for focusing too little on the threat to regional interests that the crisis posed.

Kenya argued that devoting so much attention to the internal humanitarian catastrophe in Somalia caused the UNSC to lose sight of and neglect the conflict's serious threat to the security of neighboring states and to the economic system in the broader region: "The regional dimension of the Somalia conflict has not been given the attention it deserves. The neighbouring countries, including my own, have shouldered the heavy burden arising out of the Somalia conflict. My Government would like this important concern to be given adequate consideration by the Council."[69] This represented an important evolution from the council's previous determination in Iraq that it was the effects of an internal crisis that threatened regional and international peace and security.

While humanitarian motives were primary, there is evidence of the interplay between the humanitarian impulse and more traditional understandings of national interest. According to Security Council members like New Zealand, the council was motivated by mixed motives—both humanitarian and strategic.[70] As an example, early into the Somalia crisis then U.S. president George H. W. Bush was hesitant to intervene, but changed course as his foreign policy legacy and his very presidency came under threat by his unwillingness to address humanitarian crises in either Bosnia or Somalia. Responding to increasing domestic and political pressure to act in Bosnia, President Bush authorized the humanitarian airlift to Somalia—which he and his advisors perceived to be the easier of the two crises.[71] Yet when he made the decision to intervene, Bush had already lost the presidential election and was no longer constrained by domestic considerations.[72] Similarly, the rapid withdrawal of U.S. forces by President Clinton when intervention became too costly following the death of sixteen U.S. soldiers also reveals interest-based motives. Yet just three days after that tragic incident, the United States voted to approve the United Nations Assistance Mission in Rwanda, albeit reluctantly and without U.S. ground troops, responding to humanitarian concern. The withdrawal of the United Nations Operation in Somalia shows that there are limits to the costs that Security Council members are willing to incur during humanitarian interventions. The reversal in Somalia reveals the conditions of its appropriate use, not the absence of humanitarian motives. Interests and ideas are mutually constituted and both shape UNSC decision making about humanitarian intervention. Cape Verde's statement of December 1992 illustrates this interplay well: "Cape Verde has always taken the view that the national conflict in Somalia has reached a level of destruction comparable to that of the most ferocious international conflicts, necessitating resolute and effective action on the part of the international community with a view to putting an end to the tragedy afflicting the Somali people."[73] These humanitarian concerns were not distinct from regional and international interests: "What is occurring in Somalia is a threat to the very existence of Somali society; but at the same time it represents one of the most serious challenges to the full establishment of a new international order on Earth within which the United Nations has a role of capitol [sic] importance to play. Moreover, we have no doubt that the national conflict has a second dimension—an international dimension—in view of the fact that, because of its repercussions on neighbouring states, it is imperiling the stability and security of the whole region."[74] Discursively, security interests and ideas about humanitarianism were linked. Admiral Jonathon Howe, former deputy assistant to the president of the United States for national security affairs and then special representative of the secretary-general of the United Nations for Somalia, described the situation of Somalia as falling within the realm of "universal interests"—the shared world interests that nations collectively are willing to defend, including stopping the mass killing of civilians.[75] Former U.S. assistant secretary of state for African affairs Chester Crocker similarly argued, "It is surely wise that we and others broaden our understanding of national interest to include consideration of interests related to global order (sanctity of borders, extension of the Nuclear Nonproliferation Treaty) and global standards (avoiding genocide, mass humanitarian catastrophe)."[76] Operation Restore Hope was ultimately an act of human solidarity although statelessness came to be defined as a threat to international peace and security in a world of sovereign states.[77]

Somalia, Bosnia, and the Debate About Precedent

Throughout the crisis, Security Council members, nongovernmental organizations (NGOs), the media, and other states regularly made comparisons between the international community's responses to events in Somalia and Bosnia. Early in 1992, human rights organizations, humanitarian NGOs, and the media challenged what they viewed as a lack of serious attention given to the Somalia crisis by the powerful states that were involved in humanitarian operations elsewhere. It was the precisely the lack of interests, they argued, that kept Western states from fulfilling their humanitarian responsibilities in Africa. For example, a prominent news director of NBC-TV in New York was quoted as saying that Americans identified with Bosnians because they were "shocked" by pictures of "white people starving" whereas the public had become fatigued by pictures of suffering Africans.[78] Several African states and even the secretary-seneral accused the UNSC and Western states of double standards by failing to devote as much attention to the crisis in Somalia as they did to Bosnia. In a March Security Council meeting, the Nigerian representative, speaking on behalf of the Organization of African Unity, argued, "Africa deserves the same qualitative and quantitative attention which has been paid to other regions—and perhaps much more because of its economic base. There is a need to have a strong and visible presence in the conflict areas of Africa."[79] During that same meeting, India chided the council that the situation in Somalia was of "crisis proportions, with five times as many casualties as have taken place in Yugoslavia."[80] Zimbabwe considered the Security Council response to crises in Cambodia and Yugoslavia appropriate and effective but criticized the lack of equal response to the tragedy in Somalia, which it described as "unraveling before our eyes."[81] Secretary-General Boutros-Ghali, in a report to the Security Council, criticized the UNSC for being too concerned with the problems in Yugoslavia to address "equally cruel and dangerous conflicts elsewhere, e.g. in Somalia."[82] Tensions were high around this question of equal treatment of regions; and the quantitative comparison of UNSC meetings suggest that it was preoccupied with the crises in the former Yugoslavia in general and Bosnia in particular relative to Somalia. Qualitatively, however, the Security Council engaged in earlier and more robust military action for the protection of civilians in Somalia and engaged in humanitarian intervention there over two years before doing so in Bosnia. In December 1993 Austria defended the Security Council's record in Somalia by arguing that the passage of Resolution 794 demonstrated that it could "muster the necessary political will and the resources required to deal with humanitarian disasters."[83] Austria then suggested that similar action ought to be taken in Bosnia, where the need for the secure delivery of humanitarian assistance was also ongoing.[84] Clearly, UNSC decisions are not made in a political vacuum, and council members are keenly aware of the other issues on their agenda and make repeated references to them. Council members claim to address situations purely on a case-by-case basis, yet their formal meeting records suggest that decisions in one case affect decisions in another.

The UNSC authorized two important innovations in the legitimate use of military force in Somalia. Resolution 794 established that a strictly internal humanitarian catastrophe could be a threat to international peace and security. Resolution 814 made UNOSOM II the first peacekeeping mission authorized to take enforcement action under Chapter VII of the UN Charter. Both resolutions were passed unanimously and most members considered these moves to be "historic," but not all members believed that these innovations should constitute precedent for future cases. Whether its actions in Somalia should become a model for other cases was a serious debate within the Security Council. China justified its vote in favor of Resolution 794 by arguing that the chaos engulfing Somalia resulted from the absence of sovereign authority. Its sympathy for the Somali people and the widespread support of African countries for the resolution also shaped its affirmative decision. Yet China stressed that the situation was "unique," prompting "exceptional action." Thus, the Chapter VII authorization should not alter current standards for the appropriate use of military force.[85] China explained its affirmative vote on Resolution 814 thus: "It is our understanding that this authorization is based on the needs of the unique situation in Somalia and should not constitute a precedent for United Nations peace-keeping operations."[86] Like China, India emphasized the "uniqueness of the Somali crisis" by arguing that "the rapidly deteriorating complex and extraordinary situation, with no government in control, demands an immediate and exceptional response from the international community."[87] India was unequivocal in its position that the Somalia case on its own did not constitute precedent. Rather, each situation presented to the council should be evaluated on its independent merit, irrespective of other cases: "The present action should not, however, set a precedent for the future. We would expect that, should situations arise in the future requiring action under Chapter VII, it would be carried out in full conformity with the Charter provisions and in the spirit of the Secretary-General's report 'An Agenda for Peace.'"[88] India said that it was opposed to resolutions creating precedent for future UNSC action in general and not only with regard to humanitarian intervention. Ecuador was also cautious, arguing that the decision to use force was "unquestionably an important one" but "commensurate to the complex and *sui generis* situation that besets Somalia."[89]

In contrast, at least six Security Council members (Austria, Cape Verde, Hungary, Spain, the U.S., and Zimbabwe) indicated that they intended their affirmative votes on Resolution 794 and 814 to build precedent for future UNSC actions. Zimbabwe agreed that Somalia was a "unique situation that warrants a unique approach," but noted that "any unique situation and the unique solution adopted create of necessity a precedent against which future, similar situations will be measured."[90] Cape Verde suggested that solving the crisis in Somalia "would contribute to giving fresh impetus to the United Nations activities in maintaining international peace and security."[91] Austria argued that by passing resolution 794 the UNSC was fulfilling its responsibility to the people of Somalia. The ambassador suggested that Resolutions 794 and 814 represented a "bold new step" but one that further developed 'steps recently taken by the Council, including the passage of Resolution 688 on Iraq' Both the U.S. and Hungary explicitly expressed their hope that the UNSC would undertake forcible action in the future to stop other humanitarian crises. The U.S. viewed the response in Somalia as "an important step in developing a strategy for dealing with political disorder and conflicts of the post–Cold War world."[92] The Hungarian representative said: "In adopting this resolution, the United Nations can take pride in action that might provide inspiration and guidelines to be followed in the future as well. In the light of the operation in Somalia upon which we are about to embark, it seems to tell us that it will be even more difficult, confronted with world public opinion, for the international community to avoid its responsibility to meet the challenges arising in hotbeds of crisis as serious as the one that is continuing to tear Somalia apart."[93] For these Security Council members, the emergence of a new standard for the appropriate use of military force was a desirable outcome of the Somalia case.

Several Security Council members explicitly identified other situations that would benefit from the same response given to Somalia, suggesting at least tacit support for a new standard of humanitarian intervention. Despite the council's tradition of examining situations on a case-by-case basis, members repeatedly made references to other conflicts on the agenda, illustrating that they perceived links to and articulated connections between conflicts. Repeated references to Cambodia and the former Yugoslavia during the 6 June 1993 meeting on the murder of Pakistani peacekeepers illustrated that council members perceived that their response would be directly linked to other cases. Spain argued that Resolution 837, which condemned the attacks on UN personnel and reaffirmed the authority of the UN to prosecute and punish the perpetrators, was "a warning to all those who threaten or harass the peace-keeping forces of the United Nations in any part of the world."[94] The UK argued that the resolution demonstrated that "the United Nations will not be diverted from its purpose in Somalia, any more than in other theatres in which United Nations peace-keeping forces were currently committed."[95] Venezuela was even more direct, remarking that Resolution 837 should serve as a warning to forces in Cambodia and the former Yugoslavia that they would also be held responsible for their crimes against the international community.[96] These examples support the idea that many council members intended that forcible humanitarian intervention be a precedent for future UN humanitarian action, and that they perceived their statements as conveying the symbolic power—the legitimacy and authority—of the Security Council.[97]

Lack of consensus about whether its actions in Somalia should constitute precedent for future forcible humanitarian action resulted in Security Council resolutions that both expanded conventional practice (by authorizing the use of all necessary means under Chapter VII to establish the conditions for humanitarian assistance) and emphasized the unique character of the expanded response. The second perambulatory clause of Resolution 794 reflects this compromise by "*recognizing* the unique character of the present situation in Somalia and *mindful* of its deteriorating, complex and extraordinary nature, requiring an immediate and exceptional response" (emphasis original).[98] Clearly, though united in its response, the council was divided over whether its historic decision to authorize humanitarian intervention should be a basis for future council action. Several members, including the United States, articulated an interest in advancing humanitarian intervention as an appropriate military response to intrastate conflicts. Other members, most notably China and India, expressed their willingness to make an exception for Chapter VII authorization in the case of Somalia but rejected efforts by other members to alter existing normative standards for the use of military force.

Conclusions

Two notable developments in UNSC practice occurred in Somalia between 1992 and 1995. The Security Council, for the first time, defined a humanitarian crisis as a threat to international peace and security on its own merits and not based on its effects on other states. The council also authorized the first Chapter VII peace operation in which UN peacekeepers were authorized to use force to create the conditions necessary for the delivery of humanitarian aid. Challenges in the field, however, led the Security Council to evaluate and revise its humanitarian practices, developing new and clearer conditions for humanitarian intervention.

First, widespread unity around a causal story allowed the UNSC to shift its focus from determining the cause and character of the conflict to debating the appropriate response. As I have detailed in earlier chapters, different causal stories appeal to different principles and have different policy implications. Initially, Security Council members settled on an inadvertent story about the situation in Somalia. They identified the humanitarian crisis as a threat to international peace and security and demanded that all parties to the conflict cease the violence. On the ground, UN troops tried to maintain neutrality in their dealings with the perpetrators and pursued policies of palliation and protection. By the time that military action was authorized, however, council members had shifted to a complex story to describe the conflict. Complex stories tend to generate status quo policies aimed at maintaining stability and order, yet with troops on the ground and the number of Somali deaths increasing, maintaining the status quo seemed impossible, given the new post–Cold War, post–Gulf War international context. Thus, the Security Council authorized humanitarian intervention, despite the complexity narrative. As tensions increased, rebel forces belonging to the SNA became involved in increasingly violent confrontations with UN personnel. In the aftermath of the killing of dozens of UN troops, the causal story employed by the council shifted again. Once the perpetrator-victim narrative of the intentional story was adopted, the use of military force by the UN qualitatively changed—rather than enforcing security for humanitarian deliveries, UN personnel began fighting Aideed's SNA, whom they sought to punish. In essence, the United Nations became a party to the conflict rather than a mediator within it. As the intentional story strengthened, so did the resolve of the UNSC and its commitment to the robust use of military force. Without any clear "good guys" to partner with and growing losses of personnel, the UNSC was unable to force a peace on Somalia. The Security Council decided that its humanitarian intervention had failed in part because of the complexity and chaos of the situation, suggesting that complex situations were not amenable to change through the use of military force.

Second, stories about sovereignty are just as important as stories about causation for opening and foreclosing the possibility of humanitarian intervention. The absence of government authority in Somalia lifted a principal barrier to humanitarian intervention—state sovereignty. New norms, like that of human rights—which was new, at least, to Security Council consideration—must be justified in relation to existing norms, like state sovereignty. In Somalia, humanitarian intervention became possible because the promotion of human rights norms did not significantly challenge existing norms of state sovereignty and noninterference in domestic affairs. Instead, because Somalia lacked a legitimate government and because council members vested sovereign authority in the Somali people, they were able to justify humanitarian intervention precisely because it did not destabilize existing normative standards. The move to humanitarian intervention, in turn, helped to reshape Security Council conceptualizations of sovereignty to be more consistent with the theoretical concept of popular sovereignty rather than Westphalian conceptions.

Third, Security Council action in Somalia was motivated by humanitarian concern. Council members justified their humanitarian intervention by referencing the humanitarian catastrophe—the dual threats of war and famine that the Somalis faced in the absence of Security Council assistance. The council responded to the crisis in innovative ways even though the use of military force and the provision of humanitarian assistance were costly and optional. Nonetheless, Somalia also demonstrates that there are limits to the costs that states are willing to incur for elective, international moral action. All Security Council action considers a mix of humanitarian and strategic interests.

Finally, each individual case on the Security Council agenda is unique, yet claims that the UNSC only addresses situations on a case-by-case basis are overblown. Actors inside and outside the council made comparisons between Somalia and Bosnia. Regardless of their intentions, by engaging in humanitarian intervention in Somalia, UNSC members created a new standard for the appropriate use of military force—one that would be applied and eventually expanded on in Bosnia two years later.

Chapter 4

From Nonintervention to Humanitarian
Intervention: Contested Stories
About Sovereignty and Victimhood
in Bosnia-Herzegovina

The war in Bosnia-Herzegovina acquired special significance for members
of the United Nations Security Council. It represented the emergence of a
new type of problem at the close of the twentieth century: political turmoil
within states accompanied by exclusionist ideologies leading to gross and
widespread violations of human rights. Indeed, the agenda of the UNSC in
the 1990s was characterized by intrastate conflicts with interstate dimensions and regional security implications. Yet the situation in Bosnia garnered more attention from the Security Council than others because it
destabilized core values of the United Nations, threatened regional security,
and brought into sharp relief the difficulties of adapting an international
organization designed to adjudicate interstate conflicts to mediating situations of contested sovereignty and intrastate violence. Despite this attention, the UNSC response to Bosnia was marked by incredible ambiguity
and inconsistency. Lack of agreement about the character of the conflict
generated lack of unity on an appropriate response, complicating UN efforts to stop ethnic cleansing. Members of the council disagreed about the
appropriateness of humanitarian intervention because they disagreed on
the sovereign authority of Bosnia, whether the conflict was a civil war or
an external aggression, and the identities of perpetrators and victims.

Three causal stories about the war in Bosnia emerged during Security
Council debates: an inadvertent story about a three-way civil war in which

all parties were responsible for human rights abuses, an intentional story about ethnic cleansing in which Bosnian Serbs aided by Serbia were targeting Bosnian Muslim civilians, and a complex story in which the causes of the conflict were multifaceted and human rights violations were considered structural as well as the result of political decision making. Contestation between members over the appropriate causal story prevented the early use of military force in defense of human rights and humanitarian values like that in Somalia. The UNSC was largely divided between members articulating an inadvertent story and those relating an intentional story about Bosnian Serb ethnic cleansing. Three years into the conflict, most permanent members adopted an intentional story because of mounting expert testimony, forensic evidence, and media imagery that made alternative stories untenable. Adoption of a perpetrator-victim narrative by most of the permanent members made punitive military action both a reasonable and politically possible policy response to violence. Coalescence around the intentional story cleared the way for humanitarian intervention; but the use of military force aimed at punishing the perpetrators of ethnic cleansing was triggered only after irrefutable evidence emerged that the Bosnian Serb military deliberately and systematically massacred Bosnian Muslim civilians in Srebrenica and Sarajevo in mid-1995.

Security Council members also disagreed about the source of sovereign authority. In Bosnia, stories about sovereignty mapped onto stories about causation. Supporters of the intentional story also supported Bosnia's self-defense rights based on its status as a newly independent state with a legitimately elected government headed by Alija Izetbegovic, a Bosnian Muslim. In contrast, supporters of the inadvertent story characterized sovereign authority over Bosnia as indeterminate given their interpretation of the conflict as an intrastate civil war between three parties. Finally, supporters of the complex story viewed sovereignty as contested because the conflict was diagnosed as having both intrastate and interstate dimensions since it resulted from the breakup of a preexisting federal state. As long as Bosnia's sovereignty was contested or indeterminate, humanitarian intervention brought the promotion and protection of human rights norms into conflict with the maintenance and protection of state sovereignty. The use of limited defensive military force to protect humanitarian aid convoys and civilian-dominated safe areas occurred as early as 1994, but humanitarian intervention against the Bosnian Serbs and in defense of the Bosnian Muslims did not occur until the second half of 1995 and only after most permanent members recognized the Bosnian government as the legitimate sovereign. Only then was the tension between human rights norms and sovereignty norms eliminated because the protection of human rights simultaneously protected the sovereignty of the Bosnian state.

The discourse used by Security Council members during formal meetings about the Bosnian war demonstrates that their responses to the conflict were shaped by both core values and core security interests. For many permanent members of the council, the war in Bosnia threatened fundamental norms—of equality, human rights, and justice—but did not directly threaten economic or military security interests. Over time, however, the incongruence between the professed values of European states and international institutions (like the UN and NATO) and their responses to the Bosnian conflict fundamentally threatened their international standing and legitimacy, respectively. Threats to values became threats to interests. Throughout the conflict, human rights norms shaped and transformed understandings of international peace and security and state sovereignty in the UNSC. In the case of Bosnia, the interaction of national interests and human rights norms influenced Security Council decision making; and changes in council discourse opened the possibility for humanitarian intervention.

The United Nations Security Council and the Bosnian War

Multiple wars were fought in the territory of the former Yugoslavia during the early 1990s. These conflicts occurred both within and between the constituent republics of Yugoslavia: Serbia and the autonomous region of Kosovo (1989–99), Serbia and Slovenia (1991), Croatia and its minority Serb population backed by Serbia (1991–93), and in the territory of Bosnia-Herzegovina (1992–95). In Bosnia-Herzegovina, conflict occurred in multiple stages beginning with a Serbian incursion followed by an internal conflict between Bosnian Serbs with the allied forces of the Bosnian Muslims and Bosnian Croats, and finally conflict among and between Bosnian Serbs, Bosnian Croats, and Bosnian Muslims, with the former two receiving active support from Serbia and Croatia, respectively.

Before its breakup in 1991, the socialist state of Yugoslavia was made up of six constituent republics—Serbia, Montenegro, Bosnia-Herzegovina, Slovenia, Croatia, and Macedonia—and included two autonomous regions within the Republic of Serbia, Vojvodina and Kosovo. Beginning in the late 1980s and throughout the early 1990s, Yugoslavia, like many parts of eastern Europe and the former Soviet bloc, was undergoing a process of economic liberalization and political democratization.[1] Internal tensions over the declining economic situation in the country and the future political organization of the federation gave rise to challenges to federal legitimacy from its constituent republics.[2] The opening of political space coupled with economic and political uncertainty provided an opportunity for the emergence of nationalist discourse and the rise of ethnonational political parties. In 1990, Slovene and Croatian politicians attempted to negotiate the transformation of Yugoslavia from a federation into a confederation with greater independence for its members. At the same time, Serbian nationalist politicians like Slobodan Milošević, a former Communist bureaucrat who catapulted to political popularity in Serbia on an ethnonationalist platform, sought to recentralize the federal state and enhance personal political power by manipulating Serb grievances and provoking conflicts along ethnic lines.[3]

In June 1990, the Republic of Serbia abolished the provincial assembly of Kosovo and revoked its status as an autonomous governing unit, sparking a decade-long confrontation between Serb authorities in Belgrade and ethnic Albanians in Kosovo.[4] Fear of Serbian domination, a "Greater Serbia Project," and increasing ethnic polarization pervaded much of the Yugoslav federation. The Republics of Slovenia and Croatia declared their independence from Yugoslavia and fought wars with the Republic of Serbia and in the case of the latter, also with its own minority Serb population. A brief, low-intensity conflict began in Slovenia in June 1991 but ended a few weeks later when an agreement on independence was brokered between what remained of federal Yugoslavia and the Republic of Slovenia. The war in Croatia lasted over six months and was characterized by military confrontation between the Croatian government and Serb minorities located in the Krajina and Slavonija regions who were seeking autonomy and forcibly expelling ethnic Croats from the disputed territories with the aid of Serbia. The fighting between the Croatian government and the Belgrade-backed Serb minorities resulted in the mass movement of both the ethnic Serbian and Croatian populations. The United Nations became involved in the wars in the former Yugoslavia early in September 1991 when the Security Council passed Resolution 713, condemning the fighting and establishing an arms embargo against the entire territory of Yugoslavia. The arms embargo was justified as an effort to limit the conflict and prevent its further escalation. Although the arms embargo applied equally to the entire territory, it would have unequal effects after Yugoslavia dissolved into multiple recognized sovereign states with varying military and defense capability. In February 1992 the Security Council established a United Nations Protection Force (UNPROFOR) on the territory of Croatia to monitor a cease-fire and peace settlement brokered between Serbia and Croatia.[5] UNPROFOR was equipped with a traditional peacekeeping function—to separate competing sides in a civil war. Later, UNPROFOR's presence would be expanded to include the territory of Bosnia but without a change in mission mandate, despite international recognition of Croatia and Bosnia as independent and sovereign states.

The war in Bosnia did not officially begin until 7 April 1992, the day following the recognition of its sovereign independence by the United States and the European Union (EU). Helsinki Watch, an international human rights organization, reported, however, that the military occupation of northwest Bosnia and the forced removal of its Muslim population by the Yugoslav Army had started nearly six months before its declaration of independence.[6] In November 1991 the nationalist Serbian Democratic Party organized a Bosnian Serb referendum in which a majority of ethnic Serbs voted to stay part of Serbia and Montenegro. By January 1992, the Bosnian Serb Assembly proclaimed the creation of the "independent Serbian Republic of Bosnia and Hercegovina" and Serbian nationalist Radovan Karadžić, a psychiatrist and amateur poet, became its president. Between 29 February and 1 March 1992, the democratically elected and sitting president of Bosnian-Herzegovina, Alija Izetbegovic, a Bosnian Muslim, held a republic-wide referendum on independence from the former Yugoslavia in which 64 percent of Bosnia's multiethnic population voted on this question: "Are you in favor of a sovereign and independent Bosnia-Herzegovina, a state of equal citizens and nations of Muslims, Serbs, Croats and others who live in it?" More than 90 percent of voters answered yes when the results of the referendum were announced on 2 March.[7] Bosnian voters overwhelmingly supported an independent, multiethnic state. Izetbegovic declared Bosnia's independence from Yugoslavia on 3 March but the Bosnian Serb authorities declared the vote invalid. Most Bosnian Serbs either boycotted the election or were forcibly prevented from participating by Bosnian Serb authorities, according to Helsinki Watch.[8] Following international recognition in early April, Bosnia quickly became engulfed in a war characterized by mass civilian casualties and gross violations of international humanitarian law as the parties to the conflict fought over Bosnia's national and territorial status and sought to match populations with territory.

The Yugoslav constitution had granted national rights to its constituent republics as well as its constituent nations. Bosnia-Herzegovina had been recognized by the constitution as a republic but not as a nation, unlike Serbia, Slovenia, and Croatia, which had all been recognized as both.[9] This resulted in major issues of contestation between and within republics as Bosnia descended into war. The first issue was whether rights should be vested in individuals or ethnic communities. The second issue was the "national question"—whether Bosnia could acquire titular status when traditionally the breakup of multinational states or empires led to the founding of national states.[10] Bosnians themselves were divided over what an independent Bosnia should look like—what group would control the state and what rights would be conferred on the others. The contest over rights and the national question in Bosnia also involved the powerful national states of two of the ethnic groups contesting these issues—the Bosnian Croats and Bosnian Serbs. This meant that Croatia and Serbia had compelling reasons to interfere in the politics of the newly independent Bosnia-Herzegovina.[11]

The conflict in Bosnia captured the attention of Security Council members, and much of the world, at a time when there was little international agreement on how to resolve tensions between sovereignty and territorial integrity with the right to self-determination, on the one hand, and sovereignty but also humanitarian intervention to halt gross human rights violations, on the other.[12] States disagreed on whether self-determination should be based on the 1975 Helsinki Final Act which recognized the inviolability of post–World War II borders; historicist principles that defined the nation based on its people, who were linked by common identity prior to the state; democratic principles, where the people residing in the territory have the right to choose their state; or the practicalities of realpolitik based on the ability to militarily control territory and populations.[13] At the same time, the UNSC was struggling to define the appropriate purpose of, and agreed criteria for, the use of military force. The council had already demonstrated its willingness to define the cross-border effects of human rights violations (Iraq in 1991) and an internal humanitarian crisis (Somalia in 1992) as threats to international peace and security.[14] The increasing legitimacy of human rights norms was changing the legitimate purpose of military force. Humanitarian intervention was an emerging, yet highly contested, practice.

The international response to the war occurred within a context of dramatic political change in Europe. At the end of the Cold War, European states were preoccupied with the dissolution of the Soviet Union, the emergence of newly independent states in eastern Europe, and the reunification of Germany. European countries were negotiating the Maastricht Treaty and struggling to create a common foreign and security identity as they both widened and deepened European integration. European states were under pressure to prove that they could address European problems without U.S. assistance, and the Bosnian war was happening in their neighborhood; yet they were reluctant to take the lead in Bosnia. Questions about what the post–Cold War order would look like extended well beyond Europe, however. The crisis in Bosnia raised important questions for all UN members, including what constitutes legitimate statehood, and how should situations of contested sovereignty be resolved? UN members were beginning to question whether norms of human rights or sovereignty should take precedence when they came into conflict and they wanted clarification on the Charter obligations of the Security Council for responding to war— whether between or within states. The broad importance of these issues was evidenced in the widespread international attention the Bosnian war garnered at the UN.

The *Provisional Rules of Procedure of the Security Council* allow any member of the United Nations that is not a member of the council to participate in its formal meetings without a vote. Generally, UN members are invited to participate in Security Council meetings when the interests of that member are specifically affected or when a UN member brings a matter to the attention of the council.[15] In the case of Bosnia, UN members regularly requested to participate in formal deliberations and the UNSC accommodated. Part of what is distinctive about the Bosnian case is the unusually high level of participation by UN member states (nonvoting participants) not serving on the UNSC in formal council meetings. Between 1992 and 1995, the UNSC met formally more than 130 times to discuss the conflict in Bosnia. It passed more than 70 resolutions and nearly 60 presidential statements related to the situation in Bosnia, and nonmembers in 145 instances participated in formal UNSC meetings without a vote. The high attendance by UN members not serving on the Security Council did not reflect a new trend of expanded participation of the general membership in the business of the Security Council because the high attendance rate only applied to Bosnia. In contrast, during this same period, the council held less than twenty formal meetings during which only half a dozen nonvoting participants joined the council to discuss the situation in Somalia despite the landmark humanitarian intervention. The council met almost twice as often about Rwanda than it did about Somalia but only a single UN member not serving on the council requested to participate in council meetings on Rwanda.[16]

In addition to the broad appeal of the normative and legal questions at stake in Bosnia, more traditional security interests and kinship relationships also explain high meeting attendance. Forty-five percent of the nonvoting participants in Security Council meetings on Bosnia came from Europe and 21 percent were from the Middle East and North African regions. Sixty-six percent of nonvoting participants in Security Council meetings, then, were either in the geographic proximity of the Bosnian war or shared cultural, social, and religious identification with the Bosnian population. Nonetheless, 34 percent of nonvoting participants self-selected into attending Security Council meetings in the absence of traditional military or economic security interests and with few ethnic, religious, linguistic, or cultural ties to the populations at risk.

The dissolution of Yugoslavia held enormous symbolism for UN members. Yugoslavia was respected by many of its peers for both being a founding member of the Non-Aligned Movement and for its status as a successful multiethnic and multireligious state. The Non-Aligned Movement and the Non-Aligned Caucus of the Security Council were particularly active in drafting resolutions for review by the council and calling for open debates in which non-voting members could participate. Members of the Non-Aligned Movement and the Organization of the Islamic Conference also were instrumental in calling for General Assembly debates and resolutions related to the Bosnia crisis, and in particular related to the selective lifting of the arms embargo when division among permanent members of the council prevented effective action on the issue. States in eastern and central Europe with large ethnic minorities were concerned about the demise of a symbol of multiethnic statehood and they consistently reminded the council members about the minority protections established following both world wars.

Finally, the nature of the human rights violations themselves and particularly their vivid capture by the international media garnered significant international concern. Bosnia was an "accessible war zone" in which the international media had relative ease of travel and access to necessary communications technology. Images of Bosnian civilians concentrated in camps behind barbed wire and live video footage of the shelling of civilians in public spaces including women and children provoked worldwide outrage. Many statements entered into the formal Security Council record drew direct parallels between the Bosnian crisis, World War II, and the Holocaust.[17] The now commonplace term "ethnic cleansing" entered the popular language of politics only during the Bosnian war. The phrase is a literal translation of the Serbo-Croatian–Bosnian phrase *etnicko ciscenje*. It was believed to be part of the Yugoslav National Army's military vocabulary to describe its policy of expelling Muslims and Croats from the territories it conquered.[18] The policy of ethnic cleansing included forced population transfers and the systematic use of violence against civilians, including murder and rape for the purpose of acquiring territory. Because it was happening in Europe, council members asserted that their national publics considered ethnic cleansing in Bosnia reminiscent of the Holocaust or "what the Nazis called the 'Endlösung: final solution.'"[19] Widespread participation in Security Council meetings by nonvoting states has created a significant and lengthy public record that includes not only the discourse used by Security Council members to characterize the conflict but also the international response to it. This record captured the competing narratives—the causal stories—that reflected and shaped the international response to the Bosnian war.

Causal Stories About the Bosnian Conflict and Human Rights Violations

Security Council debates about the nature of the conflict and human rights violations in Bosnia were marked by significant disagreement. Members of the Security Council disagreed on whether to authorize humanitarian intervention for Bosnia-Herzegovina because they disagreed about its sovereign authority and whether the conflict was a case of external aggression, civil war, ethnic cleansing, or something more complex. Security Council members and nonvoting participants advanced different causal stories, with each offering a different characterization of the conflict and the identity of perpetrators and victims. Each causal story also mapped onto a specific interpretations of sovereign authority. The *intentional story* described the war as external aggression against an independent and sovereign state member of the United Nations (Bosnia-Herzegovina) by Serbia (and at some points Croatia) in which Bosnian Muslim civilians were being deliberately targeted for ethnic cleansing by Bosnian Serb perpetrators and their allies. The intentional story also characterized the conflict as an ethnic cleansing or genocide—clearly identifying a perpetrator (Bosnian Serbs with backing from Belgrade) and a victim (Bosnian Muslim civilians and the Bosnian government). The *inadvertent story* described a civil war in which all parties were responsible for human rights violations and sovereign authority was indeterminate. The *complex story* characterized the Bosnian war as having multiple underlying causes—some of them structural and others behavioral—and even multiple forms (both a civil war and an interstate conflict) that led to inadvertent deaths and elite-organized human rights violations. In the case of the complex story, sovereignty was contested. Because the conflict was complex, often confusing, and lacked a point of leverage to address the underlying causes of the conflict, it was not amenable to resolution by the UNSC.[20]

These three causal stories emerged during Security Council deliberations about whether to authorize the use of military force to stop the human rights violations. In the absence of agreement on the question of humanitarian intervention, members deployed these causal stories during council debates about arms embargo policy and the protection of UN-mandated safe areas. Fundamental disagreement among permanent members over the character of the conflict resulted in the passage of compromise resolutions and presidential statements that ultimately stymied coherent Security Council action. Contestation over the cause and character of the conflict also blocked early humanitarian intervention. In the latter half of 1995, however, the Security Council coalesced around an intentional story about interstate aggression and ethnic cleansing against Bosnian Muslims, which made humanitarian intervention possible.

The Emergence of Three Causal Stories About Bosnia

Stories told by council members about the Bosnian Council varied over time. In May 1992, for example, council members and nonvoting participants articulated three different causal stories during a Security Council meeting establishing mandatory sanctions against Serbia and Montenegro under Chapter VII of the UN Charter (Table 4.1). Hungary, a nonpermanent member of the council, articulated an intentional story when it described the conflict in Bosnia as "naked aggression" against a state member of the United Nations and identified the "Belgrade leadership" as the aggressor with "overwhelming responsibility" for the war's conduct.[21] This intentional story was shared by four additional nonpermanent members (Belgium, Cape Verde, Morocco, and Venezuela) and the United States. Venezuela asserted that the crisis in Bosnia could no longer be classified as a civil war, and Cape Verde, Belgium, and the U.S. all identified the Serbian government in Belgrade as the principal perpetrator of atrocities against Bosnian civilians. Morocco went so far as to label the atrocities "genocide."[22] By August, Austria also advanced an intentional story in which it described the conflict as "an aggression against the legitimate Government of a State member of the United Nations. An insurrection, instigated, nurtured and heavily supported with materiel and personnel by Serbia and Montenegro."[23]

The Russian Federation and the UK articulated an inadvertent story that characterized the conflict as primarily a civil war with some limited external interference; the representative from the UK said, "Several speakers in the Council have mentioned that the responsibility for these events in Yugoslavia is shared among many. That is indeed the case."[24] Both countries agreed that Serbia bore some special responsibility—or in the words of Russia, "Serbia has not heeded good advice"—but both characterized the conflict as between multiple parties, none of whom was beyond reproach.[25] Initially, France and China advanced a complex story; the Chinese representative remarked, "The situation in the former Yugoslavia is complicated and the cause of the conflict is multi-faceted."[26] Although France supported the adoption of sanctions against the Federal Republic of Yugoslavia, it argued that the situation was complex with "many shared wrongs and responsibilities."[27] India shared this view. Lack of unity on the story resulted in draft resolutions that carefully maintained impartiality toward all parties despite an intentional counternarrative advanced by Helsinki Watch that most atrocities were the result of a systematic strategy of ethnic cleansing by the Serb party.[28]

While disagreements about the character of the conflict divided UNSC members, nonvoting participants in Security Council meetings were largely united, expressing an intentional story about interstate aggression. For

Table 4.1. Changes in Support for Causal Stories in Bosnia-Herzegovina,
1992–1995

	Intentional Story	Inadvertent Story	Complex Story	Unarticulated
May 1992 (S/PV.3082) Debate over humanitarian intervention	Belgium Cape Verde Hungary Morocco Venezuela **U.S.**	**Russia** **UK** India	**China** **France** Zimbabwe	Austria Ecuador Japan
November 1994 (S/PV.3454) Bosnian self-defense rights and partial lifting of the arms embargo	Argentina Brazil Czech Republic Djibouti New Zealand Nigeria Oman Pakistan Rwanda Spain **U.S.**	**China** **France** **Russia** **UK**	None	None
August 1995 (S/PV.3564) Second Markale market massacre and release of forensic evidence on Srebrenica	Argentina Botswana Czech Republic **France** Germany Honduras Indonesia Italy Nigeria Oman Rwanda **UK** **U.S.**	None	None	**China** **Russia**

example, during a series of Security Council meetings held 19–20 April 1993, thirty-five nonvoting participants addressed the council, urging it to stop human rights violations in Bosnia by expanding military protection of Bosnian Muslims or permitting the Bosnian government the means to defend itself by exempting it from the arms embargo. Ten of these nonvoting participants, including Bosnia, Afghanistan, Algeria, Comoros, the Czech Republic, Indonesia, Malaysia, Sierra Leone, Slovenia, and Turkey, specifically named the conflict "genocide" along with the representative of the Organization for Islamic Conference. Thirteen additional states articulated an intentional story about Serbian ethnic cleansing (Albania, Bulgaria, Croatia, Egypt, Germany, Ireland, Iran, Lithuania, Malta, Saudi Arabia, Senegal, Sweden, and the United Arab Emirates). Four others described the violence as interstate "aggression" (Argentina, Denmark, Italy, and Jordan).[29] In total, twenty-eight nonvoting participants (80 percent) explicitly advanced an intentional story. Only two nonvoting participants, Ukraine and the Federal Republic of Yugoslavia, articulated the inadvertent story. Those remaining did not articulate a story at all. Disunity among the council members on the explanation for the conflict, despite broader convergence around the intentional story in the international community, stymied Security Council action to halt atrocities.

On 29 June 1993, the Non-Aligned Caucus and the U.S. advanced a resolution to exempt Bosnia from the arms embargo and reinstate its self-defense rights. Twenty-four UN members requested to participate without a vote in the Security Council debate that followed. The meeting lasted for over nine hours without recess. Of the thirty-nine states in attendance (including the fifteen members of the council), twenty-one advanced an intentional story about Serbian aggression against the Bosnian state and its citizens and seventeen directly linked this story to justification for lifting the arms embargo. Yet only six of these states were Security Council members (Cape Verde, Djibouti, Morocco, Pakistan, the U.S., and Venezuela). Cape Verde argued that if a "lack of political will on the part of those who have the power and the means and bear the special responsibility to carry out, and ensure the implementation of the decisions of the Council" led to an unwillingness to defend Bosnia-Herzegovina, then Bosnia should be allowed to defend itself.[30] Venezuela similarly argued that it was gravely inconsistent for the Security Council to recognize Bosnia as a member-state but not defend it or its right to self-defense.[31] The resolution failed with only the six votes in favor (Cape Verde, Djibouti, Morocco, Pakistan, the

U.S., and Venezuela) and nine abstentions (Brazil, China, France, Hungary, Japan, New Zealand, Russia, Spain, and the UK). The nonpermanent members who abstained argued that lifting the arms embargo would escalate hostilities rather than reduce them and fail to assist those it was intended to help.[32] France argued that lifting the arms embargo was contrary to Charter principles because it would put the UNSC on the path of war rather than the path of peace.[33] Finally, Russia and China both emphasized the need for a political resolution of the dispute that would satisfy all parties.[34]

Eight months later, on 5 February 1994, a mortar shell exploded in the Markale marketplace of Sarajevo, killing more than sixty civilians. Although Sarajevo had been under siege for almost two years, it had a significant media, diplomatic, and humanitarian presence. A capital city located in Europe, Sarajevo had the basic infrastructure needed for international media coverage. Journalists had access to the city via the UN-controlled airport, food and lodging was available in part because of the black market, and the city had modern communications and broadcast equipment.[35] The shelling received extensive media coverage and provoked widespread outrage. The *New York Times* graphically described the scene at the marketplace after the mortar shell exploded, which it described as the "worst massacre in the 22 month siege of Sarajevo. . . . Blood, arms, legs and pieces of flesh were strewn about the market. People screamed hysterically, rushing about to try to give help or escape. . . . A severed head lay among what had been a display of used shoes. Torn bodies were tossed about, making relief workers ill as they tried to help the wounded."[36] Television images of the carnage and media reporting on the massacre angered many domestic populations, who in turn exerted pressure on their governments for a response to the killing. Speaking during a Security Council meeting on 14 February, the representative of Italy emphasized this point when he said that "the news and pictures of these massacres have aroused the revulsion of all Italians."[37] Similarly, the Canadian representative said, "Canadians were shocked and outraged at the deliberate killing and wounding of hundreds of innocent civilians in Sarajevo on 5 February."[38] During that 14 February Security Council meeting, forty-one nonvoting participants joined the fifteen members of the Security Council to condemn the attack and discuss a potential military response to protect Sarajevo. During a single meeting that convened four times during a two-day period and lasted for nearly ten and a half hours, fifty-six members of the UN become proponents of conflicting causal stories about the character of the Bosnian conflict.

The five permanent members of the Security Council remained divided between the three causal explanations. France and the UK advanced an inadvertent story that characterized the conflict as a civil war in which all three sides to the conflict could be labeled perpetrators, with none having clean hands. The UK urged all sides to end the violence and work toward a political settlement: "It seems clear—and this is not a value judgment but rather an analysis based on the facts—that none of the parties can achieve their aims on the battlefield. The longer the fighting goes on, the more everyone will suffer. Only a political settlement achieved at the negotiating table will bring an end to the hostilities."[39] While France and the UK agreed with the U.S. that the Bosnian Serbs bore greater responsibility than other parties, they refrained from identifying them as the sole perpetrators or describing the conflict in terms of intentionality.

Russia also emphasized the culpability of all parties but nested its critique within a complex story, characterizing the conflict as multifaceted: "It is now very important to urge all three parties to the conflict to reach a compromise. . . . We are not overdramatizing the present complex and confusing situation with respect to international efforts to settle the crisis."[40] The intentional story was the dominant narrative of the meeting, but of its thirty proponents, only eight were voting members of the Security Council (the Czech Republic, Djibouti, New Zealand, Nigeria, Oman, Pakistan, Rwanda, and the U.S.). These states identified the Bosnian Serbs as the perpetrators of "ethnic cleansing" or "genocide" directed primarily against the Bosnian Muslims. Slovenia summed up this position well: "The war in Bosnia and Herzegovina is neither a religious nor an ethnic conflict, nor is it a 'three-way civil war', as some observers tend to believe. That war started as a war of aggression against a United Nations Member State, and it has remained, in essence, a war for territorial expansion. The genocidal practice of 'ethnic cleansing' directed against Muslims of Bosnia and Herzegovina was devised and carried out as an instrument of war for territorial expansion."[41] In the competition between causal stories, however, the proponents of the intentional story were largely nonmembers of the Security Council and largely represented states from the Middle East and Africa. Although the U.S. was a vocal supporter of the intentional story, most supporters were less prominent and visible than the permanent members of the Security Council and the majority of primarily western European states advancing either an inadvertent story or failing to discuss the underlying cause at all. Material power alone was insufficient for the United States to alter the narrative of its council peers. Humanitarian intervention was not forthcoming in absence of strong support from a majority of permanent Security Council members, despite the material capabilities of the U.S. Legitimacy matters with regard to humanitarian intervention, and norms of multilateralism demanded majority support for the intentional story. The practicalities of politics, however, demanded majority support among the permanent members.

In November 1994, the UN General Assembly passed Resolution 49/10 recommending that the UNSC exempt Bosnia from the arms embargo. The council met on 8 November to discuss lifting the arms embargo. Again the meeting attracted UN member states and representatives of regional organizations who were not elected members. Tension was mounting in the international community between the general UN membership and the Security Council with regard to the latter's handling of the war. Pakistan started the arms embargo debate by describing the situation in Bosnia-Herzegovina as "one of the gravest tragedies of modern times. . . . The Bosnian people are not only the target of Serbian aggression and genocide but also the helpless victims of a double standard that on the one hand failed to respond effectively to the Serbian aggression and on the other hand denied the Bosnian people their inherent right to self-defence."[42] Cambodia appealed to Security Council members to consider the similarities between the Bosnian Serb tactics in Bosnia-Herzegovina and the attacks against Cambodians by the Khmer Rouge, urging them to lift the arms embargo so that the Bosnians could reaffirm their human dignity.[43] The United States forcefully defended the Bosnian government's right to defend itself, identifying the Bosnian Serbs as aggressors and specifically identifying Bosnian Serb president Karadžić as standing in the way of peace.[44] Yet other permanent members continued to reject the intentional story, as France and Russia did, condemning the Bosnian Muslims for provocative attacks on Serb forces.[45] The U.S. defended the Bosnian Muslims, arguing that the sides in the conflict were not equal and that it was a mistake to interpret UN impartiality to mean treating equally those who have not acted equally during the conflict:

There are those that condemn Bosnia for its recent attacks on Bosnian Serb forces in the central and western parts of the country. My Government regrets all continued fighting. But let us not confuse attacks made to recover territory lost to aggression with aggression.

Let us not confuse the actions of a Government that has declared its desire for peace with that of a faction unyielding in its pursuit of war. The Government of Bosnia did not start his war and is willing to end it. The Bosnian Serbs began this war and are determined to prolong it. These differences matter and they should be reflected in the actions and attitudes of the council.[46]

Although the United States was a forceful proponent of the intentional story, U.S. support in the absence of a strong coalition of support among permanent members of the council prevented the intentional story from winning against its competitors. Despite this lack of permanent member support, backing for the intentional story continued to grow to include more nonpermanent members, including Argentina, Brazil, and Spain, bringing the total number of Security Council supporters to eleven.

Although the intentional story had gained the support of most members of the Security Council, it had the backing of only a single permanent member—the U.S. (see Table 4.1). The four remaining permanent members rejected the intentional explanation. In November 1994, China, France, Russia, and the UK continued to articulate an inadvertent story about "all parties" in "a civil war." In response, Slovenia, a nonvoting participant, argued that "lack of coherence in characterizing the conflict for what it really is" prevented the Security Council from reaching agreement on an appropriate response. Slovenia characterized the war as territorial aggression by the Bosnian Serbs and Serb authorities in Serbia distinguished by the practice of ethnic cleansing, with Bosnian Muslims its primary victims.[47] "Only a realistic assessment of the situation," according to Slovenia, "can offer the necessary ground to define adequate remedies."[48]

Security Council Unity and Humanitarian Intervention

Momentum began to build in support of the intentional story after Bosnian Serb forces overran the "safe haven" of Srebrenica during 6–12 July 1995. In April 1993, the Security Council had declared six cities and towns safe areas (Srebrenica, Sarajevo, Tuzla, Žepa, Goražde, and Bihać) in an effort to relieve civilians from Bosnian Serb paramilitary attacks. In the absence of UNSC authorization for peacekeepers to deter attacks against them and without the ability of the Bosnian state to defend them, the safe havens became vulnerable to armed attack. In June 1993, the Security Council

passed two resolutions—Resolution 836 and Resolution 844—that permitted the use of force by UNPROFOR in self-defense, in response to bombardment or armed incursions into safe areas, and to protect the movement
of humanitarian aid convoys.[49] The resolutions created a "dual key" arrangement, whereby NATO could carry out air strikes, but only at the request of the UN, and the arrangement required approval by both bodies.
The council also made a distinction between two types of airpower: close
air support, which would be used in self-defense and to provide protection
to humanitarian agencies in their work, and air strikes, which would be
punitive.[50] Although NATO undertook close air support for the first time
in 1994, it limited strikes to individual artillery pieces in a reactive response
to Bosnian Serb attacks on safe areas. The international press described
NATO's use of close air support as "pin pricks" because of the strikes'
limited nature and results. The U.S. ambassador to the United Nations,
Madeleine Albright, argued on the floor of the Security Council chamber
that the use of force by NATO in defense of safe areas like Sarajevo in
February 1994 did not constitute humanitarian intervention because it was
not undertaken on behalf of any party to the conflict.[51] American diplomat
Richard Holbrooke similarly downplayed the importance of the use of close
air support, writing in his memoirs that limited bombing by NATO in
response to attacks on safe areas—even as late as May 1995—was neither
serious nor sustained.[52] The Bosnian Serb Army (BSA) response to its use,
however, started to destabilize the inadvertent story held by France and the
United Kingdom. The BSA responded to the self-defense strikes in 1994
and 1995 by kidnapping UN peacekeeping personnel and using them as
human shields to protect potential targets from future strikes. In June 1995,
just as hostage peacekeepers were beginning to be released, European states
began seriously debating both the increased use of force and possible
UNPROFOR withdrawal as policy options in Bosnia. On 3 June 1995, the
defense ministers of fourteen states met in Paris, where they decided to
create a rapid reaction force, staffed by European troops and supported
with airpower, airlift, and intelligence from the United States, to be used to
reinforce UNPROFOR.[53] Yet no close air support was forthcoming to protect the safe haven of Srebrenica.

Between 12 and 16 July, an estimated seven thousand Muslims who had
sought safety in Srebrenica, most of them men between the ages of seventeen and sixty-five, were killed and buried in mass graves by Bosnian Serb
forces led by General Ratko Mladić, commander of the BSA, acting directly

under orders from President Karadžić. Although the extent of the killing would not be fully known for weeks, Dutch peacekeepers assigned to Srebrenica confirmed the enclave's fall and witness testimony about systematic atrocities quickly began to emerge. During an emergency meeting of the UNSC on 12 July, the representative from Honduras used the phrase "Karadžić methods" as a synonym for Serbian ethnic cleansing and specifically identified Serbian president Milošević and Bosnian Serb leader Mladić as perpetrators. The United Kingdom, for the first time on the Security Council record, clearly and unambiguously identified the Bosnian Serbs as perpetrators of ethnic cleansing and France identified General Mladić by name as culpable for human rights abuses.[54] France also informed the council that it was ready, if the UN deemed it appropriate, for the use of punitive military force to be taken against the Bosnian Serbs.[55] This change in narration by the UK and France marked an important shift. By articulating the intentional story, rather than the inadvertent one, France and the UK signaled their willingness to consider a more forceful policy response to the conflict. With thirteen Security Council members articulating an intentional story, including three permanent members, humanitarian intervention became possible. The widespread use of a perpetrator-victim narrative in the Security Council opened the possibility of humanitarian intervention, just as widespread articulation of the inadvertent story earlier foreclosed that possibility. In contrast, Russia distributed blame equally among the Bosnian Muslims of Srebrenica for their "unprovoked attacks" and the Bosnian Serbs for their "disproportionate response."[56] China expressed deep reservations about the invocation of Chapter VII by the Security Council.[57] Nonetheless, the Security Council unanimously adopted Resolution 1004 condemning the Bosnian Serb offensive against Srebrenica and demanding its immediate withdrawal as well as the release of all detained peacekeepers. In the end, most Security Council members made an explicit public statement directly linking Bosnian Serb perpetrators with the crime of ethnic cleansing in Srebrenica—an intentional story. No alternative causal stories were advanced during the meeting by its members.

Bosnian Serb forces heightened their assaults on UN-protected safe areas during the month of July following the fall of Srebrenica, including serious assaults against Žepa and Bihać. Prime Minister John Major of the UK hosted a crisis meeting attended by European countries and the United States in London on 21 July. The meeting produced a memorandum, endorsed by both NATO and the UN, with an important policy change with regard to the future use of force in Bosnia. In effect, "the London Rules" ended the dual key arrangement between NATO and the UN whereby both had to approve the use of airpower in defense of Security Council objectives. Instead, whether to use airpower and how much to use would be determined in the future solely by NATO.[58]

During an informal meeting of the Security Council on the morning of 10 August 1995, U.S. ambassador Madeleine Albright circulated declassified CIA photos depicting evidence of mass graves around Srebrenica. International human rights organizations had been reporting deliberate and arbitrary killing by Bosnian Serb forces in Srebrenica, the arbitrary detention of thousands of boys and men, and the forced removal and disappearance of women refugees taken off transports as they left the safe haven.[59] Albright recalls the impact the aerial photos had on Security Council members: "As the photographs circulated, the council room—scene of so many noisy debates—grew still. I could hear fingers brushing the stiff photographs as they passed from hand to hand. American intelligence imagery is ordinarily highly classified, and it takes an expert to decipher what is being depicted. But the basic message conveyed by these pictures was clear. The refugees were telling the truth."[60] This material evidence, combined with other intelligence and testimony from survivors, profoundly altered the conception of the conflict articulated by Security Council members. Later that evening, during a formal meeting of the Security Council, Albright drew attention to the thousands of civilians missing from Srebrenica and Žepa and the compelling evidence of "barbarous and systematic murder by the Bosnian Serbs."[61] Albright emphasized that "we must not forget what happened in Srebrenica and Žepa, because there are strong grounds to believe especially with respect to Srebrenica, that the Pale Serbs beat, raped and murdered many of those fleeing the violence. These dead were not killed in the heat of battle; they were not killed in self-defence and they were not killed by accident; they were systematically slaughtered on the instructions of the Bosnian Serb leadership."[62] Following the fall of Žepa and faced with overwhelming evidence of Bosnian Serb culpability for massacres in Srebrenica, even Russia "sternly condemned the actions of the Bosnian Serb army in Srebrenica" and voiced its concern over reports of its "flagrant violations of the norms of international humanitarian law in Srebrenica."[63] The fall of Srebrenica grabbed the attention of Security Council leaders, shamed the UN, and further damaged the image of the Bosnian Serbs. Expert evidence supported the intentional story—that killings of Bosnian Muslim civilians were deliberate and systematic and that the perpetrators were the BSA under the direct leadership of Bosnian Serb president Karadžić and General Mladić, the latter having marched into Srebrenica with live Serbian television crews. The facts on the ground made the inadvertent story untenable. Despite the discursive movement toward the intentional story by the majority of council members beginning in late July, the UNSC did not immediately engage in humanitarian intervention. The Srebrenica massacre did, however, strengthen international resolve to respond more forcefully to Serbian atrocities in Bosnia.

While humanitarian intervention had not been undertaken in time to rescue the men, women, and children of Srebrenica, the newfound international resolve generated by the Srebrenica massacre ultimately benefited the inhabitants of Sarajevo. On 28 August, two shells were launched into the popular central marketplace of Sarajevo from Bosnian Serb positions. Television cameras and newspaper reporters witnessed and then broadcast the images of the bloodshed internationally. Roger Cohen of the *New York Times* graphically described the scene at the Markale open air market, where sixty-eight people were killed and more than two hundred wounded: "Limbs and flesh were splattered on storefronts, and bodies fell to pieces as they were lifted into cars. After 40 months of Serbian siege and bombardment, the scene was familiar, but the horrified frenzy among an exhausted population was still intense. . . . The shelling submerged the central Kosevo Hospital in a blood-soaked wave of dead and dying. Later, the hospital itself was hit, wounding two patients."[64] According to Robert Donia, Sarajevo was "the lens through which most outsiders viewed the conflict. . . . The agony of Sarajevo became the embodiment of the Bosnian war's savagery and senselessness."[65] The Security Council was under tremendous pressure to respond.

Two days later on 30 August 1995, the U.S. and European parties applied the "London Rules" in response to the Markale marketplace massacre. Operation Deliberate Force—extensive NATO air strikes of Bosnian Serb positions accompanied by a ground offensive undertaken by the Rapid Reaction Force—began with air strikes against Serb positions around Sarajevo but later extended to include Bosnian Serb positions throughout Bosnia. At the time, it was the largest military operation in NATO history. This humanitarian intervention became possible after the intentional story had won over both the complex and inadvertent stories in the Security Council. The drafting of the joint NATO-UN memorandum at the London Conference that authorized NATO to make unilateral decisions about air strikes in late July also paved the way. Yet humanitarian intervention did not occur until triggered by the violent Bosnian Serb mortar shell attack on Sarajevo. Peter Andreas notes that "while similar bombings had taken place in the past, this time Western leaders were looking for a legitimizing trigger and rationale to take more decisive military action against Serb positions encircling the city. The gruesome images from the marketplace bombing provided the opening for the launching of air strikes that had already been well planned out."[66] Although Russia continued to defend the civil war interpretation and China verbally objected to the use of force, the majority of UNSC members were united in their belief that the Bosnian Serbs were the intentional perpetrators of ethnic cleansing in Bosnia-Herzegovina (see Table 4.1). Even the Secretariat articulated the intentional story. In his report to the Security Council on 30 August, the secretary-general signaled the possibility that mass executions had taken place at Srebrenica at the hands of the Bosnian Serbs.[67] With the support of all the nonpermanent members of the council and three permanent members, the objections of China and Russia were insufficient to stop humanitarian intervention in absence of a veto, which was not forthcoming in the face of incontrovertible forensic evidence of Bosnian Serb culpability for systematic atrocities.

On 21 December 1995, the Security Council unanimously adopted Resolution 1034, which formally articulated this intentional story. The resolution strongly condemned "all violations of international humanitarian law and human rights" and condemned in particular "violations of international humanitarian law and human rights by Bosnian Serb and paramilitary forces in the areas of Srebrenica, Žepa, Banja Luka and Sanski Most." The resolution noted a "consistent pattern of summary executions, rape, mass expulsions, arbitrary detentions, forced labour and large-scale disappearances." It specifically named Bosnian Serb leaders Radovan Karadžić and Ratko Mladić for "their direct and individual responsibilities for the atrocities committed against the Bosnian Muslim population of Srebrenica in July 1995."[68]

Stories About Sovereignty and Human Rights

The Bosnia case is an example of how decision making occurs in a complicated normative environment.[69] Security Council members faced a serious ethical dilemma because the war brought multiple international norms into conflict, creating seemingly irreconcilable claims on members. Members were forced to argue and decide which norms to follow when they were in tension—sovereignty, nonintervention, human rights, self-determination, the protection of nationals. The competition between competing normative claims delayed but ultimately paved the way for humanitarian intervention. Just as they were initially divided on the cause and character of the conflict, Security Council members articulated different stories about legitimate sovereign authority in Bosnia over the course of the conflict. At its core, much of the debate surrounding the Bosnia war was about how to respond to a situation of contested statehood. Security Council members debated whether sovereign authority remained vested in the Federal Republic of Yugoslavia, whether it transferred to the democratically elected Bosnian government once its independence was formally recognized by the UN, or whether it remained indeterminate—its internal governing structure lacking legitimacy because of competing political and territorial claims. Stories about contested or indeterminate sovereignty brought human rights norms directly into conflict with sovereignty norms. Only when the majority of UNSC members (including its permanent members) conceived of sovereignty as residing in the democratically elected government of Bosnia-Herzegovina—a state member of the United Nations—did the use of force in defense of human rights actually promote respect for sovereignty at the same time. Because the Bosnian government was recognized as the legitimate sovereign authority and was identified as the principal victim of human rights abuses by the intentional story, humanitarian intervention complemented the protection of Westphalian sovereignty rather than conflicted with it. This is important because norms research shows that new norms are more likely to succeed if they can be grafted onto existing norms.[70] Alternatively, when a newly emerging norm comes into conflict with a highly established norm, like state sovereignty, we can expect the former to yield to the latter.

In the case of Bosnia, stories about sovereignty mapped onto causal stories. Thus the articulation and widespread adoption of an intentional story about ethnic cleansing and aggression combined with the story about the Bosnian government's sovereign legitimacy created the opportunity for the use of military force in defense of human rights. The articulation of normative coherence between human rights and sovereignty norms eliminated the most powerful barrier to humanitarian intervention in 1995—state sovereignty. Through their continued interaction, human rights

norms reshaped conceptions of state sovereignty and international security
for the Security Council.

Why France and the United Kingdom Changed Their Story

The inadvertent story had become untenable by the summer of 1995.
Graphic media imagery of Bosnian Serb mortar attacks on civilians in Sarajevo combined with witness accounts, expert testimony, and forensic evidence of mass executions of Bosnian Muslims in Srebrenica by the BSA
discredited the civil war explanation and the claim that sovereignty was
indeterminate. The facts on the ground no longer could be reconciled with
the explanation for the violence articulated by France and the UK. The
emergence of this evidence also highlighted the increasing gap between
their professed values—tolerance, equality, human rights, and the rule of
law—and their decision-making behavior in Bosnia. The continuation of
Bosnian Serb ethnic cleansing in the face of mounting evidence fundamentally threatened the core values of France and the UK, transforming the
protection of those values into a core security interest.

Human rights norms shaped Security Council narratives about Bosnia;
but desire for the protection of human rights norms during armed conflict
does not always produce humanitarian intervention. Why was humanitarian intervention possible in Bosnia in 1995? Nonintervention in Bosnia
between 1992 and mid-1995 followed by humanitarian intervention in
summer 1995 is not easily accommodated by international relations theories that explain state behavior based only on power politics or the pursuit
of national interests. On their own, these approaches founder because in
practice they often define state interests based on state behavior and they
fail to recognize that state interests and actions can be circumscribed by
normative discourse. If core national security interests include the economic and military security of the state, we would expect France and the
UK to have perceived the Bosnian war, the continuing human rights violations, and potential cross-border impact as a threat to European security.
They could have expected early humanitarian intervention to be in their
national interests; yet France and the UK did not perceive the Bosnian war
as central to their national interests in the early 1990s.[71] Once their troops
were on the ground, humanitarian intervention threatened the safety of
their nationals, and they were reticent to use military force in defense of
safe areas. Nonetheless, France and the UK did engage in humanitarian

intervention without withdrawing their ground troops in August 1995. Interest-based approaches tend to ignore the degree to which national interests are actively constructed by actors and shaped by ideas and norms. Alternatively, if humanitarian intervention is explained by material power—the ability of the strong to impose their will on the weak—then strong U.S. support for lifting the arms embargo and NATO air strikes in defense of safe areas as early as 1993 should have produced humanitarian intervention, but it did not. We would also expect that the winning story would begin with strong powers and diffuse to weaker ones; yet the opposite is true in Bosnia—most of the permanent members were the last to adopt the intentional story. Nonetheless, power matters—humanitarian intervention did not become politically possible until a majority of permanent members adopted the intentional story in July 1995 and publicly recognized Bosnia as an independent state with a legitimate sovereign government—but power alone is an insufficient explanation of humanitarian intervention in Bosnia (both its early absence and its later use).

Despite the importance of power and interests, norms—such as legitimacy, multilateralism, and human rights—also matter in the Security Council. The unprecedented power of transnational human rights norms in contemporary international society explains why humanitarian intervention is legitimate and politically possible for the Security Council; but the existence of these norms alone does not explain why the council decides to act on them in some cases but not others. What the Bosnia case shows is that norms shape Security Council decision making but that council decisions are shaped by a complex interaction of norms and interests and that its decisions are not immune from power politics. The Bosnian case illustrates how human rights norms interacted with geostrategic interests to produce UNSC humanitarian intervention.

Values, Norms, and Interests in the Security Council

Both norms and interests shaped UNSC decision making about humanitarian intervention in Bosnia. National interests changed over time and were shaped by the core norms and values of council members. For example, France and the United Kingdom changed their narration of the conflict, clearly identifying its principal perpetrators after incontrovertible evidence implicated the Bosnian Serbs in massive atrocities in Srebrenica and other safe areas, and after the repeated abductions of UN personnel by Bosnian Serb forces. Most of the UN personnel captured and used as human shields in May 1995 were French peacekeepers. Televised images of the hostages attracted worldwide attention, humiliating the UN and infuriating the newly elected French president, Jacques Chirac.[72] Reporter Mary Dejevsky of the *Independent* described the personal moral outrage experienced by Chirac in the aftermath of Srebrenica. During a July 1995 ceremony commemorating the deportation of Jews from Paris during World War II, Chirac called on Western democracies to "learn the lessons of history" and work together to halt ethnic cleansing in Bosnia: "The values on which our democracies are founded are being flouted in Europe before our very eyes. . . . If we have the will, we can stop an enterprise that threatens yet again to destroy our values and which is coming ever closer to threatening Europe as a whole."[73] Clearly, ideas, values, and information mattered. Nonetheless, by the time humanitarian intervention was undertaken in Bosnia, it was in the national security interests of both France and the UK to do so. By 1995 divisions within the transatlantic alliance over Bosnian policy threatened the relations between the U.S. and its European allies. The inability to solve the Bosnian crisis and stop the human rights violations fundamentally threatened the credibility of European security institutions, including NATO, the European Union, and the United Nations.[74] Indeed, what started out as peripheral concerns for human rights and international institutions became a serious security problem.

On the other hand, the U.S. repeatedly made principled arguments in support of Bosnian self-defense rights and the responsibility of the UNSC to rescue the Bosnian state and its people. In her memoirs, Ambassador Albright writes that U.S. efforts in Bosnia were about "the Bosnia idea"—"the simple premise that every person has value and that neighbor must look upon neighbor not as Serb, Croat, and Muslim, but as one individual to another."[75] Nonetheless, U.S. support for the use of military force became more vigorous after it became clear that the use of American forces in Bosnia was inevitable. Early on, the U.S. articulated unwavering political support for Bosnia but it was unwilling to deploy its troops on the ground. Only after it became apparent that its ground troops would be required to extract UNPROFOR forces from the intensified fighting going on around them did the U.S. push forcefully for humanitarian intervention.[76] Arguably, by advocating for the use of airpower by NATO, the U.S. envisioned using military force on its own terms and not needing to deploy ground troops until after the conflict had ended and a peace deal was signed.[77]

Before the 30 August air strikes began, the U.S. administration considered whether humanitarian intervention would negatively affect the peace process. When questioned about the wisdom of initiating strikes, Ambassador Richard Holbrook replied that he was willing to risk failure of the peace negotiations rather than allow the Bosnian Serbs "to get away with another criminal act."[78] Eleven days earlier, on 19 August 1995, the American diplomatic effort, headed by Holbrooke, to bring peace to the Balkans was severely disrupted when a vehicle carrying senior administration officials slid off the dangerous Mount Igman road above the Sarajevo valley, killing three Americans. The diplomatic team, which included Holbrooke, had been forced to travel the dangerous route after Serbian president Milošević and the Bosnian Serb leadership refused to grant them safe passage to Sarajevo through Bosnian Serb–held territory. Explaining the timing of the intervention, which followed Srebrenica, Markale, and the American deaths on Mount Igman, Holbrooke writes: "The August 28 mortar attack was hardly the first challenge to Western policy, nor the worst incident of the war; it was only the latest. But it was different because of its timing: coming immediately after the launching of our diplomatic shuttle and the tragedy on Igman, it appeared not only as an act of terror against innocent people in Sarajevo, but as the first direct affront on the United States."[79] Holbrooke describes the attack on Markale in a manner that reflects narrow American self-interests. Nonetheless, he defended the use of NATO airpower to the administration based on principles of justice using humanitarian frames of reference and was willing to risk the negotiating team's overall success by affirming humanitarian values ahead of the United States' interest in resolution of the conflict. U.S. motives were mixed in Bosnia; yet they reflect what Albright described as America's role in the world: "The President believed, as did I, that our country's purpose was not just to bear witness to history but rather to shape it in ways that served our interests and our ideals."[80] By 1995 the war in Bosnia challenged both Western interests and Western values. It was not possible for the U.S., France, and the UK to address the moral challenges posed by the war in Bosnia without taking into account strategic interests; yet they were unwilling to ignore normative concerns in the pursuit of those interests.[81] Humanitarian intervention policy on Bosnia, then, reflected the interplay of interests and normative concerns.

Despite early disagreement on the intentional story, Security Council members unanimously condemned the practice of ethnic cleansing in a series of presidential statements and Security Council resolutions.[82] Council members indicated by the passage of these resolutions that the protection of human rights and respect for international humanitarian law were intricately linked to the maintenance of international peace and security. For example, in explaining its support for Resolutions 770 authorizing sanctions against Serbia and Montenegro and 771 condemning ethnic cleansing, the representative from Hungary argued, "The adoption of these two resolutions is another example, in our opinion, of the strong commitment of the Security Council to human rights and humanitarian issues. To act urgently is not only a moral obligation of the Council: it is indispensable for the preservation of the credibility of the United Nations. Only a credible Organization and a credible Security Council can perform their basic functions—maintaining international peace and security."[83] Cape Verde argued that the grave violations occurring in Bosnia-Herzegovina were crimes committed against all of the international community and not just the Bosnians because "they violate our very decency and human dignity."[84] Japan similarly noted that grave implications of the conflict extended beyond the region of Europe to the entire international community.[85] Venezuela defended its vote in favor of imposing sanctions against Serbia and Montenegro "for reasons that are basically humanitarian," asserting explicitly, "respect for the norms and principles of international law is a prerequisite for peace and security in the world. Any State that violates them must be condemned."[86] But not all council members agreed that human rights considerations had a place in Security Council decision making. India, China, and Zimbabwe purposefully denied the linkage between human rights and international security. India, for example, expressed its strong reservation about the appropriateness of human rights concerns being discussed in the council at all. India argued that human rights concerns belonged in the Human Rights Commission in Geneva, whereas concerns about international peace and security were in the purview of the Security Council.[87] Notably, however, while China expressed its reservations about human rights considerations in formal meetings and abstained from voting on resolutions that linked human rights and humanitarian law to Chapter VII of the UN Charter, it did not veto them. Human rights were shaping and being shaped by norms of sovereignty and international security.

Innovations in Security Council Arguments and Practice

Security Council action in Bosnia, like that in Somalia before it, marked an important evolution for the emerging norm of humanitarian intervention.

In both cases, widespread agreement on a causal story about the conflict was necessary to prompt united Security Council action, and eventually humanitarian intervention. In Somalia, however, the council learned that complexity is not amenable to the use of force. In Bosnia, humanitarian intervention in defense of Bosnian civilians became possible only after widespread agreement among council members about the intentional story.

In both Somalia and Bosnia, humanitarian intervention became possible only after the majority of UNSC members, including most of its permanent members, discursively constructed sovereignty norms and human rights norms as complementary. In Somalia the absence of a legitimate sovereign authority eliminated conflict between norms. In Bosnia, the recognition of the Sarajevo-based Bosnian government as the legitimate sovereign authority eliminated that tension. Only when the council perceived the Bosnian government as victim of, rather than an equal party to, the conflict could the council use military force to promote and protect human rights without violating the grundnorm of state sovereignty. In Bosnia, stories about conflict causality and stories about sovereignty were linked—proponents of the intentional story identified the Bosnian government as sovereign, whereas proponents of the inadvertent story argued that sovereign authority was indeterminate because of competing sovereignty claims.

Expert testimony, forensic evidence, and graphic media imagery were essential to explaining both why the intentional story eventually displaced the inadvertent story in the Security Council and the timing of humanitarian intervention. While multiple stories were plausible throughout much of the conflict, there came a point when the facts on the ground no longer matched the inadvertent or complex explanation. The Bosnian case also illustrates not only the importance of but also the limits to great power leadership. Early U.S. support for the intentional story was insufficient to garner humanitarian intervention. Instead, stories about the cause and character of conflicts must gain the support of the majority of Security Council members, including a strong coalition of permanent members, in order to win over others. Active support for the intentional story by the most powerful permanent member of the Security Council was not sufficient to enable action until other permanent members changed their minds.

In sum, while initially divided over sovereign authority in Bosnia and the cause and character of the conflict, the UNSC coalesced around an intentional story in July 1995. Unity around the intentional story, in which Bosnian Serb leaders backed by the Serbian government were guilty of the

ethnic cleansing of Bosnian Muslim civilians, made humanitarian intervention possible. The intentional story won over its competitors only after a
majority of the permanent members articulated support for it. France and
the UK transferred their support from an inadvertent explanation to an
intentional one in the summer of 1995, in part because the inadvertent
story was no longer tenable in the face of mounting expert testimony,
media reports, and forensic evidence of Serb-led ethnic cleansing. Further,
in the case of Bosnia, Security Council members could promote human
rights and protect state sovereignty simultaneously, eliminating normative
incoherence. Ideas, information, and norms shaped Security Council decision making about humanitarian intervention in Bosnia, but national interests and power—both normative and material—also mattered. The case of
Bosnia pushed the emerging humanitarian intervention norm beyond the
limits established by the Somalia intervention before it. In Bosnia, it became
possible for the Security Council to intervene militarily in a case of contested statehood and not only in the absence of legitimate state authority.
Security Council discourse and military action in Bosnia demonstrated that
human rights norms were changing understandings of international security and sovereignty, prompting innovations in the purpose of military force.

Chapter 5

The Perpetrator State and Security Council Inaction: The Case of Rwanda

When the United Nations Security Council became involved in Rwanda's civil war in March 1993, the spirit of post–Cold War optimism that had characterized the council in the aftermath of the Gulf War had been replaced by a deepening concern over the health and reputation of the United Nations. The UN had taken on more peacekeeping operations in the five years between 1989 and 1993 than it had in the previous forty.[1] The Security Council's early success in reversing Iraqi aggression against Kuwait and the emergence of council intervention into civil wars had led to high expectations in the international community about its role in guaranteeing international peace and security. But mission failures in the field, skyrocketing peacekeeping costs, and its inability to determine effective contexts and conditions made the council apprehensive about undertaking new missions.[2] In October 1993, the UNSC authorized the United Nations Assistance Mission for Rwanda (UNAMIR)—a Chapter VI peacekeeping operation mandated to monitor the cease-fire between the parties of the civil war, assess the security situation in the lead-up to democratic elections, and investigate acts of noncompliance. The council justified its adoption due to the relatively unremarkable character of the conflict—it was a civil war that had been ended by a mutually negotiated peace settlement with both parties welcoming the UN presence. Council members perceived that Rwanda would be a straightforward, traditional Chapter VI peacekeeping operation—an easy case that could bolster the UN's reputation at a moment in which it was embroiled in the quagmires of Somalia and Bosnia.

The council was unprepared when less than six months later Rwanda became the place of "the twentieth century's fastest moving genocide."[3] Interpreting events on the ground through the civil war frame, the UNSC blamed both parties for the escalation of hostilities and threatened UN withdrawal instead of protection at the height of the genocide.

Once engaged in Rwanda, the UNSC in its decision making was tentative and inconsistent. Members offered only contingent support of the mission and mandates lacked the resources necessary to implement them. Initially, council members articulated an inadvertent story that characterized the conflict as a civil war in which both parties were responsible for civilian deaths—a by-product of the fighting. Members viewed the parties as morally equivalent and authorized a mission aimed at separating the sides and observing the implementation of the peace agreement. UN personnel were directed to apply classic peacekeeping principles of neutrality and impartiality in all their interactions with belligerents. When the force commander, Lieutenant General Roméo Dallaire, challenged this mandate because of increasing evidence of ethnically motivated killings and the discovered plans for the slaughter of Tutsis by Hutu militia, he was rebuked by Secretariat officials. In January 1994, the UNSC and Secretariat officials analyzed civilian deaths in Rwanda through the inadvertent frame and they were hesitant to use military force because UN legitimacy could not withstand another Somalia.[4] In April, international humanitarian and human rights NGOs began briefing nonpermanent members informally. Armed with independent information, witness testimony, expert analyses, and forensic evidence, they convinced a small group of nonpermanent members that the violence was ethnically motivated. By mid-April the NGO community argued that "genocide was most definitely taking place."[5] Council unity quickly broke down after several nonpermanent members began to articulate an intentional story about the systematic massacre of civilians which was distinct from, but simultaneous to, the ongoing civil war. Divided over the cause and character of the conflict, the council no longer agreed on an appropriate response. With UNAMIR troops already on the ground, it voted to decrease its presence in response to the increasing violence. This had been the compromise position between a small group of nonpermanent members that wanted to increase troops and strengthen the mandate to include civilian protection and permanent members that sought to end the mission entirely. In May, several nonpermanent members began using the term "genocide" to describe the violence. Immediately, a complex story was also advanced generating competition between three different causal stories in council meetings. When the council finally united around the intentional story in late June, more than 75 percent of the genocide victims had already been killed.[6]

Security Council narratives are powerful for their ability to interpret information, name violence, and identify perpetrators and for their ability to shape policy responses. Disunity on the causal story and unity around an inadvertent story are both barriers to the authorization of "all necessary measures" by the council. Yet the stories that members tell about the status of sovereign authority in the target state are just as powerful as causal stories. When sovereign authority is stable and the government is the perpetrator of human rights violations, sovereignty norms and human rights norms make competing claims on council members. To protect human rights in such a situation requires members to transgress Westphalian conceptions of sovereignty. In contrast, when sovereign authority in the target state is suspended, absent, contested, or displaced, council members can discursively construct the protection of human rights as complementary to, or at least not in conflict with, sovereignty norms. In Rwanda, the sovereign government was the alleged perpetrator of mass atrocity crimes, so preventing the killing would have required taking sides against a sovereign state member of the UN. In 1994, there was no precedent for such action, and the council had no history of preventive action. Humanitarian intervention had been authorized in Somalia, but for a humanitarian crisis; and because Somalia lacked a government, sovereignty considerations were irrelevant. Indeed, there was no UNSC consensus on the acceptance of humanitarian intervention in response to human rights violations.[7] Only limited military force had been used to protect civilians in Iraq in 1992, but this occurred within the context of a broader interstate war and after Iraq's sovereignty had been temporarily suspended. The UN had not used military force to prevent massacres in safe havens like Srebrenica and would not employ humanitarian intervention in Bosnia until more than a year after the Rwanda genocide was over. It did so only after its contested sovereignty was resolved in favor of the Bosnian Muslim government, eliminating perceived tensions between the protection of sovereignty and human rights. In 1994, when council members perceived sovereignty and human rights norms to be in conflict, the former trumped the latter. Sovereignty considerations were significant in Rwanda because not only was the government the perpetrator, it was also serving on the Security Council as a nonpermanent member at the time of its crimes.

The UNSC response to Rwanda had a dual character. During the period of October 1993–21 June 1994, the Security Council did not engage in

humanitarian intervention. A traditional Chapter VI peacekeeping operation was on the ground when the genocide started. The council did not
adjust the mandate to a Chapter VII peace enforcement operation, and the
Secretariat specifically ordered UNAMIR forces not to use force to protect
civilians when authorization was sought by the UNAMIR commander. Instead, General Dallaire was ordered to maintain the impartiality required
by his Chapter VI mandate.[8] On 22 June, however, the UNSC passed Resolution 929, authorizing member states to use "all necessary means" to address the humanitarian crisis caused by the exile of nearly three million
Rwandans into neighboring states. France launched a humanitarian relief
operation called Operation Turquoise before the end of June. Characterized
by France as a humanitarian intervention, the mandate authorized humanitarian relief to refugees but not the use of military force to stop the killing.
Whether the operation should be considered a humanitarian intervention
is highly contested because it was not undertaken to prevent, halt, or punish
mass atrocity; the ambassador representing the perpetrator government of
Rwanda voted in favor of the resolution, and it had the effect of rescuing
the perpetrators and not the victimized Tutsi population. While I address
both phases of UNSC involvement—during and after the genocide—I treat
the Rwanda situation as a noncase of humanitarian intervention based on
the definition applied in this study.[9] The focus here is on why, when faced
with genocide, the UNSC opted against humanitarian intervention.

The Rwanda case demonstrates how influential the naming and framing
of conflicts is on UNSC decision making. The dominant narratives about
the cause and character of the violence and the status of Rwanda's sovereign
authority foreclosed rather than opened possibilities for humanitarian intervention to stop genocide. When the most powerful permanent council
members articulated an inadvertent story, their prominence and monopoly
over information gave the narrative about the resumption of the civil war
considerable weight. The secretary-general's representative to the council
advised it repeatedly "that the situation was being driven by the civil war
and that the real need was to focus on how to produce a ceasefire."[10] Independent expertise, witness testimony, and forensic evidence were essential
for introducing the counternarrative about genocide into the council and
eventually making the inadvertent story untenable. The Rwanda case raises
the question of whether the causal stories and sovereignty stories articulated
by council members are sincerely "discovered" through information gath-
ering and analysis or strategically "chosen" to coincide with preexisting

policy interests. Indeed, there is significant evidence to suggest that permanent members including the U.S. were aware that genocide was taking place in Rwanda well before they were willing to publicly admit it.[11] Yet independently of motive, the stories that council members tell structure the realm of possibility for policy decisions, give signals to perpetrators and victims, and undermine or empower alternative explanations.

The absence of humanitarian intervention in Rwanda offers complicated lessons about the role of norms and interests in the UNSC. Interests, or rather their absence, seemed to drive great power decision making to the detriment of human rights norms. After all, a campaign of misinformation by permanent members and their active obstruction of the use of military force permitted the genocide to continue. Permanent members rescued their own nationals within days of the start of systematic slaughter but refused to use their troops to reinforce UNAMIR or provide protection to Rwandan civilians. Yet UNSC members also formally condemned violations of international humanitarian law, created an independent commission of experts to investigate atrocities, and established the International Criminal Tribunal for Rwanda to prosecute the perpetrators. Some permanent members believed that by reducing the UN role they were actually protecting the institution of peacekeeping and the newly emerging practice of humanitarian intervention, albeit at the expense of the Rwandan people. It is in the moral outrage and political backlash to the perceived breach of human rights norms and the UNSC's inability to meet the normative expectations of international society that we find evidence of their growing strength. Simply framing the Rwanda case as a contest between norms and interests misses the way that they are mutually constituted and ignores the tensions that exist between different international norms. In Rwanda, there was competition between multiple norms and values rather than an absence of them. There is not a single progressive path to the life cycle of a norm: norms may grow in strength, evolve in new ways, weaken, or die. The cases of northern Iraq, Somalia, and Bosnia illustrate the growing strength of human rights norms, their increasing legitimacy in the council, and the changing purpose of military force. The situation in Rwanda demonstrates that despite this changing normative context, significant barriers to the implementation of human rights norms exist, including the counterpull of established national interests, the absence of political will, and the persistence of preexisting highly internalized norms—state sovereignty, domestic nonintervention, and protection of nationals.

The War for Rwanda

The war that started in Rwanda in 1990 was deeply rooted in ethnic politics, replicating a long tradition of the manipulation of ethnic-based fears by political elites to maximize power and defeat political rivals. In 1990, Rwanda comprised three social groups often identified as ethnic groups: the Hutu (nearly 85 percent of the population), the Tutsi (15 percent), and the Twa (under 1 percent). The ethnic distinction between Hutu and Tutsi was socially engineered through "a complex interplay of culture, politics, and economics."[12] These ethnic categories existed in Rwanda prior to its colonization (*Tutsi* referred to a person rich in cattle while *Hutu* referred to a subordinate or ordinary person), but it was colonialism that institutionalized the "ethnic distinction" of superior Tutsi and inferior Hutu that persisted throughout the 1990s. In 1990, the president of Rwanda was Juvenal Habyarimana, a Hutu who had come to power through a 1973 military coup.

Habyarimana's rule was first threatened in the late 1980s as a result of a deep economic crisis, domestic pressure for political liberalization, and external military challenges from Rwandan Tutsis living in exile. In 1989, Rwanda experienced severe drought and famine in the south of the country. That same year, the International Coffee Agreement failed, which caused world coffee prices to plummet and plunged Rwanda into debt as its foreign earnings declined by half.[13] The World Bank imposed structural adjustment and the International Monetary Fund devalued the country's currency. By 1992 the economic crisis reached its climax: prices of fuel and consumer essentials soared, state enterprises went bankrupt, health and education services collapsed, famine became widespread in the southern provinces, and coffee production fell dramatically.[14] At this same time, opposition political leaders, intellectuals, and journalists began calling for democratic reforms including the creation of a multiparty system. It was in this context that the Rwandan Patriotic Front (RPF) invaded Rwanda from its base in Uganda in October 1990.

The RPF was a Rwandan nationalist organization composed primarily of members of the Tutsi group who had been living in exile in neighboring Uganda and who were dedicated to the repatriation of Tutsi refugees. The RPF justified its invasion as an effort to resolve the Tutsi refugee crisis in the region, to eliminate the political persecution of Tutsi in Rwanda, and to replace the Habyarimana regime with a democracy.[15] The Habyarimana government characterized the invasion as an aggressive attempt by Tutsis to reimpose Tutsi-dominated rule, the political exclusion of Hutus, and a system of ethnic apartheid, with help from Uganda. Despite some initial gains, the RPF invasion was unsuccessful in large part because France intervened militarily on behalf of its longtime political ally, President Habyarimana, which helped the Forces Armées Rwandaise (Rwandan Armed Forces, or FAR) halt the invasion, and because the RPF lacked legitimacy among the Rwandan people.[16]

The FAR and the RPF fought each other for nearly three years. During the height of the conflict, one-seventh of the population of Rwanda was internally displaced or became refugees.[17] Civil war further destabilized Rwandan society by intensifying political instability, hindering domestic political change, and pushing the country closer to economic collapse.[18] President Habyarimana capitalized on the external threat to quell internal challenges to his rule. The government arbitrarily arrested political opposition leaders and members of the Tutsi minority, accusing them of being "accomplices" of the RPF. The demonization of Tutsi by the regime, increasing anti-Tutsi–anti-RFP propaganda in print media and over the radio, and growing ethnic fear exacerbated the existing divide between the Hutu political opposition and the RPF, preventing them from aligning against the government. Military battles between the government and the RPF were followed by the massacres of Tutsi civilians by government troops. Investigations by human rights organizations revealed that President Habyarimana's regime had instigated attacks against Tutsi in an effort "to bolster crumbling solidarity among Hutu."[19]

The FAR and RPF signed an initial peace agreement in July 1992, but it took over a year of negotiations, punctuated by cease-fire violations, massacres of Tutsi civilians by the FAR, and a major RPF offensive that brought it to the outskirts of Kigali before the final agreement was concluded on 3 August 1993. The agreement, the Arusha Accords, instituted a series of political, military, and constitutional reforms including a power-sharing agreement, transfer of political power to a transitional government, a protocol on the repatriation of Tutsi refugees, and an armed forces integration agreement.[20] The Arusha Accords called for a neutral international force to be deployed in Rwanda in order to oversee implementation of the agreement, followed by French military withdrawal from the country.[21]

UNSC Involvement and Shifting Stories About the Killings in Rwanda

In October 1993, the UNSC passed Resolution 872 establishing the United Nations Assistance Mission for Rwanda. From its inception, UNAMIR was conceived as a simple Chapter VI peacekeeping mission that would monitor the Arusha Accords and report on violations. Renewal of the mission mandate was made contingent on continual success in meeting the timetables already agreed on by the parties. Though hesitant to get involved, council members were persuaded to assist the political transition after a joint delegation comprising representatives from the Rwandan Government and the RPF requested UNSC assistance. Council members interpreted the joint presentation as a demonstration of the dedication of both parties to finding a definitive solution to the conflict.[22] Council members were optimistic about the success of the peacekeeping mission for Rwanda because it would adhere to the principles of classic peacekeeping and avoid the perils of peace enforcement that hampered their efforts in Somalia and Bosnia.[23] France argued that Rwanda would be a "special" and "successful" case of UN intervention because both parties had put aside their differences in pursuit of peace.[24] Brazil, Djibouti, and Pakistan echoed this optimism, celebrating the "determination" and "clear willingness" of both parties to work together to resolve their differences. What the presentation masked, however, was the serious split between moderates and extremists within Habyarimana's governing coalition—the extremists opposed democratic elections and would repeatedly delay the transfer of authority to the agreed on transitional government.

Despite this spirit of optimism and the council's hope for an easy success, the UNSC warned the parties that UN participation in Rwanda was conditional. The council was willing to participate in Rwanda's democratic transition but it could not afford another failure in the field like those occurring in Somalia and Bosnia, and would not accept UN casualties. According to the United Kingdom, the international community was willing to help because an "African solution was found to an African problem," but primary responsibility for success would be with the parties themselves.[25] In a veiled reference to the ongoing turmoil in Somalia where eighteen peacekeepers had been brutally murdered only three days before UNAMIR's authorization, the UK linked Security Council action to the behavior of the belligerents: "Peace agreements such as this are only a success if they are pursued in good faith and sincerity by all parties involved. As recent events elsewhere have demonstrated, the United Nations cannot impose peace where there is no willingness to sustain compromise. It is therefore, in our view, essential that the parties continue to cooperate fully and stick firmly to the timetable that they have set for themselves for national reconciliation and elections."[26] The United States was more direct about the contingent nature of its support. U.S. ambassador Madeleine Albright said, "As the Council knows, my Government is deeply concerned about the increasing burden—both in terms of manpower and financial resources—which the United Nations is being asked to shoulder. . . . This body's continued support will depend in large measure on the demonstration of substantive progress towards the implementation of the peace agreement and the establishment of transitional institutions in advance of national elections."[27] These remarks made clear that Rwanda was a low-priority operation for the U.S. and that addressing its political and financial concerns would be central to its continued support of the mission. Only minutes after UNAMIR had been approved, the U.S. went on record stating its intention to decrease mission size and costs: "My Government will continue to monitor and work to reduce costs and personnel levels throughout this peacekeeping operation, and we look forward to the report of the Secretary-General called for in the resolution on ways to reduce the levels of the United Nations Assistance Mission for Rwanda and to reduce costs."[28] There was a clear limit to what council members were willing to sacrifice for Rwandans in terms of reputation and financial and human cost. The council was willing to undertake a minimal, classic peacekeeping operation but it would not take risks to enforce peace. Rather than bolstering the resolve of the parties, these remarks had a perverse signaling effect on the hard-liners in Habyarimana's government who opposed the transfer of political power: they could rid the country of the UN's presence by increasing the human and financial costs of the mission and by violating the terms of the Arusha agreement.

The Emergence of the Inadvertent Story

During the October 1993 meeting authorizing UNAMIR, council members described the situation in Rwanda as "tragic," "fratricidal," and a "civil war."[29] According to this inadvertent story, both parties to the conflict were culpable for the violence. Civilian deaths were perceived as a foreseen and logical result of conflict and not the purpose of the fighting. Council meet-ings devoted little attention to allegations of massacres, instead focusing on the implementation status of the Arusha Accords. When Rwanda joined the council as a nonpermanent member in January 1994, one party to the conflict gained full access to all secure documents, reports, and meetings available to the UNSC. This gave the regime an informational advantage on UN policy toward Rwanda and a privileged position from which to shape it. Despite the failure of the parties to meet the timeline for installing the transitional government, the UNSC renewed UNAMIR in January 1994 but warned "that continued support for UNAMIR will depend upon the full and prompt implementation by the parties of the Arusha Agreement."[30]

The inadvertent story persisted, despite an increase in violence and its characterization by NGOs as organized and ethnic-based massacres. Re-ports by independent experts including the International Federation of Human Rights, Africa Watch, the Inter-African Union of Human Rights, and the International Centre of Rights of the Person and of Democratic Development argued as early as March 1993 that government leaders in Rwanda had organized the killing of thousands of Tutsi.[31] The UN special rapporteur for the Commission on Human Rights used the term "geno-cide" to describe the killings in Rwanda, but rules of procedure required confidentiality, so the commission approached the Rwandan government on the evidence in closed session.[32] Nonetheless, the council only saw evi-dence of civil war because that is what it was prompted to expect. Council members expected ethnic violence as part of the political process, thus the solution to the problem was enforcement of the political agreement brok-ered in Arusha.[33]

By 5 April 1994, the council was losing patience with the Rwandan parties. It renewed UNAMIR for only six weeks instead of the customary three-month period because the new interim government still had not been installed. The council issued a stern warning to President Habyarimana that he must finalize the transitional institutions or the UNSC would reassess the "Organization's commitment to Rwanda."[34] Facing pressure from the UN and other African leaders during a regional meeting of heads of state in Dar-es-Salaam, Habyarimana publicly agreed to an immediate transfer of his political authority to the new interim government upon his arrival back in Rwanda.[35] The very next day, on 6 April 1994, the airplane carrying President Habyarimana and President Cyprien Ntaryamira of Burundi back to Rwanda was shot down as it prepared to land at Kigali's airport. Within thirty minutes of the crash, members of the Presidential Guard and military and civilian militias set up roadblocks throughout Kigali and began massacring Tutsis based on national identity cards and prepared lists. The assassination of the president created an initial gap in authority as Hutu moderates and extremists competed to take control of the state. The moderates initially took control but quickly lost it to the hard-liners, who sidelined moderate military officers and eliminated the domestic political opposition, including the named members of the interim transitional government.[36] Ten Belgian soldiers from UNAMIR who were guarding the president's successor, Prime Minister Agathe Uwilingiyamana, a progressive Hutu who became the constitutional head of government upon his assassination, were captured, tortured, and killed, prompting a formal withdrawal of all Belgian troops two days later. Prime Minister Uwilingiyamana was brutally raped and murdered by soldiers of the Presidential Guard. Rwandan soldiers and police also murdered the two candidates for the presidency of the transitional assembly and the president of the Constitutional Court, effectively decapitating the transitional regime.[37] In the wake of the massacres in Kigali and the failure of the UN to intervene, the RPF broke the cease-fire on 7 April and began fighting the FAR.[38] Between April and July 1994—a period of one hundred days—almost one million Rwandans were killed by the Rwandan government, military, local militia groups, and their neighbors. The Presidential Guard, troops commanded by Colonel Théoneste Bagasora and the *Interahamwe* militia (meaning those who stand together or those who attack together)—the youth wing of Habyarimana's political party that had been given military training by the regime—massacred Tutsi civilians with machetes in the streets, in their homes and even in schools, orphanages, and churches.[39] Not even children were spared. The vast majority of the victims were Tutsis targeted for death based on their ethnicity which was revealed by their identity cards, but victims also included Hutus in the political opposition, and those who opposed the genocide, or who resembled or sought to protect Tutsis.[40]

On 7 April, the UNSC issued a presidential statement in which it expressed regret over the plane crash and concern over the considerable loss of lives in Rwanda in the aftermath, including the deaths of government leaders, civilians, and the Belgian peacekeepers. The council strongly condemned the violence but placed a particular emphasis on the attacks against UN personnel. The statement reaffirmed the inadvertent story by identifying both parties as responsible for the attacks, although the RPF had not yet taken up arms. Regardless, the UNSC called on "all Rwandese" and "all parties and factions to desist from any further threats or acts of violence" and urged "all parties" to "respect the cease-fire."[41] This language implied that the deaths occurring in Rwanda following the plane crash were the direct result of a cease-fire violation and not systematic and targeted attacks against civilians by extremists in Habyarimana's government. Because it was still operating within the inadvertent framework, the council threatened UN withdrawal if the killing continued. This played directly into the plans of hard-liners, who had deliberately killed the Belgian peacekeepers in an effort to prompt the collapse of the mission. In the days that followed, foreign governments including the U.S., UK, and France launched extensive military operations in Rwanda to safely evacuate their nationals. Force commander General Dallaire insists that it might have been possible to stop the genocide had these troops stayed to reinforce UNAMIR after completing their rescue missions.[42]

Thirteen days after the massacres began, Secretary-General Boutros Boutros-Ghali submitted a special report to the Security Council on the status of UNAMIR.[43] It articulated an inadvertent story, diagnosing the problem as the resumption of civil war and the solution as reestablishment of the cease-fire. The report argued that the violence was prompted by the plane crash after which "unruly members of the Presidential Guard" initiated the killing. Although the secretary-general identified state actors as the perpetrators, he described the actors as "unruly," indicating that the killing was not part of a systematic policy. The report also contained elements of a complex story—characterizing the situation as "anarchy" and "spontaneous slaughter."[44] In contrast, within days of the start of the genocide, Dallaire had determined that the massacres "were not a spontaneous act" but a "well-executed operation involving the army, Gendermerie, Interahamwe and civil service" after unarmed military observers had witnessed a brutal yet methodical massacre of civilians at a church in Kigali.[45] In his memoirs, Dallaire described the massacre in detail: "Methodically and with much bravado and laughter, the militia moved from bench to bench, hacking with machetes. Some people died immediately, while others with terrible wounds begged for their lives or the lives of their children. No one was spared. A pregnant woman was disemboweled and her fetus severed. Women suffered horrible mutilation. Men were struck on the head and died immediately or lingered in agony. Children begged for their lives and received the same treatment as their parents."[46]

In his report, Boutros-Ghali described UNAMIR personnel as incapable of continuing the tasks under their mandate because the conditions on the ground exposed them to unnecessary risk.[47] This recommendation ignored the opinion of the force commander who sought only a modest reinforcement of troops and supplies, and who was willing to operate without them if he could get authorization to protect civilians under his control. The secretary-general advanced three options for responding to the crisis: (1) a massive reinforcement of UNAMIR and a change in its mandate to include enforcement powers under Chapter VII of the UN Charter, (2) a reduction of troops to a small contingent headed by the force commander in Kigali to broker a cease-fire and monitor conditions and the withdrawal of all other UNAMIR forces, and (3) complete withdrawal of UNAMIR from Rwanda.[48]

The UNSC met on 21 April to discuss the secretary-general's report. It adopted the second option: the dramatic reduction of UNAMIR forces. The council had taken a contractual approach to the Rwanda mission and the resumption of fighting was treated as a breach of that contract, legitimizing UN withdrawal in the absence of a cease-fire agreement between the parties. Resolution 912 demanded the immediate cessation of hostilities between the FAR and the RPF and called for UNAMIR to broker and then monitor a cease-fire.[49] In essence, the Security Council commanded its peacekeepers to engage in diplomacy and report on civilian deaths but not to prevent them. Resolution 912 expressed UNSC regret over the violence and civilians' deaths but linked them directly to the resumption of civil war, demonstrating the power of the inadvertent frame.

Two days before the vote, Kenneth Roth, the executive director of Human Rights Watch, contacted the president of the Security Council, Colin Keating of New Zealand, and described the violence as genocide.[50] According to Scott Strauss, by the third week of April, "widespread and systematic violence against Tutsi civilians had become the norm in almost every area of the country that had not yet fallen to the rebels."[51] In contrast, the UNSC continued to describe the situation as a "tragedy." When it voted to reduce UNAMIR, the UNSC was preoccupied with catastrophic events that were unfolding in Bosnia, where the UN safe haven of Goražde was under attack. The thirty-five-minute meeting on the future of UNAMIR took place during a suspension of a nearly eight-hour meeting on Bosnia. Not wanting the Rwanda meeting to be a simple intermission from the debate on Bosnia, Ambassador Ibrahim Gambari of Nigeria insisted that time be made for member comment. Reportedly, most members had wished to quietly and quickly adopt the resolution, but Gambari insisted those who wished to make public statements explaining their vote be permitted to do so.[52] This was a crucial decision, which ultimately saved the mission. U.S. ambassador Madeleine Albright had entered the meeting prepared to vote to end UNAMIR. After listening to Gambari's remarks, she changed her mind. In an interview, she recounted rushing to a booth in the UN hallway from which she phoned Richard A. Clarke, the national security official at the White House in charge of peacekeeping, who repeated her instructions to vote for withdrawal of the mission. " 'I actually screamed into the phone,' she recalled years later. 'I said they're unacceptable. I want them changed. So they told me to chill out and calm down. But ultimately, they did send me instructions that allowed us to do a reinforcement of UNAMIR.' "[53] Only five members made public comments to justify their vote. Consequently, the formal record conceals, perhaps by design, the justifications for the decision. The language of Resolution 912, however, reflects the persistence of the inadvertent story.

Contestation Between Causal Stories

Despite the persistence of the inadvertent story, several nonpermanent members rejected it by the end of April. Instead, these members argued that the killing in Rwanda was systematic and aimed at all Tutsi. They argued that the UN must respond to civilian massacres and not just the renewed fighting between the FAR and RPF. According to council president Colin Keating, a coalition of nonpermanent members actively supported a strategy to preserve the UN presence in Rwanda in the hopes of providing some protection for civilians.[54] Going into the 21 April meeting, the permanent members and troop-contributing countries wanted to terminate the Rwanda mission. The Czech Republic, New Zealand, Nigeria, and Spain saw fostering agreement for troop reduction as a short-term strategy for maintaining a UN presence in Rwanda, however minimal, in the face of strong permanent member support for complete troop withdrawal. They had been deeply affected by independent information from nongovernmental organizations about the ethnic character of the killings. By 25 April, Oxfam International had estimated that up to a half million people had been murdered in massacres that were planned and systematic and Médecins sans Frontièrs lobbied council members, including Keating, to stop the genocide. According to Médecins sans Frontièrs, Hutu military and paramilitary forces were entering its hospitals and murdering Tutsi patients, doctors, and nurses based on prepared lists.[55] Even UNAMIR had begun using the term "genocide" in all its communications, though council members did not see these documents. Keating shared the NGO reports with the council during an informal meeting preceding the formal vote and reportedly stunned the council chamber into silence.[56] Using the expert reports and eyewitness testimony of the NGO community, the nonpermanent member coalition implemented a two-pronged strategy: maintain at least a minimal UN presence in Rwanda and then persuade the council to focus on the killings that were happening in the towns and villages, rather than the fighting between the belligerents.[57]

This strategy met with limited success on 30 April when Keating forced a compromise on the permanent members. He tabled a resolution that would have publicly shamed permanent members by forcing their veto in exchange for a presidential statement that borrowed language from the Genocide Convention.[58] The text of the presidential statement reflected the compromise. It demanded "an immediate cease-fire and cessation of hostilities between the interim Government of Rwanda and the Rwandese Patriotic Front" but also included the Genocide Convention language: "The Security Council condemns all these breaches of international humanitarian law in Rwanda, particularly those perpetrated against the civilian population, and recalls that persons who instigate or participate in such acts are individually responsible. In this context, the Security Council recalls that the killings of members of an ethnic group with the intention of destroying such a group in whole or in part constitutes a crime punishable under international law."[59] The original draft version of the presidential statement included the word "genocide," but the word was removed at the insistence of the UK and the U.S. and replaced with the word "crime."[60] A confidential cable from the U.S. mission to the UN to the State Department warned that if the UNSC acknowledged that genocide was occurring it may be forced to "take such action under the charter as they consider appropriate for the prevention and suppression of acts of genocide"—an action that the U.S. government wanted to avoid.[61] The inclusion of references to the Genocide Convention (reflecting the intentional story) alongside references to Resolution 912 (reflecting an inadvertent story) in a single document illustrates the disunity that had emerged over the character of the violence. This was a compromise document brokered between two factions: the majority including the permanent members, which told an inadvertent story about civil war, and the minority completely comprising nonpermanent members, which told an intentional story about genocide.

The first mention of the word "genocide" in the Security Council record occurred on 16 May 1994. During the debate accompanying the passage of Resolution 918, which expanded the troop strength of UNAMIR and imposed an arms embargo on both parties, council members alternately articulated inadvertent stories about civil war and intentional stories about genocide. Table 5.1 illustrates the emerging division in the council over the causal story. Nine Security Council members advanced the inadvertent story—in which the killing of civilians was the result of the civil war—including three permanent members (China, the UK, and the U.S.). According to the inadvertent story, both parties were responsible for the atrocities and the solution to the deaths of civilians was the establishment of a cease-fire. Reflecting the opinion of the secretary-general's report, the inadvertent story identified the resumption of the civil war as the cause of the massacres in Rwanda.[62] For example, China demanded that the "conflicting Rwandese parties should cease forthwith massacring each other and agree to an effective and lasting ceasefire."[63] The U.S. argued that the UN could not solve Rwanda's problems, and if the Rwandese were to solve their problems then "the killing—by all parties—must stop."[64] The UK called on both sides to stop the bloodshed in the areas under their control but admitted that many of the atrocities were occurring within the territory under the control of the government.[65] Rwanda reaffirmed the inadvertent story, arguing that the deaths were the result of long-standing interethnic rivalry between Hutus and Tutsis. Although the ambassador acknowledged the deaths of Tutsi civilians, he suggested that they resulted from of a spontaneous explosion of angry Hutus who had historically and repeatedly been repressed by Tutsi. The government characterized itself as a victim of an ethnically motivated attempt to rid the country of Hutus by the RPF and of external aggression from Uganda, capitalizing on the civil framework and shifting culpability to the RPF.[66] The story of spontaneous eruption was shared by the delegation from Pakistan, which characterized the situation in Rwanda as one of "chaos and mayhem."[67]

Despite the dominance of the inadvertent story, the intentional story began to gain support. Ambassador Keating described the violence in Rwanda as the result of "genocide" and questioned why resolution 918 did not call for the protection of civilians. Argentina described the massacres as systematic but failed to specifically name any perpetrators.[68] Spain also characterized the international humanitarian law violations in Rwanda as "systematic, generalized and manifest," citing reports from NGOs and the press.[69] Ambassador Karel Kovanda of the Czech Republic provided the clearest characterization of an intentional story: genocide was concurrent with, but distinct from, the resumption of the civil war:

> So we have some 200,000 Tutsi lives lost, out of a total population of 1 million—20 percent of all of Rwanda's Tutsis. Each of us can figure out how many lives such a percentage would represent in his own country for his own people. This situation is now being described as a humanitarian crisis as though it were a famine or perhaps a natural disaster. In the view of my delegation, the proper description is genocide. . . . Now, as is well known, a civil war has been raging in Rwanda as well since 1990. But even a civil war, however awful by itself, is no excuse—never mind justification—for genocide. And civil war or not, the hundreds of thousands of civilians who have fallen victim to the butchers were not at the frontlines but far in the hinterland with no visible connection to the RPF except their ethnic background. Hence the real innocence of those whom we all too automatically refer to as "innocent civilians."[70]

Kovanda articulated all the constituent elements of an intentional story: he described a systematic policy of killing and named it genocide and he also identified the perpetrators and victims:

> By whom? Who is it who has been committing these unspeakable atrocities? Certainly not the Rwandan people at large, Hutu or otherwise. These atrocities have been committed by the Presidential Guard created by President Habyarimana. They have been committed by elements of the Rwandese Government forces loyal to him. They have been committed by the militia, the Gendarmerie. They have been committed on orders of people close to President Habyarimana and at the instigation of the incendiary broadcasts of Radio Milles Collines.[71]

He attacked the logic of the inadvertent story, citing lack of evidence of RPF massacres: "All reports indicate that these atrocities have been committed by Hutu cutthroats—and seldom has this word been literally the right one—against their Tutsi neighbours. Now, there are those that would apportion blame 'evenly'; those who would argue that there must also have been Tutsi atrocities against Hutus in the past month. And indeed, human rights organizations have assiduously sought direct evidence of massacres in areas controlled by the largely Tutsi Rwandese Patriotic Front (RPF). So far, they have found very little such evidence."[72] Only four members of the Security Council (New Zealand, the Czech Republic, Spain, and Argentina) characterized the killing in Rwanda as intentional and only New Zealand and the Czech Republic identified the perpetrators. The remaining council members, including France and Russia, expressed concern about the massacres but did not advance any causal explanation for the violence. France indicated that the violence was simply "unleashed" and was sympathetic to the inadvertent story, fluctuating between apportioning blame to both parties and characterizing the atrocities as primordial.

Evidence of the disunity on the cause and character of the violence can be found in the text of Resolution 918. The preamble contains elements of the intentional story by reproducing the language of the genocide convention and warning that "killing members of an ethnic group with intention of destroying that group" is punishable under international law. Operative paragraph A contains elements of the inadvertent story and demands "all parties cease hostilities," linking the atrocities to both parties of the civil war. In addition the resolution established an arms embargo, under Chapter VII, on both sides; however, the authorization did not include the use of force to protection civilians or to stop the killing.[73] Disunity among members and the continuing dominance of the inadvertent story both were barriers to humanitarian intervention to stop the killing.

The Intentional Story Gains Permanent Member Support

By the beginning of June, the intentional story was gaining strength in the council. Only Rwanda, Oman, and Russia denied that genocide was occurring. The latter two articulated a complex story that identified complicated social, historical, and institutional factors as the cause of the violence. Oman characterized the conflict as the tragic result of "centuries of conflict" whereas Russia acknowledged that mass extermination had been deliberate but described the situation as "highly complex" and "rapidly changing."[74] Nonetheless, there was a notable shift from the inadvertent to the intentional story in the Security Council. From the very start of its involvement, the secretary-general had characterized the violence as both connected to and the result of the civil war; but in his report of 31 May 1994, Boutros-Ghali agreed that genocide was happening in Rwanda. He identified the perpetrators as "members of the Rwandan government forces, the Presidential Guard and the *Interahamwe* youth militia of the MRND party." This was an intentional story. Paragraph 36 of the report asserts, "The magnitude of the human calamity that has engulfed Rwanda might have been unimaginable but for its having transpired. On the basis of evidence that has emerged, there can be little doubt that it constitutes genocide, since there have been large-scale killings of communities and families belonging to a particular ethnic group."[75] During the 8 June meeting to discuss the report, France, the UK, and the U.S. publicly acknowledged that genocide was happening in Rwanda for the first time. Despite this admittance, however, their language betrayed continuing discomfort with the term "genocide." It had been a policy of the Clinton administration since late April for U.S. officials not to use the legal term "genocide" because the administration believed such usage could increase the legal and moral pressure on it to act.[76] The UK agreed that the secretary-general had concluded that the massacres in Rwanda amounted to genocide but did not state its own concurrence with the finding. The U.S. persisted in describing the events as "acts of genocide" rather than "genocide"—perhaps in an effort to force consistency with past statements or to avoid the perceived requirements of the Genocide Convention.[77]

Genocide is an intentional act by definition; yet members seemed reluctant to move beyond UNSC tradition of Chapter VI neutrality and publicly name its architects and perpetrators. Ambassador Kovanda of the Czech Republic noted the contradiction by saying that where crimes occur there are criminals. He urged the council to take decisive action, arguing that preventing and responding to genocide was a reason for the creation of the UN:

> I used the word "holocaust" a moment ago, and one does not use that word lightly. But today, as we commemorate the fiftieth anniversary of D-Day, we reflect upon the Second World War as a war directed against a regime which became anathema to the civilized world precisely because of its having unleashed a holocaust. The regime in Rwanda has been attempting to do something similar— with machetes instead of gas chambers; with the notorious *interahamwe*, comparable to the SS, with the *Mouvement Républicain*

National pour la Démocratie et le Développement and the *Comité Dém-
ocratique Républicain*, comparable to the Nazi party.[78]

As Table 5.1 indicates, most council members, including most permanent
members, now articulated an intentional story, though some continued to
advance alternative explanations. The intentional story was weakened, however, by continued disagreement on who the perpetrators and victims were
(France was contemplating the existence of a double genocide) and an unwillingness to publicly name them. Reflecting continued disagreement, Resolution 925 requested that both sides stop the slaughter and still sought the
end of the civil war. Resolution 925 authorized an expanded mandate for
UNAMIR and the deployment of additional battalions but the resolution
fell short of authorizing humanitarian intervention. The resolution passed
unanimously, but member states were unwilling to contribute the troops
and resources necessary to make it operational in practice. Nonetheless, the
UK voiced a sentiment that was common among members of the council:
"The Security Council has been required to handle many difficult issues in
the past few years, but none has exceeded in its horror and intractability
the situation in Rwanda. There could not have been and never has been
any argument about the fact that in the hackneyed phrase 'something must
be done'. But it has been far more difficult to identify what the 'something'
realistically should be and then to do it."[79] Council members finally agreed
that "something must be done about Rwanda" but most lacked the capacity
or political will to support the expanded UNAMIR II mission they had
authorized. France, a political and military ally of the perpetrator government, offered to do something—to launch an intervention to stem the humanitarian crisis and maintain an international presence until UNAMIR
could get up to force level. On 22 June with most of the genocide complete
and the RPF poised to defeat the FAR and take control of the country, the
council passed Resolution 929, authorizing member states to use all means
necessary under Chapter VII to bring peace and stability to Rwanda.

   Resolution 929 was proposed by France, which sought authorization for
a military operation in the southwest of the country. It was controversial
because it focused resources on a unilateral intervention by a member state
allied to the perpetrator government rather than reinforcing the UN mission already on the ground. The mission would largely address the humanitarian crisis caused by the mass movement of Hutus as the government
began losing to the RPF. The resolution sharply divided the Security Council

Table 5.1. Changes in Support for Causal Stories in Rwanda, 1993–1994

	Intentional Story	Inadvertent Story	Complex Story	Unarticulated
October 1993 (S/PV.3288)	None	Brazil Cape Verde **China** Djibouti **France** Morocco Pakistan **Russia** **UK** **U.S.**	None	Hungary Japan New Zealand Spain Venezuela
April 1994 (S/PV.3368)	None	Resolution 912	None	None
May 1994 (S/PV.3377)	Argentina Czech Republic New Zealand Spain	**China** Djibouti Nigeria Oman Pakistan **Russia** Rwanda **UK** **U.S.**	None	Brazil **France**
June 1994 (S/PV.3388)	Argentina Brazil Czech Republic Djibouti **France** New Zealand Spain **UK**	Rwanda	Oman **Russia**	**China** Nigeria Pakistan **U.S.**

yet passed with ten votes and not much enthusiasm. Even supporters like the U.S. admitted that French intervention was an "imperfect solution" but argued "we must be flexible enough to accept imperfect solutions when no perfect solutions are available to us."[80] Five states including Brazil, China, New Zealand, Nigeria, and Pakistan abstained from voting. Ambassador Jean Bernard Mérimée of France justified the French intervention as necessary to save lives given the delays in deployment of the enhanced UNAMIR: "The goal of the French initiative is exclusively humanitarian: the initiative is motivated by the plight of the people, in the face of which, we believe, the international community cannot and must not remain passive. It will not be a mission of our soldiers in Rwanda to interpose themselves between the warring parties, still less to influence in any way the military and political situation. Our objective is simple: to rescue endangered civilians and put an end to the massacres, and to do so in an impartial manner."[81] Skeptics of its humanitarian motives questioned French unwillingness to devote resources to the UNAMIR mission and expressed concerns about the inefficiency of having two parallel missions with different mandates, enforcement authority, levels of resources, and a distinct chain of command. Brazil, New Zealand, and Nigeria worried that the French intervention would discourage and deflect support from UNAMIR, which was best positioned to intervene and had been denied the Chapter VII enforcement authority granted to the French. China preferred using a UN framework and Pakistan declined to publicly record a justification for its abstention.[82] Ambassador Keating of New Zealand suggested that France "redirect its energy, enthusiasm and resources" to supporting UNAMIR, which he described as the "operation that we believe would be effectively able to curtail the genocide."[83] He continued, "If that energy, enthusiasm and money were put at the disposal of the United Nations, we have no doubt that the delays that UNAMIR is currently facing would disappear overnight."[84] This uneasiness about the proposed French intervention was shared by UNAMIR's force commander, Lieutenant General Dallaire, and by one of the warring parties—the RPF. Both believed that the real motive for French intervention was to prevent the RPF from taking control of the whole country and to preserve the territory and legitimacy of the Rwandan government.[85] Even humanitarian organizations and human rights NGOs on the ground opposed French intervention, arguing that it would not meet its humanitarian objective and would likely worsen the situation.[86] Operation Turquoise did in fact have effects inconsistent with its stated motive, although it is estimated to have

saved between 10,000 and 17,000 lives.[87] The Chapter VI UNAMIR force
was placed between the Chapter VII French force and one of the belligerents,
and the French military zone provided protection for fleeing *genocidaires*
who were neither arrested nor disarmed.[88] The amount of firepower, types
of vehicles, and number of troops brought by the French indicated that the
mission had been planned as a fighting mission and not a humanitarian
one, hindering its ability to rescue endangered Tutsis.[89] In one particularly
egregious incident Tutsi survivors who had been hiding in Bisesero (Kibuye
province) revealed themselves to French soldiers in the belief that they
would be saved. Lacking permission for such an operation and unprepared
to transport the Tutsi survivors, the French soldiers left. When they returned
three days later, the surviving Tutsis had been massacred.[90]

Disunity among council members over the nature of conflict prevented
UNAMIR from undertaking a humanitarian intervention when it was
needed most—during the genocide. By passing Resolution 929 the council
authorized members to "use all necessary means" under Chapter VII of the
Charter, but only after much of the genocide was complete, the war was
nearly over, and the Rwandan government was in exile. The controversial
resolution that gave rise to the French Operation Turquoise was supported
by the extremist government and objected to by the RPF. When the council
met again on 1 July 1994, it adopted the intentional story, agreeing that
genocide had occurred in Rwanda and authorizing an independent commission of experts to document the atrocities. Four months later on 8 November the council established the International Criminal Tribunal for
Rwanda to prosecute the perpetrators.

The Powerful Effect of Causal Narratives About Sovereignty and Human Rights

The stories that Security Council members tell about the cause and character of conflict have significant policy effects because problem definition is
at the heart of policymaking. Defining the conflict as a civil war with multiple parties or genocide with a single perpetrator has significant policy implications for the behavior required to address the problem of the violence.
As previous chapters make clear, inadvertent stories prompt policies of palliation and observation whereas intentional stories prompt policies of interdiction and punishment. Whether these stories are adopted sincerely or

strategically, the frame a story creates can continue to shape decision making even when the facts no longer fit the frame. In her memoirs, Madeleine Albright reflects that looking back at the meeting records of early April 1994, she is struck by the relative lack of information and attention given to the killing of Rwandan civilians as opposed to the hostilities between Hutu and Tutsi militias. The initial framing of the situation as a civil war shaped how she interpreted subsequent information. She writes, "When the violence exploded, we tried to fit the situation in Rwanda into the framework we had created. . . . We tried to stay neutral and condemned the violence on all sides."[91] Albright explains that the "stickiness" of the frame shaped her decision making; the stories that were told in the council mattered. Michael Barnett argues that the social optics that council members used to bring the conflict into focus was based on a specific UN culture that had "a particular way of understanding both the nature of conflict in ethnically divided societies and the mechanisms that would facilitate the transition from civil war to civil society. Rwanda fit comfortably in that template, in part because the template shaped how the UN came to know about Rwanda."[92] After council members adopted a mandate to prevent a return to civil war, they were predisposed to see the return of civil war and not to see genocide.[93]

The Rwanda case shows not only that stories are powerful but that the prominence of their supporters and their resonance with independent expertise is also significant. It matters who the supporters of any given causal story are. Without the support of a majority of permanent members, supporters of the intentional story were unable to act. The interpretation of events advanced by permanent members was persuasive because they have better access to information due to sophisticated technology, superior intelligence-gathering practices, and the ability to host an embassy in every part of the world. The effect, according to Samantha Power, was that the U.S. (and other permanent members) deployed information strategically—in ways consistent with their policy interests.[94] Only after nonpermanent members gained access to highly reputable independent information did they challenge the inadvertent story. Independent information provided by international human rights organizations and other NGOs shifted the council debate. NGO documentation and reporting of atrocities combined with their lobbying of nonpermanent members made the inadvertent explanation less tenable. Eventually the facts on the ground including witness testimony, forensic evidence, and graphic photographic and television imagery of civilian victims made it impossible to deny that the killings were distinct from the civil war and that the primary victims were from a single ethnic group.

Council members articulated a coherent story about state sovereignty throughout the conflict, but that story was not conducive to humanitarian intervention: Rwanda was a sovereign state member of the UN and the Habyarimana government was the legitimate sovereign authority. Because the internationally recognized regime was a party to the conflict and indeed the primary perpetrator, the protection of human rights norms and sovereignty and nonintervention norms were in direct conflict, which foreclosed the possibility of more aggressive military force. In 1994, sovereignty norms were more strongly held than human rights norms by most council members. Despite evidence of widespread and systematic slaughter by government agents, the representative of the perpetrator government was permitted to retain his position as a nonpermanent member of the UNSC. This suggests that members of the council valued the norms of diplomatic procedure and sovereignty more than the value of condemning genocide. Human Rights Watch criticized the council for putting "decorum before the obligation to speak as the conscience of the international community."[95] It is telling that only a single state—New Zealand—broke with diplomatic protocol to suggest that the Rwandan ambassador lacked legitimate authority in the council. During its 16 May meeting, the Rwandan ambassador justified the deaths of Tutsi civilians as provoked by previous anti-Hutu behavior.[96] In anger, Ambassador Colin Keating appealed to a popular conception of sovereignty rather than a Westphalian one when he challenged the sovereign authority of the Rwandan ambassador and the veracity of his statement: "In the view of my delegation the first speaker in our debate should not have spoken. I say this for two reasons. First, in the view of my delegation he does not represent a State. He has no legitimacy and is merely the mouthpiece of a faction. He should not have been seated in a privileged position at this table. Second, he has, in the view of my delegation, given us a shameful distortion of the truth."[97] Other nonpermanent members including Argentina, the Czech Republic, and Spain similarly departed from diplomatic protocol by directly criticizing the remarks of the Rwandan ambassador but stopped short of disputing his authority to be present.[98] If it is difficult for members to deny a party to a conflict a coveted voting seat on the council, it is considerably more difficult to build the consensus necessary to authorize the use of force against another sovereign member, even when that state is a perpetrator of genocide. To do so would privilege human rights norms relative to sovereignty norms. Yet to this date, humanitarian intervention had only been possible when human rights norms and sovereignty norms were discursively constructed to be complementary, and in Rwanda they were not.

Interests and Norms in the Security Council

The UN failure to stop genocide in Rwanda, even in the face of widespread evidence of its occurrence, is often cited as proof that power politics and national interests trump normative considerations like human rights at the UN. According to this view, human rights norms and humanitarian values merely mask national interests and humanitarian intervention happens when it coincides with those interests and not as a principle-motivated response to humanitarian tragedy. Yet a careful review of the documentary record draws a more complicated picture: interests and norms both shaped council decision making and shaped each other in the process.

The Role of Interests

France perceived Rwanda to be on the front lines of its continuing cultural, political, and economic competition with Anglo-Saxon interests in Africa.[99] Habyarimana was an important ally in France's pursuit of *francophonie*— French interests in Central Africa that were both strategic and sentimental.[100] Africa was a key source of strategic raw materials and a captive market for French manufactured goods and central to its policy of *rayonnement*— the projection of French culture and values overseas.[101] To maintain influence, the French government pursued a policy of close personal relationships between the French president and African heads of state and political and military decisions regarding Africa were made directly from the president's office. France's *accord de coopération* with Rwanda included the training of troops, the provision of military advisors, and financial assistance. France intervened on behalf of the FAR during the civil war on the grounds that it was protecting its ally against aggression by an army that the French argued was supported, equipped, and trained by Uganda. During the Arusha negotiations, French officials reportedly threatened RPF leaders with massacres if they did not stop the fighting; and during Operation Turquoise, the colonel in charge of the French humanitarian zone publicly declared that he would personally fight the RPF if they came near the zone, but he would not disarm the FAR or militias that sought refuge there.[102] It has also been alleged that French military personnel fought alongside the FAR against the RPF during the civil war and that they had knowledge as early as 1990 about the potential for Hutu extermination of Tutsi.[103] Certainly French involvement was spurred by French interests but also French norms and values like francophonie and rayonnment shaped those interests. These norms were initially privileged above international human rights norms until the contradiction between professed French values of human rights and the rule of law and its actual behavior threatened France's reputation and standing at home and abroad.

In contrast, lack of national interests in Rwanda and powerful domestic political interests in minimizing UN peacekeeping operations shaped U.S. decision making. The Clinton administration was under considerable pressure from congressional critics of the UN to diminish U.S. participation in peacekeeping operations, particularly after the deaths of U.S. soldiers in Somalia. President Clinton signed Presidential Directive 25, which limited U.S. involvement in peacekeeping operations in the absence of a vital national interest on 3 May 1994. The considerations captured in the directive heavily influenced the Rwanda policy that was being developed at the same time.[104] A lack of civil society pressure in support of humanitarian intervention meant that U.S. government inaction carried no penalty. There was no domestic political cost for ignoring the genocide and elected officials did not pay a political price for inaction.[105]

The important role that national interests played in shaping the response of influential council members is well documented. France pursued its national interests by protecting its ally and its zone of francophone influence while the United States was preoccupied with minimizing mission costs and peacekeeping commitments because of domestic policy pressure. Belgium sought to disband all of UNAMIR in an effort to save face after withdrawing its own forces, and the risk-averse Secretariat manipulated information and promoted policies that prioritized the interests and health of peacekeeping rather than Rwandan lives.[106] Yet there is also evidence that human rights norms shaped council member decision making.

The Role of Human Rights Norms

France, the genocide government's strongest ally, bowed to the pull of human rights norms when it decided to cosponsor a resolution creating an

Independent Commission of Experts to investigate human rights violations and violations of international humanitarian law in Rwanda. France defended the need for a clear accounting of crimes in Rwanda: "Systematic violations of human rights and, indeed, genocide, have been committed in Rwanda. These acts arouse the indignation of the entire world, and it would be intolerable if those who have committed them remain unpunished."[107] By July, because of domestic and international pressure caused by the perceived gaps between its professed values and its behavior in Rwanda, it was more important for France to be seen as a protector of human rights norms than for it to pursue its national interest in protecting its Rwandan allies. In total, eight states cosponsored Resolution 935 establishing the Independent Commission to study human rights violations, including Argentina, the Czech Republic, France, New Zealand, Spain, the UK, and the U.S. The council passed it unanimously. Combined, members cited five international human rights treaties and the entire body of international humanitarian law as justification for its passage.[108] In November, the U.S. and New Zealand cosponsored a resolution creating an international criminal tribunal to prosecute individuals guilty of international human rights and humanitarian law violations. Argentina, France, the Russian Federation, Spain, and the UK endorsed the resolution. The International Criminal Tribunal for Rwanda was justified as necessary because "the gravity of the human rights violations committed in Rwanda extended far beyond that country," concerning the international community as a whole.[109] The tribunal was intended to send "a clear message that the international community is not prepared to leave unpunished the grave crimes committed in Rwanda" including violations of the fundamental rules of war, international human rights standards, and the Genocide Convention.[110] Even China, which abstained, declared publicly its condemnation of violations of international humanitarian law and genocide, publicly underscoring council consensus on the importance of humanitarian values to Security Council decision making in the mid-1990s.

Principled actors like Karel Kovanda of the Czech Republic and Colin Keating of New Zealand publicly defended human rights, and fought hard against permanent member resistance to maintain a UN presence in Rwanda. These principled actors lacked material power but held considerable moral authority. They also lacked traditional national and strategic interests in Rwanda but shared a view of common humanity and a commitment to international human rights norms that shaped their interests, defining the protection of Rwandan civilians as central to their respective national security policy. These members, along with several other nonpermanent members, sought independent and expert information on the crisis, genuinely struggled to understand what was happening on the ground, and adopted stories that described the situation as they perceived it. Their actions demonstrated that elected members are not passive recipients of norms defined by great powers and that causal stories do not flow in a single direction.

Similarly, UNAMIR forces headed by Lieutenant General Roméo Dallaire sought to provide whatever means of protection to Rwandan civilians they could and fought the Secretariat and their home governments alike to be able to defend human rights at great personal risk. Permanent members were publicly shamed and stridently criticized for failing to stop the killing and falling short of the normative expectations of international society. Despite expressed regret for failing to label the killing genocide, the Clinton administration argued that its concern with humanitarian norms explains its behavior. It acted to nurture the emerging practice of humanitarian intervention at a crucial moment when U.S. leadership in the UN was under duress and the future of UN peacekeeping was under threat: "They believed that the UN had more to lose by sending reinforcements and failing than by allowing the killings to proceed. Their chief priority, after the evacuation of the Americans, was looking after UN peacekeepers on the grounds that it would ensure a future for humanitarian intervention. In other words, Dallaire's peacekeeping mission in Rwanda had to be destroyed so that peacekeeping might be saved for use elsewhere."[111] Despite its unwillingness to engage in humanitarian intervention in Rwanda, the council passed resolutions condemning genocide, authorizing an Independent Commission of Experts to determine culpability for human rights violations, and creating the International Criminal Tribunal for Rwanda to punish the architects and perpetrators of genocide. Security Council decision making was more complicated than a simple contest between norms and interests; it actually continually occurred at the intersection between them.

Certainly the Rwanda case raises important questions about the authenticity of humanitarian justifications and appeals to human rights. In June 1994 the representative from Djibouti accused the UNSC with being so concerned with debating whether or not genocide was happening that it neglected searching for solutions to stopping the massacres. He also accused his fellow members of strategically hiding behind human rights discourse in order to appear to be doing something in order to satisfy their domestic audiences but deliberately failing to end the genocide.[112] French historian Gérard Prunier criticized Operation Turquoise, writing, "French politicians were floundering desperately in the Rwandese mire, trying to glorify the Turquoise intervention in the hope of washing off any genocidal bloodspots in the baptismal waters of 'humanitarian' action."[113] General Dallaire was similarly cynical, arguing that precious resources were wasted in the refugee camps in Goma (where the perpetrators diverted humanitarian resources from needy populations), "fueling a charade of political conscience-cleansing by the developed states in deference to the media and their con-stituencies."[114] Their skepticism is warranted; yet these very criticisms dem-onstrate the increasing influence of human rights norms on the members of the UNSC, who are compelled to appeal to human rights norms to justify their behavior whether they sincerely value them or not.

Conclusions

When the UNSC first authorized a peacekeeping operation for Rwanda in late 1993 the credibility of the United Nations was under threat, the safety of peacekeeping forces in other parts of the world was severely compro-mised, and the financial burden of ongoing peacekeeping operations was excessive. The council was only a reluctant partner in the peace process and agreed to participate in Rwanda's transition because it conceptualized the conflict as a traditional civil war, which had ended after both parties com-mitted to a peace agreement. By April 1994, the reality was much different. Rwanda's president had been assassinated, Hutu political opposition lead-ers and Tutsi civilians were being massacred in a fast-moving genocide under the direction of hard-liners in Habyarimana's government, and the RPF had broken the cease-fire. Both civil war and genocide were ongoing. Despite a rapidly evolving situation on the ground, the UNSC continued to articulate an inadvertent story that characterized the conflict as a civil war in which civilian casualties were regrettable but inevitable and both parties were culpable. The inadvertent story had powerful proponents, including all five permanent members, which lent credibility to the story. They also had a monopoly on information about the crisis, which they said at the time confirmed the inadvertent narrative. Unity around the inadvertent story began to break down after a small group of nonpermanent members began consulting with international NGOs who collected compelling evidence of the organized and systematic nature of massacres in areas under government control. They began articulating an alternative story—an intentional story about genocide—but were unable to persuade the more powerful members of the council to adopt it. The intentional story succeeded in displacing the inadvertent story in June 1994 because the latter was no longer tenable given the widespread dissemination of expert evidence, witness testimony, and photographic and forensic evidence detailing the government-directed massacre of Tutsis. The introduction of the language of the Genocide Convention into council resolutions and presidential statements also discursively transformed the decision-making environment. It became unsustainable for Western states that professed a normative commitment to the rule of law and international human rights to continue to articulate the inadvertent story because doing so exposed the gap between their professed values and actual behavior.

The divided UNSC response to Rwanda demonstrates that while some states had internalized human rights norms and identified their promotion with their national and international interests, there are limits to the financial and human costs that intervening states are willing to incur in order to protect noncitizens. In early 1994, during the height of the Rwandan genocide, the normative pull of human rights was insufficiently developed or internalized by council members to overcome the power of competing normative values like sovereignty, nonintervention, and the pursuit of national interests. One of the lessons of Rwanda is that most members are unwilling to incur the high economic and human costs associated with humanitarian intervention in the absence of strategic or national interests, particularly given the high costs the UN was enduring elsewhere. The Rwanda case shows that norms matter and shape council member behavior, but multiple norms can make competing claims on members simultaneously. In Rwanda, the Rwandan government was the principal perpetrator of human rights violations against its own people; thus the promotion of human rights would have directly challenged Rwanda's sovereign authority. Faced with competing normative demands—to promote human rights and to preserve state sovereignty—the Security Council initially could not build consensus on an appropriate response to mass killing. Even after members believed that the killings were systematic and ethnically based, they decided against humanitarian intervention and failed to interrupt the slaughter. In Somalia, the Security Council had justified its military intervention based on the absence of state authority. In Bosnia, the council intervened in a case of contested state sovereignty only after the Bosnian Muslim government in Sarajevo had been discursively constructed as the legitimate state authority and the victim rather than the perpetrator of mass atrocities. In both these cases, application of human rights norm reinforced existing norms about state sovereignty while in Rwanda, human rights norms challenged them. It is significantly more difficult to build the consensus necessary to authorize the use of force against a sovereign state member of the United Nations, even when that state is a perpetrator of genocide. For this reason, Rwanda represented a fundamentally different type of conflict than the previous cases. To undertake the emerging practice of humanitarian intervention in Rwanda, even during the genocide, was in direct contradiction of sovereignty and nonintervention norms. It was significantly more difficult to challenge state sovereignty by confronting a perpetrator state than to assist a state being victimized.

The normative backlash against council members representing democratic states for failing to stop the genocide was immense—Western democratic states had failed to live up to the normative expectations of international society. International commitment to the rule of law and international human rights and humanitarian norms prompted Security Council resolutions creating an independent commission of inquiry and an international tribunal to investigate and prosecute the perpetrators. The failure in Rwanda ultimately contributed to faster humanitarian intervention in Kosovo by NATO without UN authorization. UNSC failure to stop mass atrocity in both Rwanda and Kosovo eventually transformed the meaning of sovereignty at the UN from sovereignty as unchecked authority to sovereignty as responsibility (see Chapter 6). Security Council decision making happens at the intersection of competing norms as well as at the intersection of norms and interests. It is the articulation of these normative values and interests through stories about causality and sovereignty that open and foreclose the possibility of humanitarian intervention in response to mass atrocity and humanitarian crisis.

International Law, Human Rights, and State Sovereignty: The Security Council Response to Killings in Kosovo

The decade of the 1990s ended as it began for the United Nations Security Council, with systematic human rights violations in the territory of the former Yugoslavia threatening to destabilize the entire Balkan region. The war in Bosnia in the first half of the 1990s had its start in Kosovo, a province of Serbia that lost its constitutional autonomy to growing Serbian nationalism in 1989, which set off federation-wide fears of a "Greater Serbia Project"—a nationalist elite attempt to exert Serbian control over other nations and territories. By 1998, Kosovo's ethnic Albanians and Serb authorities were engaged in a vicious cycle of violence and reprisal that included kidnapping, unlawful detentions, and summary executions. The international human rights organization Human Rights Watch accused the Yugoslav government, and particularly Serbian authorities, of indiscriminately attacking civilian groups and targeting individuals not involved in the fighting.[1] The systematic violation of human rights and humanitarian law in Kosovo in 1998 and 1999 looked dangerously similar to the ethnic cleansing that had occurred in Bosnia between 1992 and 1995. Civilians in Kosovo were at risk along with the fragile Balkan peace agreement brokered in Dayton in 1995. Unlike the beginning of the 1990s, however, the UNSC had precedents of humanitarian intervention to draw on during its deliberations about how to respond to the increasing violence. It also had nearly a decade of experience dealing with the leadership in Belgrade whom it previously identified as culpable for the systematic violations of human rights in Bosnia. What made the case of Kosovo different from Bosnia, and similar to Rwanda, was that this debate was about how to respond to systematic human rights violations perpetrated by a sovereign state against civilians within its territory. Indeed, when faced with the similar situation in Rwanda, the council chose not to intervene. While council action in Somalia and Bosnia created precedents for humanitarian intervention, there was no precedent for a humanitarian intervention against a sovereign state for the treatment of its own citizens. Serbia was accused of systematically violating the human rights of its ethnic Albanian citizens but its sovereignty over the territory of Kosovo was not contested.

In the case of Kosovo, council members disagreed on the fundamental character of the conflict—whether it was systematic ethnic cleansing, a civil war, or a legitimate police action responding to unruly domestic elements. Permanent members held irreconcilable positions that evolved very little over time. China and the Russian Federation rejected the intentional story about Serbian ethnic cleansing of ethnic Albanians articulated by France, the United Kingdom, and the United States. Instead, they defended what they argued was a legitimate state right to defend itself against internal threats to its rule. France, the UK, and the U.S. denied that sovereignty gave states the right to terrorize their own populations. Disunity among permanent members on the rights of sovereignty, the character of the violence, and the appropriate response prevented the UNSC from undertaking humanitarian intervention. Disunity in the council, however, did not prevent an eventual humanitarian intervention by a regional organization without UN authorization. Five of the fifteen members serving on the council in 1999 were also members of the North Atlantic Treaty Organization, the military alliance of states in North America and Europe designed to secure peace and to spread liberal democratic values throughout Europe. In March 1999, in the face of a renewed Serbian offensive against its ethnic Albanian population, NATO launched a humanitarian intervention to stop what it deemed ethnic cleansing.

The use of military force against a sovereign state without Security Council authorization provoked a major political crisis at the UN. NATO humanitarian intervention threatened the legitimacy and authority of the UNSC and severely damaged relations among its permanent members. It also provoked questions about the future role of the council, the UN's relationship to regional organizations, and both the legality and legitimacy of the use of force without UN authorization, even in defense of human rights. The controversy that ensued laid bare the stark divisions in international society about the relationship among human rights, state sovereignty, and international security. At stake was nothing less than determining the limits of both state authority and state control over population and territory. In an era of increasing state commitment to human rights principles, where did the rights of the state and its duties to its population begin and end? The council also debated which institution or institutions had primary responsibility for the maintenance of international peace and security and the relevance of human rights norms to the fulfillment of that responsibility. The divergent UNSC and NATO responses to Kosovo spurred the international debate about the legitimacy of the practice of humanitarian intervention, fundamentally strained relations among great powers, threatened the workings of the Security Council, and provided skeptics of humanitarian intervention with an example of its illegal use.

During this same period, the UNSC responded differently to violence in Sierra Leone. In Sierra Leone, rebel forces were fighting against a democratically elected government and committing grave atrocities against the civilian population and particularly children. There the council authorized UN personnel to use any necessary means to protect the civilian population under its care, paving the way for an eventual humanitarian intervention by the UK that was both legal and legitimate. Comparing the council response to these conflicts underscores the importance of causal stories, stories about sovereign authority, and human rights norms to UNSC humanitarian intervention decisions.

Background to the Kosovo Conflict

Kosovo was an autonomous region within the Republic of Serbia when the Socialist Federal Republic of Yugoslavia dissolved in 1991. In large part, it was the treatment of the ethnic Albanian population there and the unconstitutional revocation of the province's autonomy by Serbia in March 1989 that heightened ethnic nationalism in Yugoslavia, which caused the Republics of Slovenia, Croatia, Bosnia-Herzegovina, and Macedonia to seek independence between 1991 and 1992. Serbia fought conflicts with Slovenia (1991) and Croatia (1991–93) and in the territory of Bosnia (1992–95) while Macedonia gained its independence peacefully in 1991. The sole remaining republics—Serbia and Montenegro—formed the Federal Republic of Yugoslavia (FRY) in 1992 and sought unsuccessfully to become the legal successor state of Yugoslavia.[2] Before becoming President of the federal republic in 1997, Slobodan Milošević, an ambitious member of the post-Communist political elite, was the president of the Republic of Serbia (1989–1997). Milošević rose to political power based on an ethnonationalist platform of taking back Kosovo, the symbolic heart of Serbia, from Kosovo's ethnic Albanians.

The territorial region of Kosovo is central to the Serbian mythology of nationhood. In 1399 Serbian forces were defeated by the Ottoman Empire at the Battle of Kosovo. The mythology and symbolism of this defeat was central to the emergence of Serbian national consciousness. Kosovo is also the seat of the Serbian Orthodox Church, making the province an important part of religious culture and political and social identity for Serbs.[3] By the 1980s, the vast majority of the province's two million inhabitants were ethnic Albanians with only a small minority of Serbs and even fewer Roma and Turks residing there. Though located geographically inside the Republic of Serbia, Kosovo was granted status as an autonomous province within the federal structure of the Yugoslav state by the 1974 constitution. This autonomous status meant that Kosovo enjoyed direct representation in the main Yugoslav legislative bodies, had its own constitution, and was granted a representative in the Presidency of Yugoslavia. Kosovo had a provincial assembly and maintained autonomous control over police, social and economic policy, and education policy.[4] The key difference between the republics and autonomous provinces was that only the former had a right of secession and were considered bearers of Yugoslav sovereignty. Albanians had been classified by the Yugoslav state as a nationality and not a nation, and only nations were granted republic status.[5] While ethnic Albanians were displeased with what they viewed as second-class status in the federation, it was the revocation of their political autonomy by Serbia in 1989 and the refusal to reinstate it that became the root of the 1998–99 Kosovo war.

In a series of political moves between 1988 and 1989, the Serbian government began to severely restrict Kosovo's governing powers. In March 1989 Serbian authorities revoked Kosovo's autonomy and dissolved its provincial assembly. The Serbian government purged ethnic Albanians from positions of authority and installed a system of ethnic apartheid.[6] The systematic repression of ethnic Albanians in Kosovo garnered little international attention, particularly after violent conflicts characterized by ethnic cleansing began occurring in other republics, with one notable exception.

On Christmas Day in 1992, then U.S. president George H. W. Bush warned President Milošević in a letter that "in the event of a conflict in Kosovo caused by Serbian action, the United States will be prepared to employ military force against the Serbians in Kosovo and in Serbia proper."[7] In January 1993 the newly elected U.S. president, Bill Clinton, repeated this "Christmas warning." The U.S. would consider a war in Kosovo a direct threat to its national interests because it would directly threaten its allies Albania, Greece, and Turkey, and the U.S. would use force to stop it.[8]

The ethnic Albanian community in Kosovo banded together to protest their loss of autonomy and demand its restoration. Massive, nonviolent marches, boycotts, and hunger strikes erupted throughout the province. Dr. Ibrahim Rugova, an outspoken intellectual and professor of Albanian literature, was elected president of the Democratic League of Kosova (LDK),[9] the first political party in Kosovo to directly challenge the ruling Communist regime. Under his leadership, the Kosovar Albanians pursued a campaign of nonviolence, deliberately fashioned in the spirit of Mahatma Gandhi and Martin Luther King. In September 1990 the Albanian members of the dissolved assembly adopted a new constitution and created "underground" institutions of government.[10] A year later, 87 percent of Kosovo's population participated in a referendum on independence. Of these voters, 99.7 percent voted in favor of declaring Kosovo a sovereign and independent "Republic of Kosova."[11] In May 1992, Rugova was elected president of the new shadow government.

The Kosovars' pursuit of nonviolent struggle in the context of the Balkan wars won international admiration but little international political support. By 1995 many Kosovars were growing weary with a nonviolent struggle that had neither garnered international assistance nor regained their freedom. The Kosovars were bitterly disappointed when their leaders were not invited to participate in the Dayton peace conference on the Balkans in 1995. The "Kosovo question" was left off the agenda out of fear that it would preclude Serb participation and thus a peace deal for Bosnia. Rugova and his nonviolent movement were severely discredited within Kosovo by their failure to gain international support to end Serb repression of the Kosovo Albanians, and Dayton became a turning point for the Kosovars. With the status of Kosovo left unresolved, many of Kosovo's Albanians abandoned the decade long nonviolent struggle. The lesson seemed to be that the international community would intervene only in response to the use of military force.[12]

Shortly after Dayton, an Albanian insurgency movement began to operate openly in Kosovo—the Ushtria Çlirimtare e Kosovës or Kosovo Liberation Army (KLA). Its ethnic Albanian members aimed to spark a violent
revolution in Kosovo by launching a guerilla campaign against Serb authorities.[13] In April 1996, the KLA launched its first guerilla attacks against Serbian police stations in various locations throughout Kosovo. The KLA
launched thirty-one attacks in 1996, fifty-five in 1997, and sixty-six in January and February 1998 alone.[14] What started as a relatively low-level conflict
with a small number of deaths escalated as it provoked severe retaliatory
measures from Serbian authorities. The Serbian police and military response to KLA attacks was excessive and often included reprisals against
ethnic Albanian civilians living in the surrounding areas. The Serbian government justified its military action as the legitimate response of a sovereign
state to domestic terrorism.

In early March 1998, Serbian police and special paramilitary units from
the Ministry of the Interior surrounded the Drenica region in central Kosovo,
known as a stronghold of the KLA. They attacked three villages (Likoshan,
Çirez, and Prekaz I Poshtëm) with heavy artillery in reprisal for the killing of
four policemen by the KLA ten days earlier. In one village, fifty-one ethnic
Albanians were killed including twenty-five women and small children, most
from a single family associated with the KLA movement. A total of eighty-
three people were killed.[15] The police assault "unleashed anger and revulsion"
among ethnic Albanians who abandoned the nonviolent movement of
Ibrahim Rugova in large numbers and swelled the ranks of the KLA.[16] The
Serbian police action in Drenica escalated the conflict and proved to be the
single most powerful recruiting tool of the KLA, triggering an escalating cycle
of violence between the rebels and the authorities.[17] The number of KLA
attacks against police escalated after March, bringing the total for 1998 to
1,470 compared to the 66 attacks of the year before.[18] President Milošević
also escalated his response by ordering military attacks against ethnic Albanian villages, which included indiscriminate shelling, summary executions,
the razing of homes, and rape.[19] The attack against Drenica provoked international outrage, further internationalizing the conflict. At an emergency meeting of the Contact Group in London, an informal grouping of countries with
an interest in the Balkans, U.S. secretary of state Madeleine Albright compared the Serbian actions in Kosovo to ethnic cleansing in Bosnia, saying,
"We are not going to stand by and watch the Serb authorities do in Kosovo
what they can no longer get away with doing in Bosnia."[20]

The UN, Causal Stories, and the International Response to the Kosovo Conflict

The situation in Kosovo made it onto the UNSC agenda in March 1998. Deliberations were characterized by fundamental disagreement between permanent members about the character of the violence, whether it warranted international attention at all, and the appropriate council response. Members articulated two causal stories. The intentional story described the violence as a deliberate campaign of ethnic cleansing targeted against ethnic Albanian civilians and directed by the Yugoslav and Serbian authorities. The inadvertent story took two forms. The first characterized the violence as a civil war in which two parties—the Yugoslav and Serbian authorities and the KLA—were responsible for a cycle of violence and reprisal. The second variation identified both parties as responsible for violence but legitimized the use of force by the state against an internal, domestic, and illegitimate challenge to its rule. Proponents argued that while the use of force by state authorities might be excessive, it was justified according to the norm of state sovereignty. Council debates became as much about the legitimacy of the use of force and the conditions for its use as they were about the specific situation of Kosovo.

On 31 March 1998, the council passed Resolution 1160 imposing an arms embargo on the entire territory of the Federal Republic of Yugoslavia. The resolution reflected an inadvertent story—it condemned both the excessive use of force by Serbian police against civilians and acts of terrorism by the KLA. Resolution 1160 reaffirmed the sovereignty and territorial integrity of the federal republic but demanded immediate compliance with a set of UNSC conditions including the initiation of dialogue on Kosovo with the participation of outside representatives, the withdrawal of special police forces from Kosovo, and the acceptance of a monitoring mission of the Organization for Security Cooperation in Europe (OSCE).[21] Resolution 1160 was well supported, passing with thirteen votes but with two permanent member abstentions—China and Russia. Divisions among members quickly emerged on two points: whether the situation warranted council attention at all, and the character of the conflict. France, the UK, the U.S., and most of the elected members argued that the situation in Kosovo was a threat to regional and international peace and security. Costa Rica and Sweden argued that the UN had a duty to respond based on the human rights violations alone. In fact, Costa Rica argued that the violation of fundamental rights in Kosovo was so serious that it constituted, in itself, a threat to international peace and security and demanded the application of the full powers of the UNSC under Chapter VII, regardless of cross-border impact.[22] Russia and China argued that the events in Kosovo were an internal matter and should be solved "on the basis of the principle of respect for the sovereignty and territorial integrity of the Federal Republic of Yugoslavia."[23] The federal republic defended its actions as legitimate state behavior: "It is the right of every state to defend itself from this evil, to protect its territorial integrity, public peace and order and the safety of its citizens. This right is not denied anywhere in the world and it cannot be denied to Serbia and the Federal Republic of Yugoslavia."[24] Germany, host to three hundred thousand ethnic Albanian refugees, was skeptical since this argument also had been used to justify the Bosnian war.[25] According to most members, the historical precedent of ethnic cleansing in Bosnia by the Serbs and the continuing fragile peace process were sufficient justification for labeling Kosovo a threat to international peace and security.[26]

Members of the council also were divided on their conceptualization of the conflict. Initially, most members characterized the conflict as a civil war in which both sides were responsible for the violence—the Serb authorities for excessive use of force and the KLA for acts of terrorism. China and Russia, however, argued that the state party had a legitimate right to use military force. Russia admitted that the Serbian police response had been excessive but argued that the police units were fighting terrorism and the "manifestation of extremism."[27] Bosnia, Croatia, and Slovenia spoke out against what they described as the manipulation of the term "terrorism" for "reasons of political convenience" and warned that state terrorism was the most dangerous of its manifestations.[28] Slovenia urged other members of the council to remember the lessons of Bosnia and that "there are forms of struggle that, albeit undesirable, are not terrorism and ought not to be labeled as such."[29] Only Slovenia, Bahrain, and the U.S. articulated an intentional story about Serbian repression and ethnic cleansing.[30] They criticized attempts to describe the actions of the ethnic Albanians and Serb authorities as morally equivalent. Slovenia directly challenged the inadvertent story. "The attempts to obscure that threat by various techniques of what commentators call 'an even distribution of guilt'—techniques that were amply on display in international discussions on some other situations in the recent past—would again bring only harm and suffering and would delay the solutions. The techniques of 'an even distribution of guilt' say little about the actual facts of the situation concerned and speak volumes about the lack of agreement at the level of the international community."[31]Nonetheless, the inadvertent story shaped the initial Security Council response (Table 6.1).

Despite lack of agreement on the necessity of UN involvement or the character of the conflict, the council was united in its commitment to preserving the sovereignty and territorial integrity of the federal republic. Council members believed that the political solution to the Kosovo problem was autonomy for the Kosovo Albanians with substantial self-administration but within the existing borders of Serbia. Most members wanted to protect human rights in Kosovo but were unwilling to challenge Serbia's state sovereignty or territorial integrity to do so.

Six months later the UNSC continued to be divided on the cause and character of the conflict but more members began to gravitate toward the intentional story in response to mounting expert testimony, media reporting, and forensic evidence detailing civilian massacres by Serb forces. In a particularly brutal case that captured international media attention, Serb forces massacred an extended family of ethnic Albanians that had fled to the forest after their village came under attack. Human Rights Watch investigated the scene and examined the dead bodies of five women and two children ages five and seven—all of whom had been shot in the head at close range, apparently while attempting to flee. In all, eighteen civilians including five children had been killed in the forest. Some of the bodies were mutilated including that of a pregnant twenty-eight-year old woman whose abdomen had been cut open and a sixty-five-year old man whose brain had been partially removed and placed next to his body.[32] Human Rights Watch characterized the conflict as one waged by the Serb authorities against ethnic Albanian civilians and criticized Western states for allowing them to operate in a climate of impunity.[33] Expert testimony and forensic evidence added strength to the intentional story. Council members came under increasing pressure to respond more decisively to breaches of their resolutions than they had in Bosnia. Mounting NGO and media pressure had an effect. On 13 October, only seven months after Kosovo appeared on the UNSC agenda, members of the NATO alliance voted to use force to compel a settlement in Kosovo. Acting to diminish the NATO threat, the Federal Republic of Yugoslavia agreed to the establishment of the Kosovo Verification Mission (KVM) under the auspices of the OSCE to monitor the federal republic's compliance and to allow NATO air verification of Serbian compliance with its international agreements.

Table 6.1. Changes in Support for Causal Stories in Kosovo, 1998–1999

	Intentional Story	*Inadvertent Story 1 (Civil War)*	*Inadvertent Story 2 (Internal)*	*Unarticulated*
March 1998 (S/PV.3868) Imposition of arms embargo	Bahrain Slovenia **U.S.**	Costa Rica Gambia Japan Portugal Sweden **UK**	**China** **Russia**	Brazil **France** Gabon Kenya
October 1998 (S/PV.3937) Endorsement of Yugoslav-OSCE-NATO agreement establishing KVM	Bahrain Brazil Costa Rica Kenya Slovenia **UK** **U.S.**	Gabon Japan Portugal Sweden **Russia**	China	Gambia **France**
March 1999 (S/PV.3988) Serbian ethnic cleansing campaign begins; NATO humanitarian intervention	Argentina Bahrain Canada **France** Gambia Malaysia Netherlands Slovenia **UK** **U.S.**	Gabon **Russia**	**China**	Brazil Namibia
June 1999 (S/PV.4011) Establishment of UN protectorate for Kosovo	Argentina Bahrain Brazil Canada **France** Gabon Gambia Malaysia Namibia Netherlands Slovenia **UK** **U.S.**	**Russia**	**China**	None

Despite the council's formal endorsement of the agreements, meeting records reveal deep divisions among members about both the character of the conflict and the legal authority of regional organizations to threaten the use of military force. Support for the intentional story continued to grow but several members continued to articulate an inadvertent story. Kenya, Brazil, and the UK shifted their support to the intentional story, arguing that the government of the Federal Republic of Yugoslavia bore primary responsibility for the well-being and security of its citizens.[34] Costa Rica specifically condemned the Serbian policy of "ethnic cleansing."[35] Nonetheless, at least a third of UNSC members blamed "both parties" for the continued violence. The language of Resolution 1203 reflected this continued ambivalence. It described the conflict within a civil war frame in which both parties were responsible but placed greater emphasis on the systematic human rights violations committed by Serb authorities.[36] Disunity in the council about responsibility for the violence was complemented by disagreement over NATO's threat to use force without UNSC authorization. In October 1998, UNSC debate centered on three interrelated issues: the credibility of the UNSC if its resolutions were flouted, the legal bases for the use of military force, and the relationship between regional organizations and the UNSC. Discussion reflected widespread concern among members about the council's willingness and ability to respond decisively to breaches of its demands. Poland argued that resolutions 1160 and 1199 had not been complied with and asked the council for decisive action in responding to the Kosovo crisis.[37] Brazil urged members, "The Council cannot allow itself to be seen as showing complacency about noncompliance or even incomplete compliance with its resolutions."[38] As the number of members pressing for military action to address Serbian noncompliance began to grow, Costa Rica pressed for "a position of political firmness vis-à-vis the Belgrade government" but stressed the importance of adhering to the rule of law and the tenets of the UN Charter when contemplating the use of military force.[39] "The Security Council alone can determine whether there has been a violation of its resolutions adopted in the exercise of its mandated powers," the Costa Rican representative argued. "Only the Security Council can authorize the use of force to ensure compliance with its resolutions, in exercise of its primary responsibility for the maintenance of international peace and security."[40] Similarly, Brazil argued that the use of force could only be used in self-defense or with UNSC authorization under Chapter VIII, Article 53, of the Charter.[41] Brazil warned that if NATO circumvented council authorization, a two-tiered security system could be created in which the council would cease to bear primary responsibility for maintenance of international peace and security in part of the world.[42] In contrast, China continued to deny that the Kosovo situation threatened peace and security and expressed its regret that "a regional organization" decided to interfere in the internal affairs of the Federal Republic of Yugoslavia without consulting the council or seeking its authorization.[43] The U.S. countered that a credible threat of the use of force was necessary to achieving a political agreement and ensuring its implementation and that NATO retained the necessary authority to use force: "The NATO allies, in agreeing on 13 October to the use of force, made it clear that they had the authority, the will and the means to resolve the issue. We retain that authority. We will not tolerate the continued violence that has resulted in nearly a quarter of a million refugees and displaced persons and thousands of deaths, and has jeopardized the prospects for peace in the wider Balkans."[44] The failure of the Security Council to authorize an early use of military force was creating discontent in an international society that placed increasing normative weight on the protection and promotion of human rights. The permanent members, however, had reached an impasse. They could not agree on the cause of, character of, or response to the conflict. The council remained notably quiet on the Kosovo problem for the next three months despite increasing violence on the ground, lack of progress toward a political solution, and Yugoslav government intransigence in response to council resolutions. A watershed moment for international involvement in Kosovo came in January 1999 when William Walker, head of the KVM and a seasoned American diplomat, publicly accused Yugoslav authorities of committing crimes against humanity in the village of Racak, Kosovo.

The Impact of Expert Testimony, Media Attention, and Forensic Evidence on NATO Members

On 8 January 1999, the KLA ambushed a group of Serbian police officers near the village of Racak, killing three officers and wounding another. Two days later, the KLA ambushed another Serbian police patrol, killing one policeman. In the days following, a significant Yugoslav military buildup occurred in the region. On the morning of 15 January, uniformed police and security forces of the Federal Republic of Yugolsavia and Serbian special police engaged KLA fighters near Racak. At the end of the firefight, Yugoslav authorities surrounded the village and a large group of officers entered.[45] The

KVM arrived in Racak that evening but was prevented from entering by Yugoslav authorities. When members of the KVM returned to the scene with William Walker the next day they discovered the mutilated body of an elderly man who had been decapitated. They found in all the bodies of forty-five ethnic Albanians, including at least one woman, a twelve-year-old boy, and a seventy-year-old man, most having been shot in the head at close range. Some had had their eyes gouged out or heads smashed in.[46] Reporters described the incident as the "bloodiest spree of the conflict."[47] Walker determined that the victims were civilians based on their clothing, physical attributes, and lack of weapons. In a news conference he described the killings as "an unspeakable atrocity" and "a crime against humanity."[48] Walker specifically identified Federal Republic of Yugoslavia security forces, uniformed members of the armed forces, and Serbian special police as responsible for massacring the civilians. In response, the UNSC and called on the International Criminal Tribunal for Yugoslavia to investigate.[49] The Yugoslav Government defended its police action, arguing that those killed were either KLA soldiers or civilians caught in the crossfire.[50] Human Rights Watch later confirmed Walker's findings: Serbian police and Yugoslav army indiscriminately attacked civilians, tortured detainees, and committed summary executions in the village of Racak after receiving direct orders to kill male inhabitants of the village over the age of fifteen.[51]

While similar massacres had allegedly occurred in Kosovo prior to Racak, this massacre had a profound international effect because it was independently verified by official observers and the international media broadcast the images around the world. The international response to the Racak massacres was quick and determined. On 19 January, the Security Council issued a presidential statement strongly condemning the massacre. Citing the OSCE-KVM report, the statement identified the Yugoslav security and armed forces and Serbian police as responsible for the massacre of civilians. The council described the events in Racak as "the latest in a series of threats to the efforts to settle the conflict through negotiations and peaceful means."[52] Yet in addition to condemning Yugoslav authorities for their actions, the statement warned the KLA against actions contributing to the tensions in Kosovo.[53]

At the end of January, NATO issued a solemn warning to the Yugoslav authorities that an air attack was impending and the leaders of the Contact Group summoned the leaders of the Albanians and Serbs to political negotiations in Rambouillet, France, in February. Despite the renewed efforts at political negotiation, human rights organizations publicly criticized the international community's handling of the crisis, accusing it of weak enforcement and acquiescence in the face of partial implementation. The intent was to shame the international community into taking more effective action to end the violations of human rights and humanitarian law in Kosovo. Human Rights Watch offered this critique:

> The pattern is familiar. The international community expresses moral outrage about an atrocity and promises "decisive action," including a possible military intervention. Milošević responds with a temporary pull-back of his forces and some vague commitments. But no one is willing to take the necessary steps to hold Milošević to his commitments. The most common refrain is the "serious threat" of NATO action against Yugoslav government forces or installations, most likely in the form of airstrikes. . . . But so far, measures by the international community have been weakly enforced, and sometimes rescinded when Milošević makes concessions on actions that he should not have undertaken in the first place.[54]

Human rights organizations demanded a stronger response to protect Kosovar civilians.

The leaders of the Kosovo Albanians and the Federal Republic of Yugoslavia ended the first round of political negotiations in Rambouillet with a verbal agreement between the parties on a plan for substantial autonomy for the Kosovo Albanians within Serbia. When the talks to discuss implementation resumed, agreement broke down. Nonetheless, acting under pressure from Western states to accept a peace deal that guaranteed Kosovar autonomy but delayed the question of independence, the leaders of the Kosovo Albanians reluctantly signed the Rambouillet Accords on 18 March. When the Serb party refused to also accept the agreement, the negotiations concluded without a deal. The very next day, Milošević launched a massive ethnic cleansing campaign, forcibly deporting ethnic Albanians, burning villages, and indiscriminately murdering and raping civilians who remained. On 24 March, NATO launched a humanitarian intervention.

Ethnic cleansing hastened after the start of NATO military strikes. At the end of February the Serbian government had 25,000 troops on the ground in Kosovo. By 24 March the number of Serbian troops in Kosovo had climbed to 36,000 and an additional 8,000 troops were in transit.[55]

Milošević's strategy included the systematic cleansing, street by street, of ethnic Albanians and attempting to provoke regional instability by coordinating attacks on NATO troops stationed in Bosnia on the ground and from the air.[56] The result was the largest population displacement in Europe since World War II.[57] An estimated 90 percent of the population was pushed out of the province by Serb forces in an effort to make the Kosovar question irrelevant by changing the demographic facts on the ground.[58]

Why NATO Humanitarian Intervention

NATO's humanitarian intervention in Kosovo was unprecedented because NATO is a collective defense organization. This was the first time that the alliance had deployed its armed forces in war, deployed out of area, used force offensively, and acted in defense of human rights. NATO justified the use of military force based on humanitarian considerations and not traditional self-defense justifications.[59] It acted, however, without explicit authorization from the UNSC. According to the UN Charter, states are permitted to use military force only in self-defense or with Security Council authorization. According to Article 53, regional organizations are permitted to engage in enforcement actions but only with UNSC authorization. In effect, all other uses of military force against a sovereign state are prohibited. The North Atlantic Treaty, which established NATO, recognizes the legal authority of the UN Charter in Article 1, which prohibits members from using military force for purposes inconsistent with the UN Charter. Article 5 establishes that an armed attack against any NATO member will be treated as an attack against all and that they will use force individually or in concert to restore and maintain security consistent with Article 51 of the UN Charter. Neither of the two treaties authorizes the practice of humanitarian intervention, although both reference the promotion of human rights principles.

NATO members articulated both a moral and legal argument to justify humanitarian intervention. NATO secretary-general Javier Solana argued that the organization acted out of necessity—to prevent a humanitarian catastrophe at the edge of its neighborhood—and that it had sufficient legal authority to do so in order to enforce previous Security Council resolutions that had defined the situation in Kosovo as a Chapter VII security threat.[60] NATO members sought legitimacy for their actions in the council's previous decisions to authorize military force for humanitarian purposes, their past failures in Bosnia and Rwanda, and a moral imperative driven by the growing legitimacy of human rights norms and changing conceptions of state sovereignty. NATO's behavior was driven by the interplay of norms and interests. Once the threat of force was made, NATO's credibility was on the line and failure could have irreparably damaged the alliance. Further violence also directly threatened European troops on the ground in Bosnia and Croatia and the security of neighboring NATO members. Finally, NATO members agreed on the cause and character of the conflict. They articulated a common intentional story about the Serbian ethnic cleansing of ethnic Albanian civilians and held a popular conception of sovereignty that incorporated minimal standards of human rights protection.

Why Not UNSC Humanitarian Intervention?

Disunity among permanent members over the cause and character of the conflict was the primary barrier to effective and unified UNSC action to halt the increasing violence. Council members not only disagreed on whether the violence was intentional, they also disagreed on whether it was a relevant matter for council discussion. The positions of the five permanent members were irreconcilable: an insurmountable barrier to UNSC humanitarian intervention. The second barrier to UNSC authorization for the use of force was the dominant interpretation of the sovereignty norm. Because Somalia had been a situation where sovereign authority was absent and Bosnia was one in which disputed sovereignty was resolved in favor of the Bosnian Muslim government, humanitarian intervention had complemented sovereignty norms. Both Rwanda and Kosovo, however, were situations where the perpetrator of atrocities was a state whose sovereign authority was uncontested. Ethnic Albanians' desire for secession meant that using force to protect them would conflict with the Federal Republic of Yugoslavia's state sovereignty and territorial integrity. Many council members wanted to defend the human rights of Kosovo's Albanians but were unwilling to alter the boundaries of the federal republic. Finally, divisions between ethnic Albanians committed to nonviolent political change and those committed to the use of force made them complex political victims and complicated partners for peace.[61]

Security Council Divisions Over the Authority to Use Force in Defense of Human Rights

NATO's unauthorized use of military force prompted serious debate within the Security Council about international authority for, and the legality and legitimacy of, humanitarian intervention. The council faced the question of what to do in the face of grave crimes against humanity and war crimes, particularly when its decision-making authority was blocked by internal divisions among its permanent members. While past unwillingness to stop ethnic cleansing and genocide was considered a UN failure, the use of military force without UNSC authorization threatened the credibility and authority of the UN.[62] Between March and June 1999 council debates about the necessity and legitimacy of NATO's use of force derived from three fundamental disagreements: (1) the cause and character of the conflict in Kosovo and different views of the conflict's perpetrators and victims, (2) the authenticity and legitimacy of NATO's human rights justifications, and (3) the contested meaning of state sovereignty and the relationship between sovereignty norms and human rights norms.

Secretary-General Kofi Annan's formal statement in response to the NATO bombing in Kosovo alluded to the dilemma of balancing new humanitarian norms, the tradition of state sovereignty, and existing international law.

> It is indeed tragic that diplomacy has failed but there are times when the use of force may be legitimate in the pursuit of peace. In helping maintain international peace and security, Chapter VII of the United Nations Charter assigns an important role to regional organizations, but as Secretary-General, I have many times pointed out, not just in relation to Kosovo, that under the Charter, the Security Council has primary responsibility for maintaining international peace and security and this is explicitly acknowledged in the North Atlantic Treaty. Therefore, the Council should be involved in any decision to resort to force.[63]

In a series of emergency meetings called by Russia between 24 and 26 March, members weighed in on the cause of the Kosovo conflict, evaluated NATO's justifications for humanitarian intervention, and discussed the implications for Security Council authority. Russia, Namibia, and China opposed the NATO bombing and argued it was a violation of international law that threatened the core institutions of international society—sovereignty and nonintervention. They called for an immediate end to the bombing and a formal censure of NATO members.[64] The NATO members of the council (Canada, France, the Netherlands, the UK, and the U.S.)

justified their military action according to the following principles: the protection of human rights norms, the duty to stop ethnic cleansing, the failure of the federal republic to live up to its commitments to the Security Council and the responsibilities of state sovereignty, and Security Council inaction.[65] Most non-NATO members (Argentina, Bahrain, Brazil, Gabon, Gambia, Malaysia, and Slovenia) cautiously supported the humanitarian intervention but regretted the inability of the UNSC to act and warned of setting a dangerous legal precedent.[66]

In March 1999, a majority of council members articulated an intentional story about ethnic cleansing. The permanent members, however, continued to be divided between the intentional and inadvertent stories. The U.S. articulated an intentional story when it summed up the case for NATO humanitarian intervention: "We and our allies have begun military action only with the greatest reluctance. But we believe that such action is necessary to respond to Belgrade's brutal persecution of Kosovar Albanians, violations of international law, excessive and indiscriminate use of force, refusal to negotiate to resolve the issue peacefully and recent military buildup in Kosovo—all of which foreshadow a humanitarian catastrophe of immense proportions."[67] NATO was undertaking humanitarian intervention to prevent an anticipated humanitarian catastrophe. According to the U.S. argument, Belgrade's systematic policy of undermining international agreements and its violation of the international human rights law and the laws of war provided adequate legal justification for humanitarian intervention.[68] Canada also articulated an intentional story that underscored the humanitarian motives of the NATO intervention: "We cannot simply stand by while innocents are murdered, an entire population is displaced, villages are burned and looted, and a population is denied its basic rights merely because the people concerned do not belong to the 'right' ethnic group."[69] The UK and France echoed the intentional story about Yugoslav repression of the ethnic Albanian population and justified that interpretation based on their past experiences with the Yugoslav government during the Bosnian war.[70] The UK argued that humanitarian intervention was undertaken on the basis of "overwhelming humanitarian necessity" and France asserted that both peace in Europe and human rights were at stake.[71] The Netherlands explained that NATO would have preferred a Security Council authorization for the use of force but such a resolution was unattainable given the opposition of "one or two permanent members." Council disunity did not justify allowing a humanitarian catastrophe to occur, the Netherlands reasoned, therefore NATO acted on the legal basis available to it.[72]

Bahrain and Malaysia also adopted the intentional story about ethnic cleansing, arguing that the systematic repression in Kosovo was reminiscent of the policy of ethnic cleansing carried out in Bosnia.[73] Malaysia argued that combating "so-called acts of terrorism in Kosovo does not in any way justify gross human rights violations or the failure to respect international norms and international humanitarian law."[74] Indeed the statements by a majority of elected council members and those participating as nonvoting participants in the formal meeting suggested widespread concurrence with NATO justifications. For example, Argentina argued that there was a humanitarian obligation to end the violence in Kosovo based on solid legal foundations, despite NATO's decision to circumvent council authority.

> Argentina also wishes to stress that the fulfillment of the legal norms of international humanitarian law and human rights is a response to universally recognized and accepted values and commitments. The obligation to protect and ensure respect for these rights falls to everyone and cannot be debated. That obligation is all the more urgent given that it has been alleged, witnessed and proven that, in that region, extremely serious international crimes have been committed, including acts of genocide, some of which are being tried in a special tribunal established by this Council.[75]

Bosnia attended the meeting as a nonvoting participant. Its delegation argued that they would still be suffering the consequences of war had the council not undertaken humanitarian intervention there in 1995: "For three and a half years in Bosnia and Herzegovina, people promoted talks, and for three and a half years, the war, the genocide, the aggression and the ethnic cleansing continued. Only after military intervention took place did diplomacy succeed."[76] The strength of the intentional story about ethnic cleansing in Kosovo was enhanced by the traumatic memory of UN failure in Srebrenica. Advocates and supporters of NATO humanitarian intervention justified its use of force by referring to international humanitarian and human rights law and the failure of the Federal Republic of Yugoslavia to abide by these international legal obligations.

The most powerful opponents to NATO intervention were China and Russia, which argued that the intervention was illegal and unjustified and that it threatened the very foundations of international relations. China insisted that only the UNSC could legitimately determine whether a situation threatened peace and security and take appropriate action. The NATO intervention was a classic example of power politics, according to China—an effort to bully the weak and interfere in the internal affairs of another state.[77] Russia expressed "profound outrage" over the NATO bombing and described it as a violation of both international law and the UN Charter. Russia chided the NATO members, insisting that they were obligated to follow Charter rules, including Article 103, which establishes the priority of Charter obligations over any other international legal obligations. Russia called for an immediate cessation of military force and warned the council that it reserved the right to take its own military measures to ensure its own and common European security.[78] China and Russia dismissed the intentional story in favor of the inadvertent one. The Federal Republic of Yugoslavia argued that it had a right to fight terrorism and defend its sovereignty and territorial integrity: "The Federal Republic of Yugoslavia has not threatened any country or the peace and security of the region. It has been attacked because it sought to solve an internal problem and use its sovereign right to fight terrorism and prevent the secession of a part of its territory that has always belonged to Serbia."[79] According to this logic, NATO's intervention was a "brutal and unprovoked aggression" against a sovereign state.[80]

Contested Bases of International Authority

On 26 March 1999 Russia introduced a draft resolution that if passed would have defined the use of force by NATO against the Federal Republic of Yugoslavia as a threat to international peace and security under Chapter VII of the UN Charter. The accompanying Security Council debate illustrated the growing consensus around a nuanced interpretation of NATO action—that humanitarian intervention in Kosovo was illegal because it lacked council authorization but was legitimate according to changing international norms. Nonetheless, the debate also showed that the NATO bombing had hardened the irreconcilable differences that were the cause of its intervention without council authority in the first place. Supporters of the NATO intervention justified it on multiple bases of authority including human rights law, international humanitarian law, and the obligations of regional organizations. Opponents argued that NATO members were acting out of national interest rather than the interest of common humanity.

Supporters of NATO humanitarian intervention further justified the organization's authority to use force on the basis of UNSC inaction coupled with the international legal obligations of state actors and regional organizations. Though NATO's actions were not sanctioned according to the UN

Charter, the U.S. pointed out that the UN Charter "does not sanction armed assaults upon ethnic groups, or imply that the international community should turn a blind eye to a growing humanitarian disaster."[81] Council members including Canada, the Netherlands, and Slovenia argued that disunity among the permanent members stymied what should have been a Security Council humanitarian intervention. Slovenia put it this way: "We regret the fact that not all permanent members were willing to act in accordance with their special responsibility for the maintenance of international peace and security under the United Nations Charter. Their apparent absence of support has prevented the Council from using its powers to the full extent and from authorizing the action which is required to put an end to the violation of its resolutions."[82] Albania, a nonvoting participant in the debate, defended NATO action, arguing that it was "saving the same values that the United Nations was created to defend" but had been prevented from doing by some members.[83] The Netherlands specifically accused Russia of acting in ways that made council pressure on the Yugoslav authorities less credible, necessitating the NATO military response.[84] Slovenia conceded that the UNSC had primary responsibility for the maintenance of international peace and security but emphasized that primary responsibility was not the same as exclusive responsibility, and that whether this primacy was respected in practice derived from the legitimacy of its behavior, regardless of the authority given to it by the Charter.[85] Making reference to the attempt to censure NATO members, Germany, speaking for the European Union, argued that the countries of the EU had a moral obligation to censure gross human rights abuses and indiscriminate violence: "We are ultimately responsible for securing peace and cooperation in the region which will guarantee the respect of our basic European values, i.e., the respect of human and minority rights, international law, democratic institutions and the inviolability of borders."[86] Canada warned the council before the vote that those who would support the censure of NATO for humanitarian intervention would "place themselves outside the international consensus, which holds that the time has come to stop the continuing violence perpetrated by the Government of the Federal Republic of Yugoslavia against its own people."[87] Through deliberately acting "inappropriately" (intervening without Security Council authorization), NATO members attempted to redefine the standards of appropriate military action. NATO humanitarian intervention reflected growing support for the idea that it is morally acceptable to use force to prevent or end humanitarian crises. An emerging standard of what was morally right, however, was in tension with existing norms of what was legally permissible.[88] Nonetheless, the draft resolution failed with only three states voting in favor of censure (China, Namibia, and Russia). All other states opposed the resolution (Argentina, Bahrain, Brazil, Canada, France, Gabon, Gambia, Malaysia, the Netherlands, Slovenia, U.K. and U.S.), signaling widespread support for the idea that states have a responsibility to protect the human rights of their peoples.

Bosnia, a nonvoting participant in the debate, noted that although its delegation was concerned by the implications of NATO military action being undertaken without UNSC authorization, it "would be even more concerned and dismayed if the Security Council were blocked and there were no response to the humanitarian crisis and to the legal obligation to confront ethnic cleansing and war crimes abuses."[89] Nonpermanent council members Gambia and Malaysia argued that UNSC authorization was required for the use of military force, but that the exigencies of particular situations may require decisive action when authorization is absent. In short, they argued that the humanitarian intervention by NATO was technically illegal but legitimate according to international legal standards. Consequently, the international community could not permit humanitarian crises to occur when irreconcilable differences between permanent members prevented Security Council action.[90]

India and Russia disputed humanitarian justifications given by NATO supporters. Russia protested the "false claim" that NATO's actions were necessitated when particular members blocked council action pointing out that no formal proposals on humanitarian intervention or draft resolutions were introduced.[91] Indeed, no resolutions had been vetoed by Russia but it had indicated to council members during informal discussions and in its consultations with NATO that it would veto any such resolution.[92] India suggested that the real conflict between members was one of diverging interests and that there was very little basis for NATO claims to be acting legitimately because of widespread international support: "They [NATO] say they are acting in the name of humanity. Very few members of the international community have spoken in this debate, but even among those who have, NATO would have noted that China, Russia and India have all opposed the violence which it has unleashed. The international community can hardly be said to have endorsed their actions when already representatives of half of humanity said that they do not agree with what they have done."[93] Tensions between permanent members were further exacerbated when in early May NATO B-2 bombers destroyed the Chinese Embassy in the Federal Republic of Yugoslavia, killing three Chinese journalists. China publicly accused NATO of a deliberate attack on its embassy for strategic purposes and condemned the organization for violating Chinese sovereignty.[94] Russia suggested that the embassy bombing was evidence that NATO was using the humanitarian banner as a cover for its attempts to destroy the present world order.[95] Whether humanitarian values or narrower national interests were driving NATO action was central to the Security Council debate.

The Interplay of Interests and Norms

The Kosovo case shows that both human rights norms and national interests shaped NATO member decision making about the use of force. Explaining NATO's decision to use force without Security Council authorization, U.S. secretary of state Madeleine Albright argued that U.S. policy was motivated by both strategic interests and moral concerns:

> We could allow Russia's threatened veto to stop us from acting, or we could use force to save the people of Kosovo even without the UN's explicit permission. I pushed hard and successfully for the second option. My reasons were partly strategic: Europe was never going to be fully at peace as long as the Balkans were unstable, and the Balkans were never going to be stable as long as Milošević was in power. My primary motive, however, was moral: I did not want to see innocent people murdered. NATO's presence in Europe gave us the means to stop ethnic cleansing on that continent, and I hoped that by doing so we could help prevent similar atrocities elsewhere.[96]

In his formal statement following the start of NATO air strikes, British prime minister Tony Blair similarly justified the humanitarian intervention as necessary to prevent continued repression of the Kosovar Albanians and because the events in Kosovo had far-reaching regional effects. Blair argued that it was in the national interests of the UK to help the Kosovars attain the fundamental freedoms enjoyed by other Europeans: "We have in our power the means to help them secure justice and we have a duty to see that justice is now done."[97] For the U.S., the UK, and many of their allies, national interests were defined in normative as well as material terms.

Peace and stability in Kosovo was in the individual and collective security interests of NATO members. The organization's principal function is
to secure and maintain a peaceful Europe. Continued fighting in Kosovo
threatened to spill beyond its borders into neighboring states, threatening
key NATO allies. Additionally, ethnic cleansing in Kosovo put the safety of
thousands of European troops in Bosnia at risk and threatened the peace
agreement brokered in Dayton.[98] Threats to its success in the Balkans directly threatened the authority, credibility, and legitimacy of NATO. Milošević's unwillingness to back down in Kosovo tested both American
leadership and the relevance and effectiveness of the transatlantic alliance.[99]
During the late 1990s, NATO's role in post–Cold War Europe was in question. As it approached its fiftieth anniversary, NATO risked falling into
irrelevance if it did not evolve its purpose and mission.[100] NATO members,
particularly those on the UNSC, had an interest in stopping the Kosovo
bloodshed.

After NATO leaders threatened the use of force, the organization's credibility was on the line. General Wesley Clark wrote: "Once the threat
surfaces, . . . nations or alliances are committed. Following through to preserve credibility becomes a matter of vital interest. Credibility is the ultimate measure of value for states and international institutions. Inevitably,
sacrificing credibility carries long-term consequences far greater than the
immediate issue, whatever it is."[101] Maintaining NATO credibility in Kosovo was a vital interest for the alliance and its members. Yet the threat to
NATO's credibility stemmed as much from perceived failure to meet the
normative expectations of its members' domestic populations as it was
from the unwillingness to follow through on past threats. NATO is a values-
based community as well as a political and military alliance. The European
security project entails creating a whole, free, and peaceful Europe based
on liberal democratic values including human rights and the rule of law.[102]
Television images of ethnic Albanians being driven out of Kosovo made it
implausible for NATO to not follow through on its commitment to humanitarian values and protecting human rights.[103]

According to General Clark, the preservation of transatlantic values became a vital interest of the military alliance—norms and interests were
intimately connected. In his memoirs, Clark writes that humanitarian intervention in Kosovo illustrated the power of ideas—ideas of human rights
and dignity, the rule of law, and self-government—and the possibility of

waging war based on values and law rather than narrower national interests.[104] Nonetheless, preserving and projecting these values was a defining feature of both European and American interests.[105] Secretary of State Albright has argued with regard to Kosovo, "I believed that it was very important to make clear that the kinds of things that Milošević does—deciding that you don't have the right to exist because of your ethnic group—is unacceptable. It is not just a lesson for Kosovo. It is not American to stand by and watch this kind of thing. That doesn't mean that we can be everywhere all the time, but where we can make a difference, with an alliance that works, we should."[106] A normative commitment to human rights united the members of NATO and made humanitarian intervention possible.

The Coevolution of Sovereignty Norms and Human Rights Norms in the Security Council

The Group of Eight highly industrialized countries—Canada, France, Germany, Italy, Japan, Russia, the UK, and the U.S.—presented the Federal Republic of Yugoslavia with principles for political resolution of the Kosovo conflict in early June 1999. The National Assembly of Serbia voted to accept those principles and by 10 June Serb forces had begun to withdraw from Kosovo and NATO humanitarian intervention was coming to an end. The UNSC passed Resolution 1244, which endorsed the political solution and established an international civil and military presence under UN auspices, marking effective reengagement of the council.[107] The debate accompanying the vote was about much more than resolving the Kosovo conflict, however. The formal discussion centered on the meaning of sovereignty and its relationship to human rights. China set the tone for a divisive debate when it argued that ethnic problems within states should be settled by its own government and peoples. Respect for sovereignty and noninterference in internal affairs are the foundation of modern international society, according to China

> Since the end of the Cold War, the international situation has undergone major changes, but those principles are by no means outdated. On the contrary, they have acquired even greater relevance. At the threshold of a new century, it is even more imperative for us to reaffirm those principles. In essence, the "human rights over sovereignty" theory serves to infringe upon the sovereignty of other

States and to promote hegemonism under the pretext of human rights. This totally runs counter to the purposes and principles of the United Nations Charter. The international community should remain vigilant against it.[108]

Responding directly to China, Slovenia conceded that international organizations must respect the sovereignty of states but argued that "it is at least equally clear that State sovereignty is not absolute and that it cannot be used as a tool of denial of humanity resulting in threats to peace."[109] The Netherlands argued that the protection of human rights is consistent with the principles of the UN Charter. Since the Charter protects both sovereignty and human rights, there is a need to find a way to reconcile them.

The Charter, to be sure, is much more specific on respect for sovereignty than on respect for human rights, but since the day it was drafted the world has witnessed a gradual shift in that balance, making respect for human rights more mandatory and respect for sovereignty less absolute. Today, we regard it as a generally accepted rule of international law that no sovereign State has the right to terrorize its own citizens. Only if that shift is a reality can we explain how on 26 March the Russian-Chinese draft resolution branding the NATO airstrikes a violation of the Charter could be so decisively rejected by 12 votes to 3.[110]

While acknowledging that all states have difficulties dealing with the shift from sovereignty to human rights, the Netherlands warned that "times have changed, and they will not change back."[111] Canada argued that there is a significant relationship between the maintenance of international peace and security and the protection of human rights. The latter, according to Canada, must be given new weight in the council's definition of security and its decisions about when and how to engage in conflicts.[112]

In his annual report to the General Assembly in September that year, Kofi Annan reflected on the Kosovo case and the divisions it brought to the Security Council.[113] In his speech, Annan affirmed the existence of a developing international norm of military intervention to protect civilians from slaughter. He argued that state sovereignty was being redefined by the forces of globalization and international cooperation to include a state responsibility for the welfare of its people. Annan suggested that the core challenge for the Security Council and the United Nations as a whole in the twenty-first century is "to forge unity behind the principle that massive and systematic violations of human rights—wherever they may take place—should not be allowed to stand."[114] He illustrated the dilemma facing the UN by comparing its responses to Rwanda and Kosovo. He asked members to consider what horrors might have been prevented in Rwanda had a regional organization intervened to stop the genocide in absence of Security Council action. He also asked members to consider the dangerous precedent set by use of military force in absence of UNSC authorization in Kosovo and how it might undermine the international security system and threaten international order, peace, and security. Annan argued that the spirit of the Charter affirms fundamental human rights but that members need to find a way to apply Charter principles "in an era when strictly traditional notions of sovereignty can no longer do justice to the freedoms and aspirations of peoples everywhere to attain their fundamental freedoms."[115]

Acrimony between permanent members in the aftermath of the Kosovo conflict prevented it from becoming a productive venue for further discussion of the relationship between sovereignty and human rights. According to Kenneth Roth, executive director of Human Rights Watch, the priority of national sovereignty gave way to that of human rights in 1999 in places where crimes against humanity were being committed. In the aftermath of Kosovo, states could no longer safely hide behind a cloak of national sovereignty.[116] Because the council remained divided over the evolving relationship between sovereignty and human rights, however, it was closed to further debate on the legitimacy of humanitarian intervention and the changing meaning of sovereignty. Instead, the government of Canada established the International Commission on Intervention and State Sovereignty (ICISS) to respond to the secretary-general's challenge.

The ICISS was an independent international body designed to bridge the concepts of human rights and sovereignty and to foster a global political consensus on humanitarian intervention in an effort to move toward action within the UN system. After a year of research and worldwide consultations, the ICISS produced its groundbreaking report, *The Responsibility to Protect*, in which it defended a conceptualization of sovereignty that includes state responsibility for the protection of human rights. Sovereignty implies dual responsibility, the Commission argued. Externally, states must respect the sovereignty of other states but internally, states must respect the rights and fundamental dignity of its citizens.[117] Acceptance of *sovereignty as responsibility* means that when a state is unable or unwilling to protect its population, the state's *responsibility to protect* must be fulfilled by the international community and specifically by the UNSC (see Chapters 7 and 8).[118]

Comparing the Council Response to Kosovo (1998–1999) and Sierra Leone (1995–2000)

The conflict in Kosovo coincided with a brutal war in Sierra Leone. Council members, the broader UN membership, and even refugees regularly made comparisons between international responses to the two crises.[119] The international community was accused of being more concerned with, acting more quickly to respond to, and dedicating more resources toward solving the problems of Kosovo than Sierra Leone. While it is certainly true that the level and character of the violence in Sierra Leone reached an incredibly high level of barbarity before ethnic cleansing in Kosovo even started, and Western states dedicated greater resources to address the crisis in Kosovo than Sierra Leone, the UNSC passed a Chapter VII resolution authorizing UN personnel to take any necessary action to protect civilians in Sierra Leone while no such authorization was forthcoming for Kosovo. Security Council Resolutions 1270, 1289, and 1299 created the context in which an eventual humanitarian intervention by the UK to push back a rebel advance on Sierra Leone's capital city of Freetown in May 2000 was both legal and legitimate. In contrast, in the absence of council authorization the NATO humanitarian intervention in Kosovo was illegal. Comparing the different responses of council members to these simultaneously occurring crises highlights the importance of causal stories, sovereign authority, and human rights norms to Security Council decision making about the legitimate purpose of military force.

Plagued by corrupt leadership, economic collapse, and state disintegration, the fragile Sierra Leone state quickly became engulfed in war in March 1991 after a rebel group called the Revolutionary United Front (RUF) invaded eastern Sierra Leone, initiating what would turn out to be "a ten year cross-border and civil war" characterized by horrendous atrocities and fueled by the exploitation of its alluvial diamond minds.[120] The war started by the RUF raged against three successive governments and accelerated decades of state disintegration before officially ending in January 2002.[121] Trained and armed by the government of Libyan president Muammar Qaddafi, Foday Sankoh's RUF fought alongside Charles Taylor, then head of the National Patriotic Front of Liberia, against the Liberian government of Samuel Doe. In exchange, Liberian forces loyal to Taylor, who would later replace Doe as Liberia's president, helped the RUF invade and control the diamond mines in Sierra Leone.[122] RUF forces looted the country's mines, swapping diamonds and other precious resources for arms, money, and drugs, which fueled the conflict.

The war in Sierra Leone has been characterized as being more about greed than political grievance and more of a cross-border incursion than a traditional civil war because the core membership was composed of Sierra Leonean, Liberian, and Burkinabe mercenaries who lacked a political agenda.[123] The RUF quickly became known for the brutality of its atrocities, which included the amputation of fingers, hands, arms, and legs of civilians.[124] RUF forces were also known for looting and burning the villages they attacked, raping women and abducting children to serve as rebel soldiers and "bush wives."[125] Over the course of the decade of war, more than ten thousand children would be separated from their families including an estimated fifty-four hundred who were forcibly conscripted to serve in the rebel army or state armed forces.[126] Children captured by the RUF were drugged and forced to commit atrocities against their own family members to bind them to the rebels and make it impossible for them to escape and return home.[127]

The UNSC first became involved in Sierra Leone's conflict in March 1995 but was distracted by the atrocities in Bosnia and Rwanda, not fully giving it its attention until the end of the decade when RUF violence spiked. The democratically elected president, Ahmad Tejan Kabbah, was overthrown in a military coup by disgruntled military officers called the Armed Forces Revolutionary Council, which was allied with the RUF. The Organization of African Unity, the Economic Community of West African States, and the UNSC condemned the military coup and demanded the immediate reinstatement of the democratically elected president. Almost a year later, the Military Observer Group of Economic Community of West African States, with the support of the UNSC, forced the military junta from Freetown, allowing President Kabbah to resume his post. Despite Kabbah's efforts at national reconciliation and state building, the RUF and the remnants of the deposed junta continued their campaign of terror against the civilian population for another two years before the international community pressured the government and the RUF to the negotiating table in July 1999. The Lomé Peace Accords established a broad power-sharing government composed of both parties, and a program for the disarmament, demobilization, and reintegration of rebel forces and Civil Defense Forces. The UNSC established the United Nations Mission in Sierra Leone (UNAMSIL) to assist in the implementation of the agreement and to provide protection to the civilian population.[128] Continuing rebel atrocities, cease-fire violations, and the abduction of five hundred peacekeeping personnel by the RUF caused the agreement to collapse in May 2000. The UK responded with a military intervention to rescue the peacekeepers and other foreign nationals but transformed the mission into a humanitarian intervention and fought against the rebels alongside UNAMSIL troops to secure the airport, defend the city, and protect civilians.

In Sierra Leone, it was the combination of gross human rights violations and the overthrow of a democratically elected government that motivated UNSC action. Unlike in Kosovo, members agreed on a causal story. They quickly united around an intentional story in which the RUF, its leader, Foday Sankoh, and ousted members of the military junta were perpetrators of horrific atrocities against the civilian population during its assault against a legitimate democratically elected government.[129] In this narrative, both the government and people of Sierra Leone were victims of the RUF, which was the clear perpetrator. Council members were particularly repulsed by the finding of its panel of experts that rebel motivation included control of the diamond mines for self-aggrandizement rather than a legitimate, political, social, economic, or humanitarian cause.[130] The intentional story had the support of the entire council and all the core resolutions were passed with unanimous support.[131] The intentional story resonated with members because it was consistent with independent expertise and the documentation and advocacy of international human rights organizations, and it matched media imagery of the conflict. Widespread agreement on the causal narrative generated widespread agreement on the appropriate response, which included political dialogue and the use of enforcement measures to protect civilians and members of the democratically elected government against rebel atrocities.

In Kosovo, the state was the alleged perpetrator of human rights violations while in Sierra Leone the state was one of the victims. This made it easy for council members to discursively construct the protection of human rights norms as consistent with the norms of sovereignty. When violations of fundamental human rights are defined as a threat to international peace and security, unless the perpetrator is a nonstate actor or lacks legitimate sovereign authority, core norms of the UN Charter come into conflict and foreclose opportunities for humanitarian intervention. The council identified the deposed democratically elected government as the legitimate sovereign authority of Sierra Leone and later, when Kabbah was back in power, it continued to identify the perpetrators as the RUF and the remnants of the NPRC, despite allegations that the Civil Defense Forces also engaged in serious human rights violations. In Sierra Leone, then, the council could protect the population from widespread atrocities and protect the sovereignty rights of the government at the same time. This normative coherence created the opportunity for Security Council humanitarian intervention in Sierra Leone just as normative incoherence closed that opportunity for Kosovo, forcing NATO to act without the Security Council authorization that was forthcoming for Sierra Leone.

Although early reaction to the Sierra Leone crisis was primarily concerned with the return of legitimate state authority and the protection of the traditional Westphalian sovereignty norm, the council's concern with rebel violations of human rights and humanitarian law was central to explaining its continued engagement with the conflict after President Kabbah had been reinstated. From the outset, presidential statements, resolutions, and meeting records condemned the atrocities carried out by the rebel forces and demanded full respect for international human rights and humanitarian law.[132] Resolution 1181, establishing the first UN Observer Mission in Sierra Leone , specifically called on factions to respect human rights and abide by international humanitarian law as a requirement for establishing lasting peace and a proper functioning of democracy.[133] More than a year later, the council altered the mission mandate, authorizing UN personnel to provide protection to civilians threatened by violence in accordance with Chapter VII of the UN Charter—this was the first civilian mandate to be authorized during a UN peace operation. This change in mandate was noted by a change in name to United Nations Mission in Sierra Leone. Resolution 1270 also required that UNAMSIL personnel be trained in international humanitarian, human rights, and refugee law and prioritized the protection of children and women.[134] The council would no longer be indifferent to indiscriminate attacks against the civilian population while it was in the field.[135]

In another striking example of commitment to human rights principles, during the Lomé peace negotiations in July 1999, the special representative of the secretary-general for Sierra Leone, Francis Okelo, refused to endorse an amnesty provision that had been negotiated between Kabbah and Sankoh. Reflecting growing consensus within the UN Secretariat that durable peace cannot be built upon impunity and that leaders who orchestrate war crimes and crimes against humanity are not immune from criminal prosecution, Okelo appended a handwritten disclaimer: "the United Nations holds the understanding that the amnesty and pardon in Article IX of the agreement shall not apply to international crimes of genocide, crimes against humanity, war crimes and other serious violations of international humanitarian law."[136] On 14 August 2000, the UNSC unanimously passed Resolution 1315, which recommended the establishment of a special court for Sierra Leone and authorized the secretary-general to negotiate an agreement with the government of Sierra Leone to create an independent court that would have jurisdiction over these grave crimes. As in Kosovo, UNSC action in Sierra Leone illustrated the increasing importance of human rights norms to the council and their perceived link to the maintenance of international peace and security.

Conclusions

In Kosovo, Security Council members initially disagreed on the cause and character of the conflict—whether it was ethnic cleansing, a civil war, or a legitimate domestic police action by a state against an internal challenge to its rule. As violence intensified over time and expert testimony and media coverage of civilian massacres increased, most members coalesced around the intentional story about ethnic cleansing. The permanent members remained divided, however, between those articulating the intentional story (France, the UK, and the U.S.) and those articulating an inadvertent story (China and Russia). Disunity in the council was a barrier to humanitarian intervention. In direct contrast, council unity around an intentional story created the possibility of the Security Council's authorization of humanitarian intervention in Sierra Leone. The divisions over Kosovo, however, were about much more than the internal conflict. In Kosovo, council debates centered on deep and vexing problems facing international relations at the end of the twentieth century—the status of human rights, the meaning of sovereignty, the appropriate source of authority over the use of force, and how to interpret and apply contested interpretations of international norms and law.

The case of Kosovo provoked the most direct confrontation among UNSC members over the place of human rights norms and sovereignty norms in the council's deliberations about the use of force, which led to a major crisis in permanent member relations. The council did not authorize humanitarian intervention for Kosovo because its members could not agree on the fundamental rights and responsibilities of states with regard to their populations and because its exercise against a perpetrator state would directly threaten traditional Westphalian conceptions of the sovereignty norm. China and Russia argued that the Kosovo conflict was an internal matter and defended a state's right to repress unruly elements of its population. France, the UK, and the U.S. argued that the Kosovo conflict was a threat to international peace and security because it was characterized by ethnic cleansing. Lack of agreement among permanent members on an intentional causal story and the lack of coherence between human rights norms and sovereignty norms stymied humanitarian intervention, even in the face of irrefutable evidence of civilian casualties and the precedent of Bosnia. In Bosnia the support of three permanent members for the intentional story of conflict was sufficient to trigger the use of force; but not in Kosovo. Russia threatened to veto military action in Kosovo but acquiesced to the intentional story in Bosnia. Once the government of Bosnia was recognized as the legitimate sovereign authority, the council could promote human rights simply by protecting state sovereignty. The case of Sierra Leone was similar. Humanitarian intervention there actually protected state sovereignty as well as human rights. In contrast, in Kosovo the perpetrator was the state acting against its own citizens, bringing the two sets of norms into conflict. UNSC responses to Rwanda and Kosovo show there are significant barriers to humanitarian intervention when the perpetrators are states.

In the absence of Security Council action in defense of Kosovo's Albanians, NATO engaged in humanitarian intervention. The NATO intervention, although widely interpreted as illegal because it lacked UNSC authorization, was widely perceived as legitimate in the absence of council action. NATO members of the council defended their intervention on the basis of shared human rights norms and as a moral duty, indeed, even legal obligation to prevent ethnic cleansing. President Clinton claimed that it was a war to protect values, not interests: "I think that there is an important principle here that I hope will be now upheld in the future. . . . And that is while there may be a great deal of ethnic and religious conflict in the world—some of it might break out into wars—that whether within or beyond the borders of a country, if the world community has the power to stop it, we ought to stop genocide and ethnic cleansing."[137] Nevertheless, the United States had at least two overlapping interests in Kosovo: prevention of a civil war–humanitarian crisis and demonstration of the utility and potential of NATO.[138] The evidence presented here suggests that NATO members were motivated by humanitarian reasons to intervene to protect Kosovo's Albanians but that human rights norms shape and are shaped by national interests. NATO humanitarian intervention was possible because its members shared a conceptualization of the conflict in Kosovo as a case of ethnic cleansing. They articulated an intentional causal story with identifiable and intentional perpetrators (Serb authorities) who were committing gross crimes (ethnic cleansing) against a specific population (Kosovo's Albanians). In sum, what the Kosovo case shows is that interests are increasingly shaped by human rights norms and that the meaning of sovereignty is continually evolving. In 1999 Security Council humanitarian intervention was not possible in Kosovo because its members fundamentally disagreed on the responsibilities of states with regard to their citizens. At the same time, human rights norms were sufficiently developed so as to garner humanitarian intervention by NATO despite the political and legal risks of acting without UNSC authority.

Chapter 7

Complex Conflicts and Obstacles to Rescue in Darfur, Sudan

When the conflict in Darfur, Sudan, caught the attention of the United Nations Security Council in early 2004, members of the United Nations were debating whether the international community has a responsibility to protect people from gross violations of their fundamental human rights when their state is unable or unwilling to do so. The idea of the international responsibility to protect was crafted in part as a response to the council's failure to stop the 1994 Rwandan genocide during which approximately eight hundred thousand people were slaughtered in one hundred days. The height of military conflict in Darfur coincided with the ten-year anniversary of the Rwandan genocide. It took little over one year from the launch of an armed rebellion in early 2003 for the fighting in Darfur to make it onto the council's agenda. In contrast, the conflict between North and South Sudan had been ongoing for twenty-one years before it garnered formal Security Council attention.[1] Despite the high public profile of the conflict in Darfur, council members would prioritize protection of the north-south peace process over the resolution of the Darfur conflict.

What began as a rebel insurgency in 2003 quickly deteriorated into the world's worst humanitarian crisis[2] and became the site of the world's largest humanitarian relief effort by 2004.[3] The council recognized the severity of the Darfur crisis relatively early but its debates about how to respond were marked by contestation over culpability for the crisis and the appropriate response, delaying meaningful action. Members disagreed whether the government of Sudan bore principal or only partial responsibility for widespread violations of human rights and international humanitarian law and whether the Security Council bears responsibility for civilian protection in absence of government protection of civilians.

Security Council members articulated three causal stories between 2004 and 2011 to characterize the conflict: an intentional story about genocide in which the government of Sudan was using proxy fighters to murder and rape civilians, an inadvertent story about civil war in which rebels and government agents were responsible for human rights violations, and a complex story about a multilayered conflict with both intrastate and interstate dimensions between multiple and fragmenting armed rebel groups and government regular and paramilitary forces where responsibility for killing was diffuse. The strength of, and support for, these causal stories shifted considerably over time. Initially, council members were divided between all three stories, but the inadvertent story soon began to dominate the council's proceedings. However, after a 2006 Security Council mission to Darfur, there was a significant shift in support for the complex story. Conflicting testimony by independent experts between 2007 and 2009, however, destabilized council unity. Individual members of the council articulated support for both the complex story articulated by the United Nations Secretariat and the intentional story articulated by the prosecutor of the International Criminal Court. Nonetheless, consensus-based Security Council documents including presidential statements and mission reports continued to reflect the complex story. Members of the council who were also members of the ICC responded to competing expert testimony by articulating a hybrid version of the complex causal story—one that incorporated the ICC prosecutor's intentional story as one aspect of a complicated and multifaceted causal narrative. According to this account, the government was responsible for an ethnically motivated mass killing campaign that was nested within a broader more complex conflict that also included a civil war, counterinsurgency campaign, and regional conflict. Both the dominance of the complex story and continuing contestation over the character of the conflict precluded humanitarian intervention in Darfur through 2011.

While council members were initially divided about the cause and character of the conflict, there was considerable unity between them on the source of sovereign authority. Members discursively described Sudan as a sovereign state member of the UN and identified President Omar al-Bashir's government as its legitimate sovereign authority. Members were only divided on the extent to which they believed the government was fulfilling its sovereign responsibilities or violating them. As previous cases in this study have shown, when the state is a perpetrator of human rights violations it is considerably more difficult to garner Security Council support for humanitarian intervention because its use contradicts preexisting sovereignty norms. Rather, in past cases, humanitarian intervention became possible when council members discursively constructed the promotion of human rights as consistent with or complementary to the protection of state sovereignty.

The discourse members used during their deliberations demonstrates that both norms and interests shaped Security Council action in Darfur. New norms—like the responsibility to protect and humanitarian intervention—emerge in a highly contested normative space where they must compete with other norms and perceptions of interest.[4] In Darfur, international norms of state sovereignty, nonintervention in domestic affairs, human rights, and the responsibility to stop genocide made competing demands on council members. In this context, members chose to protect and preserve norms that were either more highly internalized or that most closely corresponded to their national interests. However, the national interests of council members vary and are shaped, in part, by norms. Some states understand the protection of human rights to be squarely in their national interests whereas the national interests of other states correspond more directly to the protection of domestic noninterference. On the surface, the absence of humanitarian intervention in Darfur coincides with the strategic interests of some permanent members. Yet Security Council support for human rights norms does not necessarily lead to the adoption of humanitarian intervention. Nor does a failure to intervene necessarily reflect a lack of concern with human rights. Discourse during debates and language used in council texts about Darfur demonstrate that ideas about human rights shaped the council's decision making. This was not strategic "cheap talk." Security Council decision making on Darfur created two important innovations in the field of human rights: affirmation of the responsibility to protect in a case-specific council resolution and the first Security Council referral to the International Criminal Court.

The United Nations Security Council and the Darfur Conflict

Sudan is the largest country in Africa and shares its borders with nine other African states. It is home to nearly four hundred ethnic groups and more than three hundred spoken languages, reflecting the cultural, religious, and ethnic diversity that characterizes the continent. In the western region of Darfur alone there are more than thirty-five ethnic groups, making it one of the most diverse regions of Sudan.[5] Armed resistance groups in the southern, western, and eastern regions of Sudan have arisen over the past several decades in response to a lack of power sharing and unequal resource distribution between the central government and regions in the periphery.[6]

The rebel insurgency in Darfur captured international attention in April 2003 after two rebel groups—the Sudan Liberation Army (SLA) and the Justice and Equality Movement (JEM)—exercised a provocative and successful military challenge against the government of Sudan. Their joint attack on the al Fasher Air Force Base resulted in the loss of all seven planes, the deaths of more than seventy troops, pilots, and technicians, and the kidnapping of an additional thirty men.[7] The rebels left the base with an enormous cache of weapons and vehicles. The government was humiliated. Julie Flint and Alex de Waal write of the attack, "In more than twenty years' war in the South, the SPLA had never inflicted such a loss on the air force. The rebels were jubilant. . . . Indeed the attack did change everything: this was the pivotal moment that transformed Darfur's war from provincial discontent into a front-rank military danger to Khartoum."[8] Justifying their use of military force against the regime based on local complaints about governmental neglect, lack of development, and self-defense, Darfur rebel groups have attacked government institutions, state agents, and individuals perceived to support government policy. They have also attacked civilians and rival rebel groups. The government has responded to this armed challenge with dramatic levels of military force, employing the air force and regular army soldiers against the rebel groups and civilian members of the same tribes, but also by sponsoring a loose collection of irregular Arab fighters known as the *Janjaweed* to attack villages in Darfur. International human rights organizations have accused both the government and the Janjaweed of systematically targeting and attacking civilian populations suspected of supporting the rebellion as a deliberate part of its war strategy, particularly targeting the Fur, Maasalit, and Zhagawa tribes. By the end of 2004, Human Rights Watch estimated that the continued fighting between the Sudanese government and splintering armed rebel groups had resulted in the displacement of 2 million civilians and the deaths of 70,000 others.[9] The fighting in Darfur has been characterized by widespread violations of human rights and international humanitarian law. Villages across Darfur have been ravaged and burned and their inhabitants murdered, raped, or forced to flee. Approximately 2.7 million of Darfur's civilians live in camps for the internally displaced, where they are dependent on international humanitarian assistance for their protection and survival, while hundreds of thousands have found refuge in camps across the border in Chad. Experts characterized the situation in Darfur as more grave after five years of conflict than the situation in the south following twenty-one years of war.[10] By 2009, an estimated 4.7 million civilians in Darfur depended on international humanitarian assistance for their survival and approximately 300,000 had been killed.[11]

Western and African media have largely characterized the war as one between Arabs and Africans, but most scholars and area experts agree that it is better characterized as counterinsurgency warfare by proxy where the central government is exploiting existing ethnic and economic cleavages.[12] Nomadic groups (which have been classified as Arab in the media) have been trained, armed, and used by the ruling National Islamic Front government to fight sedentary communities (which have been classified as African by the media).[13] The underlying cause of the conflict is largely considered to be the unequal distribution of power and wealth by the regime leading to the denial of access to resources for communities in Darfur and elsewhere in Sudan. Recurring droughts and famine, a shrinking regional resource base, the widespread use and availability of weapons from the government, and regional conflicts, combined with intergroup tensions, have multiplied and exacerbated the conflict.[14]

The UNSC became formally involved in Darfur shortly after the April 2004 signing of a Humanitarian Ceasefire Agreement brokered by the African Union (AU) between the government, and the SLA and JEM rebel groups. Since then, the parties to the conflict have multiplied and the character of the violence has changed. Between 2003 and 2004 the majority of deaths were caused by the army and the Janjaweed militias.[15] Civilian deaths caused by violence were at their highest in September 2003 in North Darfur, between January and March 2004 in West Darfur, and later in 2004 in South Darfur.[16] In a 2004 report, the UN high commissioner of human rights determined that "what appears to have been an ethnically-based rebellion has been met with an ethnically-based response building in large part on the long-standing, but largely hitherto contained tribal rivalries."[17] Starting in 2005, however, most violent deaths were the result of fighting among armed rebel groups or between Arab militias over pasture land.

Ironically, when the most international attention was focused on the crisis in Darfur in 2005 and 2006—after the activist campaign calling for humanitarian intervention became strong—disease, not violence, was the biggest killer of civilians in Darfur.[18]

When the council added Darfur to its agenda in May 2004, it also was politically invested in peace negotiations to end the decades-long civil war fought between North and South Sudan. The government and the Sudan People's Liberation Movement/Army were in the process of establishing a power-sharing government. Consequently, council members examined and responded to the situation in Darfur within the broader political context of the North-South civil war. Throughout, council members and the Secretariat have viewed peace in Sudan as indivisible—peace between the north and south is inextricably linked to peace in Darfur and in other regions.[19]

The Security Council response to the war in Darfur has coincided with, and been shaped by, dramatic international developments in the beliefs about and practice of human rights. These include the increasing legitimacy of the idea that state sovereignty encompasses a minimal obligation to respect human rights and the practice of holding heads of states and military leaders criminally accountable for human rights violations under their authority. As earlier cases have demonstrated, debate over the meaning of state sovereignty was persistent across the 1990s. The United Nations' unwillingness to stop genocide in Rwanda in 1994 and NATO's humanitarian intervention in Kosovo without council authorization in 1999 created the impetus for norm entrepreneurs to find a way to reconcile an emerging, yet controversial norm of humanitarian intervention with the privileges and limits of state sovereignty. In 1999, Secretary-General Kofi Annan posed a vexing question to the United Nations General Assembly: "If humanitarian intervention is, indeed, an unacceptable assault on sovereignty, how should we respond to a Rwanda, to a Srebrenica—to gross and systematic violations of human rights that affect every precept of our common humanity?"[20] Responding directly to the secretary-general's challenge, as the previous chapter describes, the government of Canada and a group of major foundations established the International Commission on Intervention and State Sovereignty to study the legal, moral, political, and operational questions about humanitarian intervention.[21]

The commission issued its report, *The Responsibility to Protect*, in December 2001. In it, the ICISS argues that sovereignty implies a dual responsibility. Externally, states must respect the sovereignty of other states but internally, states must respect the rights and fundamental dignity of their citizens.[22] Acceptance of sovereignty as responsibility means that when a state is unable or unwilling to protect its population, the state's responsibility to protect must be met by the international community and specifically the UNSC.[23] The responsibility to protect was subsequently endorsed by the secretary-general's High-Level Panel on Threats, Challenges, and Change in 2004 and by the secretary-general in his report prepared for the UN's Second Millennium Summit in 2005.[24] In 2005, paragraphs 138 and 139 of the World Summit Outcome document granted the council limited authority to use humanitarian intervention based on the principles under the doctrine of the responsibility to protect:

> 138. Each individual State has the responsibility to protect its populations from genocide, war crimes, ethnic cleansing and crimes against humanity. This responsibility entails the prevention of such crimes, including their incitement, through appropriate and necessary means. We accept that responsibility and will act in accordance with it. The international community should, as appropriate, encourage and help States to exercise this responsibility and support the United Nations in establishing an early warning capability.

> 139. The international community, through the United Nations, also has the responsibility to use appropriate diplomatic, humanitarian and other peaceful means, in accordance with Chapters VI and VIII of the Charter, to help protect populations from genocide, war crimes, ethnic cleansing and crimes against humanity. In this context, we are prepared to take collective action, in a timely and decisive manner, through the Security Council, in accordance with the Charter, including Chapter VII, on a case-by-case basis and in cooperation with relevant regional organizations as appropriate, should peaceful means be inadequate and national authorities manifestly fail to protect their populations from genocide, war crimes, ethnic cleansing and crimes against humanity.[25]

A second significant normative development in international human rights was occurring at the same time that the notion of the responsibility to protect was gaining legitimacy: the erosion of sovereign immunity from prosecution.

On 17 July 1998, a total of 120 states signed the Rome Statute establishing the first permanent treaty-based international criminal court. The International Criminal Court entered into force in July 2002 after receiving its sixtieth state ratification. The ICC was established to help end impunity for the perpetrators of the most serious crimes including war crimes, crimes against humanity, and genocide. As of the end of 2011, a total of 120 UN members, including UNSC permanent members France and the UK, have ratified the treaty, becoming state parties of the court. China, Russia, and the U.S. are not members of the ICC. Although the ICC is independent of the UNSC, the Rome Statute includes a provision whereby the UNSC acting under the authority of Article 16 of the statute may refer any situation to the prosecutor for investigation. In 2005, the Security Council referred the situation of Darfur to the prosecutor of the ICC—the first such referral by the council under Article 16. In April 2007, Pre-Trial Chamber I issued arrest warrants for Ahmad Harun, then the minister of state for the interior, and the militia-Janjaweed leader Ali Kushayb for war crimes and crimes against humanity. In 2009, the court issued an arrest warrant for President Omar al-Bashir, who retaliated by expelling international humanitarian aid organizations from Darfur.[26]

The emergence of the International Criminal Court is an important manifestation of an "international justice cascade"—a rapid and dramatic international shift in the legitimacy of norms of criminal accountability for human rights abuse.[27] Elsewhere, ad hoc tribunals, special hybrid courts, and domestic courts were indicting past and present heads of states for human rights and humanitarian law violations. For example, former president of Serbia and Montenegro Slobodan Milošević was arrested and transferred to the International Criminal Tribunal in Yugoslavia in 2001 after being indicted on human rights and war crimes charges in Kosovo, Croatia, and Bosnia. His trial began in 2002 and ended when he died of natural causes in 2006. The Special Court of Sierra Leone indicted the sitting president of Liberia, Charles Taylor, in June 2003 on charges of crimes against humanity and violations of the laws of war for his part in the Sierra Leone conflict. He was convicted of war crimes in April 2012 and later sentenced to fifty years in prison. In Chile, in 2005, Augusto Pinochet—former general and dictator of Chile—was stripped of his presidential immunity from prosecution. He was subsequently charged with crimes against dissidents, including the forcible disappearance of individuals during his military dictatorship, but he died of complications of a heart attack in 2006. Similarly, in Argentina, members of the military dictatorship of the late 1970s and early 1980s have been prosecuted domestically for human rights crimes including kidnappings and disappearances.[28]

Finally, the Security Council's reaction to Darfur was also shaped by a massive civic activist movement that sought to bring attention to human rights crimes there. By 2005, the previously unknown Muslim region, which lacked natural resources and did not have historic ties to the U.S., had become the focus of "the largest American civic activist movement on Africa since apartheid."[29] The international attention and subsequent pressure on the government of Sudan forced the regime to loosen restrictions on the operation of humanitarian organizations, saving countless lives. Mass mobilization around the crisis in Darfur kept the conflict on the agenda of the council but restricted its response. Because the international movement to save the people of Darfur characterized the conflict as a clear-cut case of genocide perpetrated by the bad guys (Arabs) against the innocent good guys (Africans), policymakers were under considerable pressure to pursue policy solutions that reflected this narrative, namely humanitarian intervention.[30] Alternate solutions that considered the broader context were not considered legitimate options by many Darfur activists. Yet by the time the activist movement gained its greatest power, the character of the conflict had changed considerably, raising important questions about the efficacy of the proposed policy response. The combination of graphic media coverage of human rights violations as journalists gained greater access to information and images and widespread popular activism on the issue of Darfur in the domestic publics of democratic states made meetings on the subject politically sensitive for many council members. In fact, the high-profile character of the international debate may have discouraged external participation in council meetings, which was disproportionately low in comparison to international interest. Members became increasingly reluctant to make statements in the formal meeting record about culpability for human rights violations occurring in politically sensitive conflict areas beginning in the early 2000s. Instead, an increasing number of meetings were characterized by public briefings from Secretariat officials followed by private, informal meetings of the council. This trend is particularly pronounced in the case of Darfur, where up to 70 percent of the Security Council meetings in 2008 and 2009 were informal or closed, meaning they were off the public record, which makes tracking shifts in the belief in causal stories more difficult than in earlier conflicts. When the causal stories of individual

Security Council members were not available during a particular meeting, I derived the consensus view of the Security Council using council resolutions (which have a roll call vote) and presidential statements and mission reports, which are consensus documents.

Causal Stories About the Darfur Conflict and Human Rights Violations

Security Council debates about Darfur were characterized by regular contestation over culpability for the conflict and the subsequent humanitarian crisis as well as the appropriate response to the war's continuation. As noted earlier in the chapter, the intentional story characterized the conflict as a campaign of genocide waged by the Sudanese government and Janjaweed militias against African minorities living in Darfur. The inadvertent story characterized the conflict as civil war in which all parties to the conflict bore responsibility for human rights violations. The complex story identified multiple and fragmenting armed rebel groups and government regular and paramilitary forces with shifting alliances as culpable for human rights abuses. Some attacks on civilians were described as intentional and systematic while others were categorized as collateral damage or instrumental. The complex story also described the conflict as intertwined with other conflicts occurring within Sudan and in the broader region. In 2006, the Security Council reached agreement on a causal story for Darfur, but members coalesced around a complex causal story, precluding the use of military force without government consent. Contestation continued in the council, however, as ICC prosecutor Luis Moréno-Ocampo gave testimony on the character of the conflict that conflicted with other accounts throughout 2011. Rather than displacing the complex story, the intentional story the prosecutor advanced was viewed by the majority of council members as nested within the complex story. Multiple and varied conflicts were occurring simultaneously in Sudan, rather than a single one. Security Council meetings in 2010 and 2011 devoted very little attention to diagnosing the cause and character of the violence in Darfur and focused primarily on the broader north-south peace agreement and the Doha peace process for Darfur. Council members repeatedly called on all parties to cease the violence and commit to peace. The continuing salience of the complex story for council members persisted and can be explained by the power of causal story proponents, the uncontested status of sovereign authority, and a preponderance of media reporting and expert testimony privileging the complex story in the second half of the decade. The continuation of a counternarrative by the ICC prosecutor actually fueled the complex story rather than weakened it.

Contestation over Causal Stories

Security Council members were initially divided over the character of the fighting in Darfur. In 2004, members articulated all three stories, but the inadvertent story was dominant. In July 2004, the U.S. advanced an intentional story that accused the Sudanese government of fostering armed attacks against its civilians and creating a humanitarian disaster: "The responsibility for this disaster lies squarely with the Government of Sudan. To suppress a rebel uprising begun in early 2003, the Government commenced a campaign of terror against innocent civilians. Government aircraft bombed villages. Exploiting an ancient rivalry between Arab African herdsmen and groups of largely black Africans who are farmers, the Government armed the Janjaweed militias and unleashed them against black civilians."[31] By September, the U.S. accused the government of condoning and perpetrating genocide.[32] The U.S., however, was the lone supporter of the intentional story.

The Russian Federation, Brazil, and Pakistan initially advanced a complex story—all three members described the political and humanitarian situation in Darfur as "complex" and identified multiple parties as perpetrators guilty of human rights violations, and they also described a general situation of "lawlessness."[33] The number of members describing the conflict as complex would increase over the next two years, but the inadvertent causal story treating Darfur as a civil war was the dominant view of the Security Council in 2004. A majority of Council members in 2004 advanced an inadvertent story in which both the rebels and the government of Sudan were responsible for crimes against civilians, this majority including Algeria, Angola, Benin, France, Germany, Romania, Spain, and the United Kingdom. The UK argued that the government was failing to protect its people but also blamed the rebels for "their share of the responsibility for the present crisis."[34] Although most members of the council shared the U.S. concern about the rate of civilian deaths in Darfur and criticized the government for its failure to protect its citizens, they argued that multiple parties were responsible for the violence and demanded that all sides meet the obligations specified in the Humanitarian Ceasefire Agreement and UNSC resolutions. During formal meetings, these states demanded that the government disarm its militias and bring their leaders to justice but also demanded that rebel groups respect the cease-fire, engage in political talks without precondition, and stop their attacks on civilians.[35] Security Council Resolutions 1556 (2004) and 1564 (2004) reflected the inadvertent story. In addition to criticizing the government for not living up to its expressed commitments and the requirements of responsible statehood, both resolutions identified rebel leaders as sharing culpability with the government for the continuing violence, including violations of international humanitarian and human rights law.

Expert testimony in 2004 also supported the inadvertent explanation. In a September briefing to the Security Council on Sudan's compliance with the terms of Resolution 1556, the special representative of the secretary-general for Sudan argued that multiple parties were responsible for attacks against unarmed civilians in the context of a conflict between the government and rebel movements agitating for regional development. He noted that although the government had made progress in providing security and humanitarian access to areas with a high concentration of internally displaced persons, it had not met its commitments to stop attacks by government-supported militias and disarm them or to bring them to justice. Yet he also called on "both parties" to respect the Humanitarian Ceasefire Agreement and noted that the demands of the council applied equally to government and rebel movements.[36] In October, the special representative reported that both sides were violating the cease-fire agreement. He described attacks and counterattacks and a cycle of revenge and retaliation.[37] By the beginning of November, he noted that most of the violations of the cease-fire were the result of the SLA movement and he warned council members that Darfur might enter a state of anarchy. In short, the government was losing control over the situation in Darfur.[38] By December, he reported that a new rebel movement, National Movement for Reform and Development, had emerged and started attacking villages. The SLA was responsible for instigating government violence and the government had used disproportionate force and aerial bombing of villages in retaliation.[39] The story was evolving over time, but not without contention.

Contestation between the inadvertent and complex stories increased in 2005. During a February briefing, the special representative described the conflict in Darfur as having characteristics of a conflict that is "economic, cultural, sometimes religious, sometimes ethnic or tribal, and resource-driven, as well as political."[40] He advanced a complex story to explain the atrocities in Darfur:

> The conflict in Darfur is very complicated. It has political, economic, environmental and cultural dimensions. It is more than a civil war between a Government and rebel movements. It also encompasses a multitude of tribal conflicts—inter-tribal, as well as intra-tribal and clan fights. It certainly has some of the characteristics of a confrontation between Arabs and Africans. . . . But it is also a struggle for survival between economic lifestyles—peasants and nomads—and the borderline between those two is not the same as that between Arabs and Africans. The economic struggle has environmental dimensions.[41]

In March 2005, the International Commission of Inquiry on Darfur—created by Resolution 1564—submitted its report to the council. The commission identified the government and the Janjaweed as responsible for war crimes and crimes against humanity, but also indicated that rebel forces were responsible for serious violations that might amount to war crimes.[42] These findings were consistent with the inadvertent story. The commission also concluded that the government had not pursued a policy of genocide, rejecting the intentional story, but recommended that the Security Council refer the situation in Darfur to the International Criminal Court for further investigation, which it did later that month. At the end of 2005, permanent members remained divided over the character of the conflict. Despite contestation, however, consensus-based council documents, like presidential statements, reflected the inadvertent story.

Convergence Around the Complex Story

The Security Council achieved greater unity about the character of the conflict in 2006. In April, the chief mediator for the Inter-Sudanese Peace Talks on Darfur described the conflict: "Let us be clear: the war in Darfur is not a conventional war between contending armies, or even a war between conventional State armed forces and a guerrilla movement. Darfur is home to a myriad of armed and dangerous militias, including the Janjaweed, armed movements that are fragmenting, bandits of sorts, foreign combatants and tribal forces.[43]" The formal shift of council support from the inadvertent to the complex story came in June 2006, following a Security

Table 7.1. Changes in Support for Causal Stories in Darfur, 2004–2006

	Intentional Story	Inadvertent Story	Complex Story	Unarticulated
July 2004 (S/PV.5015)	U.S.	Algeria Angola Benin **France** Germany Romania Spain **UK**	Brazil Pakistan **Russia**	Chile **China** Philippines
February 2005 (S/PV.5120)	None	Presidential Statement of the Security Council	None	None
June 2006 (S/PV.5478)	None	None	Report of the Security Council Mission to Sudan and Chad	None

Council mission to Sudan headed by the UK (Table 7.1). In his subsequent briefing to the council, Ambassador Emyr Jones Perry emphasized the increasing complexity of the conflict, reaffirming the complex story being advanced by the Secretariat: "During its visit, the mission found that the conflict was not fully understood by the international community. It found, for example, that the terms 'Government,' 'rebel,' 'Arab,' and 'African' were often oversimplifications of a more complex situation on the ground, where alliances between tribes and groups often shift. The porous—or non-existent—border with Chad exacerbates. A number of the Council's interlocutors described the situation in Darfur as a traditional conflict between herdsmen and farmers over limited national resources."[44] Weeks later, the formal mission report was admitted into the public record. In the conclusion and recommendations section, the council concludes, "the conflict in Darfur is particularly complex, and the United Nations needs a range of policies to tackle it."[45] The council also determined that peace in Darfur was linked to the resolution of broader regional conflicts.[46] During the meeting to discuss the report, Jones Perry again emphasized the complexity of the conflict: "What we all understood clearly was how complex the situation is and how interrelated are all the different aspects in Sudan. But we also understood how it has to be put in a regional context."[47] Norway's representative's comments summed up the general Security Council response to the mission report: "My government welcomes and supports the analysis and recommendations emerging from the mission. . . . The complexity of the situation in the Sudan is illustrated by the fact that three different peace processes are going on at the same time. Each has its unique character, but they are all interconnected."[48] Following the mission's visit to Darfur the council had coalesced around the complex story. Its resonance was reflected in the briefings by the Secretariat, statements of individual council members, and consensus-based documents like presidential statements and mission reports.

Nonetheless, by 2007, experts briefing the council began to advance contradictory stories. Representatives of the UN Secretariat continued to articulate a complex story about intertribal fighting, Arab unrest, militancy, and fragmenting rebel groups. For example, the secretary-general's special envoy for Darfur, Jan Eliasson, reported, "Inter-tribal conflicts over land and water resources continue and persist. There is increasing concern of Arab unrest and militancy as well as a spillover of the conflict into Kordofan. Tensions in international displaced persons camps are growing. The raids of Government forces into camps, as well as incidents in and around camps, have led to loss of life, destruction of shelters and violations of human rights. Humanitarian access has been impeded."[49] However, Moréno-Ocampo, the prosecutor of the International Criminal Court, forcefully refuted these characterizations of the conflict. Instead, he argued that human rights violations were the result of a calculated, organized campaign by officials of the government of Sudan to destroy entire communities in Darfur, not "chaos" or "inter-tribal clashes."[50] Moréno-Ocampo asserted that "we are witnessing a calculated, organized campaign by Sudanese officials to attack individuals and further destroy the entire community. All information points not to chaotic and isolated acts, but to a pattern of attacks. We cannot and should not deny reality. Calling those crimes 'chaos' or 'sporadic violence' or 'inter-tribal clashes' is a cover-up."[51] Individual members of the Security Council criticized the government for lack of compliance with ICC arrest warrants for government officials and noted that lack of cooperation violated council resolutions. Despite widespread support for the ICC prosecutor in the council, its members continued to portray the conflict as a complex and multifaceted situation. In September 2007, for example, rebel groups had attacked African Union peacekeepers, operating in South Sudan as part of the monumental hybrid joint AU-UN peacekeeping force, killing several African peacekeepers. The council viewed multiple parties to the conflict as aggressors.

During 2008, the Secretariat continued to talk about multifaceted causes of the conflict and multiple layers of violence. The language used by Secretariat officials included terms associated with the inadvertent story (rebel movement clusters, attacks on civilians by all sides, intertribal fighting, and civil war) but the argument was nested within a broader narrative about complexity. In May 2008, for example, the under-secretary-general for peacekeeping operations argued that the situation in Darfur continued to grow "infinitely more complex."[52] In June, the special envoy of the secretary-general for Darfur said, "the complexity and scope of the conflict make it even more essential that we strengthen regional and international collaboration."[53] The ICC prosecutor, on the other hand, continued to dismiss the complex story. He compared the government to the Nazi regime and its intentions to those of Karadžić in Srebrenica.[54] Moréno-Ocampo agreed that the government has a right under international law to maintain control of its territory but argued that there was no military justification for bombing schools and raping women: "Those crimes have been carefully prepared and efficiently implemented. They are not mistakes. They are not inter-tribal clashes. They are not cases of collateral damage. They are, quite simply, criminal acts against civilians. Citizens from the Sudan are being deliberately attacked by Sudanese officials."[55] Despite these briefings by Moréno-Ocampo, council members continued to support the complex interpretation and seemed little interested in debating the character of the conflict in 2008. Council members who spoke on the public record did not deny the culpability of Sudanese officials but characterized their crimes as nested within a broader and more complex conflict in which all parties were committing human rights crimes.[56] According to Deborah Stone, causal stories are rough categories with ambiguous boundaries rather than clear dichotomies. The intentional story has strongly delineated boundaries driven by its three constituent components—identifiable perpetrator, intentional harm, and targeted victim; but complex stories may incorporate characteristics of both intentional and inadvertent stories within their complicated narratives.[57] Despite the ongoing debate between the members of the Secretariat and the ICC prosecutor over the character of the violence, Security Council documents did not deviate from the complex story, despite the mixed messages from independent experts.

Three concerns dominated Security Council meetings on Darfur in 2009. First, council members and members of the Secretariat argued that implementation of the Comprehensive Peace Agreement (CPA) between North and South Sudan was fundamental to peace in Sudan, including peace in Darfur. According to Rodolphe Adada, the joint AU-UN special representative for Darfur, "We must never forget that Darfur is part of the Sudan and that a solution to the crisis in Darfur is part and parcel of the wider national Sudanese issue."[58] Under-Secretary-General for Peacekeeping Operations Alain Le Roy argued that there were clear linkages between the CPA and the conflict in Darfur: "It is now more important than ever that we see both issues as parts of a whole and that we understand both issues to be linked to the marginalization of large portions of the population."[59] The head of the UN Mission in the Sudan, Ashraf Jehangir Qazi, also warned the council that 2009 "could be a make-or-break year for the CPA and for the prospect of peace in the Sudan."[60] Consequently, council decisions about Darfur were shaped by broader concerns about the CPA. For example, during a July council meeting, the UK clearly said, "The Sudan remains at the top of the Security Council agenda. We are focused on Darfur today, but the Comprehensive Peace Agreement remains the highest priority and the most urgent issue."[61] The need to balance the needs of multiple ongoing conflicts within the same state also reinforced the complex story.

Second, UNSC members unanimously condemned the government for its failures to address the humanitarian needs of its population. On 4 March, Pre-trial Chamber I of the ICC issued an arrest warrant for Sudanese president Omar al-Bashir on two counts of war crimes and five counts of crimes against humanity, including extermination, rapes, and killings. Within hours, Bashir expelled thirteen international humanitarian aid organizations that he accused of working for the ICC. These organizations provided between 50–60 percent of all humanitarian aid to the region, sparking a new humanitarian crisis. By 8 March, the Office for the Coordination of Humanitarian Affairs estimated that "1.5 million people no longer had access to food or health services; that drinking water, basic sanitation and hygiene services would no longer be provided to 1.16 million; that food would no longer be distributed to 1.1 million; and that 4,000 children would no longer receive assistance to address malnutrition."[62] Costa Rica reminded the government that "preventing those people's access to humanitarian assistance could result in their deaths, which could constitute another violation of international humanitarian law."[63] Condemnation of the government was universal by council members, who demanded the reversal of the government decision. The U.S. articulated an intentional story when it argued that President al-Bashir would bear individual responsibility for every death associated with his "callous and calculated actions."[64] The U.S. further asserted, "By expelling aid groups, the Sudanese Government is denying water, food, health care and sanitation to people it drove out of their homes in the first place, thereby exacerbating an already dire humanitarian crisis in Darfur. Let me be clear: this is not a made-up crisis, as the representative of Sudan would have the Council believe. On the contrary, this is a very real and urgent crisis of his Government's own making."[65] Other council members agreed that President al-Bashir should reverse his decision but they did so within the context of the complex causal story. Third, the intentional counternarrative advanced by the ICC prosecutor in June and December did not diminish Security Council support for the complex story. Council meetings did emphasize the evolving and changing character of the conflict, however. Thus, evidence of war crimes and crimes against humanity—indicators of an intentional story—were incorporated into the broader narrative of the complex causal story that identified multiple types of crimes with multiple perpetrators.

In April, Adada, the joint AU-UN special representative for Darfur and head of the AU-UN Hybrid Operation in Darfur, described the political situation in Darfur as "a conflict of everybody against everybody. . . . Government forces against the armed movements, the armed movements among one another. Government forces against the militias and tribal groups against one another. There is also endemic banditry due to a breakdown in law and order."[66] The complex story remained dominant in the UNSC even after the ICC briefings in June and December and was reinforced by expert testimony from members of the Secretariat and the African Union. In July, Alain Le Roy, the under-secretary-general for peacekeeping operations, lamented the "heart-wrenching complexity" of the Darfur crisis.[67] Le Roy briefed the council on the changing character of the conflict, which he explained was no longer characterized by large-scale civilian deaths and displacement. Instead, he described local attacks by rebels against the government and the government against the rebels along with interethnic conflicts and cross-border hostilities with Chad. Le Roy called for the UNSC to adapt "analysis and actions to correspond to the realities on the ground."[68] In December 2009, a prominent delegation from the African Union Commission briefed the council. Its chairperson, Jean Ping, explained that the violence in Sudan was connected to "the fundamental inequality that characterizes the relationship between the Sudanese centre and hinterlands." He described the crisis in Darfur as a "manifestation of the wider crisis in the Sudan as both a country and a State."[69] Thabo Mbeki, chairperson of the African Union High-Level Panel on Darfur and former president of South Africa, briefed the council on the findings of the High-Level Panel, including the underlying causes of the conflict. "It arose," according to Mbeki, "essentially from the concentration of power and wealth in an elite centred in Khartoum, resulting in the marginalization, impoverishment and underdevelopment of the so-called periphery, including Darfur."[70] Consequently, the AU determined that the resolution of the conflict would require "the restructuring of Sudan as a whole in order to address the historical legacy, the consequences of which has [sic] been the various conflicts that have afflicted Sudan for many decades."[71]

In 2010 and 2011 the Security Council's focus shifted to the CPA and the referendum that determined South Sudan's independence from Sudan. Discussions regarding Darfur were less frequent and focused principally on the joint AU-UN peace process in Doha, Qatar. On 14 July 2011 the Darfur rebel group, the Liberation and Justice Movement, signed a permanent cease-fire and comprehensive and inclusive peace settlement for Darfur with the government of Sudan. The Doha Document for Peace in Darfur was endorsed by the Security Council but several important Darfurian rebel groups were missing from the agreement, including those that had initiated the conflict, the JEM and two factions of the divided SLA—the SLA-Abdul Wahid and the SLA-Minni Minawi. Council members urged rebel groups to join the peace process and criticized those that did not. In December 2011, however, the ICC prosecutor briefed the council on the work of the Court. Moréno-Ocampo continued to challenge the complex story, announcing to the council that he had just submitted an application for a new arrest warrant for the former minister of the interior, Abdelrahim Mohamed Hussein, who was then serving as Sudan's minister of defense. The prosecutor accused the government of continuing "genocidal intentions" by orchestrating a program of rape and hunger in Darfur refugee camps. Moréno-Ocampo noted that the law does not require that the crime of extermination has been committed with bullets; deprivation of access to food and medicines qualify when they are intentionally calculated to bring about the destruction of part of a population or group.[72]

The same factors that mediated contestation between causal stories in other cases caused the complex story to win over its competitors in Darfur. Graphic media imagery kept the conflict high on the Security Council's agenda. In response to continuing death, displacement, and hunger of civilians, members regularly and harshly criticized the government for not meeting its obligations toward its citizens. Most expert testimony, however, described these atrocities as the result of a complex interaction of multiple simultaneous conflicts having to do with economics and the environment as well as power, ethnicity, and tribe. Over time, expert testimony persuaded the majority of council members, including most permanent members, to adopt the complex explanation over the inadvertent one. The council mission's 2006 visit to Sudan confirmed the complex causal story for council members, causing most of them to adopt it. As a result, the UNSC converged around a complex story, rather than an inadvertent or intentional causal story.

The complex story continued to persist even when the Security Council was confronted with new and conflicting expert testimony like the intentional story articulated by the ICC prosecutor. In fact, for some council members, the evidence presented by Moréno-Ocampo actually reinforced the argument in favor of complexity by demonstrating that elements of deliberate and systematic human rights violations coexisted alongside intertribal clashes and splintering rebel movements. Both civil war and state-inflicted violence were characterized as components, rather than the totality of the conflict. Although the United States is the most prominent and powerful member of the council, its lone support for the intentional story was insufficient to gain other adherents. Humanitarian intervention requires that a majority of permanent members adopt or at least acquiesce to an intentional story. Instead, the majority of members, including the four other permanent members, adopted the complex story.

Sovereignty and Human Rights

Security Council members articulate stories about the cause and character of the conflict and also articulate stories about sovereign authority. In meetings about the situation in Darfur, there was little disagreement among members that the government of Omar al-Bashir was the legitimate sovereign authority in Sudan. They did disagree about whether Bashir was meeting the expected requirements of a sovereign state, however, in part because they privileged different conceptions of state sovereignty. China and Russia, for example, privileged a Westphalian conception of sovereignty that emphasized noninterference in the domestic affairs of states. France, the UK, and the U.S., among others, either privileged a popular conception of sovereignty or endorsed the concept of sovereignty as responsibility. Although intended to eliminate tensions between sovereignty and human rights, the responsibility to protect was insufficiently developed to overcome the barrier to humanitarian intervention caused by a perpetrator state. In Darfur, the sovereignty of the government was neither absent, as in Somalia, nor contested, as in Bosnia. Since the government was the legitimate sovereign, its status as a principal perpetrator of mass atrocity crimes meant that humanitarian intervention would bring human rights norms into direct conflict with Westphalian sovereignty and nonintervention norms. As a result, council members were subject to conflicting normative claims. In this context, as this work has made clear, more highly internalized norms like state sovereignty tend to trump emerging ones like humanitarian intervention and the responsibility to protect. In the case of Darfur, the Security Council was unable to discursively construct sovereignty and human rights as complementary. Thus, they could not preserve government sovereignty and intervene militarily to advance human rights at the same time.

Derogations of Sovereignty in Defense of Human Rights
Protection and Prosecution

In Darfur, Security Council decision making was shaped by changing beliefs about government responsibility and accountability for human rights even though humanitarian intervention did not occur. Debates about human rights and international humanitarian law shaped council decision making and led to important innovations in council practice. In September 2004, the council signaled its concern with human rights when it authorized an Independent Commission of Inquiry to investigate allegations of international humanitarian law and human rights violations in Darfur. Later, the council affirmed that state sovereignty included the responsibility to protect civilians in the passage of resolutions 1556 (2004), 1564 (2004), 1674 (2006), and 1706 (2006). The UNSC made a historic decision when it exercised its right to refer cases to the ICC when it passed Resolution 1593

(2005) giving the ICC jurisdiction over Darfur. During debate on the resolution and in subsequent ICC briefings, many council members directly
linked the peaceful settlement of the Darfur conflict with the pursuit of
justice and human rights protection with the maintenance of international
security. Ramesh Thakur has referred to these two normative developments—
the responsibility to protect and the responsibility to prosecute—as two
sides of the same coin.[73]

During meetings, Security Council members repeatedly emphasized the
government of Sudan's responsibility to protect the people of Darfur as
well as the international community's responsibility to do so in absence
of state success. The language of responsibility to protect was used in the
preambulatory clauses of Resolution 1556 and Resolution 1564, which
passed with thirteen and ten votes respectively, reflecting reasonable agreement with the principle that sovereign states have a responsibility to protect
their populations. Justifying the passage of Resolution 1556, the UK argued,
"the adoption of this resolution underlines the commitment of the Council
to ensure that all Governments fulfill that most basic of obligations—the
duty to protect their own citizens."[74] France and Germany described the
government's responsibility to protect its citizens as a "primary responsibility" and "sacred obligation," respectively.[75] The Philippines asserted that
the UNSC bears the moral and legal authority to ensure that states fulfill
their sovereign duties: "Sovereignty also entails the responsibility of a state
to protect its people. If it is unable or unwilling to do so, the international
community has the responsibility to help that State achieve such capacity
and such will and, in extreme necessity, to assume such responsibility itself.
We voted in favour of resolution 1556 (2004) in that context."[76] The language of the responsibility to protect in Resolution 1564, authorizing the
creation of the Independent Commission of Inquiry, was explicit in "*Recalling* that the Sudanese Government bears the primary responsibility to protect its population within its territory, to respect human rights, and to
maintain law and order and that all parties are obliged to respect international humanitarian law."[77] Benin argued that the concept of sovereignty as
responsibility reflected a renewed commitment of the UN to the fundamental rights, human dignity, and worth of the human being—principles enshrined in the Charter of the United Nations.[78]

The Security Council formally affirmed the emerging norm of the responsibility to protect in Resolution 1674 on the protection of civilians in
armed conflict and Resolution 1706, which applied the principle to the

situation in Darfur. Specifically, Resolution 1674 refers to paragraphs 138 and 139 of the World Summit Outcome document, which affirms that respect for human rights is essential to international relations; declares that individual states have a responsibility to protect their populations from genocide, war crimes, ethnic cleansing and crimes against humanity; and endorses the principle that the UN has the responsibility to protect populations through the collective action of the council.[79] Resolution 1706 was the first application of the responsibility to protect in a case-specific resolution. It also was the first council resolution establishing a UN peacekeeping operation that makes an explicit reference to "the responsibility of each United Nations Member State to protect its citizens and the international community's responsibility to assist in this if the state could not provide for such protection alone."[80] China, Russia, and Qatar abstained. China and Qatar argued that the government had not yet consented to a transition from the AU Mission in Sudan to the hybrid UN-led peacekeeping force. Russia abstained based on its objection to the use of the responsibility-to-protect language in the resolution. In contrast, Argentina, Ghana, Greece, Slovakia, and the UK each argued that the UN had a moral duty and a responsibility to act to protect the civilian population of Darfur.[81] While not all council members endorsed the responsibility to protect, no permanent member vetoed Resolution 1706. This suggests that detractors either did not view it as a fundamental threat to their national interests or that their national interests are sufficiently shaped by norms of human rights protection that they did not wish to be perceived in international society as anti–human rights. Table 7.2 contains a comparison of how members voted on key Security Council resolutions for Darfur.

Member statements in support of the responsibility to protect following briefings by the ICC prosecutor indicate that council members connected the responsibility to protect civilians with a responsibility to prosecute perpetrators when human rights are violated. For example, Croatia argued in March 2009, "The Government of the Sudan has a responsibility to protect not only its people but also the international peacekeepers and humanitarian workers who are in Sudan to help the people of Sudan. There must be accountability for gross violations of international humanitarian law, and impunity cannot be tolerated."[82] Ramesh Thakur and Vesselin Popovski refer to this as the "twin protection-prosecution agenda." They argue that international criminal prosecution is another form of international intervention in response to atrocity crimes.[83] Both contribute to long-term peace

Table 7.2. Security Council Support for Key Resolutions, Darfur

	Subject	Votes in Favor	Votes Against	Abstentions
Resolution 1564 (2004)	Authorizes the creation of Independent Commission of Inquiry to investigate rights violations in Darfur	Angola Benin Brazil Chile **France** Germany Philippines Romania Spain **UK** **U.S.**	None	Algeria **China** Pakistan **Russia**
Resolution 1593 (2005)	Referral of Darfur to the ICC	Argentina Benin Denmark **France** Greece Japan Philippines Romania **Russia** **UK** Tanzania	None	Algeria Brazil **China** **U.S.**
Resolution 1674 (2006)	Protection of civilians in armed conflict; affirms idea of responsibility to protect	Argentina **China** Congo Denmark **France** Ghana Greece Japan Peru Qatar **Russia** Slovakia Tanzania **UK** **U.S.**	None	None

Table 7.2. (Continued0

	Subject	Votes in Favor	Votes Against	Abstentions
Resolution 1706 (2006)	Reaffirms the responsibility to protect in a case-specific resolution on Darfur	Argentina Congo Denmark **France** Ghana Greece Japan Peru Slovakia Tanzania **UK** **U.S.**	None	**China** Qatar **Russia**

and security, according to France's representative: "I would like to reiterate that France believes firmly both in the authority of the Security Council, as the main United Nations body for maintaining peace and security, and in that of the International Criminal Court, as the judicial body responsible for punishing the most serious crimes in violation of international humanitarian law and human rights, to which the Council has entrusted the mission of prosecuting the atrocities committed in Darfur."[84] Similarly, Croatia argued, "The International Criminal Court is an essential means of promoting respect for international humanitarian law and human rights, thus contributing to freedom, security, justice and the rule of law, as well as contributing to the preservation of peace and the strengthening of international security."[85] Not all Security Council members agreed that impunity leads to future human rights violations and that prosecution leads to peace, however. Vietnam, for example, argued that the arrest warrant for President al-Bashir was directly linked to the deterioration of the humanitarian situation in Darfur in March 2009.

> Viet Nam has been a consistent and strong supporter of the struggle against impunity. We have always maintained that those committing crimes, especially the most serious crimes such as the crime of genocide, war crimes and crimes against humanity, must be duly punished—rather sooner than later. At the same time, concerning the

situation in the Sudan in general and in Darfur in particular, we have pointed to the need to maintain a balance between promoting the political process and waging the fight against impunity, in the interest of long-term peace and security for the Sudan and for Darfur.[86]

Yet even dissenters to the ICC indictment and arrest warrant were unwilling to speak in defense of impunity. Council members were forced to defend their political positions inside the parameters of appropriateness defined by the new norm, whether they agreed, only in part or not at all, with the emerging norm against sovereign impunity.

The Interplay of Norms and Interests

The Darfur case demonstrates that consent matters when perpetrators of human rights violations are sovereign state members of the United Nations. Alongside the developing practice of humanitarian intervention are norms about the conditions under which it can be undertaken. Even acceptance of the responsibility to protect does not justify coercive military intervention in every case of large-scale loss of life.[87] Rather, the use of military force—even in defense of victims of grave crimes—must be weighed against the prospects for a successful outcome. The precautionary principles established by the Independent Commission on Intervention and State Sovereignty note that there must be a reasonable prospect for success in averting the suffering that justifies military intervention and that the use of military force must not cause more harm than inaction.[88] In short, humanitarian intervention must do more good than harm.

By definition, humanitarian intervention is undertaken without consent of authorities in the target state, but consent matters when intervening states have a limited ability to deploy troops and must literally fight their way in to protect civilians. In such cases, consent becomes a practical necessity to the act of rescue.[89] The prospect of a successful nonconsensual military intervention to protect human life in Darfur had been diminished by the U.S. wars in Iraq and Afghanistan. Western powers lacked the military capacity to intervene militarily as a result of troop commitments in Afghanistan and Iraq, and without the support of Western troops other military forces were ill equipped and lacked the political will to fight. Western powers also lacked the moral authority to engage in humanitarian intervention in Sudan. The preventive and unilateral invasion of Iraq generated fear among developing states that the doctrine of humanitarian intervention was becoming too easily justified. Opponents of the responsibility to protect argued that the U.S.-led invasion of Iraq was evidence of Western interventionism driven by national interests rather than norms of civilian protection and human rights. It was politically untenable—and even threatening to new norms—for Western states to be seen as going to war against another Muslim country.

UNSC documents also indicate that the council was also unwilling to authorize coercive military force in Sudan because it would endanger the progress of the fragile CPA agreement. In addition, Western leaders also feared that an intervention in Darfur might provoke further insurgencies throughout Sudan and threaten a political process that has made significant progress in dealing with long-standing grievance in Sudan.[90] Finally, there was a lack of moral clarity within the Security Council over who the victims and perpetrators of atrocities were. There were no clear conception of who the good guys were and a myriad of perpetrators. Intentional stories create the possibility of humanitarian intervention because they identify perpetrators who are responsible for deliberate harm. In complex stories, like the one articulated by the UNSC about Darfur, responsibility for atrocities is diffuse.

Conclusions

The widespread use and adoption of particular causal stories by Security Council members map onto their humanitarian intervention decisions. The articulation of an intentional story creates opportunities for humanitarian intervention by identifying intentional perpetrators. Conversely, stories in which responsibility for mass atrocity is diffuse, like inadvertent and complex stories, foreclose opportunities for humanitarian intervention. There was no easy distinction between good guys and bad guys in Darfur, according to the special envoy of the African Union to Darfur: "Even though, as I said, the Government of Sudan bears primary responsibility, it would be wrong to assume that on the one hand you have all the nice guys and on the other hand you have all the bad guys. That is not true. In other words, therefore, you have to deal with the nice guys and the bad guys wherever they appear, whether they come from the Government side or the side of the movements."[91] Complexity and diffuse responsibility are barriers to humanitarian intervention. The complex story won out over competitors because of the normative and material power of its proponents and its consistency with expert testimony, media imagery, and forensic evidence.

Security Council humanitarian intervention decisions are also shaped by stories about sovereign authority. In Darfur, council members agreed that Omar al-Bashir's government was the legitimate sovereign authority. Since the government was a principal perpetrator of the conflict, the promotion of human rights norms through humanitarian intervention would directly violate sovereignty norms. Though many members discursively supported the ICISS conception of sovereignty as responsibility, the responsibility-to-protect norm was insufficiently internalized to eliminate the perceived normative incoherence between sovereignty norms and human rights norms.

Despite the absence of humanitarian intervention, human rights norms shaped Security Council decision making alongside national and international interests. Council members worried that humanitarian intervention in Darfur would endanger the fragile north-south peace agreement designed to end more than twenty years of brutal civil war. They also feared that humanitarian intervention might provoke further insurgencies throughout Sudan.[92] This represents not just a conflict between interests and norms but also a conflict between different international norms—sovereignty, security, human rights, and domestic noninterference. Ideas about human rights, however, led to innovative council practices short of the use of military force in defense of human rights. For the first time, the UNSC reaffirmed the responsibility-to-protect principles in a case-specific Security Council resolution and it referred the situation in Darfur to the International Criminal Court for investigation, signaling its support for the twin protection-prosecution agenda.

The Responsibility to Protect, Individual Criminal Accountability, and Humanitarian Intervention in Libya

On 15 February 2011, the wave of protests that had been sweeping the Middle East since December 2010 came to Libya. As in other Arab states, popular protests began peacefully but were immediately met with a violent and repressive response by the ruling regime. Unlike protests in Tunisia and Egypt, however, the situation quickly escalated into a full-scale war between the opposition, which armed itself and fought for the removal of the Muammar Qadhafi regime, and the ruling authorities, who used overwhelming force against civilians and the armed opposition alike. The escalating violence in Libya quickly captured the attention of the United Nations Security Council, which held its first formal consultations on the situation within the first week of protests. When these deliberations began, it had been five years since the UNSC had formally affirmed the principle of the responsibility to protect in Resolution 1674 and more than a decade since its last humanitarian intervention. During this period, norm advocates were busy defending the doctrine of the responsibility to protect and promoting its consolidation at the UN through the passage of resolutions and its inclusion in UN reports.[1] In contrast, norm detractors questioned both the legitimacy of the principle and whether the practice of humanitarian intervention had lost its relevance in a post–September 11 world and in the shadow of the unauthorized invasion of Iraq by the United States in 2003. Humanitarian intervention in Libya demonstrated that the international normative context had been changing over the course of the previous decade. By March 2011 it was easier for the UNSC to justify the use of military force to protect civilians at risk of state-perpetrated murder in Libya than to justify its absence.[2]

In February and March 2011, the Security Council passed two historic resolutions. Resolution 1970 referred the situation in Libya to the prosecutor of the International Criminal Court and was passed unanimously by the council. This was a significant development because the UNSC had only once before made an ICC referral—Resolution 1593 (2005) on Darfur—and four members including two permanent members had abstained. In the case of Resolution 1970, both China and the U.S. voted in favor of referral despite not being members of the court. The passage of this resolution signifies that a responsibility to prosecute perpetrators of grave international crimes is gaining traction in the Security Council and is another example of the increasing legitimacy of human rights norms at the UN. The second resolution, Resolution 1973, authorized the use of "all necessary measures" short of foreign occupation to protect civilians in Libya. Resolution 1973 was remarkable because it created a no-fly zone and authorized military protection of civilian-populated areas within weeks of the outbreak of violence and on the basis of apprehended rather than actual mass atrocities. Such an expansive mandate underscored growing support for the view that states can no longer hide behind the principle of state sovereignty in order to massacre their own people, and that the international community has a responsibility to protect populations at risk when their own governments fail to do so.

Unlike most of the previous cases in this study, only a single causal story was articulated in the UNSC about Libya—an intentional story in which Libyan authorities were perpetrators of widespread and systematic crimes against innocent civilians. Security Council debates were notable for the broad agreement among members on the cause and character of the violence as well as its perpetrators and victims. In fact, members devoted little time to conceptualizing the violence. Instead, their deliberations focused on how best to respond to "the gross and systematic violation of human rights" in Libya and how to promote "the legitimate aspirations" of the Libyan people.[3] As with previous cases in this study, the dominance of any particular story is mediated by the prominence of its proponents and its consistency with expert testimony, forensic evidence, and media imagery. From the outset, senior UN officials, including the secretary-general, his special advisors, and the high commissioner for human rights characterized the violence as government repression and described the violations of human rights as potential crimes against humanity. This early framing at the UN was complemented by the stories about the violence advanced by regional organizations. Official statements by the League of Arab States (Arab League), the Gulf Cooperation Council (GCC), the Organization for Islamic Cooperation (OIC), and the African Union all characterized the violence in Libya as intentional: perpetrated deliberately and willingly by Libyan authorities acting under the direction of Colonel Muammar Qadhafi against innocent civilians.[4] Without the public calls and private requests of the Arab League for the authorization of a no-fly zone to protect Libyan civilians, it is unlikely that Security Council members would have coalesced so quickly around the intentional story, given its potential policy implications. Finally, the intentional story was highly consistent with independent expertise including the reports by Libyan human rights advocates and the research of international human rights organizations like Human Rights Watch and Amnesty International.

Resolution 1973 also was historic because it provided the first explicit authorization to use military force against a UN member to stop a perpetrator government from committing human rights atrocities. Chapter VII resolutions had paved the way for humanitarian intervention in previous situations of mass killing but they had never done so explicitly against a legitimate state member of the UN to stop ongoing atrocities. The Security Council authorized the use of military force in Somalia but in absence of a legitimate sovereign government. In Bosnia-Herzegovina, sovereign authority was initially contested and then vested in the Bosnian government, which was characterized as the victim rather than the perpetrator. In Sierra Leone, a UN peacekeeping mission preceded humanitarian intervention, but when the UN undertook the latter, it was in defense of a democratically deposed government rather than against a perpetrator one. Humanitarian intervention in Libya against a perpetrator state suggests that the meaning of sovereignty has been reconceptualized at the UN to include at least a minimal commitment to the most fundamental human rights. Sovereignty now confers state responsibility as well as state rights, opening up new debates in the UNSC about what constitutes legitimate sovereign authority, particularly in the context of mass atrocity crimes.

More remarkable than quick coalescence by the UNSC around an intentional story was its agreement on the status of Libyan state sovereignty. Though Security Council resolutions reaffirmed the sovereignty and territorial integrity of the Libyan state, Security Council members simultaneously argued that Libyan authorities, including Qadhafi, had lost the legitimate right to rule. Rhetorically, they invested sovereign authority in the Libyan people, reflecting a conceptual move toward sovereignty as responsibility and away from the traditional Westphalian conception that had dominated the UNSC in previous decades. This was a groundbreaking development and it ultimately paved the way for humanitarian intervention. The discursive characterization of the Libyan people as the sovereign authority eliminated normative incoherence by making it possible for interveners to promote human rights and protect sovereignty simultaneously.

The United Nations Security Council and the Libyan Revolution

Libya is situated between Egypt and Tunisia—two countries whose populations succeeded in deposing their autocratic leaders in the Arab Spring uprisings that began in Tunisia in December 2010 and quickly spread to Egypt and other Arab states including Libya by February 2011. Libya comprises three provinces, but the geographic, cultural, and political divisions between the eastern and western provinces of Cyrenaica and Tripolitania had led to long-standing tensions between them. Libya's two urban centers have belonged to different economic and political spheres and have had closer relations with Egypt and the Arabian Peninsula respectively than with each other.[5] Colonel Muammar Qadhafi came to power after overthrowing the monarchy based in Cyrenaica in a 1969 coup. Qadhafi privileged the Tripoli region where his native town of Sirte is located over the eastern region, which he deemed potentially disloyal because of its historic links with the monarchy and Islam. He largely neglected Cyrenaica (and its urban center, Benghazi) and often played the two provinces off of each other as part of his strategy to stay in power.[6] Qadhafi maintained control over the country for four decades through the use of arbitrary arrest, torture, enforced disappearances, and political killings.[7] Control through the use of violence was complemented by the lack of a functioning civil society, the absence of a free press, a ban on private ownership and retail trade, and underdeveloped formal institutions, with the civil service and military leadership subverted by Qadhafi. The military, in particular, was underfunded with resources and training instead directed toward elite units composed of tribal allies and mercenaries that were controlled by Qadhafi's sons.[8] Over time, kin networks became extremely important, replacing much of the public-sector bureaucracy by providing everything from security to goods and services.[9] Libya's vast oil wealth also helped maintain power by funding government subsidies for health care and education. In addition, it is estimated that nearly 70 percent of the population was on the state payroll, making the population susceptible to manipulation and control by the regime.[10]

The seeds of the February 2011 uprising in Benghazi were planted two years prior when a small group of families of disappeared prisoners began holding weekly demonstrations to protest the Qadhafi regime's failure to abide by a March 2007 court ruling requiring the government to reveal information about the fate of their missing family members. More than twelve hundred prisoners at Abu Salim Prison, many of whom were political prisoners, were massacred by the Internal Security Agency in 1996 following a prison riot over poor living conditions.[11] The arrest and detention of prominent human rights lawyer Fathih Terbil, who represented the families in their case against the government, sparked the spontaneous protests that shook Benghazi on 15 February. Several hundred family members and their supporters joined the Revolutionary Committee in Benghazi in protests outside police headquarters, eventually clashing with security forces.[12] The protest quickly escalated and within days, thousands of protesters were in the streets of Benghazi calling for the overthrow of the regime. Yet even before Terbil's arrest, opposition organizations and Libyan websites laid the groundwork for protests, calling for a "Day of Rage" to be held on 17 February. This day was symbolic because it marked the anniversary of a peaceful demonstration in 2006 that had been violently disrupted by security forces. A similar effort had been organized in 2007 but ultimately failed when the regime arrested its organizers before the protests began.[13] Media reports estimated that the number of protesters in Benghazi alone had reached fifteen thousand by 18 February 2011 and unrest was spreading to other towns in the northeast and southeast of the country.[14]

The response of Muammar Qadhafi's regime was swift and brutal as the police, security forces, and mercenaries moved to rout dissent by shooting into crowds of unarmed demonstrators and arbitrarily arresting, torturing, and killing protesters, human rights advocates, and journalists. The regime used live ammunition and heavy weaponry in the streets in an effort to crush the rebellion. The Security Council held its first consultations on the situation in Libya only one week after the protests began—the same day that Qadhafi pledged to make the streets of Benghazi run with blood.[15] During a 22 February televised address, Qadhafi alternately described the protesters as "rats" and "terrorists" and called on loyal citizens to join the regime in "securing and cleansing" their areas from "these rats." He warned, "We will issue a call to the millions, from the desert to the desert. And I and the millions will march in order to cleanse Libya, inch by inch, house by house, home by home, alley by alley, individual by individual, so that the country is purified from the unclean."[16] That same day, the international community launched an unprecedented international response to protect Libyan civilians from the Qadhafi regime.

The regional response to the violence in Libya was historic. On 22 February, Mohammad Moussa, the secretary-general of the Arab League, announced the suspension of Libya from the organization and called for an immediate end to all violence. Moussa urged the initiation of a national dialogue to respond to the legitimate demands of the Libyan people and called on Libyan authorities to respect the rights of citizens protesting and expressing opinions in a peaceful manner.[17] This was the first suspension of league membership in more than thirty years and only the second suspension in the organization's history (the league temporarily suspended Egypt in 1979). The next day, the African Union Peace and Security Council condemned the "indiscriminate and excessive use of force by Libyan authorities" against peaceful protesters as violations of international human rights and international humanitarian law.[18] Then, in early March, both the Gulf Cooperation Council and the Organization of Islamic Cooperation condemned the crimes perpetrated by Libyan authorities against civilians and called on the UNSC to take necessary measures to protect civilians, including the enforcement of a no-fly zone over Libyan territory.[19] As the seriousness of the violence increased, so did the regional response. On 12 March, the Arab League met at the ministerial level in an irregular session at the headquarters of the General Secretariat in Cairo. There the ministers reaffirmed their previous statements demanding that the regime stop committing crimes against the Libyan people, end the fighting, and withdraw its forces from cities and regions they had entered forcibly.[20] Most notably however, Arab League Resolution 7360 asked the UNSC to impose a no-fly zone to restrict the movement of Libyan warplanes immediately and to establish safe areas for civilian protection.[21] The demand for the UNSC to provide civilian protection was unanimous from the region's principal organizations.

The United Nations response to the violence in Libya was as swift and severe as the regional response. Within a week of the outbreak of violence, the Security Council received its first briefing on the situation from the under-secretary-general for political affairs during a closed meeting on 22 February. Seventy-five members of the United Nations joined the fifteen members of the Security Council at the briefing as nonvoting participants, demonstrating significant international concern with the situation.[22] That same day, the UN high commissioner for human rights, Navi Pillay, former president of the International Criminal Tribunal for Rwanda and a former judge of the ICC, issued a statement in which she declared that the widespread and systematic attacks against the civilian population by Libyan authorities might amount to crimes against humanity.[23] Two independent UN human rights investigators, the special rapporteur on extrajudicial, summary, and arbitrary executions and the special rapporteur on torture, similarly condemned the Libyan authorities for committing gross human rights violations, which they described as punishable under international law.[24] The secretary-general's special advisors on the prevention of genocide and the responsibility to protect, Francis Deng and Edward Luck, also issued a joint statement in which they warned that "egregious violations of international human rights and humanitarian law, if confirmed, may constitute crimes against humanity."[25] They reminded Libyan authorities and other countries facing similar protests that the heads of state and government at the 2005 World Summit had pledged to protect populations from atrocity crimes as well as their incitement. These official statements by senior UN officials were underscored by the secretary-general himself, Ban Ki-Moon, who quickly framed the Libyan crisis in responsibility-to-protect terms: "When a State manifestly fails to protect its population from serious international crimes, the international community has the responsibility to step in and take protective action in a collective, timely and decisive manner."[26] Secretary-General Ban Ki-Moon argued that the "obligation of the international community to do everything possible for the protection of civilians" in Libya was clear; the challenge was to determine how to provide real protection and stop the ongoing violence.[27]

Rhetorical UN condemnation of Libyan authorities, and Qadhafi in particular, quickly escalated into material action. On 25 February, fifty member states of the UN requested a special session of the Human Rights Council to address the situation in Libya, marking the first time that a member of that council became the subject of a special session.[28] The

Human Rights Council took two actions: (1) it established an independent international commission of inquiry to investigate allegations of human rights violations and crimes against humanity in Libya, and (2) it recommended that the General Assembly consider suspending Libya from the Human Rights Council.[29] The General Assembly followed that recommendation on 1 March when it unanimously passed a resolution introduced by Lebanon and cosponsored by seventy-two other states temporarily suspending Libyan membership from the council.[30] Within the first month of fighting, the UNSC also unanimously passed Resolution 1970, which referred the situation in Libya to the International Criminal Court, imposed an arms embargo on the country, and leveled a travel ban and asset freeze against Qadhafi, his family members, and high-ranking members of the government. Resolution 1973, which was passed with ten votes and five abstentions, imposed a no-fly zone and authorized member states to take all necessary measures to protect threatened civilians. Both Secretary-General Ban-Ki Moon and U.S. secretary of state Hillary Clinton said that the international community had "spoken with one voice" with regard to Libya.[31]

The Intentional Story About Libyan Atrocities

Part of what distinguishes Libya from many of the cases in this study is the rapid coalescence of the Security Council around a common story about the cause and character of the violence. During its first formal meeting on the public record, a clear majority of UNSC members explicitly framed the conflict using an intentional story that identified Libyan authorities as the perpetrators of widespread and systematic human rights violations and possible crimes against humanity. Subsequent Security Council resolutions also articulated an intentional story within the resolution text. In fact, not one alternative story was advanced in the Security Council to characterize the conflict in Libya prior to actual humanitarian intervention. Only after military intervention did the unity among council members break down. Nonetheless, there remained widespread agreement on the identities and intentional behavior of the perpetrators and on the innocence of the victims.

The violence in Libya quickly became a priority issue for the UNSC, which met to discuss the conflict three times in the first week that it appeared on its agenda. The first two meetings used private consultations, but

Table 8.1. Security Council Stories About Violence in Libya

	Intentional Story	Inadvertent Story	Complex Story	Unarticulated
February 2011 (S/PV.6491) Referral of Libya to the ICC	S/RES/1970 Bosnia **France** Germany Portugal South Africa **UK** **U.S.**	None	None	Brazil **China** Colombia Gabon India Lebanon Nigeria **Russia**
March 2011 (S/PV.6498) Authorization of all necessary means to protect civilians	S/RES/1973 Brazil **France** Lebanon Nigeria Portugal South Africa	None	None	Bosnia **China** Colombia Gabon Germany India **Russia** UK U.S.

on 26 February the Security Council discussed the situation in Libya publicly for the first time. At this meeting, Security Council members characterized the violence in Libya in strikingly similar ways, regardless of the geographic location of their states, membership in regional organizations, or permanent or elected membership status. There was widespread agreement that violations of human rights were occurring in Libya with both the knowledge and expressed authorization of Libyan authorities. Not a single UNSC member defended the violence or the Libyan authorities against accusations of criminal behavior. At least seven members of the Security Council (Bosnia, France, Germany, Portugal, South Africa, the United Kingdom, and the United States) explicitly articulated an intentional story to explain the cause and character of the violence (Table 8.1). For example, Germany stated the consensus view of the group when its ambassador explained his vote in favor of Resolution 1970: "The international community will not tolerate the gross and systematic violation of human rights by the Libyan regime. That is what we owe to the Libyan people, and that is why we imposed sanctions on the Libyan leadership."[32] Portugal described the

actions of the Qadhafi regime as "heinous crimes." France characterized the violence as a "brutal and bloody repression," and South Africa criticized the "indiscriminate use of force" against the Libyan people. The victims were Libyan civilians who were described as having "legitimate aspirations" and acting in a manner consistent with their human rights.[33] The perpetrator was identified as the Libyan government, and Colonel Qadhafi was identified by name as responsible for violations of human rights and possibly crimes against humanity.[34] The ambassador from Libya, who had defected from the regime, described Qadhafi in villainous terms as both "the criminal leader" and "the butcher of Tripoli."[35] The secretary-general repeated the intentional narrative but in so doing, highlighted that the Qadhafi regime's actions were inconsistent with international human rights norms and humanitarian law: "The actions taken by the regime in Libya are clear-cut violations of all norms governing international behavior, and serious transgressions of international human rights and humanitarian law."[36]

Even though only seven Security Council members explicitly articulated the three constituent components of an intentional story, Resolution 1970, which as noted earlier was passed unanimously by the entire council, also contained all three elements: deliberate violence named to depict its intentional character, identifiable perpetrators, and specific victims targeted by the perpetrators. The perambulatory clauses of Resolution 1970 describe the violence in Libya three times as "violations of human rights and international humanitarian law" and characterize these violations as "gross," "systematic," and "widespread." The resolution also names the violence in a manner that depicts its intentional character: potential "crimes against humanity." The perpetrators are identified generically as the "Libyan authorities," but annexes 1 and 2 of the resolution identify specific individuals alleged to have perpetrated crimes or incited violence against "the civilian population," who are identified as the victims. These individual perpetrators named in the annexes include Colonel Qadhafi, several of his family members, and senior government officials.[37]

Only three weeks after the passage of Resolution 1970, the Security Council passed Resolution 1973 enforcing a no-fly zone over Libya and authorizing the use of all necessary means by members states to ensure civilian protection. The passage of the resolution followed the formal request by the Arab League detailed in Arab League Resolution 7360 of 12 March, the purpose of which was to protect the Libyan people from "the crimes and violations perpetrated by the Libyan authorities against the Libyan people."[38] During formal deliberations of the UNSC on 17 March, many of the same Security Council members rearticulated the intentional story, but they were also joined by Brazil, Lebanon, Nigeria, and Portugal. Both Lebanon and Portugal made strong statements about the "atrocious" character of the crimes being carried out by Libyan authorities against their people.[39] The Portuguese representative said, "Portugal has consistently condemned the indiscriminate violence against civilians and the gross and systematic violation of human rights and of humanitarian law perpetrated by a regime that has lost all of its credibility and legitimacy vis-à-vis its own population and the international community."[40] Brazil and Nigeria took a softer approach but still characterized the violence as resulting from Libyan authorities' "disrespect for obligations under international humanitarian law and human rights law."[41] The violence was characterized most commonly as "crimes" committed by the Libyan authorities, with Colonel Qadhafi cited by name as responsible almost a dozen times by the four members. An additional six members identified "Libyan authorities" as responsible for crimes against the civilian population, which was described as both "innocent" and "freedom-loving."[42] In explaining its vote on the resolution, France described both the urgency and the appropriateness of an aggressive Security Council response to increasing violence: "If we are careful not to act too late, the Security Council will have the distinction of having ensured that in Libya law prevails over force, democracy over dictatorship and freedom over oppression."[43] Security Council Resolution 1973, like Resolution 1970 before it, described the violence in Libya with an intentional frame. The preamble immediately characterizes the violence as "gross and systematic violations of human rights, including arbitrary detentions, enforced disappearances, and torture and summary executions." The resolution describes these attacks as widespread and systematic in character, possibly amounting to "crimes against humanity." Libyan authorities are again identified as perpetrators, with some listed in the attached annex to the resolution. The victims remained Libyan civilians but expanded to include more specific categories including journalists and media professionals, and their associates. Specifically, Resolution 1973 under Chapter VII of the UN Charter demands the establishment of a cease-fire, requires an end to attacks against civilians, imposes tighter sanctions, establishes a ban on flights in Libyan airspace, and authorizes UN members states to "take all necessary measures" to protect civilians and

Table 8.2. Security Council Support for Key Resolutions, Libya

	Subject	Votes in Favor	Votes Against	Abstentions
Resolution 1970 (2011)	Referral of Libya to the ICC	Bosnia Brazil *China* Colombia **France** Gabon Germany India Lebanon Nigeria Portugal **Russia** South Africa **UK** *U.S.*	None	None
Resolution 1973 (2011)	Establishment of no-fly zone; authorization of all necessary means for civilian protection	Bosnia Colombia **France** Gabon Lebanon Nigeria Portugal South Africa **UK** *U.S.*	None	Brazil **China** Germany India **Russia**

civilian-populated areas under threat of attack, short of foreign occupation. The resolution describes these actions as responsive to the "legitimate demands of the Libyan people."[44]

Although the intentional story won, support for Resolution 1973 was not unanimous. Five Security Council members—one-third of the council—abstained during the vote (Table 8.2). Abstentions by permanent members, China and Russia in this case, allow council action to proceed and have become a common practice for both countries, neither of which wish to stand out as having singly blocked Security Council action that has broad international support.[45] Both states frequently emphasize the importance of regional organizations in shaping Security Council action, so when regional organizations like the Arab League, OIC, and GCC all called for strong military action by the council, vetoing the resolution became more difficult, especially when combined with the growing legitimacy of the concept of the responsibility to protect.[46] Though neither state is a supporter of an international responsibility to protect and regularly state their opposition to the use of military force, they seldom wish to be perceived as opponents to strongly held humanitarian and human rights norms. In contrast, abstentions by elected members can be interpreted in multiple ways. These abstentions function more like a "no" vote for the abstaining state but politically they can also signal acquiescence to the proposed action, if not support for it.[47] Nonetheless, abstentions in the UNSC are becoming less common than in the past. More than 90 percent of Security Council resolutions were passed unanimously by the fifteen members between 2000 and 2010.[48] This means that Resolution 1973 is among only 10 percent of Security Council resolutions that passed with a registered abstention and Resolution 1973 had five, showing a reasonably strong level of division over the possibility of the use of military force for human rights protection.

Brazil, Germany, and India were the nonpermanent members that abstained on Resolution 1973. Each of these states cited an aversion to the use of military force, which they argued would cause more harm than good, exacerbate the conflict, and exceed the call for protection requested by the Arab states in the region.[49] In addition to these concerns, all three aspire to permanent seats on the Security Council, and the authorization of military force remains considerably controversial among members of the Group of 77—an important constituency for decisions about future Security Council membership.[50] Each of these states also has strong economic interests in the Middle East. Yet it is notable that given these material interests, these states abstained rather than voted against the resolution, perhaps in part due to the groundswell of international support to halt mass atrocities in Libya and the perceived legitimacy of the use of military force for human rights protection. Indeed, people in Libya were dying to secure the very same values of democracy and human rights that the domestic populations of Brazil, Germany, and India share.[51] These abstentions show that humanitarian intervention remains controversial but that nonintervention is difficult to justify in the face of real or apprehended mass atrocity in the current international normative context.[52]

Prominence and Resonance of Security Council Stories

Frequently, there is significant contestation between Security Council members over the appropriate characterization of a particular conflict. In

Libya, initially there was none. Instead, council meetings were notable for their uncharacteristic level of agreement. Two important factors help to explain why the intentional story frame was so widely accepted: the prominence of its storytellers and the consistency of the story with independent expertise. First, it matters *who* articulates a particular story. Prominent council members—either because they are materially or normatively more powerful than others—bring considerable weight and legitimacy to a particular story. For example, France, the UK, and the U.S.—all early supporters of the intentional story—were materially powerful (and had the capability of using military force in Libya). Lebanon and South Africa were normatively powerful supporters of the resolution. Their support gave the resolution moral legitimacy because Lebanon was a regional neighbor and because South Africa is generally highly skeptical of humanitarian intervention and protective of state sovereignty. Their support helped to discredit the objections of skeptics who were advancing an imperialist narrative about the Security Council's potential use of military force in Libya. In practical terms, it is necessary to have the backing of a majority of Security Council members, including most of the permanent members, and acquiescence of the others for the adoption of an intentional story because its articulation has potential military implications. The articulation of the intentional story by prominent regional organizations and the Arab League in particular gave the story significant moral weight. In fact, without the public support of the Arab League it is unclear whether such unprecedented unity around an intentional story by the permanent members would have been possible. Certainly, without its endorsement of a no-fly zone, there would not have been adequate support for Resolution 1973. It also helped that the Libyan representative to the UN renounced Qadhafi's violent rule and declared that the Libyan mission had decided to serve as representatives of the Libyan people and their free will rather than the Qadhafi government.[53] Ambassador Abdel Rahman Shalgham characterized the Security Council response as "a sincere attempt to protect civilians."[54] As a result, the debate moved quickly from *whether* to respond to Libyan government atrocities to *how* to respond to them.[55]

Second, the story must resonate with other council members, domestic and international publics, and third-party states. A story that is consistent with expertise (often in the form of expert testimony, human rights reports, media imagery, and forensic evidence) resonates better than one at odds with independent information. Though multiple stories about the cause and character of conflict may be plausible at any one time, there are moments where a particular story is no longer tenable based on the facts on the ground or in the face of more persuasive, alternative stories. The intentional story was overwhelmingly consistent with expert and witness testimony provided by nongovernmental organizations and independent experts. Within days of the start of the violence, an international coalition of more than twenty rights groups from twelve countries accused the Libyan authorities of committing gross and systematic violations of the right to life and possibly crimes against humanity. In a joint statement, they described the deliberate killing of peaceful protesters by the regime using snipers, artillery, and helicopter gunships and characterized it in a manner consistent with the legal definition for crimes against humanity: "The Libyan government's mass killing of innocent civilians amounts to particularly odious offenses which constitute a serious attack on human dignity."[56] Directly referencing the 2005 World Summit Outcome document and the UN Charter, this international coalition directly called on the UNSC to take action under Chapters VI and VII of the Charter to protect Libyan civilians. Amnesty International also documented the lethal use of force by the Qadhafi regime against unarmed protesters and accused Qadhafi of ordering his security forces to quell the rebellion at any cost.[57] Human Rights Watch reported that government forces used lethal force against peaceful protesters and documented the arbitrary arrest, enforced disappearance, and torture of large numbers of people. The organization warned that these violations of human rights should cause deep anxiety about the safety of the civilian population in Libya given the broader context of Qadhafi's "deplorable human rights record over 41 years in power."[58] The high commissioner for human rights reported on the atrocities in Libya during her briefing at the 25 February meeting of the Human Rights Council:

Witnesses in and out of Libya consistently describe horrifying scenes. Libyan forces are firing at protestors and bystanders, sealing off neighbourhoods and shooting from rooftops. They also block ambulances so that the injured and dead are left on the streets. Reports from hospitals indicate that most of the victims have been shot in the head, chest or neck, suggesting arbitrary and summary executions. Doctors relate that they are struggling to cope and are running out of blood supplies and medicines to treat the wounded.

Images of unverifiable origin appear to portray the digging of mass graves in Tripoli.[59]

The International Red Crescent society and the International Committee of the Red Cross confirmed reports that Libyan authorities were blocking access of humanitarian workers to injured populations, and the UN high commissioner for refugees warned that the violence was creating a crisis of refugees and displaced persons as thousands of people poured across Libya's borders into Tunisia and Egypt.[60] Though its complete report would not be published until a year later, the Independent Commission of Inquiry concluded that Qadhafi forces committed crimes against humanity and war crimes in Libya as well as other breaches of international human rights law including murder, enforced disappearance, torture, and rape.[61] The threat to civilians was immediately clear for much of the international community when faced with allegations of Qadhafi's violent repression and given his previous repressive behavior and public incitements to violence in February and March, including this threat: "I will burn Libya; I will distribute arms to the tribes. Libya will run red with blood."[62] Security Council members could not plausibly argue against the intentional story based on the overwhelming evidence of regime atrocities. Even those who condemned the regime but were opposed to military action could not legitimately defend inaction in the face of what members viewed as impending crimes after they had accepted the intentional frame.

Finally, the intentional narrative fit the facts of Libya's relationships with its neighbors. Qadhafi's regime was widely distrusted across Africa and the Middle East. It was responsible for fueling regional conflicts in Liberia, Sierra Leone, Chad, and Palestine. Qadhafi regularly sought to increase his own influence at the expense of other gulf states and he had weak relations with other Arab leaders, many of whom he had personally insulted.[63] Qadhafi in many ways was the ideal villain—one with few allies regionally or internationally.[64] In his remarks to the American people on 28 March, President Barack Obama described Qadhafi as a "tyrant" who denied his people freedom, exploited their wealth, murdered his opponents, and terrorized innocent people around the world.[65] The situation in Libya resonated perfectly with the perpetrator-victim narrative of the intentional story.

Humanitarian intervention began with military strikes on 19 March, just two days after the passage of Resolution 1973. In his report to the Security Council on 24 March, the secretary-general reported that eleven states and the North Atlantic Treaty Organization had notified the Secretariat and the council of their intentions to undertake measures in line with the provisions of Resolution 1973.[66] As Operation Odyssey Dawn, as it was called, continued and as fighting on the ground between the armed opposition and Qadhafi loyalists expanded to include the south and west of the country, the intentional story retained its dominance over Security Council discourse. In May, the prosecutor of the ICC, Luis Moréno-Ocampo, presented the results of his initial investigation of Libyan violence to the Security Council. He confirmed the intentional story, arguing that there were "reasonable grounds to believe that widespread and systematic attacks against the civilian population, including murder and persecution as crimes against humanity, have been and continue to be committed in Libya."[67] Moréno-Ocampo also disclosed evidence of premeditation—Qadhafi had hired and brought foreign mercenaries into the country to prepare for potential unrest as early as January 2011.[68] Yet it was during this same meeting that the first signs of an alternate story entered the Security Council when Nigeria described the political situation in Libya as "complex" and the security environment as "fragile and mutable."[69] By May, the African Union had withdrawn its support of the NATO bombing and by June its Peace and Security Council called directly on the UN to require NATO to pause the bombing.[70] By the end of July, South Africa argued that the Security Council had allowed the implementation of Resolution 1973 to expand unreasonably beyond its original intentions and warned the UN about taking sides.[71] Despite these concerns, the complex story did not gain traction among the membership and the intentional story persisted until the end of the conflict. The Libyan Transitional National Council was formally recognized as the legitimate (interim) governing authority and assumed Libya's seat at the United Nations on 16 September 2011. The new government formally declared Libya's liberation on 23 October 2011.

The Responsibility to Protect and Reconceptualizing Libyan State Sovereignty

Humanitarian intervention is a highly contested use of military force. Previous cases in this study have shown that human rights norms were more likely to influence Security Council behavior when they could either evade conflict with, or could be grafted onto, internalized sovereignty norms.

When human rights norms were characterized as complementary to sovereignty norms, the Security Council could promote human rights and protect state sovereignty at the same time. When the two norms were characterized as in conflict, however, human rights norms—which are the weaker held by the UNSC—yielded to the highly established norm of state sovereignty. This suggested that the Security Council would not use military force against a perpetrator when doing so would bring these dual responsibilities into conflict—as when the perpetrator is the legitimate sovereign authority of a state. Rather, humanitarian intervention was undertaken when the act of rescue was justified discursively as complementing the protection of state sovereignty—when helping victims was articulated by the council as reinforcing, or at least not conflicting with, state sovereignty rather than diminishing it. Humanitarian intervention, then, was not forthcoming in the absence of normative coherence. For example, the nonstate character of Somalia made humanitarian intervention possible in 1992 because the potential conflict between promoting human rights norms and protecting sovereignty norms was eliminated by the lack of legitimate government authority. Similarly, in Sierra Leone, promoting human rights through military force in 2000 did not conflict with sovereignty norms because the primary perpetrator was a nonstate actor. Humanitarian intervention actually helped the legitimate sovereign authorities, who had been forcibly removed from power. In contrast, in Rwanda in 1994 and in Kosovo in 1999, government authorities who were internationally recognized as the legitimate sovereign authorities of their states were the perpetrators of human rights violations. Humanitarian intervention on behalf of victimized civilians by the United Nations would have meant using military force against a sovereign member of the UN, bringing human rights and state sovereignty directly into conflict. In both cases, the Security Council did not authorize the use of military force to save lives while atrocities were occurring.

The twin failures of the UN in Rwanda and in Kosovo prompted the work of the International Commission on Intervention and State Sovereignty which gave rise to the principle of the responsibility to protect. As discussed in earlier chapters, the principle of responsibility to protect defends a conceptualization of sovereignty that entails state responsibility for the protection of the human rights and the fundamental dignity of its citizens.[72] Adoption of the principle by the UN is meant to resolve the tension that can arise between the sovereignty obligations detailed in Article 2.7 of the Charter and human rights by requiring states, and when they are unwilling to do so the UNSC, to protect basic human rights as part of the responsibility of sovereign statehood. But as the previous case of Darfur demonstrated, rhetorical articulation of the responsibility to protect and its endorsement by the Security Council has not always translated into protection in practice. Until the responsibility to protect becomes more widely internalized, deference to traditional Westphalian conceptions of state sovereignty can function as a barrier to effective human rights protection unless the Security Council discursively constructs a story about sovereignty in which its protection is linked to the promotion of human rights. This was not achieved in Darfur but it was in Libya. Humanitarian intervention in Libya, then, marks a dramatic political development precisely because it was the first time that the Security Council authorized the use of "all necessary measures" against a perpetrator state to stop its human rights violations. In Libya, it appears that the responsibility to protect is finally beginning to have its intended effect—easing the tension between sovereignty norms and human rights norms by reconceptualizing the former to encapsulate the latter. By reconceptualizing sovereignty to entail responsibility, in cases of mass atrocity the realization of sovereignty norms means protecting human rights. Yet as the cases in this study have shown, the story that UNSC members articulate about sovereignty matters crucially for the prospects of humanitarian intervention. The Libya case suggests that in the future, Security Council debates will likely center more on what constitutes legitimate sovereign authority than whether sovereign states have the right to domestic noninterference during times of internal conflict.

The stories that Security Council members told about Libyan sovereignty were anchored in conceptions of popular sovereignty and the responsibility to protect, rather than the Westphalian conceptions of sovereignty that dominated Security Council debates of the 1990s. As early as 25 February, the secretary-general framed the situation in Libya as one of responsibility to protect by twice reminding Libya and the Security Council of their sovereign responsibilities during a brief twenty-five-minute meeting: "When a State manifestly fails to protect its population from serious international crimes, the international community has the responsibility to step in and take protective action in a collective, timely and decisive manner. . . . The heads of State and Government at the 2005 World Summit pledged to protect populations by preventing genocide, war crimes, ethnic cleansing and crimes against humanity as well as their incitement. The challenge for us now is how to provide real protection and do all we can to halt the ongoing violence."[73] The following day during its deliberations on Resolution 1970, Brazil, Colombia, France, and the U.S. justified their votes in favor of sanctions and the ICC referral by referencing the responsibility to protect. According to France, "the text, unanimously adopted today, recalls the responsibility of each State to protect its own population and of the international community to intervene when States fail in their duty."[74] Brazil similarly emphasized that the resolution demonstrated Security Council resolve to fulfill its responsibilities. Colombia and the U.S., however, focused their comments more specifically on the responsibilities of the Libyan government toward its people rather than those of the international community. The Colombian representative said, "The State must assume its primary responsibility to guarantee the security and the rights of its citizens, including the rights to life, freedom of expression and peaceful assembly."[75] For its part, Resolution 1970 makes explicit reference to "the Libyan authorities' responsibility to protect [Libya's] population" and affirms the Security Council's "responsibility for the maintenance of international peace and security under the Charter of the United Nations."[76] Although the violence in Libya is defined as a threat to international peace and security and the Security Council has the responsibility to stop it, the choice of wording in the text of Resolution 1970 emphasizes only part of the responsibility to protect doctrine—that of state responsibility to its population. The resolution was passed unanimously by the Security Council, signaling widespread agreement on this aspect of the responsibility to protect. That it did not specifically reaffirm paragraphs 138 and 139 of the World Summit Document—as Resolutions 1674 (2006), 1706 (2006), and 1894 (2009) did—suggests that in the UNSC, the second requirement of the responsibility to protect (international responsibility) remains somewhat controversial, and contested.

In March, a clear majority of UNSC members justified the establishment of the no-fly zone and the authorization of all necessary means to protect civilians as fulfilling an international responsibility to protect civilians. Colombia cited Libya's failure to fulfill its responsibility to protect its population as justification for approving measures aimed at protecting the civilian population from imminent attacks by the government.[77] Nigeria argued that Resolution 1973 demonstrated to the Libyan people that the international community is prepared to respond when civilians face grave danger and seek protection.[78] South Africa, a state that wields considerable normative power among developing countries as well as in Africa, asserted:

> We believe that by adopting resolution 1973 (2011), which South Africa voted in favour of, the Security Council has responded appropriately to the call of the countries of the region to strengthen the implementation of resolution 1970 (2011), and has acted responsibly to protect and save the lives of defenceless civilians, who are faced with brutal acts of violence carried out by the Libyan authorities. We believe that the establishment of these additional measures, including a ceasefire and a no-fly zone, as authorized by this resolution, constitute an important element for the protection of civilians.[79]

In a speech to the American public, President Obama declared that the coalition of states enforcing the no-fly zone was meeting "their responsibility to defend the Libyan people."[80] Security Council members who opposed the resolution largely defended their positions as motivated by an opposition to the use of military force either in principle or in this specific case but made no remarks that indicated that they were opposed to an international responsibility to protect civilians at risk. Indeed, their unanimous consent to Resolution 1970 suggests that their objection to Resolution 1973 had more to do with the *means* of response (humanitarian intervention versus sanctions and ICC prosecution) than *whether* to respond. Nonetheless, like Resolution 1970 before it, Resolution 1973 reiterated "the responsibility of the Libyan authorities to protect the Libyan population" and that parties to armed conflict are responsible for civilian protection.[81] In effect, Resolution 1973 exercised the Security Council's responsibilities under the responsibility to protect as affirmed in the World Summit Outcome document but without explicitly affirming it rhetorically in the text.

Members of the Security Council achieved normative coherence by discursively constructing sovereignty norms and human rights norms as complementary, allowing those in favor of the exercise of military force to justify humanitarian intervention as compatible with the protection of Libyan sovereignty. They did so by denying that Qadhafi and the Libyan authorities had the right to rule Libya and instead identified the source of sovereign authority as the Libyan people themselves and their delegation at the UN. This allowed Security Council members to defend the sovereignty and territorial integrity of the Libyan state while at the same time using military force against the Qadhafi regime to protect the human rights and legitimate aspirations for freedom of the Libyan population. For example, Ambassador Susan Rice of the United States argued in February, "When a leader's only means of staying in power is to use mass violence against its own people, he has lost the legitimacy to rule."[82] Lebanon, representing the Arab League, argued that the legitimacy of UNSC action against the Libyan authorities came from the calls for assistance from the Libyan people. According to the league, Qadhafi's regime lost all legitimacy through its crimes against the Libyan people.[83] The no-fly zone was undertaken to protect Libyan civilians, but territorial integrity was preserved by the prohibition on military occupation included in Resolution 1973. Sovereignty of territory was separated from the sovereign authority of leadership. Regime authorities lost their credibility, legitimacy, and sovereign authority with the Libyan people as well as the international community.[84] In effect, supporters of Resolution 1973 defined sovereignty as comprising state responsibility for the protection of human rights. Because the government authorities were failing to protect, they lost the right to rule and sovereign authority was transferred to the Libyan people and their representatives. Enforcement of the no-fly zone then, protected both human rights and sovereignty rights. Humanitarian intervention in Libya demonstrates that the meaning of both human rights norms and sovereignty norms are coevolving and is an affirmation of a reconceptualized understanding of state sovereignty by the Security Council that includes elements of both responsibility and legitimacy.

The Responsibility to Protect and Prosecute

The responsibility to protect is complemented by growing support for a responsibility to prosecute. The increasing legitimacy of human rights norms has changed the purpose of military force such that humanitarian intervention is now a legitimate military action for the Security Council. The growth of human rights norms has also altered the meaning of sovereignty such that states are now viewed as having responsibilities to protect and not harm their populations. This also means that the violation of the most fundamental human rights cannot be legitimate acts of states or their leaders. Instead, they are crimes and the individuals who commit these crimes can and should be prosecuted through judicial proceedings that protect the due process rights of the accused.[85] This commitment to the justice norm means that state leaders can no longer hide behind a norm of sovereign immunity. Instead, the culture of impunity that this fostered has given way to a culture of accountability.[86] Security Council deliberations demonstrated that there is not only a growing UN commitment to halting mass atrocities but also a growing commitment to bringing those who perpetrate them to justice. In the case of Libya, the Security Council demonstrated its commitment to the justice norm by making international prosecutions a part of its response to violations of human rights. During Security Council deliberations on Resolution 1970, members discursively linked the responsibility to protect civilians with the responsibility to prosecute perpetrators when human rights are violated. Ambassador Rice of the United States argued, "The Security Council has acted today to support the Libyan people's universal rights. These rights are not negotiable. They cannot be denied. Libya's leaders will be held accountable for violating these rights and for failing to meet their most basic responsibilities to their people."[87] Similarly, Bosnia condemned the violations of human rights and international humanitarian law and demanded that perpetrators of such crimes be held accountable.[88] Portugal stated it simply: "Impunity will not be tolerated, and the perpetrators of these crimes against civilians will be prosecuted."[89] In referring to this as the "twin protection-prosecution agenda," Ramesh Thakur and Vesselin Popovski argue that international criminal prosecution is another form of international intervention to end mass atrocity crimes.[90]

International law is central to the justice norm. During their deliberations following the passage of Resolution 1970, the secretary-general and ten UNSC members made nearly twenty explicit references to the importance of international law and particularly international humanitarian and international human rights law. They condemned the Libyan authorities' violation of international humanitarian and human rights law, spoke out against impunity, and demanded that perpetrators of violations be brought to justice in court.[91] In referring the situation to the ICC for investigation, Resolution 1970 specifically condemns "serious violations of human rights and international humanitarian law that are being committed in the Libyan Arab Jamahiriya," considers that widespread and systematic attacks against civilians may amount to crimes against humanity, and demands that Libyan

Table 8.3. Security Council Referrals to the ICC

	Subject	Votes in Favor	Votes Against	Abstentions
Resolution 1593 (2005)	Referral of Darfur to the ICC	Argentina Benin Denmark **France** Greece Japan Philippines Romania **Russia** **UK** Tanzania	None	Algeria Brazil **China** **U.S.**
Resolution 1970 (2011)	Referral of Libya to the ICC	Bosnia Brazil **China** Colombia **France** Gabon Germany India Lebanon Nigeria Portugal **Russia** South Africa **UK** **U.S.**	None	None

authorities fully respect human rights and international humanitarian law.[92] The growing legitimacy of the justice norm alongside the responsibility to protect norm is evidenced in the unanimous approval of Resolution 1970. In 2005 when the UN Security Council made its first referral to the ICC, eleven states voted in favor of referring Darfur to the Court and four states abstained including Algeria, Brazil, China, and the U.S. (Table 8.3). In contrast, all Security Council members voted in favor of Resolution 1970 in 2011, including Brazil, China, and the U.S. China and the U.S. are not parties to the ICC. Nonetheless, just as it is becoming more difficult to justify nonintervention than humanitarian intervention in the face of mass atrocities, it is similarly becoming more difficult to justify impunity over accountability in the face of grave crimes. Human rights norms are shaping views of sovereignty as well as justice in the UN Security Council.

Norms, Interests, and Unintended Consequences: Why Libya and Why Not Syria?

International norms are central to understanding how humanitarian intervention in Libya became possible, but material factors matter too. Clearly, without the normative commitment of UNSC members to international human rights, the responsibility to protect, and global justice, humanitarian intervention would not have happened. Security Council discourse in formal meetings about Libya has demonstrated a sustained commitment by its members to humanitarian values. As an example, the UK characterized Resolution 1973 as embodying UN Charter principles and Security Council action in Libya as a defense of UN values.[93] Because humanitarian intervention is politically risky and materially costly, it is difficult to explain without reference to the widely shared values held by international society. Yet as previous cases of this study have shown, adoption of these shared values does not always result in humanitarian intervention. It is important to note the political contingency of humanitarian interventions and the material factors that help answer questions like: why members of the Security Council pursued "all necessary measures" in Libya and not alternative punitive measures short of military force; and why a Chapter VII mandate was possible in Libya but not in nearby Syria.

First, widespread articulation and unanimous adoption of the intentional story about the cause and character of conflict combined with the story about sovereign authority in Libya opened the door to humanitarian intervention. There was widespread agreement among Security Council members that Libyan authorities, including Colonel Qadhafi, were deliberately killing Libyan civilians and would commit further massacres. In contrast, during this same period, there was widespread disagreement in the UNSC about the cause and character of the violence in Syria. Council members were divided between three causal stories: the intentional, inadvertent, and complex. France, the UK, and the U.S. advanced an intentional story about the brutal repression of the Syrian people by the Bashar al-Assad regime, including the deliberate targeting of civilians and the use of tanks and heavy weaponry against peaceful protesters and their families.[94] China and Russia advanced an inadvertent story about armed conflict in which multiple parties were perpetrating violence, including armed elements that were attacking the government and seeking to provoke civil war.[95] India characterized the situation in Syria as complex, and Bosnia and Lebanon condemned the killings and expressed condolences to the families but did not identify any perpetrators responsible for the violence.[96] The ambassador from Syria characterized the Syrian government as the victim of armed criminals, terrorists, and extremist groups who were targeting government officials and killing innocent civilians.[97] There was extreme diversity in these stories about the character of the conflict. There was also deep division among members about the source of sovereign authority in Syria. Some members argued that the Assad regime must honor the legitimate aspirations of the Syrian people to choose their own leaders (Bosnia, France, Portugal, the U.K., and the U.S.) while others argued that the government has a sovereign right to maintain internal law and order and that it was a domestic concern and not a threat to international peace and security (India, Russia, and Syria).[98] Despite some basic similarities in the repressive tactics used by the Libyan and Syrian governments against peaceful protesters (and Syria's were far more brutal), the discursive representation of the conflicts by Security Council members was extremely different.

Two important material factors help to explain humanitarian intervention in Libya: military capacity and reasonable prospect for success. Military capacity entails the ability to procure the necessary military forces and equipment to wage humanitarian intervention and the ability to gain legitimacy. In Libya, members of the Security Council possessed both—several members, especially those that were members of the NATO alliance, were prepared to commit the necessary troops, intelligence, military hardware, weaponry, and financial resources to enforce the no-fly zone, protect civilian areas and even provide air cover to the armed opposition. They also not only had the authorization of the UNSC for the use of military force but had been invited to intervene by the Libyan people and the defecting Libyan ambassador to the UN, as well as regional powers. While there appears to be little doubt that several countries, including the U.S., the UK, and France, might have the necessary capacity for a similar humanitarian intervention in Syria, there is no legitimacy to do so as a result of the blockage of UNSC action by Russia and China, the absence of an invitation by regional organizations, and significant divisions within Syrian society about the al-Assad regime.

The prospect for success is another important determinant of humanitarian intervention. Indeed, without it, the use of military force may cause more harm than good and no longer be humanitarian. Outside his inner circle of loyal supporters, Qadhafi suffered from a lack of depth of support among his people and had few international allies. The security forces under his command were disorganized and he employed large numbers of foreign mercenaries who lacked heartfelt support for or ideological commitment to Qadhafi's cause. The existence of a reasonably united and well-organized opposition that enjoyed early military successes created a potential partner for interveners. Rebels were joined by defecting army commanders and together they succeeded in controlling a significant and contiguous portion of Libyan territory. Though lacking in discipline and guilty of its own human rights violations, the rebel army sought domestic and international legitimacy by attempting to fight its war in ways consistent with international humanitarian law. Reportedly, rebel commanders regularly contacted the ICRC to inquire about the legality of their tactics, misunderstanding the nature of the ICRC's work in the field but fully comprehending the power of international humanitarian norms and the necessity of honoring them if they wanted to be perceived as a legitimate international actor.[99] Yet even in the case of Syria, where humanitarian intervention has been notably absent, the UNSC has met regularly to discuss Syria's internal affairs and to regularly criticize al-Assad's regime. In formal meetings, Security Council members literally dictate to the Syrian government how to manage its police force and how to appropriately respond to the demands and aspirations of its people, and demand that it protects the fundamental human rights of its people.

There is an important interplay between norms and interests when it comes to Security Council decision making. Security Council deliberations on Libya linked international security directly to respect for international law. For Colombia, the atrocities committed by the discredited Libyan regime against the civilian population constituted a threat to international peace and security in addition to its large humanitarian toll.[100] Nigeria asserted that its conscience motivated it to act but also stressed that Libya had violated the terms of earlier UNSC decisions as well as international humanitarian law. Humanitarian crisis itself was the threat to international peace and security.[101] The U.S. explicitly identified both interests and norms as the dual motives for its participation in the humanitarian intervention. President Obama, in a speech to the American people, defined national interests to include the protection of American values: "To brush aside America's responsibility as a leader and—more profoundly—our responsibilities to our fellow human beings under such circumstances would have been a betrayal of who we are. Some nations may be able to turn a blind eye to atrocities in other countries. The United States of America is different."[102] He described Libya as a situation where "our safety is not directly threatened, but our interests and values are." He defined these values as opposition to violence directed against one's own citizens; support for a set of universal rights, including the freedom of expression and the right to choose leaders; and support for governments that are responsive to the aspirations of their people.[103] President Obama argued that allowing Qadhafi to massacre his people was a threat to "our common humanity and common security."[104] These sentiments were repeated by Ambassador Rice a month later when she characterized the violence perpetrated by the government of Syria against its own people as "abhorrent" and questioned the legitimacy and international standing of a government that would brutalize unarmed demonstrators.[105]

Humanitarian intervention in Libya, like those before it, had unintended consequences. UNSC unity quickly broke down amid the use of military force. Members disagreed whether the authorization of the no-fly zone included the use of offensive measures and questioned whether NATO sought protection of civilians or regime change while others wondered if the two could be separated. The atmosphere in the Security Council was poisonous in the fall of 2011 as violence in Syria escalated. The permanent members had not been so divided since NATO's intervention in Kosovo. When China and Russia vetoed a resolution that would have condemned Syrian atrocities and threatened retaliatory action, France, the UK, and the U.S. were "outraged" at the Security Council's unwillingness to stop "crimes against humanity."[106] But four additional states abstained, including South Africa, which suggested that its lack of support stemmed from its view that humanitarian intervention in Libya had exceeded Resolution 1973's mandate: "We have seen recently that Security Council resolutions have been abused and that their implementation has gone far beyond the mandate of what was intended. . . . We are concerned that this draft resolution not be part of a hidden agenda aimed at once again instituting regime change."[107] Indeed, South Africa expressed a sentiment shared by many in the African Union, which had refused to endorse the Western humanitarian intervention in large part because of continent-wide skepticism that the intervention might be abused for instrumental and strategic purposes of its interveners.[108] While cautious skepticism is warranted, given the council's selective relationship with humanitarian intervention, states are also cautiously protecting their own sovereignty rights. It is exactly because humanitarian intervention in Libya was groundbreaking—it was the first authorized use of force against a perpetrator state explicitly for its human rights crimes and was based on a conceptualization of sovereignty as responsibility—that the push back on the responsibility to protect principle has been so strong. As sovereignty evolves to incorporate requirements for human rights protection and popular legitimacy, it is understandable that states that are protective of their sovereignty push back against these developing norms. It is possible that saving lives in Libya cost lives in Syria and that in absence of a Libyan intervention, more robust action against the Syrian regime might have been possible. Yet as this study has shown, every case is distinct and there is no one template for how the UNSC responds to mass atrocity. There has been growing consistency in principle (the responsibility to protect was affirmed in Security Council Resolutions 1975 on Côte d'Ivoire, 1996 on South Sudan, and 2014 on Yemen in 2011) but not in tactics across the cases.

Conclusions

The passage of Resolutions 1970 and 1973 marked a significant evolution in the Security Council's response to mass atrocities. Within weeks of the outbreak of violence, UNSC members referred the human rights violations in Libya to the ICC for investigation and enforced stringent sanctions against Libyan authorities. United around an intentional story about the conflict in which Libyan authorities under the direction of Muammar Qadhafi were systematically violating the human rights of Libyan civilians, Security Council deliberations focused on how to fulfill its responsibility to protect civilians instead of whether such a responsibility existed. The intentional frame had the support of prominent regional organizations and particularly the League of Arab States. The Security Council's story about Libya resonated widely because it was consistent with expert and witness testimony, media imagery, and forensic evidence. Security Council members also voted for the first time to authorize the use of military force for human protection purposes against a perpetrator government that was a state member of the United Nations. Members argued that Colonel Qadhafi and his authorities had lost their right to rule as a result of their crimes against Libyan civilians. As a result, they rhetorically transferred sovereign authority to the Libyan people. This meant that the UNSC could protect the sovereignty and territorial integrity of Libya at the same time it used military force to protect the human rights of the Libyan people. This particular discursive construction of sovereignty norms and human rights norms as interdependent eased the historic tensions that had arisen between sovereignty norms and human rights norms when UN members become perpetrators of mass atrocity. Normative coherence combined with unity around an intentional story paved the way for eventual humanitarian intervention. Justifications for humanitarian intervention by Security Council members emphasized state responsibility for civilian protection and in its absence Security Council responsibility to protect, demonstrating that the international normative context has changed such that it is now easier to justify the responsibility to protect than to justify failure to respond to mass atrocities. Evidence from Security Council meetings also shows that the responsibility to react includes both humanitarian intervention and international prosecution. The increasing legitimacy and expansion of human rights norms has changed the meaning of sovereignty for the UNSC and is developing support for both the responsibility to protect norm and the justice norm. This suggests that future Security Council deliberations about situations of mass atrocity will focus on determining where legitimate sovereign authority resides when considering whether and how the council will fulfill its responsibility to protect.

Chapter 9

Causal Stories, Human Rights, and the Evolution of Sovereignty

At the start of the twenty-first century, human rights are increasingly linked to international peace and security, and normative ideas about human rights, sovereign authority, and state responsibilities to their populations shape United Nations Security Council decision making about humanitarian intervention as much as material and geostrategic considerations. The inclusion of human rights considerations in UNSC decision making since 1991 has fundamentally changed the meaning of sovereignty over a period of two decades. Initially, the council perceived the protection of human rights norms to conflict with Westphalian conceptions of state sovereignty. In the case of Iraq in 1991, for example, council members deemed human rights considerations relevant to UNSC debates only because Iraq's sovereignty had been temporarily suspended, and because its domestic practices—political repression and widespread violations of human rights—were threatening the sovereignty of neighbor states. By 2011, however, the UNSC employed humanitarian intervention to protect Libyan civilians from the repressive practices of its government, based on those repressive practices alone. The council deemed the sovereign authority of Libyan authorities illegitimate because they failed to protect the Libyan population and grossly violated their fundamental human rights. The cases in this book have demonstrated the importance of discourse to UNSC decision making: the stories members tell about the cause and character of conflict, and the source of sovereign authority in their target states, have the power to create and foreclose opportunities for humanitarian intervention.

It has been more than two decades since human rights considerations entered UNSC deliberations, and humanitarian intervention became a legitimate purpose of military force. Yet while remarkable, UNSC humanitarian intervention remains an exceptional practice. There have been more than two hundred armed conflicts since the end of World War II, with most being intrastate rather than interstate wars.[1] This book examines eight of those conflicts, with only half having experienced UNSC humanitarian intervention. While there have been others not studied in this book, most notably in Haiti, East Timor, and Côte d'Ivoire, the number of intrastate conflicts on the council's agenda far exceeds the number that are recipients of UNSC humanitarian intervention. Though increasingly legitimate, humanitarian intervention is selective and rare; and it represents a notable departure from both the appropriate justifications for military force and UNSC behavior during the Cold War. Examining the arguments that council members make and the justifications for their behavior reveals the normative context in which they operate and illustrates how opportunities for humanitarian intervention are discursively produced in specific cases. These eight cases illustrate a systematic pattern of problem definition and the policy solutions that flow from them, both explaining past humanitarian intervention decisions and signaling when and where the UNSC is likely to do so in the future. These cases also reveal how international norms of sovereignty and human rights are coevolving at the UN and shaping crucial decisions about international security. This chapter reviews the findings from each of the cases including the stories Security Council members told about the cause and character of each conflict, and the status of sovereign authority in each target state, both of which create and foreclose opportunities for humanitarian intervention. The chapter draws attention to these discernible patterns in UNSC discourse and behavior but also addresses the importance of political contingency, intervening material factors, and historical context. The chapter concludes with observations about the responsibility to protect and the future prospects of humanitarian intervention.

Causal Stories and Humanitarian Intervention

During formal meetings, Security Council members tell stories about the source of sovereign authority and the cause and character of the conflicts on their agenda, to one another, domestic publics, and third-party states.

These stories are meaningful because they reflect the authority and legitimacy of the UNSC.[2] While most of the actual decision making occurs behind closed doors, formal public statements and official documents are important because they are scripted in advance. States take considerable care to select the appropriate language and argue about terminology that enters the public record. Council members recognize that justifications for their intervention decisions are powerful because "they draw on and articulate shared values and expectations that other decision makers and other publics in other states hold."[3] As a matter of practice, council members cannot simply make any arguments or justifications they choose because they are limited by existing institutional norms. In their statements, council members are literally justifying their decisions in relation to the standards of appropriate behavior for the UNSC. Arguments that appear prejudiced or generated purely by self-interest are viewed skeptically and are unlikely to be persuasive. In the cases of intrastate conflict examined here, council members were limited to either making appeals to norms of sovereignty and domestic nonintervention or human rights norms. The need to conform arguments to specific legal and moral norms may lead to what Thomas Risse calls "argumentative self-entrapment," whereby state representatives may accept a norm rhetorically simply as a way to adapt to external pressures, but through the process end up validating the norm and being held accountable to it.[4] Whether made sincerely or strategically, council arguments have meaning and influence independent of the speaker.

To address a conflict on their agenda, council members need to adopt a frame for understanding it—a story that identifies its causes and describes its character. Members actively construct and defend causal stories because control over the story translates into the power to define threats to international peace and security, to assign responsibility for conflicts and to shape interpretation of relevant norms like sovereignty and human rights. As used throughout the book, they are called causal stories because they make claims about causality, not because their utterance directly causes subsequent council action. Nonetheless, the cases show that causal stories create and foreclose *opportunities* for the UN to use military force.

Causal Stories and Their Relationship to Humanitarian Intervention Decisions

Using actual Security Council discourse, this book demonstrates that council members frequently articulate three types of causal stories to describe intrastate conflicts: inadvertent, intentional, and complex. Inadvertent stories characterize violent conflict deaths as the "unintended consequences of willed human action."[5] Human rights violations might be expected but are not deliberately provoked or the intended purpose of the conflict. Rather, they are negative side effects that accompany military action (acts of commission) and result from human carelessness or recklessness (acts of omission). Table 9.1 lists the causal stories articulated by council members by case. For example, the inadvertent story described the Bosnian war as a civil war in which sovereign authority was contested and all parties to the conflict were culpable for human rights violations. In Rwanda, the inadvertent story described civilian deaths as a by-product of fighting between the two warring parties—the Rwandan Armed Forces and the rebel Rwandan Patriotic Front. Similarly, in Darfur, the inadvertent story characterized the conflict as a civil war in which all parties bore responsibility for human rights violations.

Intentional stories are those "where an action was willfully undertaken by human beings in order to bring about the consequences that actually happened."[6] In the context of the UNSC, intentional stories identify and name perpetrators who are responsible for deliberate harm to their victims. These are stories about aggression, ethnic cleansing, genocide, or systematic human rights and international humanitarian law violations, which are frequently classified as crimes against humanity or war crimes. For example, one version of the intentional story for Bosnia characterized the war as an external aggression by a neighboring state in which Bosnian Muslim civilians were being ethnically cleansed by Bosnian Serb perpetrators and their allies in Belgrade. In Kosovo, the intentional story described the forced displacement, murder, and rape of the ethnic Albanian population at the hands of Serb military, paramilitary, and police. In Sierra Leone, the intentional story described a conflict in which the Revolutionary United Front and elements of the Armed Forces Revolutionary Council were perpetrating criminal violence against the legitimate government of Sierra Leone and its civilian population.

In the UNSC, complex stories describe conflicts with multiple sources of causation, situations in which the causes are a result of complex systems of interaction or are derived from institutional or historical patterns.[7] They are less effective at provoking council action because they lack "a single locus of control, a plausible candidate to take responsibility for a problem or a point of leverage to fix a problem."[8] In Somalia, the complex story

Table 9.1. Security Council Causal Stories, 1991–2011

	Inadvertent Story	Intentional Story	Complex Story
Iraq	None	External aggression against Kuwait by Iraq, in violation of the UN Charter and international legal norms.	None
Somalia	Civil war in which all parties to the conflict were harming civilians.	Somali rebel factions were killing UN personnel and the civilian population in their quest to control Mogadishu.	Battle for political power by warlords, armed thugs, criminal gangs, and multiple clans characterized by interclan rivalries, which were inflicting terror on the civilian population.
Bosnia-Herzegovina	Civil war in which all parties were responsible for human rights violations.	**Version 1:** Ethnic cleansing of Bosnian Muslims by Bosnian Serbs aided by Serbia. **Version 2:** External aggression against Bosnia by Serbia, in which Bosnian Muslims were deliberately targeted by Bosnian Serb perpetrators and their Serbian allies.	Multifaceted intrastate conflict with interstate dimensions in which human rights violations were structural as well as the result of political decision making.
Rwanda	Civil war in which both parties were responsible for civilian deaths, which were the by-product of the fighting.	Genocide of Tutsis by Hutu extremists and government-led militias.	None

Table 9.1. (Continued)

	Inadvertent Story	Intentional Story	Complex Story
Kosovo	**Version 1**: Civil war in which the parties were responsible for a cycle of violence and reprisal. **Version 2**: Both parties were responsible for violence but the use of force by Serbia, while disproportionate, was a legitimate response against an internal challenge to its rule.	Ethnic cleansing of ethnic Albanian civilians in Kosovo by the Yugoslav and Serbian authorities.	None
Sierra Leone	None	**Version 1**: Campaign of violence perpetrated by armed rebel groups against the people of Sierra Leone and their democratically elected government. **Version 2**: Civil war in which a small, well-armed, deeply alienated segment of the population unleashed organized and indiscriminate terror on the population and against the government.	None

Darfur	Civil war in which armed rebels from African minority groups and government agents including Arab Janjaweed forces shared responsibility for human rights violations.	Genocide of African minority groups by the government of Sudan, using proxy fighters.	Multilayered conflict with both intrastate and interstate dimensions between armed rebel groups and government regular and paramilitary forces, in which killing was both deliberate and targeted and inadvertent, and responsibility was diffuse.
Libya	None	Libyan authorities were perpetrators of widespread and systematic violent crimes against innocent civilians.	None

identified clans, warlords, armed thugs, and criminal gangs as responsible for inflicting terror on civilians. Human suffering was caused by the fighting but compounded by armed banditry, crime, and drought. In Darfur, the complex story identified multiple and fragmenting armed rebel groups and government regular and paramilitary forces with shifting alliances as culpable for human rights abuses. Some attacks on civilians were described as intentional and systematic while others were categorized as collateral damage. The complex story also described the conflict as intertwined with other conflicts occurring within Sudan and the broader region.

The articulation and widespread adoption of causal stories by council members have specific policy implications. Intentional stories appeal to international legal norms and principles of justice, and are more likely than alternatives to prompt military action because the perpetrator-victim narrative identifies culpable actors whose behavior can be interdicted or punished by the council. In all the cases of this study in which council members coalesced around an intentional story of conflict, council members also engaged in humanitarian intervention. Clearly, the articulation of an intentional story and its widespread adoption create a rare opportunity for humanitarian intervention, in spite of the costs associated with taking sides on the battlefield (see Table 9.3).

In direct contrast, no UNSC humanitarian intervention occurred in response to council coalescence around an inadvertent story. Because inadvertent stories are narratives of moral equivalency in which parties are equally culpable for perpetrating harm against victims, they prompt policies of mediation and palliation rather than the use of military force against one set of belligerents. In general, narratives of complexity describe confusing situations in which there are multiple parties and multiple causes of conflict, including political, structural, and historical factors. Complex stories prompt policies aimed at stability and the protection of sovereignty. Often they are status-quo oriented because policymakers lack a point of leverage for addressing the problem. Complex stories would seem to be the least likely to prompt humanitarian intervention and their articulation should foreclose rather than create political opportunities for the use of military force. However, the findings about complex stories in these cases are mixed. Military force was authorized in Somalia despite articulation of a complex story; however, after the council coalesced around an intentional story, the form of forcible intervention changed from neutral protection of relief supplies against all armed elements to the use of offensive force against specific armed factions. As the conflict wore on and in the aftermath of devastating military losses in Somalia, council members determined that situations of complexity and chaos were not amenable to the use of military force. In Darfur, neither an inadvertent story nor a complex story garnered support for humanitarian intervention.

The causal stories that UNSC members tell often shift over time, and early meetings are usually characterized by significant contestation between members over the appropriate story. Human rights violations may be portrayed as part of an ethnic cleansing campaign by one set of council members, but as the unintended consequences of a civil war by another. Any single conflict may be characterized by multiple stories at the same time or by different stories at different points in time. In situations of contestation, where council members are significantly divided and do not coalesce around any story, meaningful UNSC action is unlikely.

Fundamentally, when members cannot agree on how to define a conflict or its underlying causes, they lack the capacity to address it. In Kosovo, for example, permanent members remained divided between an intentional story and an inadvertent one until a peace settlement was achieved, precluding UN humanitarian intervention. In Bosnia, members fought over the appropriate causal story for three years before coalescing around an intentional story. Council debates about the appropriate story are about more than the empirical sequence of events: they are high-stakes "fights about the possibility of control and assignment of responsibility."[9] Because causal stories are not simply given and have significant policy implications, they need to be "fought for, defended and sustained."[10] By tracing the emergence and diffusion of causal stories in the UNSC, it is possible to identify the mechanisms that explain why members shift from one causal story to another. Two are particularly important: the proponents of the story or its "storytellers" and the resonance of the story with target audiences.

The success of a particular causal story over its competitors is mediated by the prominence of its proponents. It matters which council members articulate a causal story. Storytellers that are prominent, either because they are materially or normatively powerful, strengthen the stories they tell by either bringing material pressure to bear on other members or by increasing a story's credibility and legitimacy. In practical terms, it is necessary for a causal story to gain the support of a majority of permanent members because of the veto, though it is not necessary for a causal story to originate from them. Majority support from the council is insufficient without majority support from permanent members who must be persuaded or must acquiesce to the pressure of the larger group. In Bosnia, for example, a majority of council members, including the U.S., adopted an intentional story. However, without support from France and the UK, and the acquiescence of China and Russia, unity and thus humanitarian intervention was not possible. Material power is important to the success of a causal story but alone it may not be enough. Despite support from a unipolar power, early U.S. articulation of an intentional story in both Bosnia and Darfur was insufficient for the intentional story to beat its competitors. The Rwanda and Bosnia cases illustrate that normative power also matters to the success of a causal story and that persuasion is indeed possible in the UNSC. Examining the diffusion patterns of stories across the cases shows that stories occasionally diffuse from weaker to stronger powers through pressure and persuasion. In Bosnia, small and non-Western states in the UNSC were the earliest and strongest supporters of the intentional story, and in Rwanda, representatives from the Czech Republic, New Zealand, and Nigeria eventually convinced permanent members to adopt the intentional language of the Genocide Convention. These nonpermanent members themselves had been persuaded by international human rights organizations to change their own causal stories. In one very stark example of persuasion, Nigerian ambassador Ibrahim Gambari convinced U.S. secretary of state Madeleine Albright to change her vote on a crucial Security Council resolution, ultimately preventing the UNAMIR mission from being withdraw from Rwanda.[11] Finally, in Libya, Arab League support gave the intentional story a high degree of moral legitimacy that helped gain support from less enthusiastic members of the council like China, South Africa, and Russia.

Successful stories resonate with their target audience. Simply stated, a causal story must be convincing. While multiple stories might be plausible, there are moments when some stories fit better than others with the "facts on the ground." Stories that complement widespread and deeply held values and are consistent with legal and scientific expertise, forensic evidence, and media imagery resonate better than those that do not. Expertise, evidence, and imagery not only explain why some causal stories succeed and other fail but can also trigger the moment of actual humanitarian intervention when they support an intentional story. After the council has adopted an intentional story , documentation of particularly egregious abuses may provoke the actual use of military force. So while evidence of mass atrocity can shift council support away from an inadvertent story to an intentional one, mass atrocity may also explain the timing of humanitarian intervention if the council has already adopted an intentional story. In Bosnia, for example, council members were divided initially among those articulating inadvertent, intentional, and complex stories. Contestation over the cause and character of the conflict stymied coherent action and blocked early humanitarian intervention. In the latter half of 1995, however, members of the council coalesced around the intentional story after France and the UK gave it their support following the fall of the UN safe haven at Srebrenica. In this example, both prominence and resonance mattered. Unity around the intentional story made humanitarian intervention a possibility as early as July 1995 but it did not occur until August, when it was prompted by a highly publicized massacre of civilians in a Sarajevo marketplace and the public release of aerial surveillance photos of mass graves surrounding the fallen UN safe haven of Srebrenica.

Stories About Sovereignty and the Effects of Norm Coherence

Causal stories create and foreclose opportunities for humanitarian intervention, but Security Council adoption of humanitarian intervention also depends on the broader normative context, which includes the stories that council members tell about sovereignty and the identity of the perpetrator. The UN is first and foremost "a states' organization that seeks to forge commonly shared values and interests through the political will of its members. In turn, these values and interests are translated into policies, practices, and actions covering a variety of subjects."[12] A strong argument can be made that the UN adopted both sovereignty and human rights as core principles at its founding. Yet there was unevenness in the conceptual development of, level of member commitment to, and assignment of responsibility for sovereignty and human rights. The principle of sovereignty protected states' rights, was well defined in Article 2 of the Charter, and was safeguarded by the UNSC; while the principle of human rights protected individuals' rights, was defined by the Universal Declaration of Human Rights and subsequent international covenants, and was monitored by the Economic and Social Council. States privileged sovereignty rights, which became more highly internalized in UN practices than human rights, which empowered individuals to make claims against their states, and thus against state sovereignty. The eight cases of this study illuminate a fundamental challenge to the UNSC. Since the end of the Cold War, gross violations of human rights have come to be seen as a threat to international peace and security, and stopping mass atrocities has become a legitimate purpose of military force. Intrastate conflicts characterized by mass atrocity crimes have upended the traditional division of labor within the UN such that human rights norms now compete directly with sovereignty norms and council member interests during the formation of policy within the UNSC. These cases trace the coevolution of both norms across a period of two decades. At the start, the definition of human rights violations as a threat to international peace and security put the norms directly into conflict; yet by the end of this period, their conceptual meaning had changed in ways that allows them to be perceived and discursively constructed as complementary. Until the discursive construction of human rights as complementary to sovereignty in Libya in 2011, however, these cases illustrated a perverse finding. Council members were unwilling to engage in humanitarian intervention against perpetrator states unless they had transgressed sovereignty norms, even though the UNSC occasionally halted and even punished mass atrocity crimes of nonstate actors.

Before the conceptual meaning of sovereignty was fundamentally altered by acceptance of the responsibility to protect, UNSC decision making took place in a highly competitive and complicated normative environment. When the council defined human rights violations as a threat to international peace and security, two norms potentially came into conflict: the protection of state sovereignty and the protection of fundamental human rights. This could create normative incoherence for council members, who are forced to determine how to interpret and apply both norms simultaneously in a single case. Protection of sovereignty suggests a policy of nonintervention in state domestic affairs, whereas protection of human rights suggests the opposite. When council members face competing normative demands, they argue. Members interpret these normative claims differently and debate whether they require action from the UNSC. In the conflicts outlined in this book, members employed humanitarian intervention in cases where the promotion of human rights norms was discursively constructed as complementary to the protection of state sovereignty. These include Somalia, Bosnia, Sierra

Leone, and Libya (see Table 9.2 for a complete list of council stories about sovereignty). Members decided against humanitarian intervention in cases where the promotion of human rights was characterized as compromising state sovereignty, including Rwanda, Kosovo, and Darfur. The modest embrace of the responsibility to protect by the UNSC in 2006 and its actual application in Libya in 2011 demonstrates that the tension between these two normative principles is easing, but normative coherence still has to be actively and rhetorically constructed.

Iraq, 1990–1992

During deliberations about how to address Iraq's territorial aggression against Kuwait, human rights norms first entered the Security Council discourse as a legitimate subject. While some council members objected to any discussion of human rights in the council chamber, the majority of members decided in 1991 that the *cross-border effects* of internal human rights violations by the Iraqi government against its own people were a threat to international peace and security. Resolution 688 demanded that the Iraqi government cease violating human rights and international humanitarian law and open its sovereign territory to humanitarian relief organizations and external military observers.

Although Resolution 688 was unprecedented for redefining international security interests to include the protection of human rights, the resolution also reaffirmed the principle of noninterference in the internal affairs of member states, despite demanding immediate and unrestricted access to Iraq's sovereign territory and the end to human rights violations against its citizens. The Security Council reconciled this inherent tension between sovereignty norms and human rights norms by reasoning that the internal human rights situation extended beyond the border of Iraq, thus moving it beyond the realm of domestic affairs and justifying an international response.[13] In effect, Resolution 688 reaffirmed the national jurisdiction of states over their peoples and territories, but the human rights situation caused by Iraq was no longer an internal matter of the Iraqi state. Further, the referents for sovereignty were Iraq's neighbors, Kuwait, Iran, and Turkey, and not Iraq itself. Thus, it was the threat to the security and sovereignty of neighbor states posed by Iraq's violation of human rights norms and not human rights norms per se that enabled the passage of Resolution 688. The promotion of human rights norms occurred within the context of a conventional war in which the sovereignty of the aggressor state had been

Table 9.2. Security Council Stories About Sovereignty

	Sovereign Authority in Target State	Sovereignty Story	Referent for Sovereignty	Theoretical Conception of Sovereignty
Iraq	Illegitimate (temporarily suspended)	Iraq's sovereignty was temporarily suspended and the effects of its domestic repression threatened the sovereignty rights of its neighbors.	Turkey and Iran	Westphalian
Somalia	Illegitimate (absent)	Absent a legitimate government in Somalia, sovereignty transferred to the Somali people.	People of Somalia	Popular
Bosnia-Herzegovina	Contested Legitimate (government of Bosnia)	**Version 1:** Sovereignty was disputed as a result of an intrastate civil war with interstate dimensions. **Version 2:** The Bosnian government was recognized as the legitimate sovereign authority and a victim of human rights violations in the conflict.	**Version 1:** Contested **Version 2:** Bosnian government led by President Alija Izetbegovic	**Version 1:** International legal **Version 2:** Popular and Westphalian

Rwanda	Legitimate (government of Rwanda)	Sovereign authority resided in President Habyarimana's government and its successor after his death.	Habyarimana government and its successor	Westphalian
Kosovo	Legitimate (government of Serbia)	**Version 1:** States have a legitimate right to use military force to fight internal threats to their rule. **Version 2:** Sovereignty does not give states the right to terrorize their own populations. It incorporates a minimal standard of human rights protection not being met by the government of Serbia.	Serbian government	**Version 1:** Westphalian **Version 2:** Popular sovereignty
Sierra Leone	Illegitimate (displaced)	The legitimate sovereign authority was the deposed democratically elected government. Attacks against the civilian population represented attacks against the state's sovereign authority. Protecting human rights aided the restoration of legitimate sovereign authority.	Democratically elected but deposed government of Sierra Leone	International legal, popular, and Westphalian

Table 9.2. (Continued)

	Sovereign Authority in Target State	Sovereignty Story	Referent for Sovereignty	Theoretical Conception of Sovereignty
Darfur	Legitimate (government of Sudan)	The government of Sudan led by President Omar al-Bashir was the legitimate sovereign authority but was failing to meet its responsibility to protect its people.	Government of Sudan led by President Omar al-Bashir	Westphalian and responsibility to protect
Libya	Illegitimate	The UNSC reaffirmed the sovereignty and territorial integrity of the Libyan state but simultaneously argued that Libyan authorities had lost the legitimate right to rule, investing sovereign authority in the Libyan people.	Libyan people	Popular and responsibility to protect

temporarily suspended, removing the tension between the protection of state sovereignty and the promotion of human rights norms.[14] In this context, the council could promote human rights at the same time that it protected state sovereignty. The UNSC response created the political and normative space for human rights considerations to shape future council deliberations about humanitarian intervention.

Somalia, 1992–1995

The authorization of military force for humanitarian reasons in Somalia significantly altered the way that council members defined the legitimate use of force and marked the emergence of UNSC humanitarian intervention. Yet it was because sovereign authority was absent in Somalia that the UNSC was able to undertake early forcible military action there in defense of human rights and humanitarian principles. Resolution 746 (1992) defined the continuation of the *internal* humanitarian crisis in Somalia itself, not its cross-border effects, as a threat to international peace and security. Later, Security Council Resolutions 794 (1992) and 814 (1993) authorized the use of "all necessary means" to ensure the delivery of humanitarian aid and to foster political reconciliation. The Chapter VII authorization marked an important evolution in UNSC practice—the authorization of armed force for a strictly humanitarian cause. Unlike Resolution 688, which authorized UN protection of Iraqi minorities because of the transborder impact of internal human rights violations, Resolution 794 identified the internal humanitarian crisis *itself* as a threat to international peace and security. This move was possible because the use of coercive force posed little threat to established and highly internalized norms of state sovereignty and territorial integrity. In effect, Somalia was a failed state with no sovereign government, and thus no sovereignty to be undermined.

Bosnia-Herzegovina, 1992–1995

Humanitarian intervention in Bosnia expanded the possibility of its use to an intrastate conflict characterized by contested sovereignty. In cases of contested sovereignty, it is easier to build consensus around the use of force in defense of a sovereign state than against it. Humanitarian intervention became possible only after UNSC members described the Bosnian Muslim government in Sarajevo as the legitimate sovereign authority. Because the government and its people were the victims of the human rights violations and not the perpetrators, humanitarian intervention was justified as complementary to state sovereignty. Because Bosnian Serb perpetrators were supported by Belgrade, humanitarian intervention also was justified as a form of collective defense against aggression.

Rwanda, 1994–1995

When the 1994 genocide began in Rwanda, the UNSC did not authorize humanitarian intervention to stop it. The Rwandan government was the principal perpetrator of human rights violations against its own people; thus, the promotion of human rights directly challenged norms of state sovereignty and domestic noninterference. In the 1990s, it was hard to justify humanitarian intervention when confronted with traditional sovereignty concerns because there was no precedent for humanitarian intervention against a legitimate government that was also a perpetrator state. In Rwanda, only a small group of nonpermanent members championed the promotion of human rights norms, and their justification did not complement state sovereignty. For others, including the permanent members, sovereignty norms were an effective barrier to, or a convenient justification for, avoiding humanitarian intervention. In Somalia, the council had justified its humanitarian intervention based on the absence of state authority. In Bosnia, the council intervened only after it determined that the legitimate government authority was a victim, rather than a perpetrator, of massive human rights violations. In both cases, humanitarian intervention promoted human rights norms but was justified as either circumventing or reinforcing existing norms about state sovereignty and nonintervention, rather than directly challenging them. In the council, it is difficult to build the consensus to authorize the use of force against a sovereign state member of the UN, even when that state is a perpetrator of genocide, because to do so would challenge existing sovereignty norms.

Kosovo, 1998–1999

The case of Kosovo highlighted growing tensions within the UNSC about the status of human rights norms and the degree to which they either conformed to or conflicted with state sovereignty. Council members fundamentally disagreed about the character of the conflict—whether it was a legitimate police response to unruly elements of a domestic population or ethnically motivated killing. The issue at stake in Kosovo was state responsibility towards its citizens. Serbia was accused by members of systematically violating the human rights of its ethnic Albanian population, but its sovereignty over the territory of Kosovo was uncontested. In this case, humanitarian intervention would have directly conflicted with, rather than complemented, sovereignty norms. Council members were divided over the appropriate meaning of state sovereignty. States that supported humanitarian intervention argued that Serbia had violated its sovereign responsibilities by forcibly deporting and murdering its ethnic Albanian population, while opponents of humanitarian intervention argued that Serbia was exercising its sovereign right to neutralize internal threats to its rule. The two positions were irreconcilable. The principal justification for the absence of humanitarian intervention was the conflict between sovereignty norms and human rights norms. As in Rwanda, the perpetrator was a sovereign state and the victims were members of its own population. The North Atlantic Treaty Organization launched a humanitarian intervention in Kosovo in 1999 without Security Council authorization. Composed of a different set of members and not charged with regulating sovereignty norms, NATO members were willing to deviate from them because they perceived humanitarian intervention as complementary to both their shared interests and values.

Sierra Leone, 1995–2004

In Sierra Leone, human rights norms and sovereignty were discursively constructed as complementary. In contrast to the situations in Rwanda and Kosovo, the government was portrayed as a victim rather than a perpetrator. Rebel forces, including the Revolutionary United Front and elements of the Armed Forces Revolutionary Council, were the perpetrators, and the victims were both the legitimate sovereign government of Sierra Leone and its domestic population. Thus, the UNSC could simultaneously protect sovereignty norms by reinstalling the legitimate government authority and by intervening militarily to protect the civilian population. While council members had a vested interest in protecting state sovereignty by reversing the effects of an illegal military coup, UNSC resolutions went beyond defending state sovereignty to include important innovations in peacekeeping and peace-enforcement operations. This included the adoption of a civilian protection mandate under Chapter VII, the establishment of human rights monitors and child protection standards, extensive human rights training for UN personnel involved in peacekeeping operations, and the creation of a special court to prosecute international crimes committed during the war.

Through their justifications, a majority of council members registered their support for a broader conception of state sovereignty that included state responsibility for the protection of human rights.

Sovereignty as Responsibility, 2001–2011

Security Council decisions against humanitarian intervention in Rwanda and Kosovo were widely regarded as UN failures. In 1999, Secretary-General Kofi Annan challenged UN members to imagine what horrors might have been prevented in Rwanda if humanitarian intervention had been undertaken, but to also imagine the instability that would be generated if more humanitarian interventions without UNSC authorization like Kosovo were permitted. Annan challenged the UN to find a way to reconcile human rights principles with the tradition of state sovereignty.[15] Responding directly to the secretary-general's challenge, the International Commission on Intervention and State Sovereignty produced a groundbreaking report, *The Responsibility to Protect*, in which it defended a conceptualization of sovereignty that included state responsibility for the protection of human rights. The report argued that sovereignty implied dual responsibility. Externally, states must respect the sovereignty of other states but internally, states must respect the rights and fundamental dignity of their citizens.[16] Acceptance of *sovereignty as responsibility* means that when a state is unable or unwilling to protect its population, the UNSC has a *responsibility to protect*.[17] In 2005, the UN General Assembly passed the World Summit Outcome document, which affirmed that the respect for human rights is essential to international relations; declared that individual states have a responsibility to protect their populations from genocide, war crimes, ethnic cleansing, and crimes against humanity; and endorsed Security Council responsibility to protect populations when states fail to do so.[18] The council formally endorsed the responsibility to protect in Resolution 1674 (2006) and Resolution 1894 (2009) on the protection of civilians in armed conflict and in council resolutions on the situation in Darfur in 2006 and in Libya, Côte d'Ivoire, South Sudan, and the Middle East in 2011.[19]

Darfur, 2004–2009

During its meetings on Darfur, council members repeatedly emphasized the government of Sudan's responsibility to protect the people of Darfur, but remained divided on the responsibility of the international community when the government was unwilling or unable to do so. Responsibility-to-protect language was used in the perambulatory clauses of Resolution 1556 (2004) and Resolution 1564 (2004) and was formally affirmed in Resolution 1674 (2006) on the protection of civilians in armed conflict and Resolution 1706 (2006), which applied it to the situation in Darfur. Yet because the government was a perpetrator, the international protection of human rights would directly conflict with state sovereignty. Nonintervention was justified, in part, out of deference to state sovereignty. Because permanent members were divided on the responsibility to protect, they could not reconcile sovereignty norms and human rights norms, and thus the pattern of the 1990s persisted: sovereignty trumped human rights norms whenever the perpetrator was a state. However, formal council records illustrate that the burden of justification had shifted, making it more difficult to justify not intervening than it was to justify humanitarian intervention, even when an appeal to sovereignty norms was the basis of objection.

Libya, 2011

The UNSC endorsed and acted on the responsibility to protect in Libya in 2011. Council members invoked the concept as justification for the passage of both Resolution 1970, which referred the conflict to the International Criminal Court, and Resolution 1973, which established a no-fly zone over Libyan territory and authorized military force to defend it. Supporters of Resolution 1973 defined sovereignty as comprising state responsibility for the protection of human rights, but humanitarian intervention in Libya was not a victory of human rights norms over sovereignty norms. Rather, it reflects support for a reconceptualized understanding of state sovereignty that includes elements of both responsibility and legitimacy. Because Libyan authorities failed to protect and actually perpetrated crimes against their own civilian population, council members called into question the very legitimacy of their sovereign authority. Once their leaders were deemed illegitimate, the UNSC transferred sovereign authority to the Libyan people. This allowed council members to discursively construct the protection of the Libyan people through humanitarian intervention as consistent with and complementary to the protection of sovereignty. Consequently, UNSC resolutions reaffirmed the sovereignty and territorial integrity of Libya at the same time that they rejected the legitimacy of Libyan authorities, affirmed the right of ordinary Libyans to determine their own future, and authorized the use of all necessary means to protect civilians. This important evolution to employ humanitarian intervention against a perpetrator state suggests that future UNSC deliberations about how to address situations of mass atrocity will center on determining where legitimate sovereign authority resides when considering whether and how the council fulfills its responsibility to protect

Causal Stories, Sovereignty Stories, and Humanitarian Intervention

Security Council unity around an intentional story creates a political opportunity for humanitarian intervention, but the normative context in which the use of military force is debated is integral to its occurrence. UNSC humanitarian intervention decisions are shaped by both stories about causality and stories about sovereignty. When council members adopt an intentional story, they identify perpetrators and victims, and prompt policies aimed at interdiction and punishment, including the possibility of humanitarian intervention. Because the council is charged with safeguarding state sovereignty, it has adopted humanitarian intervention only when it has discursively constructed its use as complementary to sovereignty norms, either because the target state is not a perpetrator or because government authorities are illegitimate because they are violating their sovereign responsibilities. In either case, using military force does not compromise traditional Westphalian conceptions of the sovereignty norm. Table 9.3 summarizes both of these findings for each of the cases, and illustrates both consistency and evolution across time. Intentional stories and stories in which sovereignty and human rights are discursively constructed as complementary are associated with UNSC humanitarian intervention. Inadvertent stories, contestation, and stories in which sovereignty and human rights are conceived as conflicting are not. The cases also signal evolution over time because humanitarian intervention occurred in Somalia despite the adoption of a complex story, whereas subsequently, complexity was a barrier to humanitarian intervention in Darfur. Then, until Libya, UNSC humanitarian intervention had never been employed against a state perpetrator. It was possible in Libya, however, because Libya was also the first case with a perpetrator state in which sovereignty and human rights were discursively constructed as complementary. This change suggests that the legitimacy of sovereign authority was more important than its presence or absence beginning in 2011.

Table 9.3. UNSC Stories and Humanitarian Intervention by Case

	Dominant Causal Story	Story About Sovereignty and Human Rights	Perpetrator	Victim	UNSC Humanitarian Intervention
Somalia	Complex Intentional	Complementary Complementary	Rebel factions and clans	Innocent civilians UN	Yes Yes
Bosnia	Contested Intentional	Conflicting Complementary	All parties Bosnian Serbs	Innocent civilians Bosnian Muslims and Bosnian government	No Yes
Rwanda	Inadvertent	Conflicting	All parties	Innocent civilians	No
Kosovo	Contested	Conflicting	Serbia and Federal Republic of Yugoslavia	Kosovar Albanians	No
Sierra Leone	Intentional	Complementary	Revolutionary United Front and Armed Forces Revolutionary Council	Innocent civilians and Sierra Leone	Yes
Darfur	Inadvertent Complex	Conflicting Conflicting	Government of Sudan and Janjaweed militias Rebel groups	Innocent civilians	No No
Libya	Intentional	Complementary	Libya	Innocent civilians	Yes

a Armed Forces Revolutionary Council

The Role of Contingency and the Interaction of Material and Ideational Factors

The purpose of this project has been to draw attention to the often over-looked ways that international norms shape UNSC decisions about the use of military force. In focusing on the systematic patterns that emerge in council discourse across cases and linking that discourse to humanitarian intervention behavior, the project has emphasized continuity across cases and the evolution of international norms over time. Yet political and historical contingency is also important to explaining UNSC humanitarian intervention outcomes, and ideational factors complement material factors in shaping council discourse and behavior. It was crucially important in Libya, for example, that regional organizations adopted both the intentional causal story and the story about the illegitimate sovereign authority of Libyan authorities. Without the public support and private lobbying for a no-fly zone by the League of Arab States and the Organization for Islamic Cooperation, it is likely that contestation among UNSC members would have prevented the authorization of "all necessary means" in Libya—the same way that contestation prevented UNSC humanitarian intervention in Syria in 2011. Similarly, the last-minute decision of U.S. secretary of state James Baker to visit Kurdish refugee camps in the spring of 1991, despite his hesitancy to do so, prompted him to subsequently forcefully advocate for the creation and enforcement of no-fly zones over Iraq. Finally, council humanitarian intervention decisions in one case also shaped the UNSC response to others, despite the council's expressed commitment to examining each situation on a case-by-case basis. Success in Iraq encouraged the UNSC to intervene in Somalia and Bosnia, but significant losses of UN peacekeepers in both made the council hesitant to invest its time and resources in Rwanda. Hard lessons learned in Srebrenica about the capacity and willingness of Serbian authorities to massacre civilians to acquire territory prompted members of the North Atlantic Treaty Organization to bypass the UNSC and use military force to repel the Serbs in Kosovo without council authorization when it was not forthcoming. UN failures in Rwanda and Kosovo gave rise to the movement for an international responsibility to protect. The failure of the responsibility to protect to translate into the protection of civilians by the council in Darfur may have helped generate support for humanitarian intervention in Libya, whereas perceptions by some council members that NATO overreached in its Libyan humanitarian intervention have diminished chances for humanitarian intervention to stop the killing in Syria. Contingency, timing, and sequencing of cases matter—they also shape the content and acceptance of varying causal stories and stories about sovereignty.

Although the focus of the book has been on ideational factors in order to highlight the crucial and underrecognized contribution they make to UNSC decision making, the cases have demonstrated that material factors, like military capacity and the high economic and human costs of interventions, also affected the decisions of UNSC members. Importantly, these cases illustrate that it is most accurate to understand norms and interests as regularly interacting, more so than competing. Council members operated from mixed motives and UNSC humanitarian intervention behavior did not map neatly onto a set of a priori interests belonging to its members. Rather, the cases demonstrate that interests shape and are shaped by normative considerations, including international legal and moral norms about human rights—norms and interests were mutually constituted. The cases also emphasized that power in the UNSC was as much about normative and persuasive power as it was about material power.[20] Competition among members includes competition over which story can dominate the council, which translates into control over problem definition and the appropriate solutions. The findings of this research show that discourse has real explanatory power, and that the arguments council members make about the cause and character of conflict and the source of sovereign authority in target states shape humanitarian intervention decisions.

The Future of Humanitarian Intervention

The growing legitimacy of human rights norms is changing the meaning of sovereignty at the United Nations but does not threaten the institution of sovereignty itself. While the balance between individuals' rights and states' rights at the UN may be shifting, the act of humanitarian intervention reinforces the state as the primary actor in international relations, even as it alters the state's sovereign responsibilities.[21] Indeed, sovereignty exists only in relation to the international community of states: "Sovereignty is the constitutive principle of the nation-state system, yet it is also derivative of that system. This underlies the paradox of sovereignty: states are sovereign only within the context of a broader global system of states, and thus they can remain independent only by maintaining a system that imposes constraints on their independence."[22] Sovereignty is contingent and its meaning evolves along with the international normative order of which it is a part. Changes in the meaning of sovereignty that incorporate minimal human rights protection standards do not fundamentally undermine the institution of sovereignty, although they may change what counts as appropriate state behavior, and the conditions of recognition by other states, as was demonstrated in Libya. By saving strangers through humanitarian intervention, the UNSC reaffirms that states are the primary protectors of human rights norms. The responsibility to protect changes the meaning of sovereignty to incorporate state responsibility but it also reaffirms that states retain the monopoly over power and the legitimate means of violence in the international state system. What the recent UNSC humanitarian intervention in Libya shows is that when perpetrators are states, the fact of their sovereign authority will no longer automatically protect them from humanitarian intervention. Instead, their ability to employ Article 2.7 will depend on whether or not that sovereign authority is deemed legitimate by the Security Council in relation to an ever-evolving set of human rights norms.

Notes

Chapter 1. Constructing Humanitarian Intervention

Note to epigraph: UN Security Council, 17 March 2011 (S/PV.6498).

1. "Gadaffi's Son Warns of 'Rivers of Blood' in Libya," *Al Arabiya News*, 21 February 2011, accessed 16 July 2012, www.alarabiya.net.

2. David Kirkpatrick and Kareem Fahim, "Qadaffi Warns of Assault on Benghazi as UN Vote Nears," *New York Times*, 17 March 2011.

3. UN Security Council, 17 March 2011 (S/PV.6498), 44.

4. See also Martha Finnemore, *The Purpose of Intervention: Changing Beliefs About the Use of Force* (Ithaca, NY: Cornell University Press, 2003).

5. These cases were Indian intervention in East Pakistan (1971), Tanzanian intervention in Uganda (1979), and Vietnamese inte rvention in Cambodia (1979).

6. Nicholas J. Wheeler, *Saving Strangers* (New York: Oxford University Press, 2000), 93.

7. UN Security Council, 25 February 2011 (S/PV.6490); UN Security Council, 26 February 2011 (S/PV.6491); UN Security Council (S/PV.6498).

8. UN Security Council (S/PV.6498), 6.

9. UN Security Council (S/PV.6498), 3.

10. See Joseph S. Nye Jr., *The Future of Power* (New York: Perseus, 2011), 19–20.

11. See Stephen Krasner, *Sovereignty: Organized Hypocrisy* (Princeton, NJ: Princeton University Press, 1999).

12. Margaret P. Karns and Karen A. Mingst, *International Organizations: The Politics and Processes of Global Governance* (Boulder, CO: Lynne Rienner, 2004), 110.

13. *Provisional Rules of Procedure of the Security Council* (New York: United Nations, 1983), Rules 37, 39, http://www.un.org.

14. David M. Malone, "International Criminal Justice: Just an Expensive Mirage?" *International Journal* (Summer 2008): 731.

15. Peter Wallensteen and Patrik Johansson, "Security Council Decisions in Perspective," in *The UN Security Council: From the Cold War to the Twenty-First Century*, ed. David M. Malone (Boulder, CO: Lynne Rienner, 2004), 18–19, 26–27.

16. Wallensteen and Johansson, "Security Council Decisions in Perspective," 27. For an alternative perspective about the frequency of war see Joshua S. Goldstein, "Think Again: War," *Foreign Policy,* September–October 2011.

17. UN Security Council, 11 August 1992 (S/PV.3105).

18. Jack Donnelly, *Universal Human Rights: In Theory and Practice* (Ithaca, NY: Cornell University Press, 2003), 22.

19. Finnemore, *The Purpose of Intervention.*

20. Robert Jackson, *Sovereignty at the Millennium* (Oxford: Blackwell, 1999), 10.

21. Jackson, *Sovereignty at the Millennium,* 10.

22. Jackson, *Sovereignty at the Millennium,* 8, 12.

23. Daniel Philpott, *Revolutions in Sovereignty: How Ideas Shaped Modern International Relations* (Princeton, NJ: Princeton University Press, 2001).

24. Bruce Cronin, "Intervention and the International Community," in *International Intervention: Sovereignty Versus Responsibility,* ed. Michael Keren and Donald A. Sylvan (London: Frank Cass, 2002), 150.

25. Jackson, *Sovereignty at the Millennium,* 22.

26. Daniel Philpott, *Revolutions in Sovereignty* (Princeton, NJ: Princeton University Press, 2001), 156.

27. See Krasner, *Sovereignty: Organized Hypocrisy.*

28. Independent International Commission on Kosovo, *The Kosovo Report* (Oxford: Oxford University Press, 2000), 169.

29. For a discussion of the factors contributing to the growing legitimacy of the human rights idea, see Kenneth Roth, "Human Rights Organizations: A New Force for Social Change," in *Realizing Human Rights: Moving from Inspiration to Impact,* ed. Samantha Power and Graham Allison (New York: St. Martin's Press, 2000), 225–48.

30. See Martha Finnemore, "Paradoxes in Humanitarian Intervention," in *Moral Limit and Possibility in World Politics,* ed. Richard M. Price (Cambridge: Cambridge University Press, 2008), 198.

31. UN, "Secretary General Presents His Annual Report to the General Assembly," news release, 20 September 1999, SG/SM/7136, GA/9596, www.un.org.

32. UN, "Secretary General Presents His Annual Report."

33. UN, "Secretary General Presents His Annual Report."

34. International Commission on Intervention and State Sovereignty (ICISS), *The Responsibility to Protect* (Ottawa: International Development Research Centre, 2001), sec. VIII.

35. ICISS, *The Responsibility to Protect,* sec. XII.

36. UN General Assembly, "2005 World Summit Outcome Document," 24 October 2005 (A/RES/60/1).

37. UN General Assembly, "2005 World Summit Outcome Document."

38. Peter J. Katzenstein, ed., *The Culture of National Security: Norms and Identity in World Politics* (New York: Columbia University Press, 1996); Martha Finnemore

and Kathryn Sikkink, "International Norm Dynamics and Political Change," *International Organization* 52, no. 4 (1998): 887–917; and Ann Marie Clark, *Diplomacy of Conscience: Amnesty International and Changing Human Rights Norms* (Princeton, NJ: Princeton University Press, 2001), 28.

39. Finnemore and Sikkink, "International Norm Dynamics and Political Change."

40. See Neta Crawford, *Argument and Change in World Politics: Ethics, Decolonization and Humanitarian Intervention* (Cambridge: Cambridge University Press, 2002); and Finnemore, *The Purpose of Intervention.*

41. Alexander Wendt and James Fearon, "Rationalism v. Constructivism: A Skeptical View," in *The Handbook of International Relations*, ed. Walter Carlsnaes, Thomas Risse, and Beth Simmons (London: Sage Publications, 2002), 61.

42. Wendt and Fearon, "Rationalism v. Constructivism," 61.

43. Justin Conlon, "Sovereignty vs. Human Rights or Sovereignty and Human Rights?" *Race and Class* 46 (2010): 75–100.

44. Chaim D. Kauffman and Robert A. Pape, "Explaining Costly International Moral Action: Britain's Sixty-Year Campaign Against the Atlantic Slave Trade," *International Organization* 53 (1999): 4, 633.

45. See Nye, *The Future of Power*, 219.

46. Senior UN official, interview by author, New York, June 2007; and senior researcher on the United Nations, interview by author, New York, June 2007.

47. Donnelly, *Universal Human Rights in Theory and Practice*, 257.

48. My definition is consistent with, and draws significantly from, existing literature on humanitarian intervention. See in particular Adam Roberts, "The United Nations and Humanitarian Intervention," in *Humanitarian Intervention and International Relations*, ed. Jennifer Welsh (Oxford: Oxford University Press, 2004), 146; J. L. Holzgrefe, "The Humanitarian Intervention Debate," in *Humanitarian Intervention: Ethical, Legal and Political Dilemmas*, ed. J. L. Holzgrefe and Robert Keohane (Cambridge: Cambridge University Press, 2003),18; and Donnelly, *Universal Human Rights in Theory and Practice*, 243.

49. On the Political Terror Scale, see http://www.politicalterrorscale.org. For a detailed account of what is measured by the political terror scale, its coding scheme, and its comparison to other human rights data measures see Reed M. Wood and Mark Gibney "The Political Terror Scale (PTS): A Re-introduction and a Comparison to CIRI," *Human Rights Quarterly* 32, no. 2 (2010): 367–400. For a critique of the political terror scale see David L. Cingranelli and David L. Richards, "The Cingranelli and Richards (CIRI) Human Rights Data Project," *Human Rights Quarterly* 32, no. 2 (2010): 401–424.

50. Mark Gibney and Matthew Dalton, "The Political Terror Scale," *Policy Studies and Developing Nations* 4 (1996): 74, 79.

51. Limiting the cases to those with two consecutive years of a level 5 ranking takes into account only the most severe crises where human rights abuses might raise

the consciousness of members of international society and provide sufficient opportunity to generate an international response as well as to correct for the possibility of coding error or anomaly.

52. NATO intervened in Kosovo. The Security Council did not use military force to stop genocide in Rwanda but authorized a limited humanitarian intervention by France postgenocide.

53. See Stephen Van Evera, *Guide to Methods for Students of Political Science* (Ithaca, NY: Cornell University Press, 1997), 77–88.

54. Thomas Risse, "'Let's Argue!': Communicative Action in World Politics," *International Organization* 54, no. 1 (2001): 4–5; Ian Johnstone, "Security Council Deliberations: The Power of the Better Argument," *European Journal of International Law* 14, no. 3 (2003): 453; Crawford, *Argument and Change in World Politics*; Ian Hurd, "Legitimacy, Power, and the Symbolic Life of the UN Security Council," *Global Governance* 8 (2002): 35–51; and Nicole Dietelhoff, "The Discourse of Legalization: Charting Islands of Persuasion in the ICC Case," *International Organization* 63, no. 1 (2009): 33–66.

55. Johnstone, "Security Council Deliberations," 438.

56. See Hurd, "Legitimacy, Power and the Symbolic Life," 47.

57. Risse, "Communicative Action," 32; and Kenneth W. Abbott and Duncan Snidal, "Hard and Soft Law in International Governance," *International Organization* 54, no. 3 (2000): 429.

58. Nye, *The Future of Power*, 20.

59. See Nye, *The Future of Power*.

60. Jennifer Milliken, "The Study of Discourse in International Relations: A Critique of Research and Methods," *European Journal of International Relations* 5, no. 2 (1999): 229.

61. See Roxanne Lynn Doty, *Imperial Encounters: The Politics of Representation in North-South Relations* (Minneapolis: University of Minnesota Press, 1996), on representational practices; and Riika Kuusisto, "Framing the Wars in the Gulf and in Bosnia: The Rhetorical Definitions of the Western Powers in Action," *Journal of Peace Research* 35, no. 5 (1998): 603–20, on storytelling and enemy discourse.

62. Milliken, "The Study of Discourse," 604; and Jon Western, *Selling Intervention and War: The Presidency, the Media, and the American Public* (Baltimore: Johns Hopkins University Press, 2005).

63. David M. Malone, introduction to Malone, *The UN Security Council*, 7.

64. Finnemore, *Purposes of Intervention*,15.

65. Deborah A. Stone, *Policy Paradox: The Art of Political Decision-Making*, rev. ed. (New York: W. W. Norton, 2002).

66. Milliken, "The Study of Discourse," 232.

67. Milliken, "The Study of Discourse," 233.

68. Stone, *Policy Paradox*, 188.

69. Stone, *Policy Paradox*, 209.

70. Deborah Stone, "Causal Stories and the Formation of Policy Agendas," *Political Science Quarterly* 104, no. 2 (1989): 285.

71. Stone, "Causal Stories."

72. I thank Tim Dunne for stressing the importance of identifying the underlying normative scripts that ground each of the causal stories.

73. Stone, "Causal Stories," 281–300.

74. Stone, *Policy Paradox*, 196–97, and "Causal Stories," 289.

75. Stone, *Policy Paradox*, 196.

76. Stone, *Policy Paradox*, 204.

77. Stone, *Policy Paradox*, 197.

78. Senior UN Secretariat official, interview by author, New York, June 2007.

79. Kenneth Roth, interview by author, New York, May 2007.

80. Stone, "Causal Stories," 292. See also Donald A. Sylvan and Jon C. Pevehouse, "Deciding Whether to Intervene," in Keren and Sylvan, *International Intervention*.

Chapter 2. The Emergence of Human Rights Discourse in the Security Council

1. Middle East Watch, *Human Rights in Iraq* (New Haven, CT: Yale University Press, 1990), 83; and Physicians for Human Rights, "Winds of Death: Iraq's Use of Poison Gas Against its Kurdish Population: A Report of a Medical Mission to Turkish Kurdistan by Physicians for Human Rights," in Middle East Watch, *Human Rights in Iraq*, 80.

2. Human Rights Watch, *Whatever Happened to the Iraqi Kurds?* (New York; Human Rights Watch, 1991), accessed August 18 2012, www.hrw.org/reports/1991/03/11/whatever-happened-iraqi-kurds.

3. Middle East Watch, *Human Rights in Iraq*, 78–82.

4. Margaret P. Karns and Karen A. Mingst, *International Organizations: The Politics and Processes of Global Governance* (Boulder, CO: Lynne Rienner, 2004), 110.

5. Peter Wallensteen and Patrik Johansson, "Security Council Decisions in Perspective," in *The UN Security Council: From the Cold War to the 21st Century* , ed. David E. Malone (Boulder, CO: Lynne Reinner, 2004), 19.

6. UN Security Council, 6 August 1990 (S/PV.2933), 32, and 18 August 1990 (S/PV.2938), 21, 26, 36.

7. UN Security Council, 2 August 1990 (S/PV.2932), 21. See also Wallensteen and Johansson, "Security Council Decisions in Perspective," 17.

8. Frank Fischer and John Forester, eds., *The Argumentative Turn in Policy Analysis and Planning* (Durham, NC: Duke University Press, 1993), 2.

9. Phebe Marr, *The Modern History of Iraq* (Boulder, CO: Westview Press, 2011), 253.

10. UN Security Council, Resolution 688, 5 April 1991 (S/RES/688).

11. Marr, *The Modern History of Iraq*, 265.

12. Human Rights Watch, *Human Rights Watch World Report 1990—Iraq and Occupied Kuwait* (New York: Human Rights Watch, 1991), accessed 13 August 2012, www.unhcr.org/refworld/docid/467fca3cc.html.

13. Human Rights Watch, *Human Rights Watch World Report 1990.*

14. Peter Malanczuk, "The Kurdish Crisis and Allied Intervention in the Aftermath of the Second Gulf War," *European Journal of International Law* 2 (1991): 115, citing H. Hannum, *Autonomy, Sovereignty, and Self-Determination: The Accommodation of Conflicting Rights* (Philadelphia: University of Pennsylvania Press, 1986), 179; and Jane Stromseth, "Iraq's Repression of Its Civilian Population: Collective Responses and Continuing Challenges," in *Enforcing Restraint: Collective Intervention in Internal Conflicts*, ed. Lori Fisler Damrosch (New York: Council on Foreign Relations Press, 1993), 83.

15. Middle East Watch, *Human Rights in Iraq*, 6.

16. Human Rights Watch, *Human Rights Watch World Report 1990.*

17. Human Rights Watch, *Human Rights Watch World Report 1990.*

18. Marr, *The Modern History of Iraq*, 202.

19. Human Rights Watch, *Whatever Happened to the Iraqi Kurds?* and Physicians for Human Rights, *Unquiet Graves: The Search for the Disappeared in Iraqi Kurdistan* (New York: Middle East Watch, February 1992).

20. Human Rights Watch, *Whatever Happened to the Iraqi Kurds?*

21. Human Rights Watch, *Whatever Happened to the Iraqi Kurds?* See also Middle East Watch, *Human Rights in Iraq*, 83.

22. UN Security Council (S/PV.2932), 11.

23. Marr, *The Modern History of Iraq*, 206.

24. Marr, *The Modern History of Iraq*, 224.

25. Human Rights Watch, *Human Rights Watch World Report 1990.*

26. The vote in the Security Council was fourteen in favor, none opposed, and no abstentions; however, Yemen did not participate in the voting. See UN Security Council (S/PV.2932), 2, and Resolution 660, 2 August 1990 (S/RES/660).

27. Marr, *The Modern History of Iraq*, 231.

28. UN Security Council, Resolution 661, 6 August 1990 (S/RES/661), Resolution 662, 9 August 1990 (S/RES/662), Resolution 664, 18 August 1990 (S/RES/664), Resolution 665, 25 August 1990 (S/RES/665).

29. UN Security Council, Resolution 678, 29 November 1990 (S/RES/678).

30. UN Security Council, 29 November 1990 (S/PV.2963), 61–62.

31. UN Security Council (S/PV.2938). See especially remarks by representatives of Colombia, the U.S., and Canada.

32. UN Security Council (S/PV.2963), 6.

33. UN Security Council (S/PV.2963), 6.

34. Christine Gray, "From Unity to Polarization: International Law and the Use of Force Against Iraq," *European Journal of International Law* 13 (2002): 1, 18–19.

35. James A. Baker III with Thomas M. DeFrank, *The Politics of Diplomacy: Revolution, War and Peace 1989–1992* (New York: G. P. Putnam's Sons, 1995), 435–36.

36. UN Security Council, Resolution 686, 2 March 1991 (S/RES/686). See also Marr, *The Modern History of Iraq*, 239.

37. UN Security Council, Resolution 687, 3 April 1991 (S/RES/687).

38. Marr, *The Modern History of Iraq*, 240.

39. Marr, *The Modern History of Iraq*, 242.

40. Carol McQueen, *Humanitarian Intervention and Safety Zones: Iraq, Bosnia and Rwanda* (New York: Palgrave, 2005), 26.

41. Human Rights Watch, *Iraq and Occupied Kuwait* (New York: Human Rights Watch, 1992), accessed 13 November 2006, www.hrw.org/reports/1992/WR92/MEW 1–02.htm.

42. Marr, *The Modern History of Iraq*, 242–45.

43. Human Rights Watch, *Iraq and Occupied Kuwait*, 8.

44. Human Rights Watch, *Iraq and Occupied Kuwait*, 8.

45. Human Rights Watch, *Iraq and Occupied Kuwait*.

46. Human Rights Watch, *Iraq and Occupied Kuwait*, 7.

47. Agency for International Development, *Iraq: Displaced Persons and Refugees* (Washington, DC: Agency for International Development, 1991). See also UN Security Council (S/PV.2982), 12.

48. UN Security Council (S/PV.2932), 19.

49. UN Security Council (S/PV.2932), 22–23.

50. UN Security Council, 5 April 1991 (S/PV.2982), 62, 73, 78, 88.

51. UN Security Council (S/PV.2982), 6.

52. These included Denmark, Germany, Iran, Ireland, Luxembourg, Norway, and Turkey. UN Security Council (S/PV.2982).

53. UN Security Council (S/PV.2982), 71.

54. UN Security Council (S/PV.2982), 36, 38, 56, 61.

55. UN Security Council (S/PV.2982), 4–6.

56. UN Security Council (S/PV.2982), 13–15.

57. UN Security Council, Resolution 688.

58. UN Security Council (S/PV.2982), 67.

59. UN Security Council (S/PV.2982), 32–37.

60. UN Security Council (S/PV.2982), 64–65.

61. UN Security Council (S/PV.2982), 88.

62. UN Security Council (S/PV.2982), 53, 71.

63. UN Security Council (S/PV.2982), 72.

64. UN Security Council (S/PV.2982), 46.

65. UN Security Council (S/PV.2982), 56.

66. Malanczuk, "Kurdish Crisis and Allied Intervention," 120–21.

67. Gray, "From Unity to Polarization," 9–10.

68. United Nations, *Provisional Rules of Procedure of the Security Council* (New York: United Nations, 1983), Rule 39.

69. UN Security Council, 11 August 1992 (S/PV.3105), 7–10, 11–12.

70. UN Security Council (S/PV.3105), 12.

71. UN Security Council (S/PV.3105), 7.

72. UN Security Council (S/PV.3105), 3.

73. UN Security Council (S/PV.3105), 18.

74. UN Security Council (S/PV.3105), 22.

75. UN Security Council (S/PV.3105), 22.

76. UN Security Council (S/PV.3105), 47.

77. UN Security Council (S/PV.3105), 57.

78. UN Security Council (S/PV.3105), 53.

79. UN Security Council (S/PV.3105), 42–43.

80. UN Security Council (S/PV.3105), 62.

81. See James Mayall, "Non-intervention, Self-Determination and the New World Order," *International Affairs* 67 (1991): 3, 421–29; and Robert C. DiPrizio, *Armed Humanitarians: U.S. Interventions from Northern Iraq to Kosovo* (Baltimore: Johns Hopkins University Press, 2002).

82. Mayall, "Non-intervention, Self-Determination and the New World Order," 426; and Stromseth, "Iraq's Repression of its Civilian Population," 84.

83. DiPrizio, *Armed Humanitarians*, 147.

84. Human Rights Watch, *Whatever Happened to the Iraqi Kurds?*

85. Human Rights Watch, *Whatever Happened to the Iraqi Kurds?*

86. Baker with DeFrank, *The Politics of Diplomacy*, 431.

87. Nigel Rodley, *To Loose the Bands of Wickedness: International Intervention in Defence of Human Rights* (London: Brassey's, 1994), 52.

88. Baker with DeFrank, *The Politics of Diplomacy*, 434–35.

89. See Martha Finnemore and Kathryn Sikkink, "Norm Dynamics and Political Change," *International Organization* 52, no. 4 (1998): 887–917.

90. UN Security Council (S/PV.2982), 32–37.

91. See Robert Jackson, "Armed Humanitarianism," *International Journal* 48 (1993): 579–606.

92. Thomas Pickering, "Speech to the U.S. Council on Foreign Relations," in May 1991 in Lawrence Freedman and David Boren, "Safe Havens' for Kurds in Post-War Iraq," 82, in Nigel S. Rodley, ed., *To Loose the Bands of Wickedness: International Intervention in Defence of Human Rights* (London: Brassey's, 1993), 43–92.

93. United Nations, *Report of the Secretary-General on the Work of the Organization* (New York: United Nations, 1991).

Chapter 3. State Collapse in Somalia and the Emergence of Security Council Humanitarian Intervention

1. The Security Council passed resolutions related to eleven situations in 1990, including Afghanistan-Pakistan, Cambodia, Central America, Cyprus, Israel-Lebanon, Israel-Syria, Iraq-Iran, Iraq-Kuwait, Occupied Territories, Pacific Islands, and Western Sahara. The Security Council passed resolutions related to sixteen situations in 1992, including Angola, Bosnia-Herzegovina, Cambodia, Croatia, Cyprus, El Salvador,

Israel-Kuwait, Israel-Lebanon, Israel-Syria, Liberia, Libya Arab Jamahiriya, Mozambique, Somalia, South Africa, territories occupied by Israel, and Yugoslavia.

2. Between 1990 and 1992, the Security Council recommended twenty states for membership in the United Nations.

3. Chapter VII of the UN Charter describes the actions available to the UNSC with respect to threats to the peace, breaches of the peace, and acts of aggression.

4. Martha Finnemore and Kathryn Sikkink, "International Norm Dynamics and Political Change," in *Exploration and Contestation in the Study of World Politics*, ed. Peter Katzenstein, Robert Keohane, and Stephen Krasner (Cambridge, MA: MIT Press, 1998), 897.

5. Finnemore and Sikkink, "International Norm Dynamics and Political Change," 897–98.

6. Jeffrey Clark, "Debacle in Somalia," *Foreign Affairs* 72, no. 1 (1992): 111.

7. Clark, "Debacle in Somalia," 110; and Ioan Lewis and James Mayall, "Somalia," in *United Nations Interventionism, 1991–2004*, ed. Mats Berdal and Spyros Economides (Cambridge: Cambridge University Press, 2007), 116.

8. Lewis and Mayall, "Somalia," 117.

9. See Clark, "Debacle in Somalia"; Lewis and Mayall, "Somalia"; and Jon Western, "Sources of Humanitarian Intervention: Beliefs, Information, and Advocacy in the U.S. Decisions on Somalia and Bosnia," *International Security* 26, no. 4 (2002): 112–42.

10. Africa Watch, "Somalia Beyond the Warlords: The Need for a Verdict on Human Rights Abuses," *Human Rights Watch Reports* 5 (March 1993): 2, 4.

11. Africa Watch, *Somalia Beyond the Warlords*, 5; and Lewis and Mayall, "Somalia," 119.

12. Africa Watch and Physicians for Human Rights, *Somalia: No Mercy in Mogadishu: The Human Cost of Conflict and the Struggle for Relief* (New York: Africa Watch, 1992), 2.

13. Jeffrey Clark, "Debacle in Somalia: Failure of the Collective Response," in *Humanitarian Intervention in Contemporary Conflict: A Reconceptualization*, ed. Oliver Ramsbothan and Tom Woodhouse (Cambridge: Polity Press, 1996), 198, citing J. Stevenson, "Hope Restored in Somalia?" *Foreign Policy* 91 (1993): 138.

14. Seth Faison, "UN Head Proposes Expanded Efforts for Somalia Relief," *New York Times*, 25 July 1992, cited in Western, "Sources of Humanitarian Intervention," 124–25.

15. Jeffrey Clark, "Debacle in Somalia," *Foreign Affairs* 72, no. 1 (1992–1993), 113.

16. Jonathon Howe, "The United States and the United Nations in Somalia: The Limits of Involvement," *Washington Quarterly* 18, no. 3 (1995).

17. UN Security Council, 17 March 1992 (S/PV.3060), 21, 46–50.

18. UN Security Council (S/PV.3060).

19. UN Security Council (S/PV.3060), 48.

20. UN Security Council (S/PV.3060), 38.

21. UN Security Council (S/PV.3060), 38.

22. UN Security Council (S/PV.3060), 54.

23. UN Security Council (S/PV.3060), 16–17.

24. UN Security Council (S/PV.3060), 9–10, 44, 46, and esp. 41.

25. UN Security Council, Resolution 746, 17 March 1992 (S/RES/746).

26. UN Security Council (S/PV.3060), 58.

27. See the UN Security Council, Report of the Secretary General, 11 March 1992 (S/23693); and *UN Chronicle*, 29, nos. 2, 23.

28. Roy Laishley, "Building on the Fragile Peace in Somalia," *Africa Recovery* 16 (December 1992–February 1993): 4, 12.

29. See Sean D. Murphy, *Humanitarian Intervention: The United Nations in an Evolving World Order* (Philadelphia: University of Pennsylvania Press, 1996), 78.

30. UN Security Council 3 December 1992 (S/PV.3145), 6, 8, and UN Security Council (S/PV.3060), 21, 46.

31. UN Security Council (S/PV.3060), 31.

32. UN Security Council, 3 December 1992 (S/PV.3145), 36.

33. UN Security Council (S/PV.3145), 16–17, 26, 46.

34. UN Security Council, Resolution 794, 3 December 1992 (S/RES/794).

35. UN Security Council, 26 March 1993 (S/PV.3188), 28.

36. UN Security Council (S/PV.3145), 18.

37. Thomas G. Weiss, "The Humanitarian Impulse," in *The UN Security Council: From the Cold War to the 21st Century*, ed. David M. Malone (Boulder, CO: Lynne Rienner, 2004), 37.

38. UN Security Council (S/PV.3145), 23, 32.

39. Hirsch and Oakley, *Somalia and Operation Restore Hope*, 118.

40. UN Security Council, 6 June 1993 (S/PV.3229), 6.

41. UN Security Council, Resolution 837, 6 June 1993 (S/RES/837).

42. UN Security Council (S/PV.3229), 6–7.

43. UN Security Council (S/PV.3229), 8.

44. UN Security Council (S/PV.3229), 12.

45. UN Security Council (S/PV.3229), 16, 19, 22.

46. UN Security Council (S/PV.3229), 16.

47. UN Security Council, Resolution 794.

48. UN Security Council, Resolution 837.

49. UN Security Council, Resolution 837.

50. Lewis and Mayall, "Somalia," 131.

51. UN Security Council, 18 November 1993 (S/PV.3317), 22.

52. UN Security Council, Resolution 886, 18 November 1993 (S/RES/886).

53. UN Security Council, 4 November 1994 (S/PV.3447), 5, 8, 10, 11, 13–16.

54. UN Security Council, 30 September 1994 (S/PV.3432), 4.

55. UN Security Council (S/PV.3432), 3.

56. UN Security Council (S/PV.3447), 16.

57. UN Security Council (S/PV.3447), 17.

58. Lewis and Mayall, "Somalia."

59. UN Security Council (S/PV.3188), 8.

60. UN Security Council (S/PV.3145), 23, 24.

61. UN Security Council (S/PV.3145), 13, 17, 23–24, 46, 49.

62. UN Security Council (S/PV.3145), 13.

63. Lewis and Mayall, "Somalia," 108.

64. UN Security Council (S/PV.3145), 23.

65. UN Security Council (S/PV.3145), 11.

66. UN Security Council (S/PV.3447), 4.

67. UN Security Council, 17 March 1992 (S/PV.3060), 54.

68. UN Security Council, Resolution 794. See especially the second and eighth paragraphs of the preamble.

69. UN Security Council (S/PV/.3447), 3.

70. UN Security Council (S/PV/.3447), 4.

71. See Western, "Sources of Humanitarian Intervention," 130.

72. Western, "Sources of Humanitarian Intervention," 123.

73. UN Security Council (S/PV.3145), 18.

74. UN Security Council (S/PV.3145), 18.

75. Howe, "The United States and the United Nations in Somalia."

76. Chester A. Crocker, "The Lessons of Somalia: Not Everything Went Wrong," *Foreign Affairs* May–June (1995): 7.

77. Lewis and Mayall, "Somalia," 108.

78. Djibril Diallo, "The Bosnia Syndrome," *Africa Recovery* 6 (November 1992): 3.

79. UN Security Council (S/PV.3060), 12–13.

80. UN Security Council (S/PV.3060), 33.

81. UN Security Council (S/PV.3060), 46–47.

82. UN Security Council, Report of the Secretary General, 3 December 1992 (S/24333), para 13.

83. UN Security Council (S/PV.3145), 32.

84. UN Security Council (S/PV.3145), 32.

85. UN Security Council (S/PV.3145), 32.

86. UN Security Council (S/PV.3188), 22.

87. UN Security Council (S/PV.3145), 49.

88. UN Security Council (S/PV.3145), 51.

89. UN Security Council (S/PV.3145), 14.

90. UN Security Council (S/PV.3145), 11.

91. UN Security Council (S/PV.3145), 21.

92. UN Security Council (S/PV.3145), 38.

93. UN Security Council (S/PV.3145), 48.

94. UN Security Council (S/PV.3229), 24.

95. UN Security Council (S/PV.3229), 22.

96. UN Security Council (S/PV.3229), 16–17.

97. See Bruce Cronin and Ian Hurd, *The UN Security Council and the Politics of Authority* (London: Routledge, 2008).

98. UN Security Council, Resolution 794.

Chapter 4. From Nonintervention to Humanitarian Intervention

1. Mary Kaldor, *New and Old Wars: Organized Violence in a Global Era* (Stanford, CA: Stanford University Press, 2001); and Susan Woodward, *Balkan Tragedy: Chaos and Dissolution After the Cold War* (Washington, DC: Brookings Institution, 1995).

2. Kaldor, *New and Old Wars*, 38.

3. Noel Malcolm, *Bosnia: A Short History* (New York: New York University Press, 1994), 216; and V. P. Gagnon, "Ethnic Nationalism and International Conflict: The Case of Serbia," *International Security* 19, no. 3 (Winter 1994–95): 130–66; 2, 155.

4. Malcolm, *Bosnia*, 216.

5. UN Security Council, Resolution 743, 21 February 1992 (S/RES/743).

6. Helsinki Watch, *War Crimes in Bosnia-Hercegovina* (New York: Human Rights Watch, 1992), 25.

7. Malcolm, *Bosnia*, 231.

8. Helsinki Watch, *War Crimes in Bosnia-Hercegovina*, 27.

9. Woodward, *Balkan Tragedy*, 210, 211.

10. Steven L. Burg and Paul S. Shoup, *The War in Bosnia-Herzegovina: Ethnic Conflict and International Intervention* (Armonk, NY: M. E. Sharpe, 1999), 5–6.

11. Burg and Shoup, *War in Bosnia-Herzegovina*, 5–6, 8.

12. Burg and Shoup, *War in Bosnia-Herzegovina*, 190.

13. Woodward, *Balkan Tragedy*, 212.

14. UN Security Council, Resolution 688, 5 April 1991 (S/RES/688), and Resolution 746, 3 December 1992 (S/RES/746).

15. *Provisional Rules of Procedure of the Security Council* (New York: United Nations), 1983, Rule 37.

16. Figures in this paragraph and the next were calculated using the Security Council agenda and meeting records for the three conflicts between 1991 and 1995. Agendas, meeting records, resolutions, and presidential statements can be accessed at www.un.org/en/sc.

17. UN Security Council, 18 April 1993 (S/PV.3200), 28.

18. Jennifer Jackson Preece, "Ethnic Cleansing as an Instrument of Nation-State Creation: Changing State Practices and Evolving Legal Norms," *Human Rights Quarterly* 20 (1998): 821; and Carrie Booth Walling, "The History and Politics of Ethnic Cleansing," *International Journal of Human Rights* 4, nos. 3–4 (2001): 48.

19. UN Security Council (S/PV.3200), 28.

20. Deborah Stone, "Causal Stories and the Formation of Policy Agendas," *Political Science Quarterly* 102, no. 2 (1989): 289.

21. UN Security Council, 30 May 1992 (S/PV.3082), 16.

22. UN Security Council (S/PV.3082),16, 25, 31.

23. UN Security Council, 13 August 1992 (S/PV.3106), 24.

24. UN Security Council (S/PV.3082), 42.

25. UN Security Council (S/PV.3082), 42–43; see also India's comments, 21.

26. UN Security Council (S/PV.3082), 9–10.

27. UN Security Council (S/PV.3082), 39.

28. Helsinki Watch, *War Crimes in Bosnia-Hercegovina*.

29. UN Security Council, 19 April 1993 (S/PV.3201), 20 April 1993 (S/PV.3202), 11, 17, 23–25, 20 April 1993 (S/PV.3203), 3, 12, 49–50, 58, 66. In many cases, nonvoting participants used more than one of these three phrases to describe the violence. For counting purposes, only the most serious characterization was included.

30. UN Security Council, 29 June 1993 (S/PV.3247), 6–7.

31. UN Security Council (S/PV.3247), 131.

32. UN Security Council (S/PV.3247), 132.

33. UN Security Council (S/PV.3247), 136.

34. UN Security Council (S/PV.3247), 138, 151.

35. Peter Andreas, *Blue Helmets and Black Markets: The Business of Survival in the Siege of Sarajevo* (Ithaca, NY: Cornell University Press, 2008), 108.

36. Jon Kifner, "66 Die as Shell Wrecks Sarajevo Market," *New York Times*, 6 February 1994.

37. UN Security Council, 14 February 1994 (S/PV.3336), 116.

38. UN Security Council (S/PV.3336), 116, 137.

39. UN Security Council (S/PV.3336), 22.

40. UN Security Council (S/PV.3336), 44.

41. UN Security Council (S/PV.3336), 142.

42. UN Security Council, 8 November 1994 (S/PV.3454), 2.

43. UN Security Council (S/PV.3454), 51–52.

44. UN Security Council (S/PV.3454), 69–70.

45. UN Security Council (S/PV.3454), 5–6.

46. UN Security Council (S/PV.3454), 69.

47. UN Security Council (S/PV.3454), 23.

48. UN Security Council (S/PV.3454), 23.

49. UN Security Council, Resolution 836, 4 June 1993 (S/RES/836), Resolution 844, 18 June 1993 (S/RES/844); and U.N. General Assembly, "The Fall of Srebrenica," 15 November 1999 (A/54/549), 30.

50. Chinmaya R. Gharekhan, *The Horseshoe Table: An Inside View of the UN Security Council* (Delhi: Pearson Education, 2006), 129.

51. UN Security Council (S/PV.3336), 19.

52. Richard Holbrooke, *To End a War* (New York: Random House, 1998), 63.

53. Tim Ripley, *Operation Deliberate Force: The UN and NATO Campaign in Bosnia 1995* (Lancaster, UK: Centre for Defence and International Security Studies, 1999), 130.

54. UN Security Council, 12 July 1995 (S/PV.3553), 5, 11.

55. UN Security Council (S/PV.3553), 5.

56. UN Security Council (S/PV.3553), 9.

57. UN Security Council (S/PV.3553), 13.

58. Holbrooke, *To End a War*, 72.

59. Amnesty International, "Bosnia-Herzegovina: Amnesty International Calls on Bosnian Serb Authorities to Protect Detainees," AI Index (EUR/63/14/95), 17 July 1995.

60. Madeleine Albright, *Madame Secretary: A Memoir* (New York: Miramax Books, 2003), 239.

61. UN Security Council, 10 August 1995 (S/PV.3564), 6.

62. UN Security Council (S/PV.3564), 6.

63. UN Security Council (S/PV.3564), 5.

64. Roger Cohen, "Shelling Kills Dozens in Sarajevo; U.S. Urges NATO to Strike Serbs," *New York Times*, 29 August 1995.

65. Robert Donia, *Sarajevo: A Biography* (London: Hurst 2006), 287; see also Peter Andreas, *Blue Helmets and Black Markets*, 4–5.

66. Andreas, *Blue Helmets and Black Markets*, 105.

67. UN, Secretary-General's Report to the Security Council Pursuant to Resolution 1010 (1995), 30 August, 1995, S/1995/755.

68. UN Security Council, Resolution 1034, 21 December 1995 (S/RES/1034).

69. See Martha Finnemore, "Paradoxes in Humanitarian Intervention," in *Moral Limit and Possibility in World Politics*, ed. Richard M. Price (Cambridge: Cambridge University Press, 2008).

70. Martha Finnemore and Kathryn Sikkink, "International Norm Dynamics and Political Change," *International Organization* 52, no. 4 (1998): 908, 914.

71. Woodward, *Balkan Tragedy*; and Dana H. Allin, *NATO's Balkan Intervention* (Oxford: Oxford University Press, 2002).

72. Andreas, *Blue Helmets and Black Markets*, 107; Allin, *NATO's Balkan Intervention*, 32; and Mary Dejevsky, "Chirac Invokes History and Maintains High Moral Tone," *Independent*, 17 July 1995.

73. Dejevsky, "Chirac Invokes History."

74. Woodward, *Balkan Tragedy*, 2, 11; and Allin, *NATO's Balkan Intervention*, 9.

75. Albright, *Madame Secretary*, 244.

76. Albright, *Madame Secretary*, 240.

77. Spyros Economides and Paul Taylor, "Former Yugoslavia," in *United Nations Interventionism, 1991–2004*, ed. Mats Berdal and Spyros Economides (Cambridge: Cambridge University Press, 2007), 65–107.

78. Holbrooke, *To End a War*, 92.

79. Holbrooke, *To End a War*, 93.

80. Albright, *Madame Secretary*, xii.

81. Burg and Shoup, *The War in Bosnia-Herzegovina*, 411.

82. These include among others, a 4 August 1992 presidential statement in UN Security Council 4 August 1992 (S/PV.3103); UN Security Council, Resolution 771, 13 August 1992 (S/RES/771), Resolution 798, 18 December 1992 (S/RES/798), Resolution 808, 22 February 1993 (S/RES/808), and; Resolution 827, 25 May 1993 (S/RES/827).

83. UN Security Council (S/PV.3106), 32.

84. UN Security Council (S/PV.3082), 56.

85. UN Security Council (S/PV.3082), 60.

86. UN Security Council (S/PV.3082), 27.

87. UN Security Council (S/PV.3106), 11.

Chapter 5. The Perpetrator State and Security Council Inaction

1. See Michael Barnett, *Eyewitness to a Genocide: The United Nations and Rwanda* (Ithaca, NY: Cornell University Press, 2002), 29; See also Peter Wallensteen and Patrik Johansson, "Security Council Decisions in Perspective," in *The UN Security Council: From the Cold War to the 21st Century*, ed. David. M. Malone (Boulder, CO: Lynne Rienner, 2004), 17–33.

2. Barnett, *Eyewitness to Genocide*, 13.

3. Scott Strauss, *The Order of Genocide: Race, Power and War in Rwanda* (Ithaca, NY: Cornell University Press, 2006), 41.

4. Samantha Power, *A Problem from Hell: America and the Age of Genocide* (New York:Basic Books, 2002), 384.

5. Colin Keating, "Rwanda: An Insider's Account," in Malone, *The UN Security Council*, 508.

6. Strauss, *The Order of Genocide*, 57.

7. Robert C. Loehr and Eric M. Wong, "The UN and Humanitarian Assistance: Ambassador Jan Eliasson," *Journal of International Affairs* 48, no. 2 (Winter 1995): 491–506.

8. See Barnett, *Eyewitness to Genocide*; and Roméo Dallaire, *Shake Hands with the Devil: The Failure of Humanity in Rwanda* (Toronto: Random House Canada, 2003).

9. I define humanitarian intervention as the use of military force by a group of states inside a sovereign state without the formal consent of its authorities for the purpose of preventing, halting, or punishing widespread and gross violations of the fundamental human rights of individuals.

10. Keating, "Rwanda," 505.

11. Power, *A Problem from Hell*; Barnett, *Eyewitness to Genocide*; Dallaire, *Shake Hands with the Devil*; and Linda Melvern, *A People Betrayed: The Role of the West in Rwanda's Genocide* (London: Zed Books, 2009).

12. Barnett, *Eyewitness to Genocide*, 50.

13. Melvern, *A People Betrayed*, 45.

14. Melvern, *A People Betrayed*, 45. For an excellent critical analysis of the political economy of the genocide in Rwanda, see Isaac A. Kamola, "The Global Coffee Economy and the Production of Genocide in Rwanda," *Third World Quarterly* 28, no. 3 (2007): 571–92.

15. Human Rights Watch, "Rwanda: Human Rights Developments 1994," *Human Rights Watch Annual Report* (New York: Human Rights Watch, 1995), accessed August 30, 2012, www.hrw.org/reports/1995/WR95/AFRICA-08.htm#P397_139563.

16. For more information on French military involvement in Rwanda during the 1990s, see Mel McNulty, "French Arms, War and Genocide in Rwanda," *Crime, Law and Social Change* 33 (2000): 105–29; and Daniela Kroslak, *The French Betrayal of Rwanda* (Bloomington: Indiana University Press, 2008).

17. Human Rights Watch, *Rwanda 1993* (New York: Human Rights Watch, 1994), accessed August 30, 2012, www.hrw.org/reports/1994/WR94/Africa-06.htm#P258_112461.

18. Melvern, *A People Betrayed*, 43–44.

19. Human Rights Watch, *Rwanda 2003*; see also International Commission of Investigation on Human Rights Violations in Rwanda, *Report of the International Commission of Investigation on Human Rights Violations in Rwanda Since October 1, 1990* (London: Human Rights Watch and Africa Watch, 1993).

20. See Gérard Prunier, *The Rwanda Crisis: History of a Genocide* (New York: Columbia University Press, 1995), 192–97; and Melvern, *A People Betrayed*, 59–67.

21. For more information on the Arusha Accords and analysis of their content, see Prunier, *The Rwanda Crisis*, 159–91; and Melvern, *A People Betrayed*.

22. UN Security Council, 5 October 1993 (S/PV.3288), 12.

23. UN Security Council (S/PV.3288), 16

24. UN Security Council (S/PV.3288), 20.

25. UN Security Council (S/PV.3288), 21.

26. UN Security Council (S/PV.3288), 22.

27. UN Security Council (S/PV.3288), 22.

28. UN Security Council (S/PV.3288), 22.

29. UN Security Council (S/PV.3288), 11, 23, 28.

30. UN Security Council, Resolution 893, 6 January 1994 (S/RES/893).

31. International Commission, *Report of the International Commission*; see also Melvern, *A People Betrayed*, 64.

32. See Melvern, *A People Betrayed*, 64.

33. Barnett, *Eyewitness to Genocide*, 112–13.

34. UN Security Council, 5 April 1994 (S/PV.3358), 6.

35. Alison des Forges, *Leave None to Tell the Story: Genocide in Rwanda* (New York: Human Rights Watch, 1999), 181.

36. Strauss, *The Order of Genocide*, 49.

37. Des Forges, *Leave None to Tell the Story*, 190–91.

38. Des Forges, *Leave None to Tell the Story*, 195.

39. Des Forges, *Leave None to Tell the Story,* 4–10.

40. For a detailed analysis of the genocide and its causes, see Strauss, *The Order of Genocide*; and des Forges, *Leave None to Tell the Story.*

41. UN Security Council, "Statement by the President of the Security Council," 7 April 1994 (S/PRST/1994/16).

42. Dallaire, *Shake Hands with the Devil*; see also Power, *A Problem from Hell.*

43. United Nations, "Special Report of the Secretary-General on UNAMIR," 20 April 1994 (S/1994/470).

44. United Nations, "Special Report."

45. Dallaire, *Shake Hands with the Devil,* 280–81.

46. Dallaire, *Shake Hands with the Devil,* 280.

47. United Nations, "Special Report," paragraphs 4, 7.

48. United Nations, "Special Report," paragraph 13.

49. UN Security Council, Resolution 912, 21 April 1994 (S/RES/912).

50. Melvern, *A People Betrayed,* 190.

51. Strauss, *The Order of Genocide,* 50.

52. Ibrahim A. Gambari, "Rwanda: An African Perspective," in Malone, *The UN Security Council,* 516.

53. Stanley Meisler, *Kofi Annan: A Man of Peace in a World of War* (Hoboken, NJ: John Wiley & Sons, 2007), 98.

54. Keating, "Rwanda: An Insider's Account," 507.

55. Melvern, *A People Betrayed,* 200.

56. Melvern, *A People Betrayed,* 200.

57. Keating, "Rwanda: An Insider's Account," 508.

58. Keating, "Rwanda: An Insider's Account," 509; repeated in Keating, interview with author, June 2007.

59. UN Security Council, "Statement by the President of the Security Council," 30 April 1994 (S/PRST/1994/21).

60. Power, *A Problem from Hell,* 361.

61. Power, *A Problem from Hell,* 361.

62. United Nations, "Report of the Secretary-General on the Situation in Rwanda," 13 May 1994 (S/1994/565).

63. UN Security Council, 16 May 1994 (S/PV.3377), 9.

64. UN Security Council (S/PV.3377), 13.

65. UN Security Council (S/PV.3377), 12.

66. UN Security Council (S/PV.3377), 6.

67. UN Security Council (S/PV.3377), 7, 8.

68. UN Security Council (S/PV.3377), 14.

69. UN Security Council (S/PV.3377), 14.

70. UN Security Council (S/PV.3377), 16.

71. UN Security Council (S/PV.3377), 16.

72. UN Security Council (S/PV.3377), 15, 16.

73. UN Security Council, Resolution 918, 17 May 1994 (S/RES/918).

74. UN Security Council, 8 June 1994 (S/PV.3388), 14.

75. United Nations, "Report of the Secretary-General on the Situation in Rwanda," 31 May 1994 (S/1994/640), paragraph 36.

76. Human Rights Watch, *Annual World Report 1995* (New York: Human Rights Watch, 1996), accessed 31 December 2012, www.hrw.org/reports/1995/WR95/AFRICA-08.htm#P397_139563.

77. UN Security Council (S/PV.3388), 8 and 11.

78. UN Security Council (S/PV.3388), 4.

79. UN Security Council (S/PV.3388), 7, 8.

80. UN Security Council, 22 June 1994 (S/PV.3392), 6.

81. UN Security Council (S/PV.3392), 6.

82. UN Security Council (S/PV.3392), 2–4, 7, 10–11.

83. UN Security Council (S/PV.3392), 7.

84. UN Security Council (S/PV.3392), 7.

85. Melvern, *A People Betrayed*, 235; des Forges, *Leave None to Tell the Story*, 23; and Prunier, *The Rwanda Crisis*, 273.

86. UN Security Council (S/PV.3392), 7.

87. Kroslak, *The French Betrayal of Rwanda,* 239. Prunier, *The Rwanda Crisis*, 297; des Forges, *Leave None to Tell the Story*, 689.

88. Melvern, *A People Betrayed*, 241.

89. Prunier, *The Rwanda Crisis;* and Kroslak, *The French Betrayal of Rwanda.*

90. Kroslak, *The French Betrayal of Rwanda*, 239.

91. Madeleine Albright, *Madame Secretary: A Memoir* (New York: Miramax, 2003), 194.

92. Barnett, *Eyewitness to Genocide,*158

93. Barnett, *Eyewitness to Genocide*, 114.

94. Power, *A Problem from Hell.*

95. Des Forges, *Leave None to Tell the Story*, 25.

96. UN Security Council (S/PV.3377), 6.

97. UN Security Council (S/PV.3377), 11.

98. UN Security Council (S/PV.3377), 14–16.

99. Prunier, *The Rwanda Crisis*, 105. This dynamic is referred to as the Fashoda syndrome, which gets its name from a small southern Sudanese village where the British and French armies clashed in 1898.

100. Kroslak, *The French Betrayal of Rwanda*, 60.

101. Guy Martin, "The Historical, Economic and Political Bases of France's Africa Policy," *Journal of Modern African Studies* 23 (1985): 197; and Kroslak, *The French Betrayal of Rwanda*, 60.

102. Kroslak, *The French Betrayal of Rwanda*, 238.

103. Kroslak, *The French Betrayal of Rwanda*, 83, 86, 112–13; McNulty, "French Arms, War and Genocide in Rwanda," 110–11, 115; and Prunier, *The Rwanda Crisis*, 93–126.

104. Power, *A Problem from Hell*, 342.

105. Power, *A Problem from Hell*, 373, 374.

106. Des Forges, *Leave None to Tell the Story*, 595; and Melvern, *A People Betrayed*, 266.

107. UN Security Council, 1 July 1994 (S/PV.3400), 5.

108. UN Security Council (S/PV.3400); the international agreements and conventions included the Universal Declaration of Human Rights, the International Convention on the Elimination of All Forms of Racial Discrimination, the Convention on the Prevention and Punishment of the Crime of Genocide, the Convention Against Torture and Other Cruel, Inhuman or Degrading Treatment or Punishment, and the Convention on the Rights of the Child.

109. UN Security Council, 8 November 1994 (S/PV.3452), 6.

110. UN Security Council (S/PV.3452), 8.

111. Power, *A Problem from Hell*, 384.

112. UN Security Council (S/PV.3388), 3.

113. Prunier, *The Rwanda Crisis*, 296.

114. Jonathan Moore, *Hard Choices* (Lanham, MD: Rowman & Littlefield, 1999), 72; see also Melvern, *A People Betrayed*, 245.

Chapter 6. International Law, Human Rights, and State Sovereignty

1. Human Rights Watch, *Human Rights Watch Condemns Violence by Security Forces in Kosovo* (New York: Human Rights Watch, 1998).

2. Montenegro seceded from its union with Serbia in 2006.

3. See Spyros Economides, "Kosovo," in *United Nations Interventionism, 1991–2004*, ed. Mats Berdal and Spyros Economides (Cambridge: Cambridge University Press, 2007); Noel Malcolm, *Kosovo: A Short History* (London: Macmillan, 1998); and V. P. Gagnon, "Ethnic Nationalism and International Conflict: The Case of Serbia," *International Security* 19, no. 2 (Winter 1994–1995): 130–66.

4. Malcolm, *Kosovo*, 343.

5. Independent International Commission on Kosovo, *The Kosovo Report* (Oxford: Oxford University Press, 2000), 36.

6. Malcolm, *Kosovo*, 327.

7. Wesley K. Clark, *Waging Modern War: Bosnia, Kosovo, and the Future of Combat* (New York: Public Affairs, Perseus Books Group, 2002), 108. See also "Crisis in the Balkans: Statements of United States' Policy on Kosovo," *New York Times*, 18 April 1999.

8. Michael McGwire, "Why Did We Bomb Belgrade?" *International Affairs* 76 (2000): 1, 5.

9. Kosova is the Albanian name for the province.

10. Human Rights Watch, *Yugoslavia: Human Rights Abuses in Kosovo 1990–1992* (New York: Human Rights Watch, 1992), accessed on 30 August 2012, www.hrw.org/reports/1992/yugoslavia.

11. Malcolm, *Kosovo*, 347. Kosovo's Serbs boycotted the referendum.

12. See, for example, Peter Russell, "The Exclusion of Kosovo from the Dayton Negotiations," *Journal of Genocide Research* 11, no. 4 (2009): 487–511; Michael Salla, "Kosovo, Non-violence and the Break-up of Yugoslavia," *Security Dialogue* 26 (1995) 427–38.

13. Carrie Booth Walling, "The History and Politics of Ethnic Cleansing," *International Journal of Human Rights* 4, nos. 3–4 (2000): 75.

14. Keiichi Kubo, "Why Kosovar Albanians Took Up Arms Against the Serbian Regime: The Genesis and Expansion of the UÇK in Kosovo," *Europe-Asia Studies* 62, no. 7 (2010): 1142; and International Crisis Group, "Kosovo Spring," 20 March 1998, cited in Independent International Commission, *Kosovo Report*, 67..

15. Human Rights Watch, *Humanitarian Law Violations in Kosovo* (New York: Human Rights Watch, 1998), 3.

16. Chris Hedges, "On a Garage Floor in Kosovo, a Gruesome Serbian Harvest," *New York Times*, 10 March 1998.

17. Human Rights Watch, "Report Shows Seven Month Pattern of Yugoslav Government Atrocities: Rights Group Seeks Tougher Response from the West," news release, 4 October 1998, accessed on 30 August 2012, www.hrw.org/english/docs/1998/10/04/serbia1371_txt.htm. See also Kubo, "Why Kosovar Albanians," 1145–47.

18. Kubo, "Why Kosovar Albanians," 1148, citing testimony by General Rasim Delić of the Yugoslav Army at the International Criminal Tribunal for Yugoslavia, ICTY transcript of case IT-02–54 (Slobodan Milošević), 21 June 2005, 1242–43.

19. Human Rights Watch, "Human Rights Watch Statement to the Contact Group," news release, 10 June 1998, and "Yugoslav Military and Serbian Police Commit War Crimes in Kosovo, Some Abuses by KLA Also Documented," news release, 30 June 1998.

20. Steven Erlanger, "Yugoslavs Try to Outwit Albright over Sanctions," *New York Times*, 23 March 1998. The members of the Contact Group include the U.S., the UK, France, Germany, Italy, and Russia.

21. UN Security Council, Resolution 1160, 31 March 1998 (S/RES/1160).

22. UN Security Council, 31 March 1998 (S/PV.3868), 3–4.

23. UN Security Council (S/PV.3868), 10–12.

24. UN Security Council (S/PV.3868), 16.

25. UN Security Council (S/PV.3868), 19.

26. UN Security Council (S/PV.3868), 4, 9, 13, 26–27.

27. UN Security Council (S/PV.3868), 11.

28. UN Security Council (S/PV.3868), 26.

29. UN Security Council (S/PV.3868), 8.

30. UN Security Council (S/PV.3868), 13.

31. UN Security Council (S/PV.3868), 7.

32. Human Rights Watch, "Eighteen Civilians Massacred in Kosovo Forest: Thirteen Others Believed Executed," news release, 28 September 1998.

33. Holly Cartner, "Statements by the Executive Director of the Europe and Central Asia Division of Human Rights Watch," 4 October 1998. See also Human Rights Watch, "Report Shows Seven Month Pattern."

34. UN Security Council, 24 October 1998 (S/PV.3937), 8, 10, 12.

35. UN Security Council (S/PV.3937), 6.

36. UN Security Council, Resolution 1203, 24 October 1998 (S/RES/1203).

37. UN Security Council (S/PV.3937), 2.

38. UN Security Council (S/PV.3937), 10.

39. UN Security Council (S/PV.3937), 7.

40. UN Security Council (S/PV.3937), 7.

41. Chapter VIII, Article 53, of the Charter of the United Nations reads, in part, "The Security Council shall, where appropriate, utilize such regional arrangements or agencies for enforcement action under its authority. But no enforcement action shall be taken under regional arrangements or by regional agencies without the authorization of the Security Council."

42. UN Security Council (S/PV.3937), 10–11.

43. UN Security Council (S/PV.3937), 14.

44. UN Security Council (S/PV.3937), 15.

45. Human Rights Watch, "Yugoslav Government Crimes in Racak," news release, accessed on 30 August 2012, www.hrw.org/reports/1999/07/15/yugoslav-government-war-crimes-racak.

46. "Mutilated Kosovo Bodies Found After Serb Attack," New York Times, 17 January 1999.

47. Guy Dinmore, "Villagers Slaughtered in Kosovo 'Atrocity'; Scores Dead in Bloodiest Spree of Conflict," Washington Post 17 January 1999; see also "Mutilated Kosovo Bodies."

48. "Interview with William Walker," Frontline, PBS, 1999, accessed on 17 May 2011, www.pbs.org.

49. UN Security Council, "Statement by the President of the Security Council," 19 January 1999 (S/PRST/1999/2).

50. Human Rights Watch, "Human Rights Watch Investigation Finds: Yugoslav Forces Guilty of War Crimes in Racak, Kosovo," news release, 29 January 1999, accessed on 30 August 2012, www.hrw.org/english/docs/1999/01/29/serbia756.htm.

51. Human Rights Watch, "Human Right Watch Investigation Finds."

52. UN Security Council, "Statement," 19 January (S/PRST/1992/2).

53. UN Security Council, "Statement," 19 January (S/PRST/1999/2).

54. Human Rights Watch, A Week of Terror in Drenica: Humanitarian Law Violations in Kosovo (New York: Human Rights Watch, 1999), accessed on 30 August 2012, www.hrw.org/reports/1999/kosovo/Obrinje6–05.htm#P886>143719.

55. McGwire, "Why Did We Bomb Belgrade?" 10.

56. Alex J. Bellamy, Kosovo and International Society (London: Palgrave Macmillan, 2002), 164–65.

57. Independent International Commission, *The Kosovo Report*, 201.

58. Economides, "Kosovo," 229; and Independent International Commission, *The Kosovo Report*, 89–92.

59. Jules Lobel, "Benign Hegemony? Kosovo and Article 2(4) of the U.N. Charter," *Chicago Journal of International Law* 19 (2000): 27.

60. Clark, *Waging Modern War*; Lawrence S. Kaplan, *NATO Divided, NATO United: Evolution of an Alliance* (Westport, CT: Praeger, 2004); and Gülner Aybet and Rebecca R. Moore, eds., *NATO: In Search of a Vision* (Washington, DC: Georgetown University Press, 2010).

61. See Erica Bouris, *Complex Political Victims* (Bloomfield, CT: Kumerian Press, 2007).

62. United Nations, *Report of the Secretary-General Pursuant to General Assembly Resolution 53/35*, "The Fall of Srebrenica," 15 November 1999 (A/54/549); and UN Security Council, "Report of the Independent Inquiry into the Actions of the United Nations During the 1994 Genocide in Rwanda," 16 December 1999 (S/1999/1257).

63. Kofi Annan, "Kofi Annan Endorses NATO's Bombing of Yugoslavia," AOL video, 24 March, 1999, accessed on 30 August 2012, www.video.aol.com.

64. UN Security Council (S/PV.3988), 2–4, 10, 12–13 and UN Security Council (S/PV.3989), 5–6, 9.

65. UN Security Council (S/PV.3988), 4–6, 8–9, 11–12; and UN Security Council (S/PV.3989), 2–7.

66. UN Security Council (S/PV.3988), 6–11; and (S/PV.3989), 3–4, 7–9.

67. UN Security Council, 24 March 1999 (S/PV.3988), 4.

68. UN Security Council (S/PV.3988), 4.

69. UN Security Council (S/PV.3988), 6.

70. UN Security Council (S/PV.3988), 8–9, 11.

71. UN Security Council (S/PV.3988), 8–9, 11.

72. UN Security Council (S/PV.3988), 8.

73. UN Security Council (S/PV.3988), 7, 9.

74. UN Security Council (S/PV.3988), 9.

75. UN Security Council (S/PV.3988), 7–8.

76. UN Security Council (S/PV.3988), 18–19.

77. UN Security Council (S/PV.3988), 12.

78. UN Security Council (S/PV.3988), 2–4.

79. UN Security Council (S/PV.3988), 13.

80. UN Security Council (S/PV.3988), 13.

81. UN Security Council, 26 March 1999 (S/PV.3989), 5.

82. UN Security Council (S/PV.3989), 6–7.

83. UN Security Council (S/PV.3989), 20.

84. UN Security Council (S/PV.3989), 4.

85. UN Security Council (S/PV.3989), 4. See also UN Security Council (S/PV.3988), 19–20.

86. UN Security Council (S/PV.3988), 17.

87. UN Security Council (S/PV.3989), 3.

88. Economides, "Kosovo," 231.

89. UN Security Council (S/PV.3989), 14–15.

90. UN Security Council (S/PV.3988), 7, 10.

91. UN Security Council (S/PV.3988), 13.

92. Madeleine Albright, *Madame Secretary: A Memoir* (New York: Miramax Books, 2003).

93. UN Security Council (S/PV.3989), 16.

94. UN Security Council, 8 May 1999 (S/PV.4000), 2.

95. UN Security Council (S/PV.4000), 3.

96. Madeleine Albright, *The Mighty and the Almighty: Reflections on America, God and World Affairs* (New York: HarperCollins, 2006), 62.

97. Tony Blair, "Blair's Statement: The Fight for Peace," *BBC News*, BBC, 25 March 1999. http://news.bbc.co.uk/2/hi/uk_news/303648.stm, accessed 12/28/2012.

98. Kaplan, *NATO Divided, NATO United*, 121.

99. Albright, *Madame Secretary*, 498.

100. Clark, *Waging Modern War*, 422.

101. Clark, *Waging Modern War*, 457.

102. Aybet and Moore, *NATO: In Search of a Vision*, 2.

103. Kaplan, *NATO Divided, NATO United*, 126.

104. Clark, *Waging Modern War*, xxxi.

105. See Clark, *Waging Modern War*, 461.

106. Madeleine Albright, interview, "War in Europe," *Frontline*, PBS, accessed on 17 May 2011, www.pbs.org.

107. UN Security Council, Resolution 1244, 10 June 1999 (S/RES/1244).

108. UN Security Council, 10 June 1999 (S/PV.4011), 9.

109. UN Security Council (S/PV.4011), 11.

110. UN Security Council (S/PV.4011), 12.

111. UN Security Council (S/PV.4011), 12–13.

112. UN Security Council (S/PV.4011), 13.

113. Kofi Annan, "Speech to the General Assembly," New York, 20 September 1999.

114. Annan, 'Speech to the General Assembly."

115. Annan, "Speech to the General Assembly."

116. Human Rights Watch, *Human Rights Trump Sovereignty in 1999* (New York: Human Rights Watch, 1999).

117. International Commission on Intervention and State Sovereignty, *The Responsibility to Protect* (Ottawa: International Development Research Centre, 2001), 7–8.

118. ICISS, *The Responsibility to Protect*, xi.

119. UN Security Council, 11 August 1999 (S/PV. 4035), 4, 22 October 1999 (S/PV.4054), 4, and 11 May 2000 (S/PV.4139), 26.

120. John Hirsch, "War in Sierra Leone," *Survival* 43, no. 3 (Autumn 2001): 145–62, quotation on 150.

121. John Hirsch, "Sierra Leone," in *The UN Security Council: From the Cold War to the 21st Century*, ed. David E. Malone (Boulder, CO: Lynne Rienner, 2004), 521.

122. Hirsch, "War in Sierra Leone," 147.

123. Lansana Gberie, "Fighting for Peace: The United Nations, Sierra Leone and Human Security," *UN Chronicle* No. 2 (2000): 51–54, esp. 52.

124. Human Rights Watch, "Rebel Atrocities Against Civilians in Sierra Leone," news release, 17 May 1999, accessed on 30 August 2012, www.hrw.org/english/docs/1999/05/17/sierra912_txt.htm accessed 4/30/2007, and "Rebel Abuses near Sierra Leone Capital," 3 March 2000, accessed on 30 April 2007, www.hrw.org/english/docs/2000/03/03/sierra458_txt.htm.

125. See Chris Coulter, *Bush Wives and Girl Soldiers: Women's Lives Through War and Peace in Sierra Leone* (Ithaca, NY: Cornell University Press, 2009); and Ishmael Beah, *A Long Way Gone: Memoirs of a Boy Soldier* (New York: Sarah Crichton Books, 2008).

126. Horst Rutsch, "Peacewatch," *UN Chronicle* 2 (2000): 55.

127. Gberie, "Fighting for Peace," 53.

128. UN Security Council, Resolution 1270, 22 October 1999 (S/RES/1270).

129. UN Security Council, Resolution 1181, 13 July 1997 (S/RES/1181), and 5 July 2000 (S/PV.4168).

130. UN Security Council, 25 January 2001 (S/PV.4264).

131. UN Security Council, Resolution 1181, Resolution 1270, and Resolution 1315, August 2000 (S/RES/1315).

132. UN Security Council, "Statement by the President of the Security Council," 20 May 1998 (S/PRST/1998/13), Resolution 1181, 11 March 1999 (S/PV.3986), and "Statement by the President of the Security Council," 12 February 1999 (S/PRST/1999/6).

133. UN Security Council, 13 July 1998 (S/PV.3902), 11–12.

134. UN Security Council, Resolution 1270, see operative clauses 14, 15.

135. UN Security Council (S/PV.4054), 16.

136. William A. Schabas, "Amnesty, the Sierra Leone Truth and Reconciliation Commission and the Special Court for Sierra Leone," *University of California Davis, Journal of International Law and Policy* 11 (2004): 145–169, quotation on 149; Schabas explains that the statement by the special representative of the secretary-general does not appear in the text of the agreement published by the United Nations (UN Doc. S/1999/777). The statement was appended in handwriting on the official copy of the Lomé Peace Accord.

137. Ivo H. Daalder and Michael E. O'Hanlon, "Unlearning the Lessons of Kosovo," *Foreign Policy* (Fall 1999): 128.

138. McGwire, "Why Did We Bomb Belgrade?" 19.

Chapter 7. Complex Conflicts and Obstacles to Rescue in Darfur, Sudan

1. Julie Flint and Alex de Waal, *Darfur: A New History of a Long War* (London: Zed Books, 2008), 171.

2. Flint and de Waal, *Darfur*, 179, citing UN New Centre, "Humanitarian and Security Situations in Western Sudan Reach New Lows, UN Agency Says," news release, 5 December 2003.

3. Flint and de Waal, *Darfur*, 176.

4. Martha Finnemore and Kathryn Sikkink, "International Norm Dynamics and Political Change," *International Organization* 52, no. 4 (1998): 887–919.

5. Mansour Khalid, "Darfur: A Problem Within a Wider Problem," in *Darfur and the Crisis of Governance in Sudan: A Critical Reader*, ed. Salah M. Hassan and Carina E. Ray (Ithaca, NY: Cornell University Press, 2009), 40.

6. Salah M. Hassan, "Naming the Conflict: Darfur and the Crisis of Governance in Sudan," in Hassan and Ray, *Darfur and the Crisis of Governance in Sudan*, 164.

7. Flint and de Waal, *Darfur*, 121.

8. Flint and de Waal, *Darfur*, 121.

9. Human Rights Watch, *Human Rights Watch Annual World Report 2000* (New York: Human Rights Watch, 2001), accessed on 30 August 2012, www.hrw.org/english/docs/2001/01/13/sudan985.htm.

10. Khalid, "Darfur: A Problem Within a Wider Problem," 41.

11. Briefing by John Holmes, under-secretary-general for humanitarian affairs and emergency relief coordinator, to the UN Security Council, 11 June 2009 (S/PV.6139), 3.

12. Hassan and Ray, *Darfur and the Crisis of Governance*; and Mahmood Mamdani, "The Politics of Naming: Genocide, Civil War, Insurgency," *London Review of Books* 29, no. 5 (8 March 2007), 5–8.

13. Hassan, "Naming the Conflict," 158.

14. Atta El-Battahani, "Ideological Expansionist Movements Versus Historical Indigenous Rights in the Darfur Region of Sudan: From Actual Homicide to Potential Genocide," in Hassan and Ray, *Darfur and the Crisis of Governance*; Hassan, "Naming the Conflict," 154–69; and Mahmood Mamdani, "The Politics of Naming: Genocide, Civil War, Insurgency," in Hassan and Ray, *Darfur and the Crisis of Governance in Sudan*, 145–53. See also Flint and de Waal, *Darfur*.

15. Flint and de Waal, *Darfur*, 187.

16. Flint and de Waal, *Darfur*, 187.

17. "Situation of Human Rights in the Darfur Region of the Sudan," *Report of the High Commissioner for Human Rights* (New York: United Nations, 2004), (E/CN.4/2005/3), paragraph 6, page 4.

18. Flint and de Waal, *Darfur*, 186–87.

19. Paul D. Williams and Alex J. Bellamy, "The Responsibility to Protect and the Crisis in Darfur," *Security Dialogue* 36 (2005): 27–47.

20. Independent Commission on Intervention and State Sovereignty (ICISS), *The Responsibility to Protect* (Ottawa: International Development Research Centre, 2001), vii.

21. ICISS, *The Responsibility to Protect*, vii.

22. ICISS, *The Responsibility to Protect*, 7–8.

23. ICISS, *The Responsibility to Protect*, xi.

24. United Nations, "A More Secure World: Our Shared Responsibility," *Report of the High-Level Panel on Threats, Challenges and Change* (New York: United Nations, 2004); and Kofi Annan, *In Larger Freedom: Towards Development, Security and Human Rights for All* (New York: United Nations, 2005).

25. UN General Assembly, "2005 World Summit Outcome Document," 24 October 2005 (A/RES/60/1).

26. UN Security Council, 11 December 2011 (S/PV.6688), 3.

27. See Ellen Lutz and Kathryn Sikkink, "The Justice Cascade: The Evolution and Impact of Foreign Human Rights Trials in Latin America," *Chicago Journal of International Law* 2 (2001): 1; and Kathryn Sikkink, *The Justice Cascade: How Human Rights Prosecutions Are Changing World Politics* (New York: W.W. Norton, 2011).

28. See Ellen Lutz and Caitlin Reiger, eds., *Prosecuting Heads of State* (Cambridge: Cambridge University Press, 2009).

29. Flint and de Waal, *Darfur*, 184.

30. Flint and de Waal, *Darfur*, 184–86.

31. UN Security Council, 30 July 2004 (S/PV.5015), 3.

32. UN Security Council, 18 September 2004 (S/PV.5040), 6–7.

33. UN Security Council (S/PV.5015), 8, 9.

34. UN Security Council (S/PV.5015), 4.

35. UN Security Council (S/PV.5015), 6–10, (S/PV.5040), 9–12, and 19 November (S/PV.5082) 2–4, 13, 22.

36. UN Security Council, 2 September 2004 (S/PV.5027), 2–4.

37. UN Security Council, 5 October 2004 (S/PV.5050), 2.

38. UN Security Council, 4 November 2004 (S/PV.5071), 3.

39. UN Security Council, 7 December 2004 (S/PV.5094), 2–3.

40. UN Security Council, 8 February 2005 (S/PV.5120), 13.

41. UN Security Council (S/PV.5120), 13.

42. UN Security Council, 16 February 2005 (S/PV.5125), 3–4.

43. UN Security Council, 18 April 2006 (S/PV.5413), 4.

44. UN Security Council, 15 June 2006 (S/PV.5462), 2.

45. UN Security Council, "Report of the Security Council Mission to the Sudan and Chad, 4–10 June 2006" (S/2006/433), 14.

46. UN Security Council, "Report of the Security Council Mission," 16.

47. UN Security Council, 29 June 2007 (S/PV.5478), 2.

48. UN Security Council (S/PV.5478), 11.

49. UN Security Council (S/PV.5784), 3.

50. UN Security Council, 5 December 2007 (S/PV.5789), 4.

51. UN Security Council (S/PV.5789), 4.

52. UN Security Council, 13 May 2008 (S/PV.5892), 7.

53. UN Security Council, 24 June 2008 (S/PV.5922), 2.

54. UN Security Council, 5 June 2008 (S/PV.5905), 4.

55. UN Security Council (S/PV.5905), 4–5.

56. UN Security Council (S/PV.5905), 7–13.

57. Deborah Stone, "Causal Stories and the Formation of Policy Agendas," *Political Science Quarterly* 104, no. 2 (1989): 284.

58. UN Security Council, 27 April 2009 (S/PV.6112), 3.

59. UN Security Council, 24 July 2009 (S/PV.6170), 4.

60. UN Security Council, 5 February 2009 (S/PV.6079), 3.

61. UN Security Council, (S/PV.6170), 7.

62. UN Security Council, 20 March 2009 (S/PV.6096), 13.

63. UN Security Council (S/PV.6096), 13.

64. UN Security Council (S/PV.6096), 6.

65. UN Security Council (S/PV.6096), 6.

66. UN Security Council (S/PV.6112), 2.

67. UN Security Council (S/PV.6170), 4.

68. UN Security Council (S/PV.6170), 3.

69. UN Security Council, 21 December 2009 (S/PV.6251), 4.

70. UN Security Council (S/PV.6251), 7.

71. UN Security Council (S/PV.6251), 8.

72. UN Security Council, 11 December 2011 (S/PV.6688), 2.

73. Ramesh Thakur, "The Responsibility to Protect and Prosecute?" *The Hindu*, 10 July 2007.

74. UN Security Council (S/PV.5015), 5.

75. UN Security Council (S/PV.5015), 7, 9.

76. UN Security Council (S/PV.5015), 10–11. See also UN Security Council (S/PV.5040), 12.

77. UN Security Council, Resolution 1564, 18 September 2004 (S/RES/1564).

78. UN Security Council (S/PV.5040), 9.

79. UN General Assembly, "2005 World Summit."

80. UN Security Council, 31 August 2006 (S/PV.5519), 4. See also UN Security Council, Resolution 1706, 31 August 2006 (S/RES/1706).

81. UN Security Council (S/PV.5519), 3–4, 8–10.

82. UN Security Council (S/PV.6096), 11–12.

83. Ramesh Thakur and Vesselin Popovski, "The Responsibility to Protect and Prosecute: The Parallel Erosion of Sovereignty and Impunity," *Global Community Yearbook of International Law and Jurisprudence* 1 (2007): 50, 53.

84. UN Security Council, 4 December 2009 (S/PV.6230), 4.

85. UN Security Council (S/PV.5905), 9.

86. UN Security Council (S/PV.6096), 13.

87. Gareth Evans, "The Limits of State Sovereignty: The Responsibility to Protect in the 21st Century," Eighth Neelam Tiucheivam Memorial Lecture, Colombo, Sri Lanka, 29 July 2007, accessed on August 30 2012, www.crisisgroup.org/home/index.cfm?id+4967.

88. ICISS, *The Responsibility to Protect*.

89. Author interviews with senior political officials from the UK, Canada, and New Zealand, June 2007.

90. Author interview with member of the ICISS, June 2007.

91. UN Security Council, 24 June 2008 (S/PV.5922), 26.

92. Williams and Bellamy, "The Responsibility to Protect."

Chapter 8. The Responsibility to Protect, Individual Criminal Accountability, and Humanitarian Intervention in Libya

1. UN Secretary-General, *Early Warning, Assessment and the Responsibility to Protect, Report of the UN Secretary General* (New York: United Nations, 2010); UN Secretary-General, *Implementing the Responsibility to Protect, Report of the UN Secretary-General* (New York: United Nations, 2009) (A/63/677); UN General Assembly, Resolution 63/308, 7 October 2009 (A/RES/63/308); UN Security Council, "Resolution 1894," 11 November 2009 (S/RES/1894)

2. See Alex Bellamy, "Libya and the Responsibility to Protect: The Exception and the Norm," *Ethics and International Affairs* 25, no. 3 (2011): 263; Simon Chesterman, "Leading from Behind: The Responsibility to Protect and Humanitarian Intervention in Libya," *Ethics and International Affairs* 25, no. 3 (2011): 279; and Tim Dunne and Jess Gifkins, "Libya and the State of Intervention," *Australian Journal of International Affairs* 65, no. 5 (2011): 519.

3. UN Security Council, Resolution 1970, 26 February 2011 (S/RES/1970).

4. African Union Peace and Security Council, communiqué, 10 March 2011 (PSC/PR/COMM.2[CCLXV]); League of Arab States, Resolution 7360 on the Repercussions of the Current Events in Libya, 12 March 2011; Samir Salama, "GCC Backs No-Fly Zone to Protect Civilians in Libya," *GulfNews.com*, 9 March 2011, accessed 8 June 2012, gulfnews.com; and Jennie Matthew, "Libya No-Fly Zone Calls Mount as Air Force Strikes Again," *Agence France-Presse*, 8 March 2011, accessed 8 June 2012, reprinted on ABS-CBN News, www.abs-cbnnews.

5. Frederic Wehry, "Libya's Terra Incognita: Who and What Will Follow Qaddafi?," in Council on Foreign Relations, *The New Arab Revolt* (New York: Council on Foreign Relations, 2011), 255; and Dirk Vandewalle, "To the Shores of Tripoli: Why Operation Odyssey Dawn Should Not Stop at Benghazi," in Council on Foreign Relations, *The New Arab Revolt*, 270.

6. Vandewalle, "To the Shores," 270; and Saskia van Genugten, "Libya After Gadhafi," *Survival: Global Politics and Strategy* 53, no. 3 (2011): 64.

7. Human Rights Watch, "Libya: Benghazi Civilians Face Grave Risk: International Community Should Act to Protect Population," news release, 17 March 2011, accessed August 19 2012, www.hrw.org/news/2011/03/17/libya-benghazi-civilians-face-grave-risk.

8. Wehry, "Libya's Terra Incognita," 253.

9. Lisa Anderson, "Demystifying the Arab Spring: Parsing the Differences Between Tunisia, Egypt and Libya," *Foreign Affairs* May/June (2011): 327

10. Van Genugten, "Libya After Gadhafi," 64.

11. Human Rights Watch, "Events of Two Years Ago Sparked Current Uprisings in Libya," news release, 11 March 2011, accessed 19 August 2012, www.hrw.org/news/2011/03/11/events-2-years-ago-sparked-current-uprising-libya.

12. James L. Gelvin, *The Arab Uprisings* (Oxford: Oxford University Press, 2011), 81.

13. Human Rights Watch, "Libya: Arrests, Assaults in Advance of Planned Protests," news release, 17 February 2011, accessed 19 August 2012, www.hrw.org/news/2011/02/16/libya-arrests-assaults-advance-planned-protests.

14. Anthony Shadid, "Clashes in Libya Worsen as Army Crushes Dissent," *New York Times*, 18 February 2011.

15. "Excerpts from Libyan Leader Muammar al-Qaddafi's Televised Address, February 22, 2011," in Council on Foreign Relations, *The New Arab Revolt*, 414–20.

16. "Excerpts from Libyan Leader Muammar al-Qadaffi's Televised Address."

17. "The Arab League Suspends Libya Until Demands of the People Are Met," BBC World Service, 23 February 2011.

18. African Union Peace and Security Council, communiqué, 23 February 2011 (PSC/PR/COMM(CCLXI).

19. Salama, "GCC Backs No-Fly Zone" and Matthew, "Libya No-Fly Zone Calls Mount."

20. League of Arab States, Resolution 7360.

21. League of Arab States, Resolution 7360.

22. UN Security Council, 22 February 2011 (S/PV.6486).

23. Stephanie Nebehay, "Libya Attacks May Be Crimes Against Humanity: UN," *Reuters*, 22 February 2011, accessed 5 June 2012, www.reuters.com.

24. Nebehay, "Libya Attacks May Be Crimes Against Humanity."

25. UN, "UN Secretary-General Special Advisor on the Prevention of Genocide, Francis Deng, and Special Advisor on the Responsibility to Protect, Edward Luck, on the Situation in Libya," news release, 22 February 2011.

26. UN Security Council, 25 February 2011 (S/PV.6490), 3.

27. UN Security Council (S/PV.6490), 3.

28. UN Security Council (S/PV.6490), 3.

29. UN Human Rights Council, 25 February 2011 (A/HRC/RES/S-15/1).

30. UN General Assembly, 1 March 2011 (GA/11050); Human Rights Watch, "UN: Suspension from Rights Body Further Isolates Libya," news release, 1 March 2011, accessed August 19 2012, www.hrw.org/news/2011/03/01/un-suspension-rights-body-further-iso lates-libya.

31. UN Security Council (S/PV.6490), 3; Hillary Rodham Clinton, "Remarks at the Human Rights Council," 28 February 2011, accessed 5 June 2012, www.state.gov.

32. UN Security Council, 26 February 2011 (S/PV.6491), 6.

33. UN Security Council (S/PV.6491), 3, 5–6.

34. UN Security Council (S/PV.6491).

35. UN Security Council (S/PV.6491), 7.

36. UN Security Council (S/PV.6491), 8.

37. UN Security Council, Resolution 1970, 1–2, 8–10.

38. League of Arab States, Resolution 7360.

39. UN Security Council, 17 March 2011 (S/PV.6498), 3.

40. UN Security Council (S/PV.6498), 8.

41. UN Security Council (S/PV.6498), 6, 9.

42. UN Security Council (S/PV.6498), 3, 5.

43. UN Security Council (S/PV.6498), 3.

44. UN Security Council, Resolution 1973, 17 March 2011 (S/RES/1973).

45. Bruce D. Jones, "Libya and the Responsibilities of Power," *Survival: Global Politics and Strategy* 53, no. 3 (2011): 53–54.

46. See Jones, "Libya and the Responsibilities of Power," 54; and Dunne and Gifkins, "Libya and the State of Intervention," 525–26.

47. Jones, "Libya and the Responsibilities of Power," 54.

48. Dunne and Gifkins, "Libya and the State of Intervention," 523.

49. UN Security Council (S/PV.6491), 2, 6–7.

50. Anne-Marie Slaughter, "A Day to Celebrate, but Hard Work Ahead," *Foreign Policy*, 18 March 2011. http://www.foreignpolicy.com/articles/2011/03/18/does_the_world_belong_in_libyas_war?page=0,7 accessed 29 December 2012.

51. Kenneth Roth, "The Security Council Has Lived Up to Its Duty," *Foreign Policy*, 18 March 2011.

52. See also Dunne and Gifkins, "Libya and the State of Intervention," on this same point.

53. Quoted in Hillary Rodham Clinton, "Remarks at the Human Rights Council."

54. UN Security Council (S/PV.6491), 7.

55. See Bellamy, "Libya and the Responsibility to Protect," 265, on this point.

56. UN Watch, "Urgent Appeal to World Leaders to Stop Atrocities in Libya," 20 February 2011, accessed 6 August 2012, www.unwatch.org/site/apps/nlnet/content2.aspx?c=bdKKISNqEmG&b=1316871&ct=9096317.

57. Amnesty International, "Libyan Leader Must End Spiraling Killings," 20 February 2011, accessed 6 August 2012, www.amnesty.org/en/news-and-updates/libyan-leader-must-end-spiralling-killings-2011-02-20.

58. Human Rights Watch, "Libya: Benghazi Civilians Face Grave Risk," and "Libya: End Violent Crackdown in Tripoli," 13 March 2011, accessed 19 August 2012, www.hrw.org/news/2011/03/13/libya-end-violent-crackdown-tripoli.

59. Navy Pillay, "Situation of Human Rights in the Libyan Arab Jamahiriya," Human Rights Council, Geneva, 25 February 20111.

60. UN Security Council (S/PV.6490), 3; and Scott Sayare and Alan Cowell, "Libyan Refugee Crisis Called a 'Logistical Nightmare,'" *New York Times*, 3 March 2011.

61. UN Human Rights Council, Report of the International Commission of Inquiry on Libya, 2 March 2012 (A/HRC/19/68), 2.

62. UN Security Council (S/PV.6490), 5.

63. Alex J. Bellamy and Paul D. Williams, "The New Politics of Protection? Cote d'Ivoire, Libya and the Responsibility to Protect," *International Affairs* 87, no. 4 (2011): 842.

64. Roth, "The Security Council Has Lived Up to Its Duty."

65. Barack Obama, "Obama's Remarks on Libya," *New York Times*, 28 March 2011.

66. UN Security Council, 24 March 2011 (S/PV.6505), 3.

67. UN Security Council, 4 May 2011 (S/PV.6528), 2.

68. UN Security Council (S/PV.6528), 3.

69. UN Security Council (S/PV.6528), 10.

70. UN Security Council, 31 May 2011 (S/PV.6541), 3, and 27 June 2011 (S/PV.6566), 4.

71. UN Security Council, 28 July 2011 (S/PV.6595), 4.

72. International Commission on Intervention and State Sovereignty (ICISS), *The Responsibility to Protect* (Ottawa: International Development Research Centre, 2001).

73. UN Security Council (S/PV.6490), 3.

74. UN Security Council (S/PV.6491), 5.

75. UN Security Council (S/PV.6491), 5.

76. UN Security Council, Resolution 1970.

77. UN Security Council (S.PV.6498), 7.

78. UN Security Council (S.PV.6498), 9.

79. UN Security Council (S.PV.6498), 10.

80. Obama, "Obama's Remarks on Libya."

81. UN Security Council (S/RES/1973).

82. UN Security Council (S/PV.6491), 3.

83. UN Security Council (S/PV.6498), 3.

84. UN Security Council (S/PV.6498), 8.

85. Kathryn Sikkink, *The Justice Cascade: How Human Rights Prosecutions Are Changing World Politics* (New York: W. W. Norton, 2011), 13.

86. Sikkink, *The Justice Cascade*, 13.

87. UN Security Council (S/PV.6491), 3–4. See also UN Security Council, 20 March 2009 (S/PV.6096), and 4 December 2009 (S/PV.6230).

88. UN Security Council (S/PV.6491), 6.

89. UN Security Council (S/PV.6491), 5.

90. Ramesh Thakur and Vesselin Popovski, "The Responsibility to Protect and Prosecute: The Parallel Erosion of Sovereignty and Impunity," *Global Community Yearbook of International Law and Jurisprudence* 1 (2007): 50, 53.

91. UN Security Council (S/PV.6491). See especially the remarks by Bosnia-Herzegovina, Brazil, Colombia, Germany, Lebanon, Nigeria, South Africa, the United Kingdom, the United States, and the secretary-general.

92. UN Security Council, Resolution 1970.

93. UN Security Council (S/PV.6498), 4.

94. See, for example, UN Security Council, 27 April 2011 (S/PV.6524), 5

95. See, for example, UN Security Council (S/PV.6524), 7.

96. UN Security Council, (S/PV.6524), 8–10.

97. UN Security Council (S/PV.6524), 11–13.

98. UN Security Council (S/PV.6524), 4–8, 10–13.

99. Senior ICRC official, "Public Remarks of a Senior ICRC Official," Glasgow, Scotland.

100. UN Security Council (S/PV.6498), 7.

101. UN Security Council (S/PV. 6498), 9.

102. Obama, "Obama's Remarks on Libya."

103. Obama, "Obama's Remarks on Libya."

104. Obama, "Obama's Remarks on Libya."

105. UN Security Council (S/PV.6524), 4.

106. UN Security Council, 4 October 2011 (S/PV.6627), 9.

107. UN Security Council (S/PV.6627), 11.

108. See the writings by Johns Hopkins University political scientist Siba Brovu-gui, especially his scholarly blog, "Looking Beyond Spring for the Season: An African Perspective on the World Order after the Arab Revolt," *The Disorder of Things Blog*, accessed 9 August 2012, thedisorderofthings.com.

Chapter 9. Causal Stories, Human Rights, and the Evolution of Sovereignty

1. Lotta Harbom and Peter Wallensteen, "Armed Conflicts, 1946–2009," *Journal of Peace Research* 47 (2010): 501.

2. Ian Hurd, "Legitimacy, Power, and the Symbolic Life of the Security Council," *Global Governance* 8 (2002): 47.

3. Martha Finnemore, *The Purposes of Intervention: Changing Beliefs About the Use of Force* (Ithaca, NY: Cornell University Press, 2003), 15.

4. See Thomas Risse, "'Let's Argue!': Communicative Action in World Politics," *International Organization* 54, no. 1 (2001).

5. Deborah Stone, "Causal Stories and the Formation of Policy Agendas," *Political Science Quarterly* 104, no. 2 (1989): 285.

6. Stone, "Causal Stories and the Formation of Policy Agendas," 285.

7. Deborah Stone, *Policy Paradox: The Art of Political Decision-Making*, rev. ed., (New York: W.W. Norton, 2002), 195–96.

8. Stone, *Policy Paradox*, 195–96.

9. Stone, "Causal Stories and the Formation of Policy Agendas," 283.

10. Stone, "Causal Stories and the Formation of Policy Agendas," 293.

11. Madeleine Albright, *Madame Secretary: A Memoir* (New York: Miramax, 2003), 194.

12. Cherif Bassiouni, "Advancing the Responsibility to Protect Through International Criminal Justice," in *Responsibility to Protect: The Global Moral Compact for the 21st Century*, ed. Richard H. Cooper and Juliette Voïnov Kohler (New York: Palgrave Macmillan, 2009), 32.

13. UN Security Council, 5 April 1991 (S/PV.2982), 32–37.

14. See Robert Jackson, "Armed Humanitarianism," *International Journal* 48 (1993): 579–606.

15. Kofi Annan, "Secretary-General Presents His Annual Report to the General Assembly," UN, news release, 20 September 1999, accessed on 1 September 2012, www.un.org.

16. International Commission on Intervention and State Sovereignty (ICISS), *The Responsibility to Protect* (Ottawa: International Development Centre, 2001), 7–8.

17. ICISS, *The Responsibility to Protect*, xi.

18. U.N. General Assembly, "2005 World Summit Outcome," 24 October 2005 (A/RES/60/1).

19. UN Security Council, "Resolution 1970," 26 February 2011; UN Security Council, "Resolution 1973," 17 March 2011; UN Security Council, "Resolution 1975," 30 March 2011; UN Security Council, "Resolution 1996," 8 July 2011; UN Security Council, "Resolution 2014," 21 October 2011; and UN Security Council, "Resolution 2016," 27 October 2011.

20. Joseph S. Nye Jr., *The Future of Power* (New York: Perseus Books Group, 2011), 19–20.

21. I thank Bud Duvall for drawing attention to this point. See also the Independent International Commission on Kosovo, *The Kosovo Report* (Oxford: Oxford University Press, 2000), 297.

22. Bruce Cronin, "Intervention and the International Community," in *International Intervention: Sovereignty Versus Responsibility*, ed. Michael Keren and Donald A. Sylvan (London: Frank Cass, 2002), 150, 156.

Index

Acknowledgments

This project is the culmination of many years of research and writing at multiple institutions including the University of Minnesota, the Gerald R. Ford School of Public Policy at the University of Michigan, and Albion College. Many people have helped and encouraged me in this research. I especially thank Ken Booth, Barbara Frey, and Kathryn Sikkink for encouraging my interest in human rights and for showing me the importance of teaching through their own example. I owe a special debt of gratitude to Kathryn Sikkink, who helped me at the early stages of development of this project and who inspired me through her own scholarship and professional example. She read multiple versions of the entire manuscript over the course of several years. I thank her for her generosity of time and the thoughtfulness of her comments, which have done much to strengthen the overall argument. I also want to thank Michael Barnett, Sonia Cardenas, Colin Kahl, Eric Weitz, and two anonymous reviewers for reading and commenting on earlier versions of the manuscript. Many colleagues read and commented on some portion of the manuscript, and I am grateful to them all: John Ciorciari, Tim Dunne, Maryam Zarneger Deloffre, Isaac Kamola, Susan Kang, Hunjoon Kim, Audie Klotz, Jonneke Kooman, Elise Lipkowitz, Julie Mertus, Meghana Nayak, Jennifer Rutledge, Deborah Stone, and Dayne Walling. Many others provided comments at invited talks, presentations, and conferences, including the International Studies Association, the Midwest Political Science Association, the University of Minnesota, the University of Michigan, and the University of Glasgow. Lisa Disch and Richard (Bud) Duvall helped me to think in new and creative ways about the project. I also benefited from a community of intellectually engaging and unusually supportive colleagues in the political science department at the University of Minnesota and as a member of the Michigan Society of Fellows. The conversations I have had with them and their observations about the project have also shaped the final product. I am grateful for other forms of advice, assistance, and encouragement from Margot Bokanga, Amer Hawari, Bert Lockwood, Donald Lopez, Philip Rogers, Rebecca Sestili, and Susan Waltz. Jordan Adams was especially helpful in the preparation of the final manuscript. My editor, Peter Agree, was encouraging and helpful at every stage of the publication process. I want to thank Peter and the University of Pennsylvania Press for believing in the project and guiding me faithfully through the trials and tribulations of publishing my first book.

For financial and institutional support, I thank the Borderlands Research Project at the Center for Global Studies, University of Minnesota, for a research grant; the Women's Caucus of the International Studies Association for a Deborah Gerner Professional Development Grant to conduct interviews; the Department of Political Science at the University of Minnesota for a fellowship; the Michigan Society of Fellows and the Gerald R. Ford School of Public Policy at the University of Michigan for a postdoctoral research fellowship; and the Department of Political Science and Provost's Office at Albion College for research support.

It is difficult to write ethically about the subject of mass atrocity. There is a risk of exploiting the horror or unduly minimizing it. I have tried to avoid both and to be respectful in my treatment of the subject matter. I am thankful to Ibadete for showing me the strength of the human spirit to overcome exceptional hardship and adversity.

To my parents (Raymond and Susan Booth and Paul and Reba Walling), my husband Dayne, and my children Bennett and Emery, I offer special appreciation. I could not have completed this project without your patience, support, and encouragement.